Queer Objects

Pursuing the discursive or material effects of relational queerness, this book reflects on how objects can illuminate, affect, and animate queer modes of being.

In the early 1990s the queer theorist Eve Kosofsky Sedgwick defined queer as "multiply transitive . . . relational and strange," rather than a fixed identity. In spite of this, much of the queer theoretical scholarship of the last three decades has used queer as a synonym for anti-normative sexual identities. The contributions to this volume return to the idea of transitivity, exploring what happens when queer is thought of as a turning toward or turning away from a diverse range of objects, including bodily waste; frozen cats; archival ephemera; the writing of Virginia Woolf; the Pop art of Ray Johnson; the podcast *S-Town*; and Maggie Nelson's memoir *The Argonauts*.

Relevant to those studying queer theory, this book will also be of wider interest to those researching identity and the way in which it is represented in a variety of artistic disciplines.

This book was originally published as a special issue of *Angelaki*.

Guy Davidson is Associate Professor of English Literature at the University of Wollongong, Australia. His most recent book is *Categorically Famous: Literary Celebrity and Sexual Liberation in 1960s America* (2019).

Monique Rooney teaches literature, film and television in the English Program at the Australian National University. She is the author of *Living Screens: Melodrama and Plasticity in Contemporary Film and Television* (2015). She is the editor of *Australian Humanities Review*.

Queer Objects

Edited by
Guy Davidson and Monique Rooney

LONDON AND NEW YORK

First published 2019
by Routledge
2 Park Square, Milton Park, Abingdon, Oxon, OX14 4RN

and by Routledge
605 Third Avenue, New York, NY 10017

First issued in paperback 2020

Routledge is an imprint of the Taylor & Francis Group, an informa business

© 2019 Taylor & Francis

All rights reserved. No part of this book may be reprinted or reproduced or utilised in any form or by any electronic, mechanical, or other means, now known or hereafter invented, including photocopying and recording, or in any information storage or retrieval system, without permission in writing from the publishers.

Trademark notice: Product or corporate names may be trademarks or registered trademarks, and are used only for identification and explanation without intent to infringe.

British Library Cataloguing in Publication Data
A catalogue record for this book is available from the British Library

ISBN 13: 978-0-367-72944-8 (pbk)
ISBN 13: 978-0-367-20293-4 (hbk)

Typeset in Bodoni MT
by RefineCatch Limited, Bungay, Suffolk

Publisher's Note
The publisher accepts responsibility for any inconsistencies that may have arisen during the conversion of this book from journal articles to book chapters, namely the inclusion of journal terminology.

Disclaimer
Every effort has been made to contact copyright holders for their permission to reprint material in this book. The publishers would be grateful to hear from any copyright holder who is not here acknowledged and will undertake to rectify any errors or omissions in future editions of this book.

Contents

Citation Information vii
Notes on Contributors xi

Foreword 1
Guy Davidson and Monique Rooney

Introduction 3
Guy Davidson and Monique Rooney

1. Eve Sedgwick's "Other Materials" 5
   Scott Herring

2. Acts Against Nature 19
   Elizabeth A. Wilson

3. Solid Objects and Modern Tonics, or, who's Afraid of the Big Camp Woolf? 32
   Alexander Howard

4. Library Trolls and Database Animals: Kenneth Halliwell and Joe Orton's Library Book Alterations 48
   Melissa Hardie

5. Ray Johnson's Anti-Archive: Blackface, Sadomasochism, and the Racial and Sexual Imagination of Pop Art 61
   Benjamin Kahan

6. On Ray Johnson's Sexuality, Loves, and Friendships: An Interview Between William S. Wilson and Benjamin Kahan 85
   Benjamin Kahan

7. The Shameless Performativity of Camp in Patrick White's *The Twyborn Affair* 88
   Jackson Moore

8. Tom Ripley, Queer Exceptionalism, and the Anxiety of Being Close to Normal 102
   Victoria Hesford

9. Capote's Frozen Cats: Sexuality, Hospitality, Civil Rights 116
   Michael P. Bibler

10. Cooper's Queer Objects 131
    Marcie Frank

11. Objects of Desire: Masculinity, Homosociality and Foppishness in
    Nick Hornby's *High Fidelity* and *About a Boy* 144
    Nikola Stepić

12. Queer Objects and Intermedial Timepieces: Reading *S-Town* (2017) 156
    Monique Rooney

13. Ephemeraphilia: A Queer History 174
    Gillian Russell

Dossier: *The Argonauts* as Queer Object **186**

14. Medea's Perineum 187
    So Mayer

15. "Feral with Vulnerability": On *The Argonauts* 193
    Kaye Mitchell

16. Theory and the Everyday 198
    Monica B. Pearl

17. On Being a Good-Enough Reader of Maggie Nelson's *The Argonauts* 203
    Jackie Stacey

18. In the Margins with *The Argonauts* 208
    Robyn Wiegman

    Index 213

Citation Information

The chapters in this book were originally published in *Angelaki*, volume 23, issue 1 (February 2018). When citing this material, please use the original page numbering for each article, as follows:

Foreword
Foreword
Guy Davidson and Monique Rooney
Angelaki, volume 23, issue 1 (February 2018), pp. 1–2

Introduction
Editorial Introduction
Guy Davidson and Monique Rooney
Angelaki, volume 23, issue 1 (February 2018), pp. 3–4

Chapter 1
Eve Sedgwick's "Other Materials"
Scott Herring
Angelaki, volume 23, issue 1 (February 2018), pp. 5–18

Chapter 2
Acts Against Nature
Elizabeth A. Wilson
Angelaki, volume 23, issue 1 (February 2018), pp. 19–31

Chapter 3
Solid Objects and Modern Tonics, or, who's Afraid of the Big Camp Woolf?
Alexander Howard
Angelaki, volume 23, issue 1 (February 2018), pp. 32–47

Chapter 4
Library Trolls and Database Animals: Kenneth Halliwell and Joe Orton's Library Book Alterations
Melissa Hardie
Angelaki, volume 23, issue 1 (February 2018), pp. 48–60

Chapter 5
Ray Johnson's Anti-Archive: Blackface, Sadomasochism, and the Racial and Sexual Imagination of Pop Art
Benjamin Kahan
Angelaki, volume 23, issue 1 (February 2018), pp. 61–84

Chapter 6
On Ray Johnson's Sexuality, Loves, and Friendships: An Interview Between William S. Wilson and Benjamin Kahan
Benjamin Kahan
Angelaki, volume 23, issue 1 (February 2018), pp. 85–87

Chapter 7
The Shameless Performativity of Camp in Patrick White's The Twyborn Affair
Jackson Moore
Angelaki, volume 23, issue 1 (February 2018), pp. 88–101

Chapter 8
Tom Ripley, Queer Exceptionalism, and the Anxiety of Being Close to Normal
Victoria Hesford
Angelaki, volume 23, issue 1 (February 2018), pp. 102–115

Chapter 9
Capote's Frozen Cats: Sexuality, Hospitality, Civil Rights
Michael P. Bibler
Angelaki, volume 23, issue 1 (February 2018), pp. 116–130

Chapter 10
Cooper's Queer Objects
Marcie Frank
Angelaki, volume 23, issue 1 (February 2018), pp. 131–143

Chapter 11
Objects of Desire: Masculinity, Homosociality and Foppishness in Nick Hornby's High Fidelity *and* About a Boy
Nikola Stepić
Angelaki, volume 23, issue 1 (February 2018), pp. 144–155

Chapter 12
Queer Objects and Intermedial Timepieces: Reading S-Town *(2017)*
Monique Rooney
Angelaki, volume 23, issue 1 (February 2018), pp. 156–173

Chapter 13
Ephemeraphilia: A Queer History
Gillian Russell
Angelaki, volume 23, issue 1 (February 2018), pp. 174–186

Chapter 14
Medea's Perineum
So Mayer
Angelaki, volume 23, issue 1 (February 2018), pp. 188–193

Chapter 15
"Feral with Vulnerability": On The Argonauts
Kaye Mitchell
Angelaki, volume 23, issue 1 (February 2018), pp. 194–198

Chapter 16
Theory and the Everyday
Monica B. Pearl
Angelaki, volume 23, issue 1 (February 2018), pp. 199–203

Chapter 17
On Being a Good-Enough Reader of Maggie Nelson's The Argonauts
Jackie Stacey
Angelaki, volume 23, issue 1 (February 2018), pp. 204–208

Chapter 18
In the Margins with The Argonauts
Robyn Wiegman
Angelaki, volume 23, issue 1 (February 2018), pp. 209–213

For any permission-related enquiries please visit:
http://www.tandfonline.com/page/help/permissions

Notes on Contributors

Michael P. Bibler is Associate Professor of Southern Studies at Louisiana State University, USA. He is author of *Cotton's Queer Relations: Same-Sex Intimacy and the Literature of the Southern Plantation, 1936–1968* (2009); and co-author of *Just Below South: Intercultural Performance in the Caribbean and the U.S. South* (2007).

Guy Davidson is Associate Professor of English Literature at the University of Wollongong, Australia. His most recent book is *Categorically Famous: Literary Celebrity and Sexual Liberation in 1960s America* (2019).

Marcie Frank is Professor of English at Concordia University in Montreal, Canada. She is the author of *How to be an Intellectual in the Age of TV: The Lessons of Gore Vidal* (2005) and *The Novel Stage: Narrative Form from the Restoration to Jane Austen* (forthcoming in 2020).

Melissa Hardie is Associate Professor and Associate Dean (Undergraduate Programs) at the University of Sydney, Australia. She is currently completing a book on the closet after queer theory.

Scott Herring is James H. Rudy Professor of English at Indiana University, USA. He is the author, most recently, of *The Hoarders: Material Deviance in Modern American Culture* (2014).

Victoria Hesford is Associate Professor of Women's, Gender and Sexuality Studies at Stony Brook University, State University of New York, USA. She is the author of *Feeling Women's Liberation* (2013) and the co-editor of *Feminist Time against Nation Time* (2008).

Alexander Howard is Lecturer in Writing Studies at the University of Sydney, Australia. His research focuses on modern and contemporary literature and film, gender, and critical theory.

Benjamin Kahan is Associate Professor of English and Women's and Gender Studies at Louisiana State University, USA. He is the author of *Celibacies: American Modernism and Sexual Life* (2013) and *The Book of Minor Perverts: Sexology, Etiology, and the Emergences of Sexuality* (2019).

So Mayer is the author of several poetry collections, most recently *(O)* (2015) and *kaolin* (2015); of two critical film studies, *Political Animals: The New Feminist Cinema* (2015) and *The Cinema of Sally Potter: A Politics of Love* (2009); and a member of both the queer feminist film curation collective Club des Femmes, and of Raising Films, a campaign and community for parents and carers in the UK film and television industry.

Kaye Mitchell is Senior Lecturer in Contemporary Literature, and Co-Director of the Centre for New Writing at the University of Manchester, UK. She is the author of *A.L. Kennedy: New British Fiction* (2007) and *Intention and Text: Towards an Intentionality of Literary Form* (2008), editor of *Sarah Waters: Contemporary Critical Perspectives* (2013), and co-editor (with Nonia Williams) of *British Avant-Garde Fiction of the 1960s* (2019). She is the UK editor of the Oxford University Press journal, *Contemporary Women's Writing*.

Jackson Moore is a PhD candidate at the Australian National University's School of Literature, Languages and Linguistics. His current research investigates the representations of queer sexualities in the novels of Patrick White.

Monica B. Pearl is Lecturer in Twentieth Century American Literature at the University of Manchester, UK. She is the author of *AIDS Literature and Gay Identity: The Literature of Loss* (2013).

Monique Rooney teaches literature, film and television in the English Program at the Australian National University. She is the author of *Living Screens: Melodrama and Plasticity in Contemporary Film and Television* (2015). She is the editor of *Australian Humanities Review*.

Gillian Russell is Professor of Eighteenth-Century Literature in the Department of English and Related Literature at the University of York, UK. She specializes in the theatre and cultural history of eighteenth and nineteenth century Britain and Ireland. Her monograph, *The Ephemeral Eighteenth Century: Print, Sociability, and the Cultures of Collecting* is forthcoming with Cambridge University Press.

Jackie Stacey is Professor of Media and Cultural Studies at the University of Manchester, UK, and Co-Director of the Centre for the Study of Sexuality and Culture. Her publications include: *Star Gazing: Hollywood Cinema and Female Spectatorship* (1994); *Teratologies: A Cultural Study of Cancer* (1997); *Queer Screen: A Screen Reader* (2007; co-edited with Sarah Street); *The Cinematic Life of the Gene* (2010); and *Writing Otherwise: Experiments in Cultural Criticism* (2013; co-edited with Janet Wolff).

Nikola Stepić is a PhD candidate in Humanities at Concordia University's Centre for Interdisciplinary Studies in Society in Culture in Montreal, Canada. His research focuses on gender and sexuality, material cultures of masculinity, popular culture, porn studies, HIV/AIDS, and urban life in cinema and literature.

Robyn Wiegman is Professor of Literature and Gender, Sexuality and Feminist Studies at Duke University, USA. She has published *Object Lessons* (2012) and *American Anatomies: Theorizing Race and Gender* (1995), and numerous anthologies, including *Women's Studies on its Own* (2002) and *Feminism beside Itself* (1995).

Elizabeth A. Wilson is Samuel Candler Dobbs Professor of Women's, Gender and Sexuality Studies at Emory University, USA. She is the author of *Gut Feminism* (2015) and is currently writing an introduction to the work of psychologist and affect theorist Silvan Tomkins with Professor Adam Frank.

FOREWORD

guy davidson
monique rooney

QUEER OBJECTS

What does queer have to do with objects? The essays collected in this special issue explore what happens when queer is thought of as a turning toward or turning away from certain objects or objectified states of being. Pursuing the discursive or material effects of recasting queer as transitive and relational, these essays reflect in intersecting and divergent ways on how queer subjectivity might be rethought in relation to a range of historically, culturally and naturally situated objects and on how such objects can illuminate, affect and animate queer modes of being.

This issue, the first one of *Angelaki* devoted to queer matters, appears at a time when the object is receiving close attention across the humanities. Part of the broad theoretical trend of the "post-human" attention to the object includes modes of inquiry such as the new materialism, the study of "nature-cultures" and theories concerning "object-oriented ontologies." In tandem with and overlapping with these approaches has been a "post-critical" turn that has questioned the dominance of hermeneutic and symptomatic readings in favour of "surface reading," "thin description" and "actor-network" accounts of meaning-making. Situating subjects and objects in complex networks that comprise the human, non-human life, and the inanimate, these approaches have challenged the subject-centred premises of "the humanities."

In the context of these shifts, "Queer Objects" explores how queer objects shape their subjects. In contrast to positions taken in some recent debates, the essays collected here do not so much speculate about the capacity for animacy, vitalism or consciousness in the non-human world; rather, they engage with the reciprocal interactions between subjects and objects, exploring what happens when subjects become fascinated, beholden and sometimes even repulsed or abjected by the objects on which they focus.

what does queer have to do with objects?

In her influential discussion of *queer* in *Tendencies*, Eve Kosofsky Sedgwick defines it as "transitive – multiply transitive [...] Keenly it is relational and strange" (xii). The conception of queerness as a relation to an object ("recurrent, eddying, troublant" ibid.) is elaborated in the many critical projects that take "queering" (*Queering the Renaissance*, *Queering Criminology*, *Queering Masculinities*, *Queering the Colour Line* – to name a random selection of book titles) as their organizing principle. However, much of the queer work that has followed *Tendencies* – including much that sets out "to queer" – has used queer as a synonym for putatively anti-normative (homo)sexual identity, or, contrastively, has been fixated on a queer subject, positioned as "solitary and outside history," and shot through with "decollectivizing, shame-inducing, or ego-shattering death drives" (Castiglia and Reed 5). The essays collected in this special issue return to the idea of transitivity. What happens when queer is thought about as an orientation toward certain objects or objectified states of being? What are some of the discursive or material effects of recasting queer as either a turning toward or a turning away from certain objects, things or persons? In intersecting and divergent ways, these essays reflect on how queer subjectivity might be rethought in relation to a range of historically, culturally and naturally situated objects and on how such objects can illuminate, affect and animate queer modes of being.

This issue, the first one of *Angelaki* devoted to queer matters, appears at a time when the

INTRODUCTION

guy davidson
monique rooney

QUEER OBJECTS

object is receiving close attention across the humanities. Part of the broad theoretical trend of the "post-human" attention to the object includes modes of inquiry such as the new materialism, the study of "nature-cultures" and theories concerning "object-oriented ontologies." In tandem with and overlapping with these approaches has been a "post-critical" turn that has questioned the dominance of hermeneutic and symptomatic readings in favour of "surface reading," "thin description" and "actor-network" accounts of meaning-making. Situating subjects and objects in complex networks that comprise the human, non-human life, and the inanimate, these approaches have challenged the subject-centred premises of "the humanities."

In the context of these shifts, "Queer Objects" explores how queer objects shape their subjects. In contrast to positions taken in some recent debates, the essays collected here do not so much speculate about the capacity for animacy or vitalism in the non-human world (see, for example, the recent "Tranimacies" issue of *Angelaki* (22.2), or Jane Bennett's *Vibrant Matter*); rather, they engage with the reciprocal interactions between subjects and objects, exploring what happens when subjects become fascinated, beholden and sometimes even repulsed or abjected by the objects on which they focus.

acknowledgements

We wish to acknowledge the Gender Institute and the Humanities Research Centre at the Australian National University for supporting the early stages of this project. We also wish to thank Robyn Wiegman for her curation of the section of "Queer Objects" devoted to Maggie Nelson's *The Argonauts*. Thanks are due to Gerard Greenway for his enthusiasm and support in publishing this special issue, and to James Hypher and Fergus Armstrong for copyediting.

bibliography

Castiglia, Christopher, and Christopher Reed. *If Memory Serves: Gay Men, AIDS and the Promise of the Queer Past*. Minneapolis: U of Minnesota P, 2009. Print.

Sedgwick, Eve Kosofsky. *Tendencies*. Durham, NC: Duke UP, 1993. Print.

for jonathan goldberg and michael moon, in appreciation

scott herring

EVE SEDGWICK'S "OTHER MATERIALS"

"Eve Sedgwick's 'Other Materials'" refers to a seminar that Sedgwick offered several times at the CUNY Graduate Center entitled "How to Do Things with Words and Other Materials." According to its digitally archived syllabus, the seminar's graduate students participated in an "experimental seminar/studio workshop" with "each exploring different aspects of the complex relations among language, materiality, and visuality" via literary and non-literary objects, including those of their own creation ("How to Do Things").[1] With their "unconventional use of the materiality of both the written word and its support," these classes were a pedagogical riff on J.L. Austin's 1955 lectures ("How to Do Things"). But Sedgwick's title not only gestures to this British philosopher or to her own revisions of his speech act theory that she put forth in works such as her co-edited collection *Performativity and Performance* (1995) or *Touching Feeling* (2003). It also nods to her established interest in creating material things – what her memoir *A Dialogue on Love* (1999) refers to as "THE BUDDHIST STUFF, MANIA FOR MAKING UNSPEAKING OBJECTS" which assist "EMOTIONAL REGISTERS THAT WEREN'T AVAILABLE WHILE GENERATING FIRST PERSON" (*Dialogue* 207).[2] These course offerings coincided with her art pieces as well as their exhibition at Stony Brook University, Dartmouth College, and elsewhere before her death in 2009.

Eve Sedgwick's "other materials" also refers to her fecal matter. The two titles are inextricable, as Sedgwick herself acknowledges. This should come as no surprise given her avowed interest in anality. Think of her close reading of Henry James's "Golden Bowel" and his "anal poetics" in "Is the Rectum Straight?" (*Tendencies* 102, 98); her shared glee in filmmaker John Water's "toilet bowl mentality" featured in her collaborative essay with Michael Moon ("Divinity" 236); and her commitment to "female anal eroticism" in "A Poem Is Being Written" (*Tendencies* 178). All this constituted what Sedgwick, quoting James, calls "accumulated good stuff," and it is fitting, then, that the CUNY Graduate Center held a two-day symposium in 2010 juxtaposing public discussion of Sedgwick's course materials with academic talks organized under the theme of

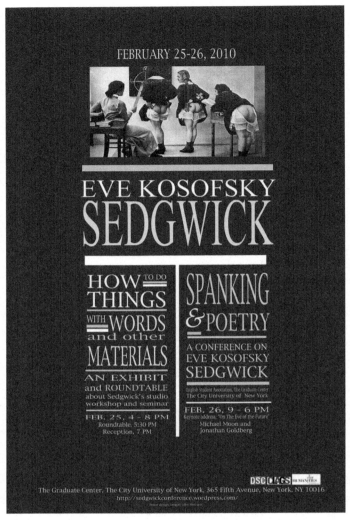

Fig. 1. Promotional poster for CUNY Graduate Center conference and exhibition on "Eve Kosofsky Sedgwick," 25–26 February 2010.

"Spanking & Poetry" (*Touching* 60; Fig. 1). Anality and erotics as well as the rear and its material output regularly went hand-in-hand for this theorist. "SOMEHOW," Sedgwick writes in a line from *A Dialogue on Love* that *Touching Feeling* repeats, "THE SILK AND SHIT GO TOGETHER" (*Dialogue* 206; *Touching* 22).

She was, as usual, on to something. This essay teases out Sedgwick's not-so-tenuous link between material cultures such as cloth and socially abject matter such as feces by thinking more about the relationship between queer object relations and queer material cultures. As I have argued in previous writings on unorthodox collecting and material deviance, queer theorists and queer studies scholars would do well to appreciate how our organizing keywords – perversion, normativity, normalization – impact persons, subjectivities, and their possessions far beyond any identifiable sex/gender system (Herring). Regimes of normalization do not fade away like old soldiers after homonormativity's successful march across the

West for many LGBTQ individuals and populations. They take on new life in material perverts such as hoarders, or in relationships with what Sedgwick and Moon call the "chemical, cultural, and material garbage – our own waste – in whose company we are destined to live and die" ("Divinity" 235).

These observations have had good company. In his recent book-length evaluation of Sedgwick, art historian Jason Edwards cites my last quoted line above and notes that "Sedgwick's writing pays particular attention to matters anal" (74). Finding that "she places in centre stage her own rear end," Edwards zeroes in on how Sedgwick negotiated "a theoretical context in which ideas of 'fecalisation' as necessarily negative were commonplace among Kleinians" (75, 74). Picking up on the queerness of this Sedgwickian "SHIT," my essay's aim is not to desexualize anality even as Sedgwick noted that the last book she published "includes so little sex" (*Touching* 13). It is instead to consider how her writings on gendered anal erotics from the late 1980s met up with her crafty interest from the mid-1990s onward in what Melanie Klein terms "the anal object relation" (123). She – and I – are interested not just in the bottom or the bowels but also in what comes out of our digestive tracts. While I acknowledge and discuss her reliance on Kleinian thought below, I nevertheless show that Sedgwick offered her own queer theory of anal affairs, or, to be more precise, of fecal object relations. Following scholars such as Edwards, Renu Bora, Kathryn Bond Stockton, Robert Reid-Pharr, and others, I consider the critical issue of Sedgwickian bowels as they materialized into an idiosyncratically queer theory of objects and stuff, one that was never not a matter of life and death in this critic's thought.[3] My basic argument is that, while we have extensively detailed Sedgwick's contributions to literary studies, sexuality, gender, affect, and performativity, we should also see her writings as theorizing queer material relations given how her rearticulating of psychodynamic object relations theory overlapped with the organic and inorganic matter that the workshops of our bodies daily produce. Indeed,

Sedgwick listed her intersecting professional fields on her CUNY Graduate Center faculty website page as "the Victorian novel; queer studies; performativity and performance; experimental critical writing; material culture, especially textiles and texture; early modernism and Proust; Romantic fiction; artists' books; non-Lacanian psychoanalysis; Buddhism in the West" (Bklynbiblio). I detail how part of her lasting investment in material culture studies was waste matter, including that of her own doing as she made things and, as a practicing Buddhist, also tried to empty herself out.

This piece consequently makes good on Sedgwick's dedication to material culture and "material garbage" of all sorts, including feces, which is and is not part of personhood given that human waste matter consists of a body's unprocessed, partially undigested food, drink, and bacteria. But shit, as Freud taught us and as the word's various usages imply, can also be an emotional thing released into the world, a queer social bond, and, for an infant, a "first 'gift'" to family members (*Three Essays* 52).[4] Sedgwick felt similarly. "In an essay that has influenced me a lot," she writes in *Touching Feeling*, "Renu Bora uses James's intense fecal interest as his point of departure for a remarkably productive discussion of the whole issue of texture" (13). My point of departure for this argument will thus be her own.

Some quick words of caution before this close reading begins: I do not intend to dishonor Sedgwick by attending to her own thinking on her own ordure. She took this subject matter seriously throughout her academic essays, her poetry, and her creative non-fiction. I follow her example and do so as well. Her writings have been formative to my own writing on queer entities as well as my development as a white gay male academic who came to US queer theory with Sedgwick's works in my pocket. With this debt in mind, my piece is not a paranoid reading of her excrement. Neither, however, is it an unabashedly reparative one. I have come to think that Sedgwick's other materials – unlike those of Klein and many of our queer theories today – suggest one way of "envision[ing] a further space beyond the depressive position" even as she tried "to get a little distance from *beyond*" (*Weather* 136; *Touching* 8). How waste matter facilitates this task is one of my essay's subsidiary concerns.

Let's start, then, with her poem "Bathroom Song," first published in the afterword to a special 2006 issue of *Women and Performance* on the topic of reparations. Reprinting the piece in the posthumously released *The Weather in Proust*, her editor Jonathan Goldberg informs us that "Bathroom Song" was earlier included in a 1997 essay entitled "Come as You Are" – the same year that Duke University Press's Series Q released one version of "Paranoid Reading and Reparative Reading; or, You're So Paranoid, You Probably Think This Introduction Is about You" in Sedgwick's edited collection *Novel Gazing*. I present the four stanzas of this free verse poem in full:

I was only one year old;
I could tinkle in the loo,
such was my precocity.
Letting go of Number Two
in my potty, not pyjama,
was a wee bit more forbidding
– and I feared the ravening flush.
So my clever folks appealed
to my generosity:
"What a masterpiece, Evita!
Look! We'll send it off to Grandma!"

Under the river, under the woods,
off to Brooklyn and the breathing
cavern of Mnemosyne
from the fleshpotties of Dayton –
what could be more kind or lucky?

From the issue of my bowels
straight to God's ear – or to Frieda's,
to the presence of my Grandma,
to the anxious chuckling
of her flushed and handsome face
that was so much like my daddy's,
to her agitated jowls,
Off! Away! To Grandma's place!

As, in Sanskrit, who should say
of the clinging scenes of karma,

"Gaté, gaté, paragaté"
(gone, gone, forever gone),
"parasamgaté; bodhi; svaha!"
(utterly gone – enlightenment –
svaha! Whatever svaha means),
Send the sucker off to Grandma.
Gaté, gaté, paragaté;
parasamgaté; bodhi; svaha!

(*Weather* xv; reproduced by kind permission of Hal Sedgwick and Duke University Press)

Riffing on nineteenth-century American writer Lydia Maria Child's 1844 hymn "The New-England Boy's Song about Thanksgiving Day" ("over the river, and through the wood / To Grandfather's house we go"), this poem concentrates numerous facets of Sedgwickian thought (91). First, the toss-off translation of "Whatever svaha means" evidences her non-expert interest in "BUDDHIST STUFF" as the fourth stanza quotes the Heart Sutra, a meditation that she elsewhere defines as "a key text of East Asian Buddhism" (*Weather* 105). By the initial publication date of "Bathroom Song," Sedgwick had written extensively about her own relationship to Buddhism – as well as American translations of Buddhist thinking – in her personal memoir, in the closing chapter of *Touching Feeling* titled "Pedagogy of Buddhism," in an essay titled "Reality and Realization," and elsewhere. The primacy of this subject reveals itself in "Bathroom Song" as well. Here the Heart Sutra not only closes down the poem. It also occupies close to a quarter of its thirty-four lines as its persona – an *I* that we can safely assume to be a literary version of Sedgwick given references to "Evita," her childhood home of Dayton, Ohio, her commitments to life writing, and her earlier mentions of being "toilet trained at one!" in *A Dialogue on Love* – provides parenthetical English translations of Sanskrit that don't really give a shit if they are translated all that well (191).

Of equal importance to the "whatever" fidelity of her Buddhist thinking is the poem's "whatever" relation to Oepidalized accounts of feces, one beholden yet nonetheless distinct from both Freudian and Kleinian doctrine. For Freud, as earlier noted, poop can be a delightful present, but it is also "unclean and disturbing and should not be part of the body" ("Character" 296). Though her "kind or lucky" toilet suggests timeworn metaphors of stool-as-gift, this primal bathroom scene does not exemplify an environmental hostility that induces repression typified by "neurotic thought," as Freud's "Character and Anal Eroticism" outlines (297).[5] Given her parent's encouragement ("what a masterpiece"), there is not much prohibition despite some anxiety over "the ravening flush." Evita fears the loss of her "Number Two," not the waste matter, and the act of "letting go" is "a wee bit more forbidding" rather than the item itself.

As much as it thinks beyond a classically Freudian framework with regards to fecal matters, "Bathroom Song" also does not restage a Kleinian fracas with your nearest and dearest. The speaker's waste matter is not "a representation of anal and urethral dirtying attacks" that a child slings with a smile at their mother, father, or closest sibling in a clichéd tableau straight out of *Love, Guilt and Reparation and Other Works, 1921–1945* ("Contribution" 126). Klein's descriptions of these family squabbles for patients in treatment are choice. "[Felix]," she writes in a 1925 essay, "had also experienced the repressed wish to insult the master with coprophilic language and to smear him with faeces" (114). Later in this piece, another of her analysands similarly familializes Klein: "Werner [...] made attempts to dirty me as well, threatened me with his fists and with scissors, tried to kick me, produced flatus-like sounds by blowing out his cheeks, abused me in all kinds of ways, pulled faces and whistled" (122). Werner is nine years old and, quite literally, talks shit to best deal with his fiery (one can only imagine petrifying) wish to annihilate his parents. This is what Klein refers to as "aggressive motor discharges provoked by the primal scene" and what Sedgwick, extending Klein's thought, terms "the devouring invasion of the feces" (122; *Weather* 126).[6]

Yet none of this angst – this psycho-drama, this raspberry blowing – shows up in "Bathroom Song." Hers is a gesture of sweetness. With parents lending solid support to her solid excrement, Sedgwick's feces widens beyond the nuclear family as it ships off to grandmother's house and, eventually, to the Goddess of Memory (Mnemosyne) and "God's ear." By the poem's closing lines, her intimate "issue" becomes a defamilialized mantra that "Bathroom Song" links to Buddhism with an extended simile: "As, in Sanskrit, who should say / of the clinging scenes of karma, / "Gaté, gaté, paragaté" / (gone, gone, forever gone)." What starts off as the ego-enhancing "masterpiece" of a precocious tot is, by its end, a piece of matter that belongs to no one and everyone but the universe.[7] Working through an icon of intrapersonal object relations – an infant's "WASTE PRODUCTS" – the poem invokes and materializes foundational psychoanalytic theory in its opening lines yet moves beyond this framework by the closing stanza (*Dialogue* 206).[8]

"Bathroom Song," I mean by this last claim, gestures to the queer otherness of our most intimate materials. With this in mind, it is important to again remember that the poem was originally part of her 1997 talk "Come as You Are," even though it was published in 2006. The title of this talk is an explicit reference to a 1991 song by the grunge-rock band Nirvana (their song also an allusion to Mnemosyne with its repeated refrain of "memoria"). In this lecture Sedgwick theorized feces, impersonality, and the object relations of our object matter – material selves included. Acknowledging that she "drew from object relations," Goldberg gives us a glimpse into these links as he reproduces a portion of the talk in an endnote included in *The Weather in Proust* for her essay "Making Things, Practicing Emptiness" (284). This endnote is lengthy but illuminating for my argument and so I offer it in full with Goldberg's embedded commentary:

> "Teachings on this sutra emphasize that 'emptiness' here – or indeed emptiness anywhere – should be thought of as like the empty space on the inside of a bell – emptiness not blank but vibrant and gravid with subtle energy, potential, and arising. But maybe we can also think of the

experimentally fantasied 'emptiness' of a child's voided insides, as the child learns to link that to the power of material formation, of the formal and of what is not herself." The latter point picks up from a discussion just before the citation from the Heart Sutra that compares dying to toilet training: "Suppose that getting toilet trained is about learning, forcibly, to change the process of one's person into a residual product – into something that instead exemplified the *im*personal in its lumpishly ultimate and taboo form. Isn't this one of the tasks of dying, as well? Suppose the many, stubborn, transformational negotiations with chosen cloth objects at that period are a medium for experimenting with the dimensions and the new possibilities of this unwelcome imperative." (*Weather* 120)

The silk and the shit again go together.[9] Collapsing preliminary activities of a life's first years with those of its final days, Sedgwick's talk contextualizes her infant self in "Bathroom Song" as a lump of incipient dead stuff, as part-object, as non-speaking fabric. Stated differently: the poem's persona is Eve Kosofsky Sedgwick as impersonal matter, Eve Kosofsky Sedgwick as "other materials." As much as it is about the vivifying delights of the loo, "Bathroom Song" also functions as one of our "dying modern poems," according to Diana Fuss's incisive survey of this genre (2). With its emphatic "(gone, gone, forever gone)," the poem is as much about not becoming beholden to our lumpish matter – to object relations of all kinds including our own persons and their insides as well as, heartbreakingly, "the person you love, who also loves you" (*Weather* 120).

I hope this close reading gives us a stronger sense of how, for Sedgwick, anality and its by-products are not exclusive to sexual or psychoanalytic experimentations but to material-metaphysical ones as well. Referring to one of her later exhibitions, she calls this creative interaction with loose materials "a first person at the very edge of its decomposition" (*Weather* 111). This "very edge" references the threshold of biological existence, but the phrase also invokes foundational aims of a highly individualized avant-garde, of living and dying and practicing dying as experimental processes that "Come as You Are" gestures toward in terms of Sedgwick's relation to the fabrics that may shroud her corpse-to-be. Or, as Nancy K. Miller, one of her CUNY Graduate Center colleagues, observes when she quotes Sedgwick on her craftwork:

> The pieces in this show are also meant to span such productive, highly-charged, and permeable boundaries as those between craft and art; between woven fiber (cloth) and nonwoven (paper, felt, soie mariée); between feeling and meditation, or gravity and lightness; at last, between making and unmaking. (221)[10]

This last threshold, we may assume, connotes a life lived and whatever afterlife may be to come.

But – in keeping with the poetic logic of "Bathroom Song" – what does it mean to *unmake* personhood before subjectivity conventionally begins to establish itself in the early stages of a human lifespan? Why desire this "freedom from the first person" at the tender age of one? (Hawkins 273). Does a baby have a death drive? Does the speaker transpose her middle-aged adult self (Sedgwick was around fifty-six when she published the poem) into a toddler's frame of mind? What kid from Ohio translates Sanskrit at twelve months – even Sedgwick, who, we can agree, was really good at "BEING GIFTED" (*Dialogue* 133)? In some respects the poem theorizes a stunning reversal of maturational processes as well as an affront to conventional notions of psychodynamic object relations. Her "precocity" outstrips conventional timelines of psychological development, and her use of "my potty, not pyjama" also confirms an observation made by her Durham-based psychotherapist, William Shannon Van Wey: "it's pretty far out of the line of physiological development" (*Dialogue* 191). Hence not only are the persona's actions potentially and potently non-familial as they go from the American Midwest to "Grandma's place" to "enlightenment." As a "supraindividual phenomenon" they are also profoundly supra-developmental (Hawkins 279).

At the same time, they may also be non-psychoanalytic and *non*-developmental. In order to better grasp how this last observation informs a Sedgwickian theory of queer object relations, it is useful to briefly review the psychotherapeutic theories of object relations – not just classical Freudian psychoanalytical concepts – that most influenced her. I have already pinpointed how the poem's subject matter of feces speaks to repression and anal eroticism. Its scenario of advanced toilet training, parental recognition and approval, and expressed love toward her "clever" parents likewise holds key ingredients for a child's emotional and psychic maturation, one steeped in "precocity." Such being the case, it looks from the poem's opening stanza as if Evita had reached the reparative stage at "one year old." In classic Klein-speak that the psychotherapist developed from the 1920s to the mid-1940s and that Sedgwick rehearses at length in her essay "The Weather in Proust," the infant begins her unconscious life within a "paranoid/schizoid position" whereby its most intimate objects – prototypically, a mother and a father – are psychically riven into "all good" or "all bad." This is what Sedgwick translates as "the awful storms of the paranoid/schizoid world" in which one's psychosomatic sense of these familial objects is "exclusively, magically good or bad" (25, 26). As non-Lacanians such as herself well knew, this stark divide is emotional life-and-death given the "greed and aggression" of a baby relying on the external world to meet her needs (25). Only later (and this cannot be stressed enough) does an infant ideally reach a "developmental achievement" – a stage different than a developmental *given* – and enter into a psychic arena of "open ambivalence" which characterizes a turn away from the paranoid/schizoid (ibid.).

If you are lucky enough (and Evita certainly is at the start of "Bathroom Song") then this move is not only made by an infant at age one but also the child that infant may become, or the graduate student studying deconstruction at Yale in the 1970s, or a leading queer theorist at the CUNY Graduate Center starting in the late 1990s, or the lay reader curious about a special journal issue on "Queer Objects" in the second decade of the twenty-first century. "The depressive position," Sedgwick rehearses, "by contrast, is an anxiety-mitigating achievement that the infant or adult only sometimes, and often only briefly, succeeds in inhabiting" (*Weather* 136). Momentarily dwelling in this "achievement," these individuals can then experiment with something like the depressive/reparative position whereby cherished object relations such as friends, family members, and even the critics we read are ambivalently seen as both good and bad ("good and bad tend to be inseparable at every level"; *Weather* 136). For instance, you might hate me right now for this piece of writing. You might love me for it. But chances are that you may already identify its argumentative flaws, its stylistic tics, its organizational turbulence, its over-reliance on other thinkers, and its awkward phrasings but nevertheless still be interested in reading on. Your achievement may not last, and, as Sedgwick herself stressed, the two positions "interdigitate" (*Touching* 145).[11] If so, my congratulations: your psyche runs like a well-oiled engine of object relations theory.

Yet, as I have hinted, a poem such as "Bathroom Song" shows Sedgwick's object relations moving beyond the psychodynamic accomplishment of attaining a depressive/reparative framework and of "opening out new relations to the depressive position" (*Weather* 142). By the time it reaches its closing lines, the piece invests less in making reparation via overcoming psychic Manichaeism or healing the wounds of psychic aggression than it does in voiding the self of objects all together. Further, I venture that "Bathroom Song" is more intrigued in letting matter stay matter rather than turn objects into the stuff of psyche, or vice versa. It is as if the arc of the poem's stanzas moves beyond Freudian and Kleinian psychodynamics even as it relies upon some of the most timeworn tropes of their psychoanalytic theories – "Number Two" – to beget this wish.

What I think this poem featured in "Come as You Are" desires, then, is an attempt to position one's self at a remove from conventional notions of Kleinian object relations theory that inform "paranoid/schizoid" and "depressive/reparative" positions (and, by proxy, the critical readings that Sedgwick inaugurates with this critical apparatus). I believe the poem tries to queer the orthodoxy of Klein via its novel take on waste. Sedgwick, it turns out, was well aware of the intellectual congestion that a paranoid-schizoid stance *as well as* a reparative stance produces. In a criminally neglected line from her essay "Melanie Klein and the Difference Affect Makes," she notes that "it becomes increasingly unclear in Klein's writing after 1940 whether she envisioned a further space beyond the depressive position" (*Weather* 136). What, following this insight, can one achieve after achieving the Kleinian reparative/depressive position? One answer – insufficient to me, to Sedgwick, and to "Bathroom Song" – would be ever more theorizations of psyche in the same vein that Klein built upon Freudian notions of repression to launch her own school of thought, or what two psychoanalysts describe as "the growing differences of opinion between the English school, which was now called the Kleinian school, and the Viennese school of thought" (Geissmann 173).

Sedgwick certainly incorporated non-Lacanian, post-Kleinian psychoanalytic theorists into her writings. D.W. Winnicott (a member of the British Independent Group) and Michael Balint as well as more contemporary theorists are cited or referenced across the pieces collected in *The Weather in Proust*. But more often than not she used Klein as the touchstone of her thinking for almost a decade as these theories offered her "the whole world of creative possibility" (*Weather* 25). Yet the case stands that what lies beyond post-1940 Kleinian-based reparative reading remained a black box for Sedgwick – a possibility amidst so many others given how closely linked "the depressive position" was with reparative interpretation. To be clear: I do not presume that Sedgwick ever fully departed from Klein. I observe that, here and there in her writings, queries emerge into *non-Kleinian* – not just non-Lacanian – modes of being in the world that might give "some possibilities of opening out new relations to the depressive" (*Weather* 142). When cast in this light the reparative starts to look something like an impasse.

This is important for how contemporary queer theory has adopted her theorizations of the reparative, especially given how invested Sedgwick was in the concept of *possibility*. This word and its plural form are constant refrains in her corpus. In an interview published in 2002, she calls for "new techniques, new materials and imaginative possibilities" ("Piercing" 261). Her definition of *queer* in the opening moments of *Tendencies* cites "the open mesh of possibilities, gaps, overlaps, dissonances and resonances" (8). *Epistemology of the Closet*, too, is a hymn to possibility-production: "more liberating possibilities" (6); "mapping out the possibilities" (23); "crucial possibilities" (68); "the world of possibilities" (74); "filled with possibilities" (78); and "new possibilities" (159). Then there are the closing moments of her reading of *The Professor's House* in "Willa Cather and Others." Sedgwick takes the ship name *Berengaria* – the ship transporting Godfrey St. Peter's family back from Europe at the end of Cather's 1925 modernist novel – and turns it into an anagram "of any vital possibility" (*Tendencies* 176). We also find her commitment to the relentless expansion of the discipline of queer studies and its "new possibilities of surprise" given that "something about queer is inextinguishable" (*Weather* 31, 188).

Possibilities entice in that they present chances for betterment and opportunities for novelty. Little wonder that possibility is an extraordinarily appealing concept that often becomes synonymous with reparative reading practices. In the years since her passing, numerous critics in queer studies have built upon this desire "to think of something *else*" (ibid.). In a widely shared methodology we may call Critical Possibility-Production, these scholars usher us toward utopian horizons and ask us to perpetually conjure alternatives, to think outside the givens of the everyday.[12] Yet something else may be going on with the "something *else*" for which the reparative often functions as shorthand. As I have suggested, the reparative was not solely a "developmental achievement" but also something to be thought through –

thought past – for Sedgwick. In spot-on recognition of this critical state of affairs, Lee Edelman, dialoguing with Lauren Berlant, points to "the unstable place of the reparative in her own thought, a place by no means final from her critical *performance*, however frequently it may be vaunted as her ultimate critical *statement*" (45). Berlant, in turn, identifies the prospect of "occupying a separateness from the circuit of attachment and repair" given "multiple paradigms of Sedgwickian relationality" (46), and she then asserts that "what we're facing is an unspectacular space in Eve's work, of the subject's own capacity not to be caught up in the tangle of her own circuits of abjection, grandiosity, and aggression" (48–49).[13] I find their conversational insights on "the plenitude of possibility" instructive for considering how Sedgwick turned to waste in order to queer – estrange – her familiarity with reparative-based Kleinian object relations and consider even less fathomed possibilities for object relations (57). This is never to neglect the promise that reparative relations offer, but it is to stress that even this mode of object-interaction is not always all good or always desirable or always the only answer to a paranoid-schizoid take on things. Why, we might ask, have we been unable to let go of the reparative? Why do we cling to it? Is it a way of still clinging to Sedgwick? What else is out there besides a paranoid or reparative position? Might a full-throated embrace of the reparative reconfirm a paranoid-schizoid reading in sheep's clothing in that it treats the reparative as "all good" and the paranoid as "all bad"? These are latent questions in Sedgwick's post-*Epistemology of the Closet* writing and ones that have, with few exceptions, been left untended.

So what if, following Berlant's lead as well as the little girl in "Bathroom Song," we experiment with letting go of the objects inside of us rather than perpetually split them in two or piece them together reparatively? What would that post-Kleinian relation to the world of things feel like, that empty child with her voided special issue? Given that her critics have viewed her fabrics as "possible object relations,"

and given her associations between the material cultures of cloth and the materiality of Number Two in "Come as You Are," the poem presents another potentially queer version of objecthood (Sedgwick, Barber, and Clark 249). This is what Sedgwick elsewhere termed "possibilities of emptiness and even of nonbeing," and I realize how ironic this may sound coming from a scholar who mastered the writerly art of the first-person (*Weather* 69). But this also is the same scholar who made a collage of the English alphabet – "Book/Alphabet: Untitled (Panda Alphabet)" – with the letter F standing for "friends *and* fans," the letter Q for "questioning," and the letter N for "non-attachment" that her memorial website archives ("Book"; Fig. 2). In this collage it is interesting to witness intimate relations to loved ones mix with the art of impersonal non-attachment as it does in "Bathroom Song" as well as her "MANIA FOR MAKING UNSPEAKING OBJECTS." This is how "the stuff of self" becomes "a motive in nonbeing," and it may be an opening beyond the depressive/reparative position (*Dialogue* 64; *Touching* 169).

To return to the role of queer waste matter in this schema: the fuel for this phantasmatic conversion seems to rest, in part, on the dogged insistence of the materiality of our lumpish self-relations. Sedgwick on Klein: "It's she who put the objects in object relations [...], things with physical properties, including people and hacked-off bits of people" (*Weather* 126). But so too does Evita in her poem's insistence on the materiality of our psychic objects. "Bathroom Song" takes Klein a step further by imaging personal things inside of you that you cannot or do not need to hold onto: the stuff of our own waste that both is and is not of our own making, the nonbeing of fecal matter, "bits of people" that become impersonally lumpish bits of human waste. In fact, the poem attempts to venture past Kleinian thinking on "lumpish matter" as it moves into its Buddhist framework of impersonality. Her Number Two becomes what she elsewhere calls "the stuff *of* the universe" as the poem tries on "intimacy with nonbeing" (32, 70). Hence even as readers witness Evita

Fig. 2. Eve Kosofsky Sedgwick, from "Book/Alphabet: Untitled (Panda Alphabet)." No date.

and her parents "send the sucker off to Grandma," they also find this waste-object relation transfigure into "a beauty, that wasn't myself, wasn't any self, and didn't want to be" (75). Buddhism, we can infer, trained Sedgwick in the arts of the toilet (she called this "an unexpected psychological leverage"; 141). Kleinian thinking does mildly "interdigitate" here as the closing stanza of "Bathroom Song" invokes an aggressive cast on feces ("sucker") and as stool weaves itself into the intestinal lines of the last stanza (*Touching* 145). But we can also interpret this closing stanza as formally enveloping this conventional object relation to fecal matter with its repeated citations of Buddhist philosophy. There's not a completely clean break with Kleinian thought, and nor should there be – just "a separateness from the circuit," again to quote Berlant.

Rephrased: thanks to writings such as the Heart Sutra a middle-aged Sedgwick toilet-trained herself into non-psychoanalytic modes of living and dying. Given that "Bathroom Song" appeared in a 1997 lecture only to be published almost a decade later (and republished in her posthumous edited collection of writings), we might view the last decade and a half of Sedgwick's writing, teaching, and turn to fiber arts and crafts as a playful return to her body's "*im*personal" arts and crafts.[14] Figuratively, this means taking the risk of trying to stick your head (your ego, your selfhood) up your "UNSPEAKING" ass. To quote from "Bathroom Song," might this state produce "enlightenment" rather than what Divine termed "assholism" in *Pink Flamingos*? After "THE SHIT AND SILK," Sedgwick cites "THE WASTE PRODUCTS, FANTASIES OF SELF-SUFFICIENCY, SPINNING STRAW INTO GOLD" (*Dialogue* 206). Her allusion to the German fairy tale of Rumpelstiltskin is there for the taking, but her reference to the bodily arts of decomposing the world into human, inhuman, or phantasmatic objects that do not stay inside us less so. Maybe we already know what this ephemeral practice feels like but we repress it with every flush. Elimination is, after all, a process of emptying the self of physiologically intimate objects that most do at least once a day and all of us have done at one time or another. How can we be relationally unrelated to these beloved objects, or emotionally attach to something structured around non-attachment? Then again, don't we do this all the time when we lose our shit, our eyelashes, our hair, our scabs, our skin, our youth, our hips, our capacities to reproduce, our minds, our lovers, our parents, our bodies, our selves? "SHE WONDERS IF SOME OF THE FEELINGS ABOUT DEATH AND DEADNESS IN HER HAVE TO DO WITH TOILET TRAINING, WHICH HER MOTHER FINISHED WITH HER BY AGE 1" (*Dialogue* 192). There is nothing shittier than losing something, or someone you love. In my experience, there is nothing worse than seeing that something "(gone, gone, forever gone)." The change forced upon us can feel like an "unwelcome imperative" as much as a pleasing interface. Hence my desire to temper any romance of self-otherness for self-otherness's sake as this piece nears its conclusion. Letting go is not the easiest thing, and the literal or figurative elimination of self into "thing making" can leave others feeling self-eliminated as we try out "the art of loosing," of being-no-more or, from a Buddhist perspective, of being-no-more-of-this-thing (*Weather* 79; *Touching* 3).

Her poem's searching model for a queer object relation beyond the Kleinian reparative position, I think, seems simple enough but its follow-through may not be. It is an attempted practice of emptiness even if not always a successful achievement. This recognition may, however, be a welcome imperative as we perpetually relieve ourselves: there should be no perfectionism here given its "departure from the vanity of achieving perfect form" and Sedgwick's contention that "in these circumstances perfectionism, for me, would make no sense at all" (*Sex* 49; *Weather* 83).[15] But let's also hold onto her emphasis in "Come as You Are" that this queer form of object relation may be a "stubborn" one, something "forcibly" put upon us, an "unwelcome imperative" that Goldberg helpfully terms "material recalcitrance" (287). Or the mournful rage (a return to Klein at the point of departing from Kleinian thinking) at this letting-go in "Bathroom Song": "Send the sucker off to Grandma!" Elsewhere this practice even produces a personal sense of filthiness and shame: "SHE FEELS SOMEHOW THAT HER PRESENT WAY OF MOVING BETWEEN THE LIVING AND THE DEAD IS OBSCENE, DIRTY (DIRT AS MATTER OUT OF PLACE)" (*Dialogue* 198). Quoting and confirming anthropologist Mary Douglas that "reflection on dirt involves reflection on the relation of order to disorder, being to non-being, form to formlessness, life to death," the poem nonetheless manages to offer possibility beyond ego-deflating abjection thanks to Eastern religious thought (7). It shamelessly embraces the "material garbage – our own waste – in whose company we are destined to live and die" ("Divinity" 235).

Part of the difficulty of this "transformational negotiation" as I imagine it is that it materializes as something like an oxymoronic *involuntary practice*, or what Sedgwick terms "a space of suspended agency" (*Weather* 83). I wager that most readers of this essay are potty-trained, and chances are good that some of us may not have had much control over that initiation. I gamble that you have an expiration date, and chances are high that some of us may not have control over that either. "The great majority of people," surgeon Sherwin B. Nuland remarks in his classic *How We Die*, "do not leave life in a way they would choose" (265). No one has absolute rule over their most intimate bodily functions, whether it is the issue of your bowels or the pumps of your heart. To quote the titular insight of an Americanized Asian text – the 1977 Japanese children's book *Minna Unchi* – that came out the same year as *Tendencies*: *Everyone Poops*.

This is another iteration of How to Do Things with Words and Other Materials, a keystone of "Bathroom Song," and one of Sedgwick's unacknowledged axioms: everyone has a tendency to poop. Everyone is transforming into decomposed bits of things. Is there gratifying if not completely satisfactory freedom – day in, day out, every waking minute, every wink of sleep – in making something of a mess inside of us that you don't have or need to hold onto? I well know that there is delight to constipation – to holding on and to holding in. But Sedgwick reminds us so too is there some jittery fun in letting loose, in "a dread-free coexistence with mess" (*Sex* 58). The lessons she learned at age one about Number Two are not all that different from those she learned in her mid-fifties when she published her poem. They are neither earth-shattering revelations nor ones that take decades to sink in: it's a chance to become anal unretentive as our bowels allow for different forms of psychic, physiological, and *aesthetic* movement beyond standard object relations. "Bathroom Song" is, I remind myself, a poem.

"What am I doing?," Sedgwick asks no one in particular in *A Dialogue on Love*. Her abbreviated answer: "Messing with 'stuff'" (199). To which aspect of "ARTS AND CRAFTS FASCINATION" she refers is unclear, and it is this queer understanding of one's foreignness – at once profound, banal, and anal – that I have been trying to grasp (ibid.). Like the crafty grads in her CUNY seminars, we are all expert rookies as we repeatedly experiment in this medium, one that "does seem," as Sedgwick found, "quite a strangeness" (*Dialogue* 205). So thank the powers that be for Little Evita's ode de toilette. Schooled at the University of Illinois at Urbana-Champaign, I was unable to take one of her classes, but these are a few of the queer things that reading up on Sedgwick's waste materials – from her earliest work to her latest on "BUDDHIST STUFF" – brought to my mind for this journal's special issue on queer objects. Treat this piece as a belated going-away gift for all the intimate stuff she never meant to give me, even though Sedgwick and I had absolutely no personal relationship whatsoever.

disclosure statement

No potential conflict of interest was reported by the author.

notes

1 Online records document that Sedgwick offered this class in the spring semester of 2004 and the semester of 2008.

2 This is not to neglect her earlier interests in material objects. See her extended discussion of kitsch in *Epistemology* (155–56) and her moving account of her close friend Michael Lynch's eyewear in *Tendencies* (252–66).

3 Besides Edwards, other thinkers on this front include Wiegman on "the socially ignored topic of female anal eroticism" ("Eve" 169); Berlant, "Eve"; Bond Stockton, 15–17; Bora on "the wonders of digestive, anal, and fecal pleasures" (95); Bersani on "cultural droppings" (*Homos* 181); Dean's psychoanalytic observation confirming that "the phallus is less a figure for the penis than, more fundamentally, a figure for the turd" (266); and Reid-Pharr on "our dirty prehistory" (409).

4 Freud in *Three Essays on the Theory of Sexuality*:

> They are clearly treated as part of the infant's own body and represent his first "gift": by producing them he can express his active compliance with his environment, and, by withholding them, his disobedience. From being a "gift" they later come to acquire the meaning of "baby." (52)

5 In a 1920 footnote on Lou Andreas-Salomé's theorizations, Freud writes:

> the prohibition against getting pleasure from anal activity and its products – has a decisive effect on his whole development. This must be the first occasion on which the infant has a glimpse of an environment hostile to his instinctual impulses, on which he learns to separate his own identity from this alien one and on which he carries out the first "repression" of his possibilities for pleasure. From that time on, what is "anal" remains the symbol of everything that is excluded and repudiated from life. (*Three Essays* 53)

6 Within this ur-scene, writes Jean-Michel Petot,

> anal aggression is aimed not so much at the feces as objects to be expelled as at objects – in the first instance the mother's body – which are attacked in these fantasies by means of the feces, identified with dangerous substances. (153)

7 Or, as Katherine Hawkins puts it, this is "a practice that teaches us to detach love from individual objects and, through creative work, to restore its generality to the universal spirit (*l'esprit universel*)" (279).

8 I'm deeply influenced here, as I have been elsewhere, by Bill Brown's thinking on what he terms "object relations in an expanded field."

9 Given this formulation, Sedgwick clearly anticipates queer scholarship on craft work. See Cvetkovich 168, 188; and Vaccaro.

10 In her contribution to the edited collection *Regarding Sedgwick*, Miller lovingly details "the craft of weaving and the practice of Buddhism" (221) as they informed Sedgwick's tenure at the CUNY Graduate Center. See also Cohen; and Edwards 132–34.

11 For more on the blurring between the paranoid-schizoid and the reparative, see Huffer, who elegantly writes in a Foucauldian reading of Sedgwick that "the antagonistic dualisms of the *mise en abyme* – Foucault versus Sedgwick, paranoid versus reparative – begin to collapse in on themselves, as lovers who have been fighting often do" (39); and Hanson.

12 Wiegman gets to the heart of this matter in a recent essay: "As I read it, the problem [Sedgwick] tracks in the literary humanities throughout the 1990s is the sheer impossibility of thinking otherwise" ("Times" 23). See also Love on how "reading her work tends to open up unexpected conceptual possibilities" (235).

13 Berlant elaborates this thought in *Cruel Optimism*: "I love the idea of reparative reading insofar as it is a practice of meticulous curiosity. But I also resist idealizing, even implicitly, any program of better thought or reading" (124).

14 Though these two theorists are often seen in respectful opposition, there exist uncanny parallels between Bersani's theorization of "impersonal intimacy" and Sedgwick's notion of "the *impersonal*" (Bersani, *Is the Rectum* 60).

15 See also Edwards's observation that "since she does not have a natural facility or particularly high level of acquired skills as a textile artist, the question of her formal mastery was happily out of the question" (133).

bibliography

Barber, Stephen M., and David L. Clark, eds. *Regarding Sedgwick: Essays on Queer Culture and Critical Theory*. New York: Routledge, 2002. Print.

Berlant, Lauren. *Cruel Optimism*. Durham, NC: Duke UP, 2011. Print.

Berlant, Lauren. "Eve Sedgwick, Once More." *Critical Inquiry* 35.4 (2009): 1089–91. Print.

Berlant, Lauren, and Lee Edelman. *Sex, or the Unbearable*. Durham, NC: Duke UP, 2014. Print.

Bersani, Leo. *Homos*. Cambridge, MA: Harvard UP, 1995. Print.

Bersani, Leo. *Is the Rectum a Grave? And Other Essays*. Chicago: U of Chicago P, 2010. Print.

Bklynbiblio. "The Passing of Eve Kosofsky Sedgwick." Personal blog. 14 Apr. 2009. Web. 17 Nov. 2017. <http://bklynbiblio.blogspot.com.au/2009/04/passing-of-eve-kosofsky-sedgwick.html>.

Bond Stockton, Kathryn. *Beautiful Bottom, Beautiful Shame: Where "Black" Meets "Queer."* Durham, NC: Duke UP, 2006. Print.

Bora, Renu. "Outing Texture." *Novel Gazing: Queer Readings in Fiction*. Ed. Eve Kosofsky Sedgwick. Durham, NC: Duke UP, 1997. 94–127. Print.

Brown, Bill. "Object Relations in an Expanded Field." *differences* 17.3 (2006): 88–106. Print.

Child, Lydia Maria. "The New-England Boy's Song about Thanksgiving Day." *The Columbia Anthology of American Poetry*. 1844. Ed. Jay Parini. New York: Columbia UP, 1995. 91–92. Print.

Cohen, Ed. "The Courage of Curiosity, or the Heart of Truth (A Mash-Up)." *Criticism* 52.2 (2010): 201–07. Print.

Cvetkovich, Ann. *Depression: A Public Feeling*. Durham, NC: Duke UP, 2012. Print.

Dean, Tim. *Beyond Sexuality*. Chicago: U of Chicago P, 2000. Print.

Douglas, Mary. *Purity and Danger: An Analysis of Concepts of Pollution and Taboo*. 1966. New York: Routledge, 2002. Print.

Edwards, Jason. *Eve Kosofsky Sedgwick*. New York: Routledge, 2009. Print.

Freud, Sigmund. "Character and Anal Eroticism." 1908. *The Freud Reader*. Ed. Peter Gay. New York: Norton, 1989. 293–97. Print.

Freud, Sigmund. *Three Essays on the Theory of Sexuality*. 1905. Ed. and trans. James Strachey. New York: Basic, 1962. Print.

Fuss, Diana. *Dying Modern: A Meditation on Elegy*. Durham, NC: Duke UP, 2013. Print.

Geissmann, Claudine, and Pierre Geissmann. *A History of Child Psychoanalysis*. Trans. Melanie Klein Trust. London: Routledge, 1998. Print.

Goldberg, Jonathan. "On the Eve of the Future." *Criticism* 52.2 (2010): 283–91. Print.

Hanson, Ellis. "The Future's Eve: Reparative Reading after Sedgwick." *South Atlantic Quarterly* 110.1 (2011): 101–19. Print.

Hawkins, Katherine. "Re-Creating Eve: Sedgwick's Art and the Practice of Renewal." *Criticism* 52.2 (2010): 271–82. Print.

Herring, Scott. *The Hoarders: Material Deviance in Modern American Culture*. Chicago: U of Chicago P, 2014. Print.

Huffer, Lynne. "Foucault and Sedgwick: The Repressive Hypothesis Revisited." *Foucault Studies* 14 (2012): 20–40. Print.

Klein, Melanie. "A Contribution to the Psychogenesis of Tics." 1925. *Love, Guilt and Reparation and Other Works, 1921–1945*. New York: Dell, 1975. 106–27. Print.

Love, Heather. "Truth and Consequences." *Criticism* 52.2 (2010): 235–41. Print.

Miller, Nancy K. "Reviewing Eve." Barber and Clark 217–25. Print.

Nuland, Sherwin B. *How We Die: Reflections on Life's Final Chapter*. New York: Vintage, 1993. Print.

Petot, Jean-Michel. *Melanie Klein: Volume I: First Discoveries and First System, 1919–1932*. Trans. Christine Trollope. Madison, CT: International UP, 1990. Print.

Reid-Pharr, Robert F. "Clean: Death and Desire in Samuel R. Delany's *Stars in My Pocket Like Grains of Sand*." *American Literature* 83.2 (2011): 389–411. Print.

Sedgwick, Eve Kosofsky. "Bathroom Song." *The Weather in Proust*. Ed. Jonathan Goldberg. Durham, NC: Duke UP, 2011. xv. Print.

Sedgwick, Eve Kosofsky. "Book/Alphabet: Untitled (Panda Alphabet)." *Eve Kosofsky Sedgwick*. H.A. Sedgwick. 2010. Web. 17 Nov. 2017. <http://evekosofskysedgwick.net/art/panda-alphabet.html>.

Sedgwick, Eve Kosofsky. *A Dialogue on Love*. Boston: Beacon, 1999. Print.

Sedgwick, Eve Kosofsky. *Epistemology of the Closet*. Berkeley: U of California P, 1990. Print.

Sedgwick, Eve Kosofsky. "How to Do Things with Words and Other Materials." *Eve Kosofsky Sedgwick*. H.A. Sedgwick. 2010. Web. 17 Feb. 2017. <http://evekosofskysedgwick.net/teaching/how-to-do-things-with-words-and-other-materials.html>.

Sedgwick, Eve Kosofsky. *Tendencies*. Durham, NC: Duke UP, 1993. Print.

Sedgwick, Eve Kosofsky. *Touching Feeling: Affect, Pedagogy, Performativity*. Durham, NC: Duke UP, 2003. Print.

Sedgwick, Eve Kosofsky. *The Weather in Proust*. Ed. Jonathan Goldberg. Durham, NC: Duke UP, 2011. Print.

Sedgwick, Eve Kosofsky, Stephen M. Barber, and David L. Clark. "This Piercing Bouquet: An Interview with Eve Kosofsky Sedgwick." Barber and Clark 243–62. Print.

Sedgwick, Eve Kosofsky, and Michael Moon. "Divinity: A Dossier, A Performance Piece, A Little-Understood Emotion (written with Michael Moon)." Sedgwick, *Tendencies* 215–51. Print.

Vaccaro, Jeanne. "Feelings and Fractals: Woolly Ecologies of Transgender Matter." *GLQ: A Journal of Lesbian and Gay Studies* 21.2–3 (2015): 273–93. Print.

Wiegman, Robyn. "Eve, At a Distance." *TransScripts* 2 (2012): 157–75. Web. 17 Nov. 2017. <http://sites.uci.edu/transscripts/files/2014/10/2012_02_11.pdf>.

Wiegman, Robyn. "The Times We're In: Queer Feminist Criticism and the Reparative 'Turn.'" *Feminist Theory* 15.1 (2014): 4–25. Print.

Edwards, Jason, ed. *Bathroom Songs: Eve Kosofsky Sedgwick as a Poet*. Brooklyn: Punctum, 2017. Print.

introduction

In their introduction to a special journal issue on *Queer Inhumanisms* Dana Luciano and Mel Y. Chen register a hope that their two key terms (queer, inhumanism) will be read as both "alongside" and "athwart" each other (189). The queer and the inhuman aren't juxtaposed in order to generate a whole new identity; rather, Luciano and Chen explain that these proximate terms remake each other – each changes, magnifies or transverses the other. Specifically, the inhuman "expands the term *queer* past its conventional resonance as a container for human sexual nonnormativities" (ibid.). Contrariwise, the twisting logics of queer remind us that things inhuman are both dynamic and brutal.

This chiasmatic relation (the inhumanism of queer, the queerness of the inhuman) structures the reading that Luciano and Chen offer of a Laura Aguilar photograph (*Grounded #114*). In this image, Aguilar sits naked in front of a large boulder. Her back is to the camera, her limbs are tucked out of view, she is leaning forward in a way that only part of her head and a long ponytail of hair are visible. Aguilar's body is broadly similar in shape to the boulder that occupies much of the frame; she "seems to mold her body into an echo of the boulder behind her – the pose concealing sex and gender, obscuring race, and making her status as human difficult, at first, to discern" (184). The composition of the photograph prompts Luciano and Chen to read for the traffic between human and mineral form: "the folds of her flesh counterpoint the dents in the stone, both marking textured, untouchable bodies. Her skin brings out the softness in the stone;

elizabeth a. wilson

ACTS AGAINST NATURE

the boulder lends her body an air of durability" (ibid.). They argue that this inversion of flesh and stone also speaks to sexuality: there is something queer in the manner by which conventional boundaries between human and non-human are dissolved in the image. Indeed, this breakdown of a boundary between the human and the non-human brings Luciano and Chen to an important political claim about queer sexualities:

> To say [...] that there is no clear division between the natural world and the human body, is also to say that there is no natural law to oppose human deviance [...] (185)

If the natural world and the human world are not in opposition, as the Aguilar image contends, then the usual logics of deviance no longer hold: there is no foundation or origin (self-contained, static, straight) from which certain behaviours and bodies could be said to have strayed. Deviance seems to have been emancipated from an imperious natural world. The oppositional violence that a charge of deviance usually enacts (nature and propriety here, aberration and dissipation there) is weakened, Luciano and Chen suggest, when we pay attention to work like Aguilar's which envisions more dynamic configurations of the natural world. In particular, the politics of queer become more expansive: our capacity for "intrahuman connection" multiplies, as does "our ability to imagine other kinds of trans/material attachments" (ibid.). In short, we can now think of the natural world as an ally for progressive sexual politics.

I will return shortly to this deployment of nature as a co-conspirator in the fight against sexual pathologization. In fact, my reservations about this kind of tactic will be the central concern of this essay. But first I want to consider the difficulties that Luciano and Chen have in managing negativity and how this shapes their sexual and natural politics. Having made the case for multiplicity and attachment in the queer inhumanism of Aguilar's photograph, Luciano and Chen read for the everyday violences that nonetheless persist in and around the image. For example, they note that the desert terrain of the US Southwest in which Aguilar's image is situated "belongs to a region overlaid with histories of occupation, of settlement, displacement, colonization, and genocide" (ibid.). That is, they don't want their interest in what might be expansive or queer in the image to distract the reader or viewer from other kinds of political concerns: "To follow Aguilar's turn toward the boulder [...] is not to turn away from questions of objectification or dehumanization" (186).

It is hard to follow, in these opening pages of Luciano and Chen's introduction, what the difference is between the non-human, the inhuman and the dehumanized. As usually understood, the term *inhuman* means not just not-of-the-human but also brutal, savage, barbarous and cruel.[1] However, the toxicity of the term has been more-or-less neutralized in Luciano and Chen's reading for connection and attachment. The inhuman has become synonymous with the non-human and with nature, and together all these terms are situated by Luciano and Chen as emancipatory sources from which "other forms, other worlds, other ways of being" (ibid.) can emerge.[2] The brutality, savagery, barbarity and cruelty conventionally understood to be part of the significatory force of the term *inhuman* emerge at another location: in the anti-emancipatory and dehumanizing events of occupation, settlement, colonization and genocide. This transposition of brutality from the inhuman to the dehumanized has the effect (no doubt unintended) of preserving a very traditional model of the human in their argument: for what other reason do we decry dehumanization if not to restore and protect a humanity that has been violated? Somewhere along the way in Luciano and Chen's explication of a queer inhuman a model humanism has materialized, the inverted, athwart logics of the queer inhuman have been disarmed, and the political field is divided again, as it just about always is, between the good (inhuman) and the injurious (dehumanization). Luciano and Chen break their promise that the chiasmatic relation of the inhuman and the queer would make "brutality" and "dynamism" more conceptually and politically available, and they find themselves endorsing the very notion of humanity that they initially seemed to spurn.

Nonetheless, the negativity (brutality, dynamism) put in play by the inhuman proves to be remarkably difficult to contain in this way. Let me offer a small example of how it returns to disrupt Luciano and Chen's conceptual ecosystem. Championing the liberatory promise of their newly reconfigured natural world, they wonder if the boulder in the Aguilar image is more agential (to use the Baradian term) than perhaps we might first assume. Wanting to avoid a conceptual claim about agency that is oblivious to what many think of as more urgent political matters, they note, somewhat defensively, that "giving attention to the boulder's potential agency within the image need not negate or marginalize concerns relating to Aguilar's identity" (ibid.). The alliterative pleasure of the phrase "need not negate" ought not distract us from the double negative ("not negate") that Luciano and Chen deploy to keep a certain kind of identitarian politics (Chicana, lesbian) in play. That is, their affirmative politics (humanist, identitarian) have proceeded, not coincidentally I am arguing, through an intensification of negativity. Their need to use Aguilar's identity as a foothold against the ravages of queerness has impelled them, curiously enough, to double down on queer's ruinous, negative logics.

What follows is an attempt to intensify arguments about negativity in queer engagement with biological or natural systems. I am focusing on one particular paper by Karen Barad ("Nature's Queer Performativity (The Authorized Version)"). Barad has expanded on her early articulations of intra-action to become directly engaged with the queerness of nature ("Queer Causation and the Ethics of Mattering"; "TransMaterialities"). I will argue that this work (like Luciano and Chen's) tends to under-read the negativity and confusion that queer entails, and so it renders nature, and the politics we might extract from it, more palatable than perhaps they should be. I have chosen to focus on "Nature's Queer Performativity (The Authorized Version)" not only because it exemplifies the problematics at play when we juxtapose queer/nature, but also as a testament to the extraordinary influence of her theory of intra-action on feminist sciences studies, in particular, and feminist theory, more broadly.[3]

I start where Barad starts: with sodomy.

natural sodomy

"In an important sense," Barad argues, "there are no 'acts against nature'" ("Nature's Queer Performativity (The Authorized Version)" 47). This is a conclusion to a much longer argument that engages what she calls the "queer performativity" of the natural world: slime moulds, lightning, stingrays, unicellular dinoflagellates and atoms are read as "queer critters" (33) that exemplify the constitutive entanglements of the material world. Expanding her early work on agential realism (*Meeting the Universe Halfway*), Barad argues that the world's intra-active entanglements are a kind of queerness and that an examination of certain critters "will help make evident the agentially intra-active, that is, queer performative, nature of (their) being/becoming" (ibid.).

What will interest me here is that Barad's longer argument about nature's queer performativity begins and ends with sodomy ("acts against nature"). Sodomy has been an important site for LGBT politics in the United States (e.g., *Bowers* v. *Hardwick 1986*; *Lawrence* v. *Texas 2003*) and transnationally (e.g., recent rulings on section 377 of the Indian Penal Code).[4] While it has also been a highly cathected site of analysis for some early and influential work in queer theory (Bersani; Edelman (*Homographesis*; "Ever After"); Goldberg (*Sodometries*; *Reclaiming Sodom*)), sodomy has been little discussed in feminist science studies where Barad's work has been so influential.[5] I am interested in how sodomy resonates in this particular milieu (feminist/critical engagements with nature, the inhuman, the animal, the quantum and inorganic realms). If sodomy has so often been the exemplar of a violation of nature ("world-destroying," as Goldberg (*Reclaiming Sodom* 5) notes) and if at the same time it has been an "utterly confused category" (Foucault 101), then how might that negativity and disorientation circulate in research interested in a close and critical engagement with the natural realm?

Barad opens her paper on the queerness of nature with an examination of the homophobic views that call sodomy a violence against the natural order of things (for example, the claim that "sodomy is to be condemned because the rational ground of all morality is nature, and sodomy is against nature" ("Nature's Queer Performativity (The Authorized Version)" 28)). For Barad, such charges of "acts against nature" are incoherent: it is not clear in such accusations whether the sodomite stands outside the natural order (a pervert, a criminal and vandal of both natural and cultural laws) or whether the sodomite is entirely too much of nature (acting like a beast, completely consumed by animality):

> "Acts against nature" – what beastly images are conjured by this phrase? [...] On one hand, it is clear that humans are understood to be the actors, the enactors of these "acts against nature." The sense of exteriority is absolute: the crime is against Nature herself, against all that is natural. Nature is the victim, the victimized, the wronged. At the same time, humans who commit "acts against nature" are said to be acting like animals. In other words, the "perpetrator" is seen as damaging Nature from the outside, yet at the same time is reviled for becoming part of Nature. ("Nature's Queer Performativity (The Authorized Version)" 30)

These confusions have been commented on frequently in the literatures on sodomy: historically and textually, sodomy is often understood to be a danger to the social order, and it has often been confused with bestiality (Goldberg, *Reclaiming Sodom*). More specifically for Barad, the charge of acts *against* nature makes no sense because, following the logic of intra-activity that she has so meticulously outlined in previous work, "there is no outside of nature from which to act" (47). If there is no place to stand outside of and against the natural order, then "there are no 'acts against nature' [...] there are only 'acts of nature'" (ibid.).

Like Luciano and Chen's claim that "there is no natural law to oppose human deviance," Barad's argument that sodomy is *of* nature rather than *against* it has an intuitive appeal for any reader who wants to rethink a conventional (social constructionist) feminist politics that tries to detach sexuality from nature.[6] Barad is urging us to rethink the nature of nature itself: if the natural realm is conceptualized in less deterministic and intransigent terms, perhaps there is no need to mark an opposition between it and sodomy. While I am on board for readings that generate a more expansive and dynamic understanding of natural events, I am apprehensive about how this deviant/sodomitical nature has been configured by Barad. My initial suspicion is this: in making sodomy an act *of* nature rather than an act *against* nature, Barad has subdued the negativity and inhumanity that queer theorists such as Leo Bersani, Lee Edelman and Jonathan Goldberg have so lovingly exhumed from sodomy. If "nature is perverse at its core" ("TransMaterialities" 412) then surely the toxic effects of perversity (etymologically related to acts that are deformed, abnormal, awry, and turned the wrong way) need to be closely specified. As Barad locates sodomy inside the entangled, intra-active realm of nature, she forgets the long histories and textualities of sodomy as indecency, bestiality, and ecstatic menace. That is, Barad's anti-homophobic move to make sodomy *of* nature seems to take from sodomy its distinctive capacity to breach "world, law and nature" (Goldberg, *Sodometries* 19); and this makes the logic of entanglement more pastoral than perhaps it should be. Consequently, there is something about the spacetimemattering of sodomy, I will argue, that spoils the ethics with which Barad concludes her argument ("making connections and commitments"; "Nature's Queer Performativity (The Authorized Version)" 47) and that compels me to think of nature in a more destructive register.[7]

sodomitical readings

Let me start by explicating this intimacy of long standing between sodomy and negativity and disorientation. Bersani's essay "Is the Rectum a Grave?," written during the first years of the US AIDS crisis, is important for the argument that I want to build here as it gives a lucid articulation of the confusions that have historically been gathered under the name sodomy, and it tracks a foundational destructiveness in sexuality that needs to be clearly formulated in any queer account of nature. Bersani argues that the "homophobic rage" (19) that emerges in the early years of the AIDS crisis in the United States targets anal sex between men as the specific act that threatens the culture at large. In this sense, the viciousness of some responses to the epidemic (and the preoccupations these commentators had with the transmission of the virus through certain kinds of sexual activity) seems to be narrowly about anality. Nonetheless, Bersani claims, there is also a pervasive confusion (in heterosexual and homosexual men) between fantasies of anal and vaginal sex and the threats that they each entail. He argues that the homophobic sentiments of the US AIDS crisis draw some of their energy from the confusion of anus and vagina and the fantasy of female sexuality as insatiable and diseased: after all, both "women and gay men spread their legs with an unquenchable appetite for destruction" (18). Bersani uses the gravity of the US AIDS crisis to show, amongst other things, that regimes of gender (the conventional alliance of masculinity with activity and femininity with passivity, for example) are always disorganized and confused; entangled, we could say. Moreover, the gender-non-specific character of the anus makes it an ideal place for these mobile figurations, practices and fantasies to prosper.

The aversion to specific kinds of sodomitical acts is but one example, Bersani argues, of a more intense and malignant aversion in sexuality itself. If what makes anal sex between men so objectionable for some is the inevitability of a penetrated and therefore passive man, this objection masks a violent pleasure in this scene and others like it: the "strong appeal of powerlessness, of loss of control" (24). Indeed, the appeal of powerlessness, the enjoyment of a "radical disintegration and humiliation of the self" (ibid.), is the sine qua non of any sexual scene for Bersani. Drawing on Freud's work on infantile sexuality, Bersani argues (famously) that sexuality is "the *jouissance* of exploded limits [...] the ecstatic suffering into which the human organism momentarily plunges when it is 'pressed' beyond a certain threshold of endurance. Sexuality [...] may be a tautology for masochism" (ibid.). This is not masochism in the behavioural sense of the enjoyment any individual may consciously take in being powerless or pained by a sexual partner or a sexual act. This Bersanian masochism is a disturbance of psychic organization in which "the opposition of pleasure and pain becomes irrelevant" (ibid.); its value

rhetorically and politically is that it annihilates, even if only momentarily, the coherence of the self and its desires for connection and commitment. Its obligations, to use a term that Barad deploys, are inhuman: "anticommunal, antiegalitarian, antinurturing and antiloving" (22). Because it emerges through a painful–pleasurable violation of psychic integrity, sexuality in Bersani is both *of* the human and *against* it.

In a close reading of Freud's case history of the Wolf Man, Edelman strengthens the claims we might want to make about the confusions of sodomy and how this reverberates epistemologically and politically. In the first instance, Edelman notes that sodomy has come to be "more than an assault upon the flesh," it is "an assault upon the logic of social discourse" (*Homographesis* 174). That is, the indecency of sodomy does not just ruin persons, it also infects and ravages the rhetorical and representational systems by which we make sense of the world. The specific indecency of sodomy is rendered in an inversion of positionality and temporality that he names *metalepsis*: "a rhetorical term that denotes the substitution of cause for effect or effect for cause, a substitution that disturbs the relationship of early and late, or before and behind" (176). Psychoanalysis, Edelman argues, is notorious for such temporal inversions (making it, perhaps, a sodomitical science). It is often not clear, for example, which comes first in psychoanalysis: the childhood event or the analytic interpretation of it. Moreover, the logic of *nachträglichkeit* consolidates in psychoanalysis the expectation that psychic events may be constituted backwards, birthed breech, or arse first.[8]

What this metaleptic method effects in psychoanalysis is a systemic uncertainty about the ordering of causes and their effects. Edelman reads for these metaleptic doubts and confusions of chronology in the Wolf Man case history. Central to this case is the Wolf Man's childhood memory of having witnessed *coitus a tergo* between his parents. What Edelman shows is that this primal scene is a site of considerable epistemological difficulty for both Wolf Man and Freud: did Wolf Man see vaginal or anal sex between his parents? Did he, in fact, see any sex between his parents? Might he, instead, have witnessed sex between animals that he transposed onto his parents? What has been seen and what has been fantasized? When? What positions are being taken (active or passive? Before or behind? Male or female?). Edelman is concise in his answer to these questions: "it is not clear" (*Homographesis* 181).

Sodomitical scenes, in psychoanalysis and elsewhere, refute "the possibility of defining clear identities or establishing the security of fixed positions" (191). Moreover, because these metaleptic perturbations have "widespread and uncontrollable implications" (183) it is not possible to determine what effects any epistemological or political act (including our own) will have. Jonathan Goldberg (*Sodometries*) reads these disorientations of sodomy through another rhetorical figure: *histeron proteron* ("a form of disordered speech in which the cart is put before the horse" that was Anglicized in the early modern period as "the preposterous" 4). Moving between early modern and contemporary concerns, Goldberg analyses the logics of a T-shirt advertised during the US/Iraq Gulf War that declares – over an image of the US flag, a camel and Saddam Hussein's head – "America will not be Saddam-ized." Exploiting the unstable significations of image and word, Goldberg argues that the T-shirt is preposterous (i.e., sodomitical): "If this shirt says we will not be sodomized, it also demystifies what must be done in order not to be in that supposedly passive position [...] In a word, 'America' says, 'we will sodomize'" (4). That is, the anti-sodomitical sentiments of the T-shirt are effected, absurdly, through an act of sodomy: the disordering of position and identity of sodomitical scenes ensures that the act we find repugnant is the act we will inevitably, enthusiastically undertake. Importantly for the argument I want to build here, sodomy doesn't just violate identities and positions that attach themselves to racist, homophobic, or misogynist demarcations of nature/culture or male/female or self/other. It also ruins the consolations of those political gestures, closer to home, that under the rubrics of social justice or queer critique attempt to set the world to right. For example, analysing a scene of sodomy in a strip from the underground feminist publication *Tits and Clits Comix* ("I had always had this fantasy about fucking a man with a strap-on dildo"; *Reclaiming Sodom* 1), Goldberg observes that "heterosexual difference, gender difference, the borders between human and animal behavior, are being dissolved, *not, it should be added, in some entirely comfortable and comforting way*" (2; emphasis added). As the world is constituted and destabilized by *metalepsis* or *histeron proteron*, so too our own political ambitions (e.g., anti-homophobia) will be inverted and thrown into doubt. Which returns me to Barad's sodomitical anxieties.

breaching nature

By making sodomy (and its violations of flesh and logic) explicitly of nature, Barad is theorizing a universe in which her/our political aspirations are party to the disorienting logic of inversion, substitution and causal indeterminacy. In this regard, I want to find a way to articulate more fully what Barad gestures towards but seems unable to entirely countenance: that negativity, never under our control, has a permanent place in the space-timemattering of the world. Let me show one place where that negativity finds its way, unnervingly, into her text. In her extended prelude to the idea of a queer nature, Barad calls on the politics of anti-homophobia in order to dispute the moralism that names sodomy as a crime against nature. Initially she draws our attention to the work of the biologist Bruce Bagemihl who has generated a catalogue of "'homosexual, bisexual, and transgendered creatures of every stripe and feather'" (quoted in "Nature's Queer Performativity (The Authorized Version)" 29). Barad extends Bagemihl's project to encompass not just the animal world but nature more broadly:

> Even this extraordinary zoological catalogue of queer animals covers only a small fraction of the universe [...] It is my contention that

the world in its exuberance is far more queer than [this] [...] I will even entertain the possibility of the queerness of one of the most pervasive of all critters – atoms. (Ibid.)

In a depathologizing move identifiable to almost every reader of feminist and queer theory, Barad declares that queer is "a desiring radical openness, an edgy protean differentiating multiplicity, an agential dis/continuity, an enfolded reiteratively materializing promiscuously inventive spatiotemporality" (ibid.). Contesting binarized structures like nature/culture as a frame for thinking about these critters, and wanting to render queer universally and intraactively available, Barad asks: "What if queerness were understood to reside not in the breech of nature/culture, per se, but in the very nature of spacetimemattering" (ibid.).

Given that sodomy and its ruinous logics bookend Barad's essay, it cannot be certain whether "breech" is what it appears to be: a copy-editing error, a simple infringement of the protocols of spelling (on the following page, the spelling "breach" is used).[9] It is important to emphasize here that "Nature's Queer Performativity (The Authorized Version)" is a different version of a paper that had previously been published (presumably without authority) in the journal *Qui Parle*. Curiously, *breach* is spelled correctly in the *un*authorized version and the spelling *breech* has been introduced into the authorized and seemingly correct version. As we consider that "Nature's Queer Performativity (The Authorized Version)" is an attempt to remedy an earlier infringement, and as we note that the vowel substitution (of *e* for *a*) seems overdetermined in an argument that relies explicitly on the logic of *différance* and comes from an author who has made her reputation on the difference between the prefixes inter and intra, the logics of breaching and breeching surely demand our attention.[10] If "breech" is an error, I would claim, it is an error of a preposterous kind: the *Oxford English Dictionary* states that *breech* is not only a garment used to cover the loins and thighs (now always used in the plural: breeches), it is also "the part of the body covered by this garment; the buttocks, posterior, rump, seat." Barad's ambitions for the queerness of spacetimemattering now have a different, and discomforting, valence. The queerness of spacetimemattering has been purchased through an anti-sodomitical gesture. She is asking: what if queerness were understood to reside not in the arse of nature/culture? That is, what if queerness could be here (as spacetimemattering) but not there (in the breech)? In this substitution, and under the sway of sodomitical performances that are "widespread and uncontrollable," Barad's political ambitions have been inverted: she has staked the political efficacy of spacetimemattering against the sodomy she has previously been at pains to defend.

This confusion (is the breech/arse here or not?) and the political havoc it wreaks on Barad's argument need greater attention in any theory of the queerness of nature. Barad's "breech" is not an error to be corrected, typographically or otherwise; it is instead a negativity (intrinsic to what Barad calls intraaction) that attacks the persons, places and ideals to which we are attached, a menace that cannot be erased from the political or conceptual landscape. If, as Barad rightly notes, there is no outside-nature (*il n'y a pas de hors-texte*), then violations of this kind are part of the fabric of the world: impossible to locate, to predict, or to properly ameliorate. Importantly for the argument I have been building here, these breaches against/of nature are also of the breech. That is, the logics of sodomy (confusion, substitution, inversion) cannot be removed from natural scenes and the politics we extract from them.

Barad concludes her argument about nature's queer performativity with an ethical call: "entanglement entails possibilities and obligations for reworking the material effects of the past and the future. There can never be absolute redemption, but spacetimemattering can be productively reconfigured, reworking im/possibilities in the process" (47). The logics of sodomy undermine the certainty in this reading that spacetimemattering can be a handmaid to our ethical aspirations. The capacity to productively reconfigure and rework is constituted through violations that make the ground on which political and conceptual and ethical claims are made perpetually uncertain, and fundamentally negative. The vicissitudes of sodomy will always spoil our capacity to do good with nature and to do good by nature.

cuts both ways

In a short commentary piece in Luciano and Chen's special issue, Susan Stryker describes the conditions in which her now canonical paper "My Words to Victor Frankenstein above the Village of Chamounix: Performing Transgender Rage" was written. Struggling to find a position from which to articulate transsexual subjectivity in the face of censure, stereotyping, pathologization and ridicule, her strategy was to "forgo the human, a set of criteria by which I could only fail as an embodied subject" ("Transing the Queer (In)human" 227). In "My Words to Victor Frankenstein," Stryker had named the transsexual body unnatural and monstrous: "it is flesh torn apart and sewn back together again in a shape other than that in which it was born" (238). She identified not simply with the corporeal construction and social exclusion of Frankenstein's monster but also with its destructive affective orientation to the world:

> Like the monster, I am too often perceived as less than fully human due to the means of my embodiment; like the monster's as well, my exclusion from human community fuels a deep and abiding rage in me that I, like the monster, direct against the conditions in which I must struggle to exist. (Ibid.)

In an articulate account of a bitterness almost too intense to bear ("I burst apart" 245), Stryker positioned herself as inhuman. Reflecting on this work twenty years later, she finds comfort in the designation inhuman because it *"cuts both ways,"* toward remaking what human meant and might yet come to be, as well as toward what should be turned away from, abandoned in the name of a better ethics" ("Transing the Queer (In)human" 228; emphasis added). That is, through an identification with monstrosity and the inhuman, Stryker hopes that her rage will effect a double transformation: the reconstruction of what we take to be the human into something politically and personally tolerable and, relatedly, a move away from exclusionary politics and towards a better ethics of gender and desire. In a longer piece in the same special issue, Barad repeats the locution "cuts both ways," and, like Stryker, finds conceptual and political solace in this rhetoric of laceration. For Barad, monstrosity *"cuts both ways.* It can serve to demonize, dehumanize, and demoralize. It can also be a source of political agency. It can empower and radicalize" ("TransMaterialities" 392; emphasis added).

The idiom "cuts both ways" usually means "to have a double or mixed effect; to have both favourable and unfavourable aspects or implications" (*Oxford English Dictionary*). In Stryker, however, the cutting force of the monstrous and the inhuman is deployed primarily with constructive and non-injurious goals in mind:

> I want to lay claim to the dark power of my monstrous identity without using it as a weapon against others or being wounded by it myself [...] words like "creature," "monster," and "unnatural" need to be reclaimed by the transgendered. By embracing and accepting them, even piling them one on top of another, we may dispel their ability to harm us. ("My Words to Victor Frankenstein" 240)

Barad's formulation of monstrosity as a force that can both "demonize" and "empower" brings the doubled politics of the inhuman into sharper view. However, like Stryker, she is less interested in the vicissitudes of demonization, dehumanization, or demoralization than she is in how these forces might be harnessed for politically benevolent ends: "empowering rage, self-affirmation, theoretical inventiveness, political action, and the energizing vitality of materiality in its animating possibilities" ("TransMaterialities" 392). While I am broadly sympathetic with the figuration of an intra-active universe in which agency is not contained by, nor originating in, the human, I am curious about how monstrosity (for Stryker and Barad and for those, like Luciano and Chen, who follow in their wake) seems to cut only one way. In other words, too often, it seems, the politics of the queer inhuman are oriented towards affectively defanged, anti-sodomitical ends – clarity, identity, and the transformation–affirmation of world, law and nature.

The early deconstructive work of Lee Edelman, while not concerned directly with questions of nature, testifies to a foundational negativity that is so far missing in Stryker and Barad's accounts, and so it may enable us to intensify Barad's claim that "nature itself is an ongoing deconstructing of naturalness" ("TransMaterialities" 412) and more closely specify what such deconstruction looks like. In response to a request to speak at a conference on the possibility of "a gay criticism" (*Homographesis* 3), Edelman contemplates how that request seems to demand of him that he see homosexuality as "a determinate entity rather than as an unstable differential relation" (ibid.). Tracking the historical and discursive forces that have rendered homosexuality a legible and stable object/identity, and noting that homosexuality has, at the same time, been conceptualized as a volatile textuality, Edelman argues for a paradoxical situation: "we enter an era in which homosexuality becomes socially constituted in ways that not only make it available to signification, but also cede to it the power to signify the instability of the signifying function *per se*" (6). That is, homosexuality has become a legible identity at that same time as it has come to figure the metonymic instability of meaning more generally ("the potential permeability of every [...] signifier [...] by an 'alien' signification" 7). To this condensed, confounding formation Edelman gives the name *homographesis*. On the one hand, the *graphesis* of homographesis calls on "Derrida's post-Saussurean characterization of writing as a system of 'différance' that operates without positive terms and endlessly defers the achievement of identity as self-presence" (9); on the other, the graphesis of homographesis also names the culturally conventional account of writing that extracts determinate, identitarian differences from *différance* (ibid.). That is, the term homographesis is forged by Edelman to take on two conflicting tasks: to name the conditions by which homosexuality might become personally and culturally intelligible, and also to name the conditions by which that intelligibility is always provisional, never self-present, and thus not fully available to ground a politics of self-empowerment or an ethics of connection and commitment. Which is to say, homographesis cuts both ways. It

> would name a double operation: one serving the ideological purposes of a conservative social order intent on codifying identities in its labor of disciplinary inscription, and the other resistant to that categorization, intent on *de*-scribing the identities that order has so oppressively inscribed. (10)

Homographesis is, therefore, sodomitical, in the ways I have been describing here – it traffics in disorder and erodes political and conceptual clarity:

> That these two operations [de-scribing and inscribing], pointing as they do in opposite directions, should inhabit a single signifier, must make for a degree of confusion, but the confusion that results when difference collapses into identity and identity unfolds into différance is [...] the problematic of homographesis. (Ibid.)

The difficulty, as I see it, in Barad's queer performativity is that the sodomitical character of homographesis (conceptual inversion, political disorder, and the negativity of a system of differences without positive terms) has been only partially acknowledged. Some of this difficulty lies in a technical matter: sodomy is a much broader category than anal sex between men. As Goldberg notes, in both the early modern and contemporary periods, sodomy is "the name for every form of sexual behavior besides married, heterosexual, procreatively aimed sex" (*Reclaiming Sodom* 3). Sodomy "designates neither a specific act nor actors" (4) and so it stands athwart conventional sexual politics that seek to represent minoritarian or marginalized sexualities. Because Barad tends to equate the sodomite with the homosexual (or with a reasonably stable identity or position that might be captured by anti-homophobic politics), she inadvertently limits the queer reach of her account of spacetimemattering. To the extent that Barad tends to equate sodomy with a determinate, identitarian homosexuality, to the extent that she asks us to "align ourselves with the raging nothingness" ("TransMaterialities" 416) of Stryker's pain in the name of progressive politics, to the extent that she describes the materializations of the world (acts of nature) in terms that are largely benevolent, Barad draws on only one function of homographesis: the inscription of identities that are readable within projects of sexual justice and amelioration, and so she overlooks how writing and breeching also de-scribe such identities and the politics that serve them.

The queer politics of nature (here, exemplified by Barad's work, but by no means contained to it and by no means excluding my own) will need to engage this double operation that Edelman names homographesis. I have outlined here one symptom of how such engagements always fail: how queer readings of nature that valorize the inhuman and re-valorize nature in order to impeach conventional scientism have ended up reinforcing the legibility of the human or the homosexual as a site to be protected against dehumanization. Such "failures," as Edelman reminds us, are inevitable:

> Even as I call for it, though, I call such a project impossible because it aims, with an insistence I link to the pure repetition of the death drive, to expose within the social something inherently unrecognizable, something radically nonidentical, that functions to negate whatever is, whatever is allowed to be by the various regimes of normativity to which, however inconsistently, we all, as subjects, subscribe. ("Ever After" 473)

If it is not possible to disentangle the regulatory and deconstructive functions of homographesis, or to choose one function over the other, then the confusions in Luciano and Chen and Barad and Stryker are not errors to be corrected but rather one more iteration of a sodomitical economy to be found underwriting and undermining every text/material/world. My goal here has not been to demand that this work be corrected, but rather to argue that nature, thus sodomized, cannot be captured for affirmative politics. It is both with and against Barad, Luciano, Chen and Stryker that I am suggesting that queer readings of nature try to remain alive to the ceaseless, confusing, spoiling negativity of nature's homographematic operations.

disclosure statement

No potential conflict of interest was reported by the author.

notes

1 Elsewhere Luciano ("The Inhuman Anthropocene") calls "inhuman humanism" a contradiction suggesting a usage of inhuman to mean cruelty; whereas Chen (*Animacies*) pairs human and inhuman, taking them to be roughly equivalent to live and dead, animate and inanimate. Interestingly, a Google Scholar search for the terms "queer" and "inhuman" ranks first a paper from the *Journal of Child Psychology and Psychiatry* that reports on a case of severe domestic deprivation and abuse of twin boys: "the people next door [to where the boys lived] testified that they often heard queer, inhuman shrieks which resembled howling" (Koluchová 107). Furthering the semantic proliferation of "inhuman" (animalistic/howling) and intensifying the depravity of "queer," this conventional psychological report and its proximity to the Chen and Luciano introduction (ranked second by Google Scholar) suggest that queer/inhuman, already in circulation, will breach the confines of Luciano and Chen's introduction. My goal here is not to delineate the correct uses of these terms but rather to pay some attention to this polysemy and its effects.

2 While she much more clearly distinguishes the inhuman from the non-human, Karen Barad nonetheless seems to make a similar kind of move. For Barad, the inhuman (usually understood as a lack of compassion) becomes, ironically, the means by which we may be more compassionate. That is, the inhuman "may be the very condition of possibility of feeling the suffering of the other, of literally being in touch with the other, of feeling the exchange of e-motion in the binding obligations of entanglements" ("On Touching" 219). As I will argue below, Barad tends to under-read for the constitutive violence of such touchings, exchanges and obligations:

> living compassionately requires recognizing and facing our responsibility to the infinitude of the other, welcoming the stranger whose very existence is the possibility of touching and being touched, who gifts us with both the ability to respond and the longing for justice-to-come. (Ibid.)

3 Hollin et al. graph the exponential increase in citations of Barad's work since the publication of *Meeting the Universe Halfway* in 2007.

4 Section 377 of the Indian Penal Code (*Unnatural Offences*) states "Whoever voluntarily has carnal intercourse against the order of nature with any man, woman or animal, shall be punished with imprisonment for life, or with imprisonment of either description for a term which may extend to ten years, and shall also be liable to fine" (<lawcommissionofindia.nic.in/1-50/report42.pdf>; see also Arondekar; Puri). Even though the Supreme Court in the United States has deemed sodomy a constitutionally protected practice (*Lawrence v. Texas*), sodomy returned as a criminal act in the 2016 US election cycle in the state of Georgia when 83.3 per cent of voters approved an amendment to the constitution of Georgia to create the "Safe Harbor for Sexually Exploited Children Fund." The ballot question read:

> Shall the Constitution of Georgia be amended to allow additional penalties for criminal cases in which a person is adjudged guilty of keeping a place of prostitution, pimping, pandering, pandering by compulsion, solicitation of sodomy, masturbation for hire, trafficking of persons for sexual servitude, or sexual exploitation of children and to allow assessments on adult entertainment establishments to fund the Safe Harbor for Sexually Exploited Children Fund to pay for care and rehabilitative and social services for individuals in this state who have been or may be sexually exploited? (<https://ballotpedia.org/Georgia_Additional_Penalties_for_Sex_Crimes_to_Fund_Services_for_Sexually_Exploited_Children,_Amendment_2_(2016)>)

5 There is an extensive historical literature on sodomy, especially in the early modern period in Europe and the New World (e.g., Betteridge; Bray; Jordan; Traub). In addition, there are excellent readings of sodomy as a legal, racialized or cultural category (e.g., Huffer; Rodríguez; Puar; Puri; Ruskola; Thompson) and a number of critical readings of anality and its value for queer theory (Nash; Sedgwick; Stockton). The idea that sodomy might circulate as a conceptual rubric (rather than as a historical, behavioural or legal event) has been much less common since the early work by Edelman (*Homographesis*; "Ever After"), Goldberg and Bersani cited here. For recent queer work about nature, see Chen; Giffney and Hird; Mortimer-Sandilands and Erickson; Morton. I don't claim here to offer a survey of this emergent work, but I do wager that the difficulties in Barad's work in relation to negativity will be found in these texts as well. This is not because all these texts are in error, but because the operations of negativity are enduring in, and constitutive of, scenes of queerness.

6 See, for example, Wilson for a detailed examination of how Gayle Rubin claims a conceptual and political space for sexuality by detaching it from biology.

7 "The imploded phrase 'spacetimemattering' (without the usual hyphens to separate out the nouns) refers to the entangled nature of what are generally taken to be separate features" (Barad, "Nature's Queer Performativity (The Authorized Version)" 49).

8 *Nachträglichkeit* is translated in the Standard Edition of Freud's work as "deferred action." Jean Laplanche has suggested that the term "afterwardsness" might be a better rendering of the idea that a "second" psychic event may become the cause for a "first" psychic event that has happened earlier. Laplanche and Pontalis note that "human sexuality, with the peculiar unevenness of its temporal development, provides an eminently suitable field for the phenomenon of deferred action" (112).

9 It is worth noting that grammatology, in the conventional sense of the term that Derrida redeploys in *Of Grammatology*, includes within its purview the science of orthography (which studies, amongst other things, the norms of spelling). Spelling is, of course, a central concern for his deployment of the neologism *différance*:

> I will speak, therefore, of the letter *a*, this initial letter which it apparently has been necessary to insinuate, here and there, into the writing of the word *difference*; and to do so in the course of a writing on writing, and also of a writing within writing whose different trajectories thereby find themselves, at certain very determined points, intersecting with a kind of gross spelling mistake. (Derrida, "Différance" 3)

10 Arguing for the "possibility of *empirical* support for deconstructive ideas like *différance*" ("Nature's Queer Performativity (The Authorized Version)" 45), Barad sees a broad similarity between *différance* and her ideas of diffraction ("*identity is diffraction/différance/differing/deferring/differentiating*" 32) and agential realism ("There is no pure external position, only agential separability, differences within, *différance*" 47) that she has formulated through close engagement with the specifics of quantum physics. Breaching (and the differences between breaches) has been an important part of Derrida's formulation of *différance*:

> The two apparently different values of *différance* [differing and deferring] are tied together in Freudian theory [...] The concepts of trace (*Spur*), of breaching (*Bahnung*), and of the forces of breaching, from the *Project* on, are inseparable from the concept of difference. The origin of memory, and of the psyche as (conscious or unconscious) memory in general, can be described only by taking into account the difference between breaches. Freud says so overtly. There is no breach without difference and no difference without trace. (Derrida, "Différance" 18)

bibliography

Arondekar, Anjali. "Without a Trace: Sexuality and the Colonial Archive." *Journal of the History of Sexuality* 14.1 (2005): 10–27. Print.

Bagemihl, Bruce. *Biological Exuberance: Animal Homosexuality and Natural Diversity*. New York: St. Martin's, 1999. Print.

Barad, Karen. *Meeting the Universe Halfway: Quantum Physics and the Entanglement of Matter and Meaning*. Durham, NC: Duke UP, 2007. Print.

Barad, Karen. "Nature's Queer Performativity." *Qui Parle: Critical Humanities and Social Sciences* 19.2 (2011): 121–58. Print.

Barad, Karen. "Nature's Queer Performativity (The Authorized Version)." *Women, Gender and Research (Kvinder, Køn og Forskning)*. Spec. issue of *Feminist Materialisms* 1–2 (2012): 25–53. Print.

Barad, Karen. "On Touching – The Inhuman That Therefore I Am." *differences* 23.3 (2012): 206–23. Print.

Barad, Karen. "Queer Causation and the Ethics of Mattering." Giffney and Hird 311–38. Print.

Barad, Karen. "TransMaterialities: Trans*/Matter/Realities and Queer Political Imaginings." *GLQ: A Journal of Lesbian and Gay Studies* 21.2–3 (2015): 387–422. Print.

Bersani, Leo. "Is the Rectum a Grave?" 1987. Bersani 3–30. Print.

Bersani, Leo. *Is the Rectum a Grave? And Other Essays*. Chicago: U of Chicago P, 2010. Print.

Betteridge, Tom, ed. *Sodomy in Early Modern Europe*. Manchester: Manchester UP, 2002. Print.

Bray, Alan. *Homosexuality in Renaissance England*. New York: Columbia UP, 1982. Print.

Chen, Mel Y. *Animacies: Biopolitics, Racial Mattering, and Queer Affect*. Durham, NC: Duke UP, 2012. Print.

Derrida, Jacques. "Différance." 1972. *Margins of Philosophy*. Chicago: U of Chicago P, 1978. 3–27. Print.

Derrida, Jacques. *Writing and Difference*. Chicago: U of Chicago P, 1978. Print.

Edelman, Lee. "Ever After: History, Negativity, and the Social." *South Atlantic Quarterly* 106.3 (2007): 469–76. Print.

Edelman, Lee. *Homographesis: Essays in Gay Literary and Cultural Theory*. New York and London: Routledge, 1994. Print.

Foucault, Michel. *The History of Sexuality, Volume 1: An Introduction.* London: Vintage, 1978. Print.

Freud, Sigmund. "From the History of an Infantile Neurosis [Wolf Man]." *The Standard Edition of the Complete Psychological Works of Sigmund Freud.* Vol. XVII. London: Hogarth, 1918. 7–122. Print.

Giffney, Noreen, and Myra J. Hird, eds. *Queering the Non/Human.* Aldershot and Burlington, VT: Ashgate, 2008. Print.

Goldberg, Jonathan. *Sodometries: Renaissance Texts, Modern Sexualities.* 1992. New York: Fordham UP, 2010. Print.

Goldberg, Jonathan, ed. *Reclaiming Sodom.* New York and London: Routledge, 1994. Print.

Hollin, Gregory, et al. "(Dis)entangling Barad: Materialisms and Ethics." *Social Studies of Science* 47.6 (2017). 918–41. Print.

Huffer, Lynne. *Are the Lips a Grave? A Queer Feminist on the Ethics of Sex.* New York: Columbia UP, 2013. Print.

Jordan, Mark D. *The Invention of Sodomy in Christian Theology.* Chicago: U of Chicago P, 1998. Print.

Koluchová, Jarmila. "Severe Deprivation in Twins: A Case Study." *Journal of Child Psychology and Psychiatry* 13.2 (1972): 107–14. Print.

Laplanche, Jean. *Essays on Otherness.* New York and London: Routledge, 1999. Print.

Laplanche, Jean, and Jean-Bertrand Pontalis. *The Language of Psychoanalysis.* 1967. London: Karnac, 1988. Print.

Luciano, Dana. "The Inhuman Anthropocene." *Avidly: A Channel of the Los Angeles Review of Books* 22 (2015). Web. 14 Dec. 2017. <http://avidly.lareviewofbooks.org/2015/03/22/the-inhuman-anthropocene>.

Luciano, Dana, and Mel Y. Chen. "Introduction: Has the Queer Ever Been Human?" *GLQ: A Journal of Lesbian and Gay Studies* 21.2 (2015): 183–207. Print.

Mortimer-Sandilands, Catriona, and Bruce Erickson. *Queer Ecologies: Sex, Nature, Politics, Desire.* Bloomington: Indiana UP, 2010. Print.

Morton, Timothy. "Guest Column: Queer Ecology." *PMLA* 125.2 (2010): 273–82. Print.

Nash, Jennifer C. "Black Anality." *GLQ: A Journal of Lesbian and Gay Studies* 20.4 (2014): 439–60. Print.

Puar, Jasbir. *Terrorist Assemblages: Homonationalism in Queer Times.* Durham, NC: Duke UP, 2007. Print.

Puri, Jyoti. *Sexual States: Governance and the Struggle over the Antisodomy Law in India.* Durham, NC: Duke UP, 2016. Print.

Rodríguez, Juana María. *Sexual Futures, Queer Gestures, and Other Latina Longings.* New York: New York UP, 2014. Print.

Ruskola, Teemu. "Gay Rights versus Queer Theory: What is Left of Sodomy after *Lawrence v. Texas?*" *Social Text* 23.2–3: (2005): 235–49. Print.

Sedgwick, Eve Kosofsky. "Anality: News from the Front." *Studies in Gender and Sexuality* 11.3 (2010): 151–62. Print.

Stockton, Kathryn Bond. *Beautiful Bottom, Beautiful Shame: Where "Black" Meets "Queer."* Durham, NC: Duke UP, 2006. Print.

Stryker, Susan. "My Words to Victor Frankenstein above the Village of Chamounix: Performing Transgender Rage." *GLQ: A Journal of Lesbian and Gay Studies* 1.3 (1994): 237–54. Print.

Stryker, Susan. "Transing the Queer (In)human." *GLQ: A Journal of Lesbian and Gay Studies* 21.2 (2015): 227–30. Print.

Thompson, Katrina Daly. "Discreet Talk about Supernatural Sodomy, Transgressive Gender Performance, and Male Same-Sex Desire in Zanzibar Town." *GLQ: A Journal of Lesbian and Gay Studies* 21.4 (2015): 521–59. Print.

Traub, Valerie. *The Renaissance of Lesbianism in Early Modern England.* Cambridge: Cambridge UP, 2002. Print.

Wilson, Elizabeth A. "Underbelly." *differences* 21.1 (2010): 194–208. Print.

I

alexander howard

SOLID OBJECTS AND MODERN TONICS, OR, WHO'S AFRAID OF THE BIG CAMP WOOLF?

Marsha Bryant and Douglas Mao tell us that "there can be neither camp nor modernism without someone's going over the top" (2). This exploratory paper seeks in part to build on the theoretical advances made by critics such as these. The first section comprises a broad theoretical overview. The second part demonstrates just how easily high modernism can tip over into outright camp. The third considers the manner in which bawdy camp can be read in relation to late iterations of literary modernism. In both instances, Bryant and Mao write, "[i]n camp as in modernism, critical evaluation involves distinguishing successful excess from excess that fails, and in both, such judgments often hinge on how gender is constructed or construed" (ibid.). We need to pay attention to the notion of evaluative judgement that Bryant and Mao evoke in this passage, not least of all because both camp and modernism are critical concepts that have often proved difficult to pin down and assess. Consider, for example, the manner in which Sean Latham and Gayle Rogers open their recent account of the evolution of the idea otherwise known as modernism. In their shared estimation, the term itself "has now beset, driven, and often befuddled generations of students and scholars alike" (1). Why might this be so? Their initial answer has to do with the paradoxical fact that, for them, "there is no such thing as modernism – no singular definition capable of bringing order to the diverse multitude of creators, manifestos, practices, and politics that have been variously constellated around this enigmatic term" (ibid.). The concept as traditionally understood is also peculiarly removed, as Latham and Rogers point out, "from political history (unlike the crisply defined Victorian era) and even from the Western calendar itself, leaving it unmoored from something as vague as twentieth-century studies" (ibid.). All this, we might add, before the question of theoretical evaluation even gets a chance to rear its ugly head. In short: it seems as if we have our critical work cut out for us when it comes to modernism.

In this sense, then, if we were to adapt the delightfully pithy axiom of an older and much wiser writer, we could say that the pure and simple truth of modernism is that it is rarely pure and never simple. This, it seems fair to say, is the sort of critical line that gets repeated from time to time by critics working in the remarkably capacious and rapaciously profitable arena of modernism studies. We see this in the discipline-defining work of critics such as Susan Stanford Friedman. "Modernity," Friedman declares, "has no single meaning, not even in one location" (473). Global or local? It apparently makes no difference. This explains why, from Friedman's vantage point at least,

> modernity appears infinitely expandable. Listening to these diverse voices, reading their scripts, I despair – especially for the new scholar just entering the field of dreams, a Tower of Babel with too many levels to climb; but also for the older scholar, trained in the old modernist studies: vertigo out on a limb, whirled up into a vortex of the new. Yet I also rejoice. Change is what drew me to modernism in the beginning. Why should it ossify? Why should the fluid freeze over, the undecidable become decided? (Ibid.)

I wonder, occasionally, as to just how far critical stances such as this might be able to carry us. I wonder, too, about purported objects of study and sometimes about the very idea of critical objectivity itself. What strikes me, reading passages like the one above, is the all-too-easy way in which the personal – that is, the purely subjective reflection – threatens to overwhelm anything approaching a properly critical position. In the interests of full disclosure, I should add that I have fallen into such a trap more than once, as the pronominal register of this paragraph should suggest. Having said that, without wishing to dispute the veracity of the important claims made by critics such as Friedman, Latham, and Rogers, I do think it possible to establish something that might at least pass muster as a workable – and coherent – definition of modernism. In order to do so, however, we have to turn briefly to the work of a self-confessedly ossified critical thinker.

According to Fredric Jameson,

> "Modernity" always means setting a date and positing a beginning, and it is in any case always amusing and instructive to make an inventory of the possibilities, which tend to move around in chronological time, the most recent – nominalism (and also McLuhanism) – being among the oldest. (31)

Such an assertion doesn't seem all that far removed from the argument put forth by critics such as those mentioned above. Jameson certainly seems unable – in this volume at least – to make his mind up when it comes to the dating of modernity. He details how some critics have argued that the modern age started around the time of the Protestant Reformation. But he also describes how more philosophically minded people disagree. The philosophers tend, Jameson tells us, to plump for Descartes's discovery of the cogito when it comes time to determine when we moved into the modern period proper. The list of possibilities as it currently stands in this sense appears to be seemingly endless. And yet commentators continue to offer up more and more alternatives. It is almost as if critics simply cannot help themselves. This leads Jameson to pose the following question in turn. "What purpose can the revival of the slogan 'modernity' still serve," Jameson ponders,

> after the thoroughgoing removal of the modern from all the shelves and shop windows, its retirement from the media, and the obedient demodernification of all but a few cantankerous and self-avowedly saurian intellectuals? It must somehow be a postmodern thing, one begins to suspect, the recrudescence of the language of an older modernity: for it is certainly not the result of any honest philological and historiographic interest in our recent past. (7)

What we have been witnessing over the past couple of decades is nothing less than, in Jameson's recounting, "the reminting of the modern, its repackaging, its production in great quantities for renewed sales in the intellectual marketplace" (ibid.). In Jameson's deliberately provocative reading,

> this means that there can be a modernity for everybody which is different from the standard or hegemonic Anglo-Saxon model. Whatever you dislike about the latter,

including the subaltern position it leaves you in, can be effaced by the reassuring and "cultural" notion that there can be a Latin-American kind, or an Indian kind or an African kind, and so forth. (12)

Yet this would be to miss the economic forest for the cultural trees. It would be, as Jameson suggests,

> to overlook the other fundamental meaning of modernity which is that of a worldwide capitalism itself. The standardization projected by capitalist globalization in this third or late stage of the system casts considerable doubt on all these pious hopes for cultural variety in a future world colonized by a universal market order. (12–13)

Irrespective of whether one agrees with everything Jameson has to say about cultural exceptionalism in the early stages of the twenty-first century, this account of what he describes as the other primary meaning of modernity furnishes us with a firm conceptual base from which to bear down on the interrelated notion of modernism. "Why not simply posit modernity as the new historical situation," Jameson suggests, "modernization as the process whereby we get there, and modernism as a reaction to that situation and the process alike, a reaction that can be aesthetic and philosophico-ideological, just as it can be negative as well as positive" (99). Indeed, why not? If nothing else, Jameson's historicized account of the condition of modernity and the emergence of modernism affords us the opportunity to take a step back critically, to consider how exactly we got here, and to think a while about where we might be heading. Before we do that, though, I think it worth spending just a touch more time getting to critical grips with modernism and modernity. Consider if you will, for a moment or two, certain of the prefatory remarks contained in the second edition of Marshall Berman's famous account of the way in which one experiences modernity. Berman defines "modernism as any attempt by modern men and women to become subjects as well as objects of modernization, to get a grip on the modern world and make themselves at home in it" (6). Berman's expansive definition of modernism dovetails nicely with the one proffered subsequently by Jameson. As we can see, they both emphasize the fact that one cannot have modernism without modernity. By the same token, however, they are both clear on the following point: modernism and modernity are not one and the same. Aesthetic or otherwise, modernism should always be thought of as outcropping of modernity. In this very real sense then, modernism should at all times be thought of – and I recognize that I run the risk of sounding slightly repetitive here – as a thoroughly and unremittingly historical phenomenon.

What, though, of the second of our chosen theoretical terms? Critics at least seem to agree on dates when it comes to camp. Fabio Cleto reminds us that the word "camp" "first entered the sanctioned space of 'the language' in a dictionary of late-Victorian slang" (9). As defined at that particular moment in history, the term pertained to a number of loosely grouped actions and gestures of exaggerated emphasis, which were favoured by – to parse the entry recorded in J. Redding Ware's seminal *Victorian Dictionary of Slang and Phrase* – anonymous persons of a highly questionable character. Picking up the indexical and linguistic thread a century or so later, Cleto details the manner in which the freshly minted notion of camp soon began to accrue a certain amount of "currency in the slang of theatricals, high society, the fashion world, showbiz, and the underground city" (ibid.). From the very outset, then, camp has always been tied in a certain sense to the arts. But there is slightly more to the matter than this. David M. Halperin details how "camp was first elaborated by gay men as a collective, in-group practice before other social groups, seeing its subversive potential and its wide applicability, claimed it for their own purposes" (135). We will return shortly to the problematic notion of appropriation that Halperin evokes in his discussion of camp. Before we do, though, I want first to say a few things about the wider world into which camp was born. Lest we forget, this was a period in history when industrialized societies began to privilege, in the words of Michel Foucault, "[the] exchange of discourses, through questions that extracted admissions, and confidences that went beyond the questions that were asked" (41). Foucault is referring, of course, to the manner in which budding psychoanalysts such as Sigmund Freud and prominent sexologists including Havelock Ellis and Richard von Krafft-Ebing, reacting as they were in a professional capacity to the burgeoning late Victorian interest in the relationship between the circuits of erotic desire and societal value, sought to render overtly visible the latent secrets of personal sexual conduct. This speaks directly to the issue of camp. Or rather, it speaks to a large-scale societal tendency that those invested in the ideas and practice of camp sought, with good reason, to sidestep. Historical context is again important here. It is generally accepted amongst contemporary critics that camp was an integral part of a specifically homosexual form of social discourse. It was a practice grounded in the necessity of passing for straight in an overwhelmingly heteronormative and legally oppressive world – a social realm in which visibility was, to borrow from Leo Bersani, "a precondition of surveillance, disciplinary intervention, and, at the limit, gender-cleansing" (11). Camp as broadly conceived at the outset thus provided queer subjects with a necessarily clandestine, tactical means with which to forge a relatively secure path through life. Recognizable only to those in the know, clandestine signs, theatrical role-play, and verbalized innuendo functioned in a very specific capacity as an efficient and necessary means of indirect communication amongst queer peers moving through otherwise hostile public spaces in the latter stages of the nineteenth century and the first half of the twentieth.

This all seems fairly clear-cut. Yet we soon find that we're on remarkably slippery critical footing when it comes to the question of what camp has come and continues to mean. "If perversion is the last word in certainty," Allan Pero argues, "then camp has the last word in uncertainty" (28). Richard Dyer would most likely agree with this suggestion. Dyer notes that "arguments have lasted all night about what camp really is and what it means" (48). These all-nighter arguments about camp tend to cleave along two main lines. There are, in Dyer's admittedly selective reading, "two different interpretations which connect at certain points: camping about, mincing and screaming; and a certain taste in art and entertainment, a certain sensibility" (ibid.). I want to start by dealing with the second of these interpretations. Dyer is alluding to the line of critical inquiry pursued by Susan Sontag in her seminal, if perpetually problematic "Notes on 'Camp'" (1964). In these "Notes," which are dedicated to the memory of Oscar Wilde, Sontag describes the camp "eye" as having "the power to transform experience" (277). The camp "eye," or "sensibility" is, for Sontag, "one that is alive to a double sense in which some things can be taken" (281). This, she posits, "comes out clearly in the vulgar use of the word Camp as a verb, 'to camp,' something that people do" (ibid.). "To camp," in the sense that Sontag understands in her essay, is thus to engage with, or to seek recourse to, "a mode of seduction" – a mode of seduction which, in her stylistically inclined treatment of the matter, "employs flamboyant mannerisms susceptible of a double interpretation; gestures full of duplicity, with a witty meaning for cognoscenti and another, more impersonal, for outsiders" (ibid.). Sontag is, without a shadow of a doubt, clearly aware of the historical significance of camp. That much is clear in the lines just quoted. In the end, however, it all comes down to a question of taste for Sontag. "There is taste in people," Sontag writes, "visual taste, taste in emotion – and there is taste in acts, taste in morality. Intelligence, as well, is really a kind of taste: taste in ideas" (276).

There is taste in art, too, of course. This is where Sontag's intervention begins to come into its own. Brian M. Peters and Bruce E. Drushel stress that Sontag "is responsible for not only initiating the first serious discussions of its cultural impact but also for her attempts at describing (though not defining) the phenomenon" (viii). Peters and Drushel also foreground the fact that Sontag's

> understanding of camp (and somewhat problematized position on it) rests on the notion that what some consider to be a

lower cultural form at best and a celebration of bad taste at worst can become incredible and certainly worth of study. (Ibid.)

Pay close attention to the emphasis being placed on the cultural side of things here. This aesthetically weighted interpretation of camp has proved influential and controversial in equal measure. According to Fabio Cleto, "Sontag's essay disseminated camp as the cipher for contemporary culture, as a refined – and, most infamously, apolitical – aesthetic taste for the vulgar and the appreciation of kitschy middle-class pretensions" (10). Certain critics have bridled at Sontag's treatment of camp. Moe Meyer has, by way of example, been extremely critical of Sontag for "detaching the signifying codes from their queer signified" (4). To put this in slightly simpler terms, in Meyer's caustic reckoning, the understanding and treatment of camp has – post-Sontag – become increasingly watered-down. That is to say, Meyer is of the opinion that critics and spectators alike have forgotten the important social function and potentially life-saving role that camp could and indeed did play for a host of legally and psychologically oppressed people. Meyer thinks this state of affairs simply unforgivable. All the more, given that historical analysis confirms the specifically sexualized origins and politicized connotations pertaining to the term. This leads Meyer to assert that prominent cultural critics such as Sontag have effectively, if unwittingly, "killed off the binding referent of Camp – the Homosexual" (6). As a result, in Meyer's reading, the discourse of camp has become increasingly "confused and conflated with rhetorical and performative strategies such as irony, satire, burlesque, and travesty; and with cultural movements such as Pop" (ibid.). This, in Meyer's eyes, simply will not do. Meyer argues there was, is, and will always be only one kind of camp. "And it is queer. It can be engaged directly by the queer to produce social visibility in the praxis of every-day life," Meyer writes, "or it can be manifested as the camp trace by the un-queer in order [...] to provide queer access to the apparatus of representation" (4).

It remains to be seen whether Meyer gets it absolutely right here. It certainly seems worth noting that some critics have moved to productively complicate Meyer's theorization of camp. For instance, Cleto posits that Meyer's rather rigid definition of queer subjectivity leaves no room for strategic manoeuvre, and also discloses "a will to ascertain a unified definitional ground [that] would thus devoid that very subjectivity of a specific positioning within culture" (18). In Cleto's estimation, Meyer's account of queer subjectivity is simply "too specific" (ibid.). Cleto suggests that Meyer's account of queer subjectivity forecloses certain avenues of potentially revealing critical inquiry. To take a specific example, Meyer's insistence that there can be only one (queer) kind of camp effectively forces him to ignore what Cleto describes as "the complex relation of camp to the phenomenology of pop and Kitsch, for that relation partakes of the Sontagian expropriation of a specifically gay formation" (19). There is a lot to be said about critical disagreements such as these. If nothing else, they serve to remind us of the fact that camp continues to dazzle and bedazzle in equal measure. But the basic point I want to emphasize here is this: camp has been, can be, and continues to be understood in a variety of ways. On the one hand, we are dealing with a historically and socially specific term that necessarily depends on indirection and innuendo. On the other, we are dealing with a culturally weighted concept that privileges a sense of flamboyance, excess, theatricality and exaggeration.

So much, then, for critical consensus about camp. How, I want now to ask, might we start to bring camp and modernism together? Much critical discourse concerning the ostensibly unrelated concepts of modernism and camp foregrounds the fact that both are difficult to define. This much we already know. Interestingly, Corey K. Creekmur and Alexander Doty suggest that camp is "perhaps gay culture's crucial contribution to modernism" (2). Whilst a little short on detail, I think this suggestion worth bearing in mind when reading through the remaining pages of the present paper. We might also bear in mind the way in which critical attempts to define and theorize both camp and modernism occasionally converge in an interesting and productive fashion. Pero argues that "[c]amp resides neither in the eye of the beholder nor in the gaze of the object; rather, camp resides in the unconscious relationship between them" (31). We would do well, I think, to pay close attention to the issue of relationality as evoked by Pero. The enigmatic and at times downright elusive quality of much of what we now call camp has directly to do with the idea of relations, unconscious or not. Robyn Weigman's recent intervention in the realm of "object relations" theory has much to offer us in this regard. To be clear, Weigman's appropriation of this concept is not indicative of

> a theoretical commitment to a distinct body of psychoanalytic thought, but a reflection of [her] interest in the simplest idea the phrase helps to deliver: namely, that objects of study are as fully enmeshed in fantasy, projection, and desire as those that inhabit the more familiar itinerary of intimate life, such as sex, lover, parent, sibling, friend. (20)

To this, Weigman adds the following:

> By object, I mean to designate targets of study that reflect a seemingly material existence in the world (as in people, goods, laws, books, or films) and those that do not reveal such materiality in any immediately graspable way (as in discourse, ideology, history, personhood, the unconscious, and desire itself). By relation, I mean the constitutive dependence of one thing on another, such that no critical practice can be considered the consequence of its own singular agency. (Ibid.)

I quote at length from Weigman because the points raised and terms defined in this passage help us better appreciate what it is about camp that proves so elusive. Camp resides in the murky constitutive space between subject and object. That is what makes this most relational and most constitutively dependent of concepts – and indeed, objects – so difficult to conceptualize. In other words, in order to understand camp, we need to be able to carve out a critical path through a forest of potentially competing associations and shifting relations. Cleto glosses precisely this point in a suitably dazzling manner. Cleto argues:

> The camp gem requires a discerning eye or, in critical jargon, a certain deployment of (cultural) capital, not only to ratify the refined stone as a desirable ornament, but also to distinguish it from its cheap counterpart – a banal, and rather vulgar, zircon – which virtually anybody can have access to, and which brings with itself the seamless, dreadful realm of anonymity. (2)

To appreciate camp and the attendant camp gem, then, we need to be able to position ourselves accordingly as critics. We need, that is, to be able to distinguish between the radiant camp object and the pale kitsch imitators that more often than not surround it. We need, in effect, to show that we are in the know, that we are capable of reading the appropriate signs. This, in a roundabout fashion, brings us back to the issue of modernism. If we are to fully appreciate modernism and the various art objects associated with modernism, we need, in a manner not all that dissimilar to the position outlined by Cleto in the passage just mentioned, to distinguish it from what it is not. We have to demonstrate, in essence, that we are truly in the know when it comes to modernism, and that we are fully capable of knowing modernism when we see it – that is, to put the matter in the simplest terms possible, that we really get modernism, and that, finally, we can demonstrate that we know that we really get modernism to an equally informed and critically aware audience that also gets modernism and knows that it gets modernism.

But herein lies a particularly tricky analytical problem. Bryant and Mao caution that "modernism and camp invite questions about whether they die as soon as they're coherently named, as soon as they're discussed routinely by intellectuals, or as soon as they become palatable to populations outside the original cognoscenti" (3). As soon as we get near to establishing a stable critical fix on camp and modernism, then, despite what critics such as Moe Meyer and Fredric Jameson might say about the respective terms they discuss, we also run the risk of spoiling them to a certain extent, of doing them a critical disservice, potentially diminishing their respective conceptual charges and charms. One thinks here, of course, of certain of the influential critical reading strategies developed by Eve Kosofsky Sedgwick. I have in mind here the specifically "reparative" model of reading privileged by this important critic in her late work on the question of affect. Differentiating her own approach from that of more hermeneutically suspicious theoreticians (such as the aforementioned Jameson), Sedgwick, as is well known, comes to privilege a model of textual criticism that encourages readers to consider not only what works of art have to tell us and how they might be thought of – and indeed chastised – as aesthetically compromised or conceptually deficient, but how they might in fact delight, entertain, and even surprise. Bearing all this in mind, we need, I think, to find an appropriate way of both thinking and writing about camp and modernism that acknowledges the importance of and pays sufficient attention to the notion of periodization and which proves capable of encouraging and sustaining open-ended critical investigation. I want to explore the potential merits and test the respective limits of just such a method in the rest of the space afforded me here. Specifically, I want to see how a historicized understanding of camp can be brought to bear on modernism, and how a historicized understanding of modernism might be brought to bear on camp. Without further ado, then, I propose that we proceed by way of example – or rather, that we spend some time approaching a specific example, a dazzling gem of a literary object plucked almost at random from a couple of different critical angles. My intuition is that in so doing we will soon find that camp and modernism do indeed coalesce in some particularly delightful, entertaining, and unexpectedly revealing ways. All it takes, I want to suggest, is one little push.

2

An up-and-coming – if easily distracted – parliamentarian is walking along a beach. His name is John. It transpires later that he is an inveterate collector of various trinkets and trophies. He is currently weaving his way towards an abandoned maritime vessel of sorts. It soon becomes apparent that he is also engaged in a spirited verbal debate with a trusted intimate, Charles:

"Politics be damned!" issued clearly from the body on the left-hand side, and, as these words were uttered, the mouths, noses, chins, little moustaches, tweed caps, rough boots, shooting coats, and check stockings of the two speakers became clearer and clearer; the smoke of their pipes went up into the air; nothing was so solid, so living, so hard, red, hirsute and virile as these two bodies for miles and miles of sea and sandhill. (54)

This passage was penned by none other than Virginia Woolf. It is taken from her tonally oblique short story "Solid Objects" (1920). Beci Carver is of the opinion that the story is best understood in terms of doubleness. This is a serious and intellectually high-minded text that wears its modernist and post-Kantian traces clearly on its sleeves, Carver tells us, displaying as it does "a simultaneous sense of the significance of matter and of its insignificance" (20). There are certainly at least two simultaneous senses in which we might read Woolf's curious account of one man's burgeoning obsession with solid matter. We can, following the lead of literary critics such as Carver, adopt a broadly philosophical stance when striving to interpret the story. In equal measure, however, we might choose instead to foreground the latently queer occurrences contained in the text. I am, as the following overview of "Solid Objects" demonstrates, significantly more interested in the second of these critical approaches. Of course, I am hardly the first person to work along lines such as these. Think, for instance, as Madelyn Detloff would have us do, about all those repeated and "hyperbolic spoofs of normative gender performance" (19) on display in Woolf's glorious – and endlessly scrutinized because outwardly gender-bending – *Orlando* (1928). That novel delights precisely, as Detloff notes, "because it is so bawdy, grotesque, hyperbolic" (21). Not so, though, the short story that preoccupies us at the present moment. Hence the need for that gentle nudge I mentioned before.

Consider afresh the long extract cited above. Much could be made, were one so inclined, of the sheer physicality of the two "hard, red, hirsute and virile" masculine subjects striding purposefully across the sandy landscape – a seaside setting with nary a beached fisherman or salty seadog in sight. Consider, too, their vigorous actions upon reaching their destination. Woolf's physically chiselled and heroically hairy protagonists launch themselves immediately, as if possessed and ravenous in equal measure, "down by the six ribs and spine of the pilchard boat" (54). Casting political discussion aside for a moment or two, John, having mistaken himself momentarily for one of the primary male characters in *Women in Love*, throws himself down onto the roughly granular turf in a manner that would most likely have a phallically inclined psychoanalyst such as Jacques Lacan yelping for joy. His fingers begin to burrow, "down, down, into the sand" (ibid.). Before long, these probing, grasping, and – appropriately enough – most Lawrentian of digits happen upon and curl "round something hard – a full drop of solid matter – and gradually dislodged a large irregular lump, and brought it to the surface" (55). Woolf describes the strangely charged and curiously weighted object now secured firmly in John's manly grip in the following way:

> It was a lump of glass, so thick as to be opaque; the smoothing of the sea had completely worn off any edge or shape, so it was impossible to say whether it had been bottle, tumbler or window pane; it was nothing but glass; it was almost a precious stone. You had only to enclose it in a rim of gold, or pierce it with a wire, and it became a jewel; part of a necklace, or a dull, green light upon a finger. Perhaps after all it was really a gem; something worn by a dark Princess trailing her finger in the water as she sat in the stern of the boat and listened to the slaves singing as they rowed her across the Bay. Or the oak sides of a sunk Elizabethan treasure-chest had split apart, and, rolled over and over, over and over, its emeralds had come at last to shore. (Ibid.)

Now, after the imagining of what seems to be a perfectly Freudian sort of receptacle, comes the calm after the deluge of the storm. Having first slipped this indeterminate glass object surreptitiously into his pocket, our urbane subject then sets off back to the city. This pipe-smoking and ruggedly handsome figure comes across as decidedly house-proud. Ensconced safely in the domestic realm once more, John places the solid object "upon the mantelpiece, where it stood heavy upon a little pile of bills and letters" (56). There it "served not only as an excellent paperweight, but also as a natural stopping place for the young man's eyes when they wandered from his book" (ibid.).

We can only speculate as to which book John has placed on his desk. Some sort of dull governmental treatise or paper? Probably. But perhaps he could be reading something more interesting. A work of fiction perhaps. Something by, say, the notorious Oscar Wilde or even Leopold von Sacher-Masoch? Unfortunately, we are not in a position to say either way. Your guess is in this respect just as good as mine. What we can say with a fair degree of certainty, however, is that wander from the pages of the book on the desk in question this reputable young man's eyes indeed continually do. Woolf emphasizes as much in the next passage:

> Looked at again and again half consciously by a mind thinking of something else, any object mixes itself so profoundly with the stuff of thought that it loses its actual form and recomposes itself a little differently in an ideal shape which haunts the brain when we least expect it. (Ibid.)

Things start to get a little strange at this point. Taking unexpectedly to the streets, John finds "himself attracted to the windows of curiosity shops when he was out walking, merely because he saw something which reminded him of the lump of glass" (ibid.). It appears that the mere presence of the previously salvaged object has triggered in him a simultaneously obscure and profound reaction – a hitherto unknown and wholly insatiable desire of sorts. "Anything," Woolf writes, "so long as it was an object of some kind, more or less round, perhaps with a dying flame sunk in its mass, anything – china, glass, amber, rock, marble – even the smooth oval egg of a prehistoric bird would do" (ibid.). Increasingly obsessive, John begins, almost fetishistically one might say, "to haunt the places which [were] most prolific of broken china, such as pieces of waste land between railway lines, sites of demolished houses, and commons in the neighbourhood of London" (57–58). Taken aback at first by the sheer variety of trinkets now seemingly within his grasp, John rapidly amasses quite the collection of solid objects. As Woolf notes, "The finest specimens he would bring home and place upon his mantelpiece, where, however, their duty was more and more of an ornamental nature, since papers needing a weight to keep them down become scarcer and scarcer" (58).

John's evermore compulsive search for pleasing solid objects precipitates – as the previous lines suggest – something approaching a loss of professional control. He begins to neglect his duties as a career politician. He also seems to forget about poor old Charles. At the same time, this curious extra-professional obsession takes on what might well be described as a feverish quality:

> Provided with a bag and a long stick fitted with an adaptable hook, he ransacked all deposits of earth; raked beneath matted tangles of scrub; searched all alleys and spaces between walls where he had learned to expect to find objects of this kind thrown away. As his standard became higher and his taste more severe the disappointments were innumerable, but always some gleam of hope, some piece of china or glass curiously marked or broken, lured him on. (59)

Woolf's peculiar narrative begins to rush forward at quite a pace: "He was no longer young. His career – that is his political career – was a thing of the past. People gave up visiting him. He was too silent to be worth asking to dinner. He never talked to anyone about his serious ambitions; their lack of understanding was apparent in their behaviour" (ibid.). John's erstwhile colleague Charles is one such figure lacking in understanding. Shocked by the shabby appearance of John's usually well-maintained living room, a by now discombobulated Charles prepares to take leave of his dear friend for what will prove to be the final time. As he does, he notices something fixed, distant, and finally alarming in John's expression. Charles then departs, breaking away from – and perhaps up with – John "for ever" (ibid.).

Thus "Solid Objects." But what are we to make of it? Mark Booth suggested a long time ago that "[a] work of art may be verified as camp if we catch in it a reflection of a camp ambiguity in the mind of its creator" (19). Can we talk of this short modernist text in terms of camp ambiguity? We are, to be sure, dealing with a modern text quite unlike the later, overtly queer *Orlando*. Douglas Mao's detailed account of "Solid Objects" is helpful in this regard. Mao points out that the narrative of the text "seems at once intimate and allegorical; like many [of Woolf's shorter stories], its curiously affectless yet earnest mood gives it the feeling of an argument somehow premised on the metamorphosis of vague desire into a singular pathology" (26). Things are not quite that simple though. In this instance, Mao argues,

> the pathology in question has something like a tradition behind it, since as a doomed devotee of beauty who forsakes the world's proffered vulgarities in favor of the obscurely fine, John can trace an authentic descent from the Byronic wanderer and the Baudelairean flâneur, from the Huysmanian decadent and the *poète maudit*; and though he may not accede to the glory of one of Shelley's unacknowledged legislators of the world, his choice of the *res* proper over the *res publica* does lend him the distinction of having sacrificed to his profounder calling the chance to become an acknowledged legislator of England. (Ibid.)

Put another way, we might say that Woolf's early twentieth-century text is very much interested and invested in contemplating specific artistic energies and legacies that can be traced back into the nineteenth century. This is something that begins to come to the fore at the very end of the story. Woolf describes the way in which a single utterance from John leaves Charles

> profoundly uneasy; the most extraordinary doubts possessed him; he had a queer sense that they were talking about different things. He looked round to find some relief for his horrible depression, but the disorderly appearance of the room depressed him still further. (59)

Charles, to reiterate, simply does not get it: he lacks the requisite means – or the requisite taste perhaps – with which to properly understand his friend, or to fully appreciate his friend's preoccupation with solid objects. Mao asserts:

> Like a character in a Victorian novel, or rather a reader working with nineteenth-century narrative and decorative codes, Charles tries to determine how John's interior expresses its inhabitant's character; but in this unusual case the room's distinctive elements speak not of an ability to purchase expressive objects but of a profound possession by things, where this possession itself might figure as a demystification of Victorian fantasies of self-fashioning through acquisition. (27)

Without getting ahead of ourselves, there is, I think, a lot we might say here. Think, for instance, on the emphasis that Mao puts on the notion of profound possession, of seemingly all-encompassing obsession, of passionate attachment. Having done so, think a little on the idea of demystification.

This well-trodden critical notion gets at the heart of precisely what is at stake in Woolf's story. Given what we have just established, it comes as no surprise to find that the idea of demystification is tied in some sense to the accumulation of those aforementioned pieces of glass and china. Mao writes:

> The point of these objects is not what they do or say, but their sheer capacity to be appreciated within a setting that conjoins a certain freedom in manner of living to an intense aesthetic devotion – which is to say, amid the kind of domestic informality that was for Woolf the very emblem of passage from constraint, middle-class correctness, and the nineteenth century to freedom, moderate bohemianism, and modernity. (Ibid.)

This makes a lot of sense. It certainly chimes with certain of the remarks contained in what is indubitably Woolf's most widely reprinted and celebrated essay. "In the first place," Woolf writes, "to have a room of her own, let alone a quiet room or a sound-proof room, was out of the question, unless her parents were exceptionally rich or very noble, even up to the beginning of the nineteenth century" (40). This passage – lest anyone need reminding – appears in the seminal "A Room of One's Own" (1929). The next extract appears slightly later in the same tract. It seems fairly obvious, to Woolf,

> that even in the nineteenth century a woman was not encouraged to be an artist. On the contrary, she was snubbed, slapped, lectured and exhorted. Her mind must have been strained and her vitality lowered by the need of opposing this, of disproving that. (42)

All of which is perhaps to say that large swathes of patriarchal Victorian society took a particularly dim view of women expressing an interest in aesthetic matters, let alone those foolhardy women willing to devote themselves intensely to the production of aesthetic objects. Such threatening tendencies were thereby to be stamped out by those who simply could not tolerate such a prospect, by those who simply refused to understand.

Such a state of societal affairs is – issues of class mobility and gender imbalance notwithstanding – somewhat akin to the one that we find in Woolf's short story. We recall that the bourgeois politico Charles simply does not understand John's attachment to solid objects, aesthetically pleasing or otherwise. Try as he might, Charles cannot dissuade his former trusted confidante from what he perceives as the error of his ways. In no small part is this due to the fact that John is simply past caring. In John's cherished and closely guarded domestic sphere, Mao tells us, "contemplation displaces action; sheer existence takes precedence over significance; collecting usurps politics; and the ornamental or aesthetic supplants the instrumental" (29). I am keenly interested in the last of these points. Peter Nicholls has written of the manner in which famous late nineteenth-century decadent novels such as Joris-Karl Huysman's exemplary *Against Nature* (1884) are characterized by, amongst other things, a pursuit of artifice that is "complicit with a violent rejection of sociality" (54). Do we not see something similar occurring at the end of Woolf's short story? After all, as Mao reminds us,

> [i]t is in this transformation of means into ends that John most clearly marks himself an inheritor of those rebellions in which the aesthetes and decadents pitted a doctrine of beauty as terminal value against the renowned Victorian tendency to stress art's powers of moral instruction. (29)

Grounded as they are in the decadent aesthetic traditions of the nineteenth century, John's extra-professional preoccupations and commitments also – as should by now be self-evident – establish him as a staunchly queer subject of sorts. But this is not all. John's behaviour at the end of – and indeed throughout – the story serves simultaneously to position him as a connoisseur of a decidedly camp persuasion. In marked contrast to his former friend Charles, and long before critics such as Sontag arrive on the scene, Woolf's central character in this particular story seems on some level cognizant of the fact that there is a double sense in which certain things – and recently unearthed objects – may be taken. Woolf also seems on some level to know this. Think here, for example, of the previously cited passage in which Woolf moves to describe the solid object that John has just wrenched from the sand. We might simply be looking at a discarded piece of glass. This much is most certainly true. But we could just as soon be looking at some precious stone. Woolf's deliciously ambiguous and self-conscious use of connective punctuation in this passage leaves the reader hanging. This is perhaps the point. Insignificant or all important. Ordinary or exceptional. Workaday or fabulous. Conventional or camp. Things can just as easily swing either way when it comes to this modernist artwork. Woolf almost seems, we might well say, to be suggesting in this moment that everything hinges on a particular sort of critical discernment. So much depends, that is, on whether one is able to read the signs, on how one chooses to relate to objects, and possibly even indeed how one chooses to view the world. It is ultimately up to the reader to decide, to determine as to whether they are alive to the fact that other kinds of understanding are possible and desirable.

3

Perhaps more so than any other modernist, Charles Henri Ford always understood that other kinds of understanding were both possible and desirable. Ford was an important writer, editor, and filmmaker. He published his first little magazine as a restless teenager whilst based in Columbus, Mississippi. He named it *Blues: A Magazine of New Rhythms*. The first issue appeared in 1929. He is also often referred to as American's first fully-fledged surrealist poet. He founded the influential art journal *View* whilst living in New York in 1940. This vital periodical served as a textual refuge for the various illustrious members of the displaced European intelligentsia during the Second World War. Ford continued to explore the possibilities of surrealism and the arts all the way up until his eventual death in 2002. He was also interested in and most definitely understood camp. He sought recourse to the strategies associated with camp whilst growing up in the Deep South and living in New York City in the late 1920s. Ford makes his feelings about the value of camp known in the following piece of poetry, which was published posthumously in an obscure collection of freeform haiku and collaged images entitled *Operation Minotaur* (2006):

A truly candid
Novella is tonic. One
Without camp
Falls flat. (N. pag.)

This brief poem operates in a self-referential fashion, as a hypothetical statement of artistic intent. Ford is referring in this passage to the novel he started working on with the queer New Orleans-born poet and film critic Parker Tyler not all that long after Woolf delivered her seminal lectures, in Cambridge, on the importance of personal space. Significantly, the noted historian George Chauncey has described *The Young and Evil* as "perhaps the campiest novel of them all" (17). Camp is quite literally foregrounded in Ford and Tyler's co-authored and semi-autobiographical text:

baggage grand cocksucker
fascinated by fairies of the Better
Class chronic
liar fairy
herself sexual
estimate crooning I'M A CAMP fire girl. (164)

Published by Jack Kahane's English-language, Paris-based Obelisk Press in 1933, *The Young and Evil* is important for a host of reasons. Featuring depictions of characters dolled-up in drag and all "*camp like mad*" (167), Ford and Tyler's text utilizes textual tactics such as parody, whilst simultaneously eschewing fixed conceptions of character. In this manner, the various non-normative figures populating the social fringes of New York in this avowedly camp novel anticipate Moe Meyer's subsequent Butlerian proposition that "identity is self-reflexively constituted" (4) by visual acts of gendered performativity. *The Young and Evil* also prefigures certain of the comments that the novelist Christopher Isherwood penned about camp in 1954. In his *The World in the Evening*, Isherwood makes the following claim:

High Camp always has an underlying seriousness. You can't camp about something you don't take seriously. You're not making fun of it; you're making fun out of it. You're expressing what's basically serious to you in terms of fun and artifice and elegance. (110)

Isherwood contrasts what he terms "high camp" with "low camp" in this particular text. In Isherwood's reckoning, low camp should be conceived as of "a swishy little boy with peroxided hair, dressed in a picture hat and a feather boa, pretending to be Marlene Dietrich" (ibid.). Unlike Isherwood, Ford and Tyler have absolutely no reservations about low camp. *The Young and Evil* celebrates and indeed revels in what some might wrongly term as vulgarity in an anarchic, quasi-Rabelaisian, and brazenly queer fashion. In the words of Joseph Allen Boone, Ford and Tyler's novel "links configurations of urban space to the marginalized sexual identities and the practices that such sites engender" (254). We get a sense of this throughout the novel. Ford and Tyler describe regular forays into the popular sites of so-called low culture: Manhattan dive bars, Greenwich Village dance clubs, and Harlem drag balls "too large to be rushed at without being swallowed" (152). Standing in for the authors, the characters of Karel and Julian offer a running commentary on the various scenes they witness in underground venues such as these:

The negro orchestra on the stage at one end was heard at the other end with the aid of a reproducer. On both sides of the wall a balcony spread laden with people in boxes at tables. Underneath were more tables and more people. The dance-floor was a scene whose celestial flavor and cerulean coloring no angelic painter or nectarish poet has ever conceived. (Ibid.)

There is, of course, a self-consciously poetic dimension to this co-authored depiction of the heavenly dance-floor. However, Karel and Julian's attention soon wanders elsewhere:

They found Tony and Vincent at a table with K-Y and Woodward. Vincent spoke with the most wonderful whisky voice Frederick! Julian! Tony was South American. He had on a black satin that Vincent had made him, fitted to the knee and then flaring, long pearls and pearl drops. (153)

It seems fair to say that our narrators are less interested in aesthetic representations of the "angelic painter" or the gauchely "nectarish poet" in moments such as these than they are in meeting interesting sorts of people. They are particularly interested in meeting figures like the "black satin" clad Tony and Vincent:

> Vincent had on a white satin blouse and black breeches. Dear I'm master of ceremonies tonight and you should have come in drag and you'd have gotten a prize. He had large eyes with a sex-life all their own and claimed to be the hardest boiled queen on Broadway. Frederick he said you look like something Lindbergh dropped on the way across. (Ibid.)

Much like their fictional counterparts, the creators of *The Young and Evil* are evidently enchanted with the figure of this wide-eyed drag queen. In this regard, we might say that Ford and Tyler seek to capture something of that which Justus Nieland describes as "the joyous hum of public being, physically undone by collective scenes of sympathy, and ever-attentive to intimate potential of public spaces, finding new homes for feeling in uncanny places" (2). Read in this way, it thus soon becomes clear that the authors of *The Young and Evil* are striving to depict suitable public spaces capable of producing and sustaining new, intimately charged, and queerly camp regimes of feeling.

Analysis such as this certainly provides us with a useful critical vantage point from which to approach *The Young and Evil*. But I can't help but also wonder what a high modernist writer like Woolf might have made of it. I like to think that she would have approved of the queer conceptual aims underpinning Ford and Tyler's collaborative project. Yet I begin to doubt that she would have had anything particularly positive to say about the manner in which Ford and Tyler choose to present their autobiographically inflected anecdotes and arrange their sexually explicit literary materials. In any case, what we do know for sure is that Woolf's modernist story and Ford and Tyler's camp novel appear to be poles apart when it comes to questions of form and content. We have to dig deep as critics when it comes time to unearth the (camp) gems of matter and meaning contained in Woolf's modernist story. Not so *The Young and Evil*. We do not need to dirty our critical hands whilst sifting through analytical sand when reading Ford and Tyler's work. In this masterpiece of camp pretty much everything is always on show and already up for grabs – provided that one appreciates just what it is that Ford and Tyler are getting at. To be absolutely clear though: this should not be taken as a criticism of *The Young and Evil*. Nor should it be taken to suggest that we are wrong to compare the work of established modernist writers such as Woolf with that of the younger Ford and Tyler. These two ambitious and camp young men – both of whom came of literary age not all that long after the classificatory term "modernist" first appeared in print – most definitely knew modernism when they saw it. In Tyler's words, both he and Ford were "dreadfully impressed by modern poetry, and we were trying to create our own brand of it. What we didn't realize too consciously was that we *were* (I hope this isn't too much of a boast!) *modern poetry*" (n. pag.). We get a sense of the scale of Ford and Tyler's engagement with literary modernism in passages such as this:

> Theodosia was reading. Julian was lying on his back and heard her voice: Wyndham Lewis says that a page of a servant-girl novel smashed up equals a page of Gertrude Stein.
>
> What Julian said Mr. Lewis means is that he thinks Miss Stein is purely negative, but he has no better word for the behavior of the organism than negative; Miss Stein is writing or walking. In one way these are the same. In neither case is she smashing the pages of a servant-girl novel.
>
> Theodosia was pleased. Suppose we go dancing tonight at the Tavern. (98)

This name-dropping passage is wholly characteristic of *The Young and Evil*. Notice that Ford and Tyler move to splice together potentially serious discussions of avant-gardism with infinitely more pressing requests to go out dancing. And they do so with specific references made in this passage to those old warhorses of high modernism: Wyndham Lewis and Gertrude Stein. *The Young and Evil* is replete with mentions such as these. The bearded spectre of one of Stein's most crushingly heteronormative of modernist protégés, Ernest Hemingway, looms particularly large over the text of *The Young and Evil*. Ford recalled that "many of us had been introduced to *The Sun Also Rises* and everyone wanted to write a novel about their life like that novel" (n. pag.). Yet it is important to recognize that Ford and Tyler were not interested in acts of mere modernist hero-worship. Whilst they know their high modernist history (having already scoured the libraries and pored over the pages of many a little magazine and literary manifesto), these precocious late moderns had absolutely no intention of merely emulating what had come before. They sought instead to repurpose existing models of modernism. Boone emphasizes this point in his comparative reading of *The Sun Also Rises* and *The Young and Evil*. According to Boone, Ford and Tyler's collaborative venture is one that bends "modernist technique to queer purposes with a vengeance" (255). Boone notes that, at the level of content, "the experimental text that [Ford] and Tyler produced is not stylistically but thematically worlds removed from Hemingway, for its 'lost generation' is composed of the queer fringe that Hemingway's novel continually attempts to excise" (ibid.). But what of form? The answer to that is relatively straightforward if we know what we're looking for in the first place, if we know how to read and interpret the relevant signs. If the reader proves adequately alive to the signs, then, they will soon find that the punctuation-free passages of what might appear on first inspection to be a curious admixture of not-so-subtle innuendo and verbiage and almost unintelligible chunks of prose are in fact self-consciously theatrical and deliberately overblown formal fusions that want nothing less than to yoke together, in Juan A. Suárez's words, the energies of "experimental modernism [and] the camp idiom of gay street culture" (261). That, to be sure, is what we encountered in the foregoing passages.

Sam See perhaps puts the matter best when he describes how

> Ford and Tyler's text shuttles between two collective, and to them, similar, experiences – those of the queer community and literary modernist culture at large – to blur the line between the strange and common, the queer and the mainstream, in American modernism. (1076)

Two things stand out in this nuanced and sensitive reading. The first point of interest concerns the critical vexed notion of queer community. See posits that many of the critics working in the field of queer theory have emphasized the fact that the very concept of a specifically queer community is in a sense utterly paradoxical, "for queerness is by most definitions anti-communitarian" (ibid.). The second point of interest relates to the first and also serves to bring the current conversation full circle. See goes on to acknowledge the fact that Ford and Tyler strive in a wholly dialectical fashion to "historicize the local communities and ethnic traditions that formed around the criterion of sexual difference throughout the twentieth century, even as they acknowledge such a criterion as paradoxical" (ibid.). And this reading, finally, brings us full circle: while, and for good reason, queer theorists and literary historians of modernism both remain uneasy with fixed definitions, this essay has sought to demonstrate that, following Ford and Tyler but also Jameson, if we properly historicize our objects, be they camp or modernist, we not only arrive at fascinating and refreshing new interpretations, we also affirm a fresh and solid object of critical study: camp modernism.

disclosure statement

No potential conflict of interest was reported by the author.

bibliography

Berman, Marshall. *All that is Solid Melts into Air: The Experience of Modernity*. 1982. New York: Penguin, 1988. Print.

Bersani, Leo. *Homos*. Cambridge, MA: Harvard UP, 1995. Print.

Boone, Joseph Allen. *Libidinal Currents: Sexuality and the Shaping of Modernism*. Chicago: U of Chicago P, 1998. Print.

Booth, Mark. *Camp*. New York: Quartet, 1983. Print.

Bryant, Marsha, and Douglas Mao. "Camp Modernism: Introduction." *Modernism/Modernity* 23.1 (2016): 1–4. Print.

Carver, Beci. *Granular Modernism*. Oxford: Oxford UP, 2014. Print.

Chauncey, George. *Gay New York: Gender, Urban Culture, and the Making of the Gay Male World, 1890–1940*. New York: Basic, 1994. Print.

Cleto, Fabio. "Introduction: Queering the Camp." *Camp: Queer Aesthetics and the Performing Subject: A Reader*. Ed. Fabio Cleto. Ann Arbor: U of Michigan P, 2002. 1–42. Print.

Creekmur, Corey K., and Alexander Doty. "Introduction." *Out in Culture: Gay, Lesbian and Queer Essays on Popular Culture*. Ed. Corey K. Creekmur and Alexander Doty. Durham, NC: Duke UP, 1995. 1–11. Print.

Detloff, Madelyn. "Camp Orlando (or) *Orlando*." *Modernism/Modernity* 23.1 (2016): 18–22. Print.

Dyer, Richard. *The Culture of Queers*. London: Routledge, 2002. Print.

Ford, Charles Henri. *Operation Minotaur*. Woodstock, NY: Shivastan, 2006. Print.

Ford, Charles Henri, and Parker Tyler. *The Young and Evil*. 1933. London: Gay Men's P, 1989. Print.

Foucault, Michel. *The History of Sexuality: The Will to Knowledge, Volume 1*. 1976. Trans. Robert Hurley. London: Penguin, 1998. Print.

Friedman, Susan Stanford. "Planetarity: Musing Modernism Studies." *Modernism/Modernity* 17.3 (2010): 471–99. Print.

Halperin, David M. *How to be Gay*. Cambridge, MA: Harvard UP, 2012. Print.

Isherwood, Christopher. *The World in the Evening*. 1954. Minneapolis: U of Minnesota P, 1999. Print.

Jameson, Fredric. *A Singular Modernity: Essay on the Ontology of the Present*. London: Verso, 2002. Print.

Latham, Sean, and Gayle Rogers. *Modernism: Evolution of an Idea*. London: Bloomsbury Academic, 2015. Print.

Mao, Douglas. *Solid Objects: Modernism and the Test of Literary Production*. Princeton: Princeton UP, 1998. Print.

Meyer, Moe. "Reclaiming the Discourse of Camp." *The Politics and Poetics of Camp*. Ed. Moe Meyer. London and New York: Routledge, 1994. 1–19. Print.

Nicholls, Peter. *Modernisms: A Literary Guide*. Berkeley: U of California P, 1995. Print.

Nieland, Justus. *Feeling Modern: The Eccentricities of Public Life*. Urbana and Chicago: U of Illinois P, 2008. Print.

Pero, Allan. "A Fugue on Camp." *Modernism/Modernity* 23.1 (2016): 28–36. Print.

Peters, Brian M., and Bruce E. Drushel. "Introduction: Some Notes on 'Notes.'" *Sontag and the Camp Aesthetic: Advancing New Perspectives*. Ed. Brian M. Peters and Bruce E. Drushel. Lanham, MD: Rowman, 2017. vii–xv. Print.

Sedgwick, Eve Kosofsky. *Touching Feeling: Affect, Pedagogy, Performativity*. Durham, NC: Duke UP, 2003. Print.

See, Sam. "Making Modernism New: Queer Mythology in *The Young and Evil*." *English Literary History* 76 (2009): 1073–105. Print.

Sontag, Susan. *Against Interpretation and Other Essays*. 1966. London: Penguin, 2009. Print.

Suárez, Juan A. *Pop Modernism: Noise and the Reinvention of the Everyday*. Urbana and Chicago: U of Illinois P, 2007. Print.

Watson, Steven. "Introduction." *The Young and Evil.* Charles Henri Ford and Parker Tyler. London: Gay Men's P, 1989. N. pag. Print.

Weigman, Robyn. *Object Lessons.* Durham, NC: Duke UP, 2013. Print.

Woolf, Virginia. *The Mark on the Wall and Other Short Stories.* Oxford: Oxford UP, 2008. Print.

Woolf, Virginia. *A Room of One's Own and Three Guineas.* Oxford: Oxford UP, 2015. Print.

the pliable object

In Michelangelo Antonioni's 1966 film *Blow-Up*, the successful commercial photographer Thomas moonlights as an artist. While he earns his living through commercial photography, on the side he is compiling his first art book, a photographic record of London that features, for instance, gritty portraits of aged men in a doss house. One photo session is prompted by his happening upon a mock-pastoral scene of lovers in a park, but as Thomas develops, enlarges, and fixes the image he recorded there he detects in this scene of seduction the event of a crime about to take place. The book of photos represents Thomas as "artist," intimately rendered documentarian portraits of an "other" London paired with distant vistas of pastoral anonymity, a critical differentiation of cultural from other forms of capital in the film's diegesis, and an instance of Thomas's ambivalent status in his world. The film sits on the cusp of, and borrows its *mises-en-scène* from, mid-60s pop art, and, you would expect, pop art's disinterest in keeping art and commerce at arm's length in favour of a concerted interrogation of that relationship. By fetishizing a distinction between "commercial" and "artistic" photography Thomas lags historically precisely as his capacity to "register" what he is seeing in the shot he takes and then repeatedly "blows up" lags in conformity with the de-acceleration of the moving image that is of aesthetic concern to the film.

Thomas's forensic analysis of the image he captured is driven by an epistemological desire never precisely sited in a world of consequential action: he investigates the image of a crime because he is driven by curiosity, not a desire for justice or resolution. At best his motivation is psychological as he tries to understand what it is a woman he has photographed is looking at out of the shot. Her glance, we discover, is directed toward a hidden gunman, and more abstractly to the future, to a crime just about to take place. Thomas's photograph becomes both clue and symptom of that crime, which is, in one sense, the fate of the photograph, to be indexical. Thomas's urge to capture the image is identified as a form of "artistic" activity, at odds with his commercial ventures, the shoot itself a busman's holiday after strenuous sessions of commercial shooting and perfunctory, contemptuous seduction.

melissa hardie

LIBRARY TROLLS AND DATABASE ANIMALS
kenneth halliwell and joe orton's library book alterations

However, even Thomas's presence "at" or around this scene, replayed through the film first as pastoral and then as evidentiary, is motivated by capital. Thomas has gone to the park after visiting an antiques shop he wishes to buy because the area in which it is located is about to "take off": Thomas confirms as much in a conversation he conducts after visiting the area, a conversation conducted via a futuristic/utopian walkie-talkie. In that conversation his evidence of gentrification is that "there are queers and poodles in the area." Simultaneously pointing to the past and to the future in its concatenation of antiques and walkie-talkie, the scene unites as well the film's own history and its scanning of the present moment. Thomas's desire to profit from the future – speculation – draws him into the ontological puzzle that forms the heart of the film, and Antonioni effects this by displacing the original sexual "crime" at the heart of the Julio Cortázar short story on which the film is based. Whereas in Antonioni's film seduction is a ruse to distract a victim before he is murdered, in Cortázar's story the narrator witnesses a seduction between a boy and an older woman that upon further forensic investigation proves to be a triangular affair: the older woman is procuring the boy for a man, lurking in a car:

> The real boss was waiting there, smiling petulantly, already certain of the business; he was not the first to send a woman in the vanguard, to bring him the prisoner manacled with flowers. (Cortázar 113–14)

In the case of *Blow-Up* we might rephrase this to say "the real crime was waiting there," namely homosexual seduction or abduction in a public place. And its ontological "reality" is similarly displaced onto two other forms of criminality, the mundane puzzle of a crime scene that introduces a corpse, and the reviled "queers and poodles" who index both the profit and loss entailed by gentrification. Thomas relies on the photo-book object as index of cultural capital aesthetically a notch or two above the camp artefacts of the antiques shop that draw or mimic "poodles and queers," but developmentally reliant on them. Just as Thomas is "certain of the business" when it comes to poodle-led gentrification, what remains formally occluded from view in Antonioni's version of the set-up is the "crime" of homosexuality, only decriminalized in England by the Sexual Offences Act a year after the film's release, in 1967. In *Blow-Up*'s classic account of 60s London as the ground zero for a certain kind of radical adventure and radical disclosure, the pursuit of capital, cultural and economic, entails happening upon a (queer) crime.

Blow-Up allies homosexuality, criminality, photos, and books to frame a question about the relationship between commercial and "artistic" activity. Most commonly read as a narrative concerned with the ontological problem posed by cinema's reliance on photographed, "documentarian" images, my reading brings to the fore a problem I've outlined in a structurally paranoid, Sedgwickian way: beneath one "layer" of representation rests an epistemology of secrecy whose secret is constitutively that of male homosexuality. Thomas's reliance on the photo-book object as index of cultural capital – his own, idiopathic gentrification, if you like – generates a cinema-like object (the photo-book) whose distinguishing feature is that it is not a film. Equally, the apparently motiveless drive to discern the "reality" of the image gains traction as a closet epistemology, parsing first the "secret" business transacted between the woman and the hidden scene of homosexual seduction/rape embedded in the source text for the film. Thomas, then, can be cast as the sedulous though ambivalently motivated detective, caught in the intricacies of a plot or project that can never be deciphered, only documented.

In their coding of homosexual seduction and subterfuge, and urban gentrification, the series of objects that Thomas creates and inspects – photo-books, antiques, poodles, "queers" – are notably pliant: in the two common senses of that term they are able both to be manipulated or bent, and to be influenced or directed by contextual codes of interpretation. As such they offer one variety of a "queer object," where that much manipulated modifier can be taken to speak to the question of manipulation and modification itself. "Queer" as a term has come to represent a capacious hold-all for speculation over the ways in which what goes against the grain or "athwart" (in Sedgwick's definitive and memorable term) is tied, etymologically as well as epistemologically, and in fact ontologically, to the concept of a movement *against*.[1] It remains undertheorized how a queer *object* might be one that moves towards, or in favour of, affirmatively with, a grain, groove, or interpretative strategy.[2] For all that Thomas encounters his "queer objects" delaying or interrupting the streamlined activities he pursues (real estate speculation, reputation building, self-aggrandisement) their very capacity to facilitate the "stream" of interpretation – Thomas's and mine as well – suggests that rather than working against the flow they increase its capacity and pressure.

In the sense I mean it, the term "pliant" as a collocation of "queer" moves against the explicit historical usage of the latter term contemporary with Antonioni's film and the "queer objects" this paper addresses. Matt Cook notes how in London "varied yet loosely connected associations of oddity, badness, malformation or foreignness resonate through the proliferating and then narrowing meanings of queer" (*Queer Domesticities* 7). At the same time, however, in a different regime of circulation the pliant object promotes transformation because it yields to influence; the pliant object is queer not because it is odd, bad, or malformed, nor because it is athwart in any simple sense, but because it is susceptible to change or metamorphic. The volatility of such an object relies, then, on its context for both the capacity to be given shape and to lose it. It is in its collections or contexts that the pliant object makes meaning, and the remainder of this article provides an example of a set of objects that demonstrate the way in which the pliant queer object proliferates rather than thwarts, aligns rather than disturbs, impresses rather than inhibits. These objects engendered an arduous task of detection not unlike Thomas's whose motivation is likewise difficult to describe, and whose object similarly constructed around arguments regarding the relationship between art and commerce. Its *mises-en-scène* now furnished by Antonioni's meditation on medial ambiguity, I'll spend some time detailing the "facts" of the detection and prosecution of Joe Orton and Kenneth Halliwell for altering library books before considering the novel ways in which theirs was a practice of crafting queer objects of exemplary pliability.

In May 1962 Joe Orton and Kenneth Halliwell were convicted and sentenced to six months' time for "malicious damage" of library books, a sentence they served in different penal institutions. Across a period of years, from the late 50s to early 60s, Orton and Halliwell had removed library books from their local circulating library, sometimes borrowing them and sometimes stealing them. Many of the books were plundered for an extensive collage that covered walls in their one-bedroom flat at 25 Noel Rd, in Islington. Alterations of covers included the redrafting of blurbs, the removal of images and their substitution, and the creation of surreal juxtapositions that reflected an ironic commentary on the contents of the book, although the covers have not been robustly mined for these intertextual ambitions. While some of the covers were frankly parodic, many were elegant collages, commentaries on the contents of the volume, as, for instance, with their alterations of Arden editions of Shakespeare.[3] Some seventy covers still exist, and from their original use as evidence in the prosecution of the men they have now becomes "art objects" in their own right, featuring in exhibitions three times since the prosecution of the crime, with a couple of covers on permanent display at the Islington Local History Centre and the collection preserved in "exact reproduction" for researchers. The books they returned with altered covers and content created out of the public resource an ambivalently private and public queer archive. Its existence was formally detected and documented by an assiduous librarian and clerk for whom Halliwell and Orton's activities constituted damage to the organizing premise of the circulating library.

The collaboration of Orton and Halliwell on this project has been overlooked in favour of the catastrophic end to their joint lives, when in August 1967 Halliwell murdered Orton, and then committed suicide, in the Islington flat. Their creative lives were revised in light of their deaths and the schism between the two that forecast them. Halliwell's 1962 incarceration was deeply and permanently damaging, whereas Orton's subsequent success and fame as dramatist was initiated in part, it seems, by their separation and the severing of their creative projects. In later interviews and appearances Orton discussed the library pranks as though they were his alone; elements of his work as a dramatist that were indebted to Halliwell were only enumerated by Orton on sufferance. The impetus for collage might have come from Halliwell, however, since Halliwell contemplated a serious career as an artist and exhibited his work at an antiques shop on the Kings Road (a revisionist exhibition of Halliwell's collages was mounted at the Islington Local History Centre in 2014). The collaboration on the books joined other pranks or "leg pulls" they worked on together, such as the creation of the character Edna Welthorpe, an older woman who wrote letters of complaint to jam manufacturers and deliberately naive, incendiary requests of vicars to host events that supported toleration of homosexuality (Lahr 136–40).

When asked to explain the apparently extraordinary pursuit and prosecution of the pair, Orton remarked that it happened "because we're queers," locating homosexuality as the covert object of prosecution or form of "malicious damage." In 1994 Simon Shepherd used this quotation for the title of his book on the pair, *Because We're Queers*, identifying in their activity a general "irreverence" and extending Orton's observation. He writes:

> The court reports were silent about sex. There is no hint that Orton and Halliwell might be lovers. Instead both were depicted as unstable character types. In the words of the senior probation officer, "both defendants were frustrated actors and frustrated authors." The crime was described as "childish [...] prompted by feelings that are unusual." The prosecutor pointed out that Halliwell had been employed as an actor and that Orton had attended RADA. Enough was known about them to know they had lived together for some time. But there's no mention of homosexuality, only descriptions of childishness, bohemians, people without proper jobs. Also failures. These are categories which can suitably replace the mention of homosexuality. (14)

In a 1967 interview not long before his death, Orton recounted that his desire to deface library books came not from "childish" or "unusual feelings" but from a general dissatisfaction with the quality of books on the shelves of their local library, and associates that dissatisfaction with the duty of the library to furnish decent books. Rather than emphasize the prankish elements of their activity, Orton aligns the defacement of library books with a frustrated desire to have unfettered access to "good books":

> The thing that put me in a rage about librarians was that when I went to quite a big library in Islington and asked for Gibbon's *Decline and Fall of the Roman Empire* they told me they hadn't a copy of it. They could get it for me, but they hadn't one on their shelves. This didn't start it off but it was symptomatic of the whole thing. I was enraged that there were so many rubbishy novels and rubbishy books. It reminded me of the phrase in the Bible: "Of the making of books, there is no end," because there isn't. Libraries might as well not exist; they've got endless shelves for rubbish and hardly any space for good books. (*Transatlantic Review* 97–98)

Figuring shelf space as a zero sum, the proliferation of "the making of books" is at personal and intellectual cost. Pitting themselves against popular taste, Orton and Halliwell became its most active consumers as well as critics, smuggling hundreds of books out of the library (Orton's sister Leonie Barnett reports that theft was not out of line with family tradition: their mother was dismissed from her job in a hosiery factory for theft and she herself was likewise sacked after stealing a twin set at her own workplace (9)). The work done by Orton and Halliwell was extensive, constituting a secondary circulating beside the sanctioned circulations through the loans desk, and was noted and even anticipated by the staff of the library, who confessed to looking forward to discovering the altered books.

Shepherd's explanation, and Orton's – that the prosecution and arrest occurred "because we're queer" – align the case with the scene of queer seduction in *Blow-Up* in complex ways. Both constructions suggest an alliance between homosexual action and gentrification; in *Blow-Up*'s case through the collocation of poodles, queers, and real estate prices, in Orton's through the representation of the activity as a protest against second-rate books. Orton and Halliwell's subversion of the library stacks as a place of criminal trespass collocates with the cottaging and other illicit seductions in public places (most isomorphically, public toilets), and also with queer appropriation of public places as orthogonal to their interests. Orton's explanation, of course, falls short: he acknowledges both ready access to Gibbon and that the story is "symptomatic" rather than causative. Presenting the Gibbon, and metonymically an ideal library, as forbidden, a primal pedagogical scene from which he is formally excluded, Orton revises their activities as a kind of protest against the circulation of "rubbish," that is, as an index of taste. At the same time, though, altered covers mocked both "high" literary culture and "low," and sometimes offered merely dreamy interpretations of classical texts such as Shakespeare. Their thievings also furnished raw material for a separate art practice, the collaged flat whose conditions are always recounted as claustrophobic in documentaries and biographical writings but which suggest exorbitant access to ornamental culture symmetrically counterposed to the fantasy of the library as venue for the demonstration that aesthetic experience is institutionally occulted from view.

In his *Transatlantic Review* interview Orton notes that in 1953

> I used to write ... None of the novels were successful, none of the plays were put on. I was really occupying myself with these library books. It used to be a full-time job. I would stagger home from libraries with books which I'd borrowed and also stolen, and then I used to go back with them a couple of times a day. (Gordon 99)

For Orton and Halliwell, the circulating library constituted a bulwark against ennui, but their adaptive manipulation of the material exceeded regulated dictates concerning the public's attachment to a public resource. They cared too little or too much, depending on your perspective, about the material of the collection: they cared *queerly* for these objects. Their book alteration continued for three years and occupied so much of their time that Orton later claimed that the alteration practices themselves, their preparation and execution, were "full-time" occupations (Gordon 99). Without the commercial activity of a Thomas (that comes later, for Orton), the creation and recirculation of the queer object becomes an aesthetic modus vivendi. Its execution in the couple form (resembling other artist couples and in particular the contemporary East London pair Gilbert and George, who were more fortunate in the contours of their careers) literalized the queerness and the "wastefulness" of the activity: two working lives were colonized by these activities, executed by a pair of men in too-close proximity. As important as the books themselves are in terms of the constitution of a queer object, the aesthetics of their practice viewed as a performance or as a form of employment critically orients a queer relationship to the library's collection. Orton and Halliwell surreptitiously observed the registration of shock and surprise on the faces of library patrons as they encountered the images, suggesting something more thoroughgoing and deliberately interactive in the circulation of material than the kind of private perversity attributed to the crime at the time. Even taking his characteristic hyperbole into account, their work was consuming and extensive, and directly competed with, or perhaps rather constituted, serious "literary" activity.

Equally interesting are the assiduous tasks taken on by the librarian who both carefully laid a trap for their revelation as the miscreants, and later documented the extensive catalogue of defaced and altered books. In an article called "A Successful Prosecution," published in *The Library Association Record* in March 1963, Alexander Connell describes the meticulous and even excessive work done to apprehend Orton and Halliwell, and to trace the plundered images to their original source. Here, images of 25 Noel Road are represented as evidence of theft and "malicious damage." Connell recounts in detail the sheer bulk and variety of books, covers, and plates that were recovered from the flat, which he visited with police after Halliwell and Orton's arrest. A criminal enterprise in full swing was unveiled by that visit: books in the process of alteration, books waiting for attention, and a hoard of loose plates. In particular, issues surrounding the stamping of plates with identifying marks was an impediment to the Library's claiming ownership: in cases where plates held reproductions on both sides the library had not stamped the plate, and where a stamp may have been impressed on a plate's reverse, their pasting onto the wall rendered such identification impractical. Nonetheless, the article reports that "of the 1653 loose plates found in the flat, only 30 remained unidentified" (104). For this remarkable achievement Connell is commended in a short addendum from the Chief Librarian and Curator of Islington who does so by citing the judge's own commendation of Connell as "highly experienced" and "extremely capable." This experience and capacity was litigiously registered in the Council's pursuit of financial recompense after Halliwell and Orton had served their time.

Islington has now embraced the men and the work: the manager of the Centre, Mark Aston, reports bidding on a cover at an auction to retrieve it for their collection:

> Joe Orton and Kenneth Halliwell were only in the borough for 15 years but created a cult. They defaced book covers 50 years ago but they are still attracting interest. It's a way into a local library collection. One of the pieces they defaced I had to bid for as it was filmed by the BBC's Flog It programme.

I was a bit nervous with the camera up my nose, but Orton and Halliwell get the youngsters in! (*Islington Faces*)

In fact the "piece" was one of Halliwell's collages, single-authored. Here, the circulation of images turns again, where the commercial imperative (Flog It!) meets artistic "production" in the choreographed space of the televised auction, venue for the "attraction of interest." The auction resolves in this sense the contradictions that frame Thomas's artistic practice in *Blow-Up* as the counterpoint to commercial activity. As I've noted, Thomas happens upon the murder scene in his search for commercially viable property, a search that brings him to an antiques shop, precisely the venue for the interposition of the logic of a secondary market (resale/recycling). The auction similarly dramatizes the resolution of contradictory impulses implicit in the library work too, where Orton and Halliwell introduce a "secondary market" into the library's authorized circulation, a form of circulation that equally can be understood as a "blockage," the interruption of access. Their activities interleaved an irregular venue for the exercise of taste between the shelves of the "rubbishy" and the "good book."

Where contemporary accounts of their activities reach for words such as "childish" to describe the pair, and "unusual feelings" to describe their motive, the contemporary term "troll" might be more apt. Orton and Halliwell altered both visual and textual material and targeted a wide variety of books in their activities, and defended their actions, politically and aesthetically, as an intervention in the circulation of substandard and/or boring material, or "rubbish." The word "troll," commonly used now in the context of the internet to describe a disruptive intervention to the harmonious interactions in online communities, conveys the nature of the "serious play" around the books: a private circulating library of altered documents fed back into the institutional circulation of the library, experienced, as Orton said, as a kind of theatre where the stimulation of affect – startle and surprise – leverages new experiences from the "rubbishy" stock.

A recent definition of the troll as internet identity runs as follows:

> "Troll," as a term of moral opprobrium, indicates an online actor who is not interested in deliberation, but in derailing it [...] Trolls are not interested in redeeming democracy through deliberation, and they mock attempts to do so. Trolls respect no procedural rules, though they may be generative of them. Trolls are the constitutive outside of online communities of political discussion, they are the intolerable of the most tolerant communities. Trolls are usually someone else, defined from our own position and interests. When they are not, and we inhabit trolling, we discover that trolling requires knowhow, close reading, experience, sometimes sympathy with those we would disrupt. (Wilson, McCrea, and Fuller)

In the version of this story that focuses on the prankish aspect of their performance, Orton and Halliwell are library trolls, disrupting or mocking the circulating library's access to knowledge not (only) by the siphoning off of books but by their alteration. Key to their trolling activities (and key to an identification of it as trolling) is their delight in witnessing the disruption effected by the altered books, tracking an audience built from the contingent passage of people through the democratizing library as public venue. Wilson, McCrea, and Fuller's description highlights the way in which trolling, like the cover alterations, is a practice of "derailment," sending the circulation of ideas off its predictable tracks or, in the case of the library books, the circulation of the objects themselves. Although Orton identifies a frustrated access to information as "symptom" of the malaise of the library, this explanation after the fact barely accounts for the variety and range of alterations, which only make sense when the project is read together, that is as a self-sustained project imbedded within the circulations of the library. The recirculation of images and content through the altered books miniaturized the library's circulation of objects on page and cover, and the alterations, like trolling, required "know-how, close reading, experience" and "sympathy with those we would disrupt." The extensive labour exerted by Orton and Halliwell in their doctoring of material involved both the appropriation of material intended for public use and the recirculation of that material in distinct senses. Their reintroduction of altered books into the library served to derange the orderly state of the collection, a derangement that relied on their books recirculating "hidden in plain sight." In this sense their disruption was of the library network, conceptualized as an imperfect or damaged circulatory system mirrored by these doctored covers. The covers represent failures of taste or discrimination that ape the failed perfection of the library as a finite resource: never enough, never the right books. As the library itself furnished all the materials for this internal critique of its workings, the collages offer an autotelic rendition of abrupt failures or aporetic over-circulation of images, where unlike meets unlike. In this sense, and in the way in which the covers served to counter the marketing and distribution of the books, the library trolls made possible unlikely juxtapositions that were argumentative in nature.

Halliwell and Orton's trolling involved more than the desire to, as Angela Nagle puts it, "rustle people's jimmies" (55) and execute a dazzling "leg pull." These corporeal metaphors emphasize the way in which the recirculated objects created a physical and libidinal attachment to the person whose shock and surprise is registered as the doctored volume is happened upon amongst the "business as usual" items of the collection. With their obvious closeness to other forms of sexual circulation in public places, and the kind of detoured "glance" that signifies homosexuality in *Blow-Up*, the doctored books materialize a form of liaison between library patrons, surreptitiously executed in the ambiguously public and private shelves of the library. As such the queerness of the objects relies not merely on their extant qualities but on their contextual apprehension, the way in which they amplify or materialize the queer potential of the circulation of objects qua objects. Equally, the work and the works, according to Matt Cook, constitute a material queer disclosure:

in the book-cover collages and in the mural in their bedsit formed from over 1,600 library book-plates we encounter something immediate and revealing about the playwright, his partnership with Halliwell and their joint interaction with queer, artistic and institutional cultures. ("Orton in the Archive" 176)

The circulation of the books in the library is matched by the circulation of images on the doctored covers of the books. These recirculated images, removed from their original context and queerly repurposed in collage, betray in other ways the "know-how, close reading" (Wilson, McCrea, and Fuller) and sympathetic relationship to the texts that were being covered. The collage presented as the new cover of *The Secret of Chimneys* gives an idea of the "close-reading" at work in them. The cover of this otherwise forgettable Agatha Christie novel is refigured in a collage that merges images of Venice with a trio of gigantic cats. The pairing of Venice and the cats offers an exemplary puzzle. Either the cats are gigantic, striding the ancient streets of the preserved city, or the city is miniature, suddenly cute beside its feline inhabitants, and where human actors are mouse-sized. This play with scale is matched with play of another kind: the two larger cats are paired in the style of a bride and groom, complete with bouquet of flowers. A smaller cat – kitten – pops out of the luxurious tail of the cat holding the bouquet, the bride-cat. Here, several improprieties are coyly presented: the allusion to childbirth, a kitten exiting from the nether regions of its mother cat, and a birth which has taken place prior to the nuptials represented. The very coy nature of these allusions is intrinsic to the work: where sometimes the collages use nudity and bodily representation to make sexual references explicit, here the very instruments of coy allusion are turned to subversion of the discretion implied. These manipulations – of scale and temporality – are exemplary trolling, making it complex to determine the disruptive nature of the image at first glance. Although the cover otherwise seems unrelated to the contents of the novel, it does encrypt the identity of the aristocratic owner of the Chimneys of the title, the Marquis of *Caterham*. The implication is, of course, that the book was read, and that Orton's relationship to "rubbishy" books was more complex than that presented in the *Transatlantic Review* interview. In a widely disseminated portrait of Orton taken in the flat, he is holding, as if reading, a copy of Harold Robbins' *The Carpetbaggers*. My guess would be that this is not a library book; both its appearance and its contemporary reputation would suggest otherwise. Although Orton could presumably have been photographed with a more bourgeois text, this selection is illuminating as it tells us that he bought (or obtained) mainstream and relatively risqué bestsellers, and was not concerned to be photographed reading them. Such a disclosure militates against a reading of the play with collage on the altered library books as confined to cultural critique.

The covers were not always altered to demonstrate disdain but sometimes a more "sympathetic" relationship to the books can be shown in several ways. The hoarding of book materials, including both the raw material and the instruments with which the collages were created, demonstrated at the least an ambivalent attachment to these objects. Identifying the attachment to the books themselves as queer could proceed if one were to understand the disassemblage and reassemblage as moving "athwart" the continence or integrity of the book object to make it queer. Certainly, that is how the alterations were read by the librarians and courts, where altered books were "restored" to their original state where possible, and along with a prison sentence Halliwell and Orton were required to pay compensation based on the value of the altered books prior to their alteration. Reading the images as a form of mimetic paraphrase suggests that their initial visual absurdity hides a more complex set of exchanges that orient these queer objects to the library and the literary. For all that their work resembles a situationism *avant la lettre*, deploying classic situationist techniques such as *détournment*, their practice suggests a more structural redefinition of the resource through which they were able to practise textual attachment.

An exemplary case is provided by the collage work done to the cover of Naomi Jacob's novel *Three Men and Jennie*. The altered cover of the book shows a pipe-smoking man beside a giant cat, whose surreal juxtaposition offers a tableau for collaboration: not merely of Orton and Halliwell, but of the duo and the library institution. The altered cover of *Three Men and Jennie* uses scale in a fashion analogous to *The Secret of Chimneys* collage – to miniaturize a human head proportioned against another giant cat, with these two portrait-like heads situated amidst a collection of artworks. Here, critical elements – frames and portraits – are drawn from the original cover, a portrait of the eponymous Jennie. The substitution of a kilted man for Naomi Jacob's author's portrait on the back of the cover slyly refers to Jacob wearing a suit, complete with tie and pocket square, in the original author photo, a more local and complex paraphrase of Jacob's own queer impersonations. Jacob's author photo (obscured by the kilted figure) showed her scrutinizing a photographic plate in a book on a table, as if modelling the very activity of the furtive collagists. Paul Bailey's *Three Queer Lives: An Alternative Biography of Naomi Jacob, Fred Barnes, and Arthur Marshall* recounts serving Jacob in Harrods and mistaking her for J.B. Priestley (22). Jacob as a publicly queer identity is not merely cited by the kilted figure but denoted an ally as well; the collage offers a simple affirmation of identity between the trolls and the book form as material testament to queer alterity.

Both the covers discussed above featured cats substituted for human figures to distort scale and introduce a creaturely presence of queer alterity: cats occupying space and cavorting as human-like where cavorting is not encouraged. In their alterations Orton and Halliwell returned repeatedly to animals and in particular cats and monkeys: creatures associated with mischief but also with the simulation of human-like behaviour (the monkey) and (the cat) with disdain, destruction, and narcissism, a queer troll triad. Orton later noted that a cover that depicted a monkey's head superimposed on a rose was a source of particular umbrage on the part of the magistrate during their trial (Gordon 98) and a press report on the trial was headed "Gorilla in the Roses." The repetitious use of monkeys in particular suggest that the monkey's head operates on two axes: first, in close commentary (absurd, or embedded/closely read), second, across the life of the project. In this sense, the monkey images are mined from a portfolio of images that operates like a database.

In his 2001 book *Otaku: Japan's Database Animals*, Hiroki Azuma coins the expression "database animal" to describe the specific relationship between otaku culture and postmodernity.[4] According to a brutally succinct Wikipedia definition, otaku "is a Japanese slang word which means someone who has a hobby that they spend more time, money, and effort on than normal people do." More specifically, the term derives from fandom around anime, and from a charged or queer relationship to typologies within anime tradition. Otaku, for instance, are sometimes drawn to a quality termed "moe," a particular kind of feeling associated often with traits of cuteness (a kiss curl, for instance, perhaps a certain kind of cat or monkey).[5] As Azuma describes it, the "database animal" is one for whom access to the proliferating field of interest (for otaku, manga) is modelled on the database, rather than through recourse to liberal humanism's rendering of textual history in terms of taste culture, and rather than to the experience of an original and its inferior copies. Images multiply and proliferate, not in terms of degradation from an original (no auratic artwork here) but in a database structure of enumerated examples. In this sense, the database animal represents an antithetical subjectivity to the one Orton models in his *Transatlantic Review* interview. For the database animal, accumulation of database-located types is the source, rather than the record, of images and types. In the face of the collapse of grand narratives, grand "non-narratives," according to Azuma, frame the work of the database animal, who is an animal precisely because the humanist narratives of liberal humanism no longer provide surety for the individual subject. In practice, the database animal mines databases for the construction of these non-narratives, a practice exemplified, for instance, in the building of what Azuma describes as the "world of differing layers in parallel" (104). As Schäfer and Roth explain:

> According to Azuma, *otaku* actively intervene in commodities by breaking down the narratives into their compounds, like screenplay, character, background in digital games, or single "*moe*-elements" in manga (Azuma 39–47). They thereby gain access to the database lying in the "depth" behind the small narrations and are hence able to produce "derivative works" (*niji sōsaku*) and new narrations or pictures themselves. (Schäfer and Roth)

Azuma's analysis is particularly rich when it turns to "novel games," forms of writing in the style of "choose your own adventure" books of the 1980s and a suggestive form alongside which to read the interposition of "differing layers in parallel" that could be transposed to account for the difference instantiated in the altered books. His model for the database is a powerful one for the library book alterations where the books themselves become a kind of mediated point of access or interface, not with the material of "high" literary culture per se but the circulation of types, iterations of the image usually characterized as a leading flaw of lowbrow and middlebrow literature as exemplified by a prolific author such as Naomi Jacob. The collection of altered covers can be reoriented as a collection of items, iterations across a literary field valued not for its conformity to generic or conventional narrative or symbolic structure but operating as a series of apertures onto a database of queer types.

Reframing the troll behaviour of Halliwell and Orton in terms of an attachment to a database, rather than to the disruptive activities of the troll per se, is a critical way to reframe the positive valency of "queer" as it modifies the "queer object." Trolling occupies "negative space" (Wilson), the conceptually deadening activity of miming epistemological structures to thwart their facilitating actions. In this sense, trolling's "know-how" can be regarded as a form of "the reassuring exhilaration of knowingness" (Sedgwick, *Epistemology* 204), a type of posture that comports with a queer object athwart the capacity to encounter or engage. It is usefully amplified, then, but the activity of the database animal, for whom attachment proceeds positively through the accumulation of image-objects that are queer because they are pliant, resistant to context-limited forms of knowing and capable of generous and non-conventional forms of association and accumulation.

This potential can be foreshadowed by the altered cover of Thigpen and Cleckley's 1956 *The Three Faces of Eve*. This best-selling non-fiction narrative introduced the notion of Multiple Personality Disorder (MPD) to public consciousness, aided by the 1957 film that featured actor Joanne Woodward as "Eve," or rather "Eve White," "Eve Black," and "Jane," the "three faces" of the eponymous character. The invention of MPD delivered a pathological–psychological resolution of cultural contradictions around femininity and its utility. Eve "splits" as a consequence of childhood mistreatment – abuse gives her the "skill" of dissociation – but also as a way to manage the contradictions implicit in the ways her femininity was to be practised by her, compliantly, as a form of generative identity. Eve cannot reconcile her sexual and domestic duties owed her husband, for example. Such cultural contradictions would be analysed through a different formal apparatus soon enough with the advent of Betty Friedan's *The Feminine Mystique* (1963) but in the meantime *The Three Faces of Eve* presented a popular narrative of the iteration of "types" as a way of managing and maintaining social orientation *as well as* a way of reshaping identity in contextual practices: different faces for different places. That the book and the film ultimately require of their hero an "integration" that denudes her life of its variety doesn't undercut the queer thrill of seeing Eve easily glide from church mouse to ingénue. The implication of secret sexual transgression as a core if diffuse identity for the otherwise downtrodden Eve implies an identity that is pliant: metamorphic, adaptable, premised on change. As character or type, Eve represents a pliant object, and as such the narrative presents in the three different Eves a narrative of the mutability of forms that is queer. Elsewhere I have written about the way in which the case study's story of mutability mediates a consideration of highbrow, middlebrow, and lowbrow culture.[6] Here, another argument arises. The original cover of the paperback that Halliwell and Orton altered depicts actor Joanne Woodward's performance of the three "faces" of Eve. These have been pliantly revised as a man's face, a woman's face, and a cat's face. The cat is also collaged over another image formally occluded by this process of alteration. Orton and Halliwell have intuited the iterative nature of the images as pointing devices aimed at distinct ideas of subjectivity, "differing layers in parallel." The non-narrative transformation of Thigpen and Cleckley's normalizing and disciplinary saga of the "integration of personality" stands as metonym for the transformations rendered by the database animal, mining the resources of a private circulating library to produce queer objects that function to "increase the flow" rather than stymie its potential. As such, these objects are forms of pliant association within the material of the library itself precisely because in reality the work was far more complex than a mere cry for the amping up of cultural capital made available at a municipal library. Precisely as the objects were made to promote a libidinal attachment to the collection, one experienced through the stimulating procedures of the trolling of the library space, they were made equally not merely to mock but also to create new contexts and associations for the typology of images they bared.

Orton and Halliwell's remarkable work helps us to think about the ways in which arguments about cultural capital and the circulating library can alibi more inchoate or symptomatic, structural issues concerning the mediation of books and book-like objects, the troll as a figure for close reading and differentiation, the database as a central resource for creative action. Substituting the figure of the database animal for the figure of the troll makes clearer the ways in which these attachments to queer objects were not subject to the kind of negativity persistently attributed to them as acts of alteration when the men were prosecuted and incarcerated. Instead, the figure of the "database animal" releases other more positive attributes of the "queer object" for closer inspection. These include the generative and tactically flexible acts of accumulation that were performed by the men, which identify alternative ways of seeing the work of literary canons and archives. The resolution of the extant material into an oeuvre, a body of work with attendant catalogues and even papers such as this seems a fittingly queer – flexible, recuperative, enhancing – response to the extraordinary labour of the library trolls, for whom alienation from the usual structures of belonging produced a powerful practice of attachment. In 2013 the first edited collection of covers was published by Ilsa Colsell and Donlon Books. Extant covers are given art monograph style reproductions, a thorough reversal of fortune. At the time of the detection and prosecution of the books, the covers were removed, books sometimes discarded, efforts made to "restore" to their original condition the altered objects. The compilation of the charge sheet, so to speak, and the calculation of damages and costs, proleptically anticipates the movement of the covers into an art catalogue. Orton and Halliwell's flat, meanwhile, bears no traces of that equally remarkable artwork. The ephemeral artwork turns out to be the more monumental because there it was executed on ambiguously public property.

disclosure statement

No potential conflict of interest was reported by the author.

notes

Versions of and extracts from this article have been presented to a variety of audiences whose different disciplinary perspectives on the material helped me enormously. It was presented at a session on "Queer Collage: The Defaced Library Books of Joe Orton and Kenneth Halliwell" at the MLA convention in Philadelphia, January 2017, organized by Ashley Shelden, chaired by Joseph Litvak, and where I spoke with Ashley and Emma Parker. I presented an early version at the Book:Logic conference at the University of Newcastle at the invitation of Patricia Pender and Rosalind Smith, and at The Image In Question conference at Sydney College of the Arts at the invitation of John di Stefano. I presented a draft version of the article to the English Department Research Seminar at the University of Sydney. I presented a version of the article at the Queer Objects Symposium organized by Monique Rooney at the ANU. Research for the article was assisted by the librarians at the Islington Library and Museum. Thanks to Sam Dickson for his work on *Blow-Up* and the opportunity to discuss this film with him at length. Thanks to Kate Lilley for lots of things.

1 "Queer is a continuing moment, movement, motive – recurrent, eddying, *troublant*. The word 'queer' itself means *across* – it comes from the Indo-European root -*twerkw*, which also yields the German *quer* (transverse), Latin *torquere* (to twist), English *athwart*" (Sedgwick, *Tendencies* xii). Alluded to in Wiegman and Wilson (12).

2 In my conjecture of a "queer" that is not "athwart" but rather provides apertures of access, I am both following and moving away from the discussion of "anti-normativity" offered by Wiegman and Wilson, for whom it is important to find "value" in commitments beyond one to "anti-normativity" (1) but for whom the movement "athwart" is distinct from "against" (11). For Wiegman and Wilson, "athwart" is a "more intimate and complicit gesture" (12) than "against." This article is interested in a queer that lessens resistance rather than one that "troubles," torques, or otherwise impedes flow.

3 See Parker for more on these collages and the way in which they amplify and illuminate a critical take on Shakespeare that irreverently resists his gentrification.

4 In fact, Azuma refers to "otaku-like" culture, an important modification for my purposes: already the figure that Azuma describes is an abstraction contextualized by but distinct from its immediate historical context.

5 Azuma notes "The term moe is used within otaku jargon to refer to the strong sense of sympathy felt toward anime characters. Within the otaku world, moe has come to point to a longing for something in particular" (128).

6 See Hardie.

bibliography

Azuma, Hiroki. *Otaku: Japan's Database Animals*. Trans. Jonathon E. Abel and Shion Kono. Minneapolis: U of Minnesota P, 2009. Print.

Bailey, Paul. *Three Queer Lives: An Alternative Biography of Naomi Jacob, Fred Barnes, and Arthur Marshall*. London: Penguin, 2004. Print.

Barnett, Leonie Orton. "Foreword." *Malicious Damage*. By Ilsa Colsell. London: Donlon, 2013. 9–10. Print.

Christie, Agatha. *The Secret of Chimneys*. London: Pan, 1957. Print.

Colsell, Ilsa. *Malicious Damage*. London: Donlon, 2013. Print.

Connell, Alexander. "A Successful Prosecution." *The Library Association Record* 65 (Mar. 1963): 102–05. Print.

Cook, Matt. "Orton in the Archive." *History Workshop Journal* 66 (2008): 163–79. Print.

Cook, Matt. *Queer Domesticities: Homosexuality and Home Life in Twentieth-Century London*. London: Palgrave Macmillan, 2014. Print.

Cortázar, Julio. "Las babas del diablo." *Blow-Up and Other Stories*. Trans. Paul Blackburn. New York: Pantheon, 2014. 100–15. Print.

Gordon, Giles. "Joe Orton." *Transatlantic Review* 24 (1967): 94–100. Print.

Hardie, Melissa Jane. "The Three Faces of Mad Men: Middlebrow Culture and Quality Television." *Cultural Studies Review* 18.2 (2012). Web. 20 Jan. 2018. <http://epress.lib.uts.edu.au/journals/index.php/csrj/article/view/2762/2952>.

Jacob, Naomi. *Three Men and Jennie*. London: Hutchinson, 1960. Print.

Lahr, John. *Prick Up Your Ears: The Biography of Joe Orton*. Harmondsworth: Penguin, 1978. Print.

"Mark Aston: Islington Museum & Local History Centre Manager." *Islington Faces*. 24 Sept. 2014.

Web. 1 June 2017. <http://www.islingtonfacesblog.com/2014/09/24/mark-aston-islington-local-history-centre-manager/>.

Nagle, Angela. *Kill All Normies: Online Culture Wars from 4chan and Tumblr to Trump and the alt-right*. London: Verso, 2017. Print.

Parker, Emma. "Joe Orton and Shakespeare: Collage, Class and Queerness." *Studies in Theatre and Performance* 37.2 (2017): 237–68. Print.

Schäfer, Fabian, and Martin Roth. "Otaku, Subjectivity and Databases: Hiroki Azuma's *Otaku: Japan's Database Animals*." *Digital Culture and Education* 16 Sept. 2012. Web. 1 June 2017. <http://www.digitalcultureandeducation.com/uncategorized/dce_r005_schafer/>.

Sedgwick, Eve Kosofsky. *Epistemology of the Closet*. Berkeley: U of California P, 1990. Print.

Sedgwick, Eve Kosofsky. *Tendencies*. Durham, NC: Duke UP, 1993. Print.

Shepherd, Simon. *Because We're Queers: The Life and Crimes of Kenneth Halliwell and Joe Orton*. London: Gay Men's Press [GMP], 1989. Print.

Wiegman, Robyn, and Elizabeth A. Wilson. "Introduction: Antinormativity's Queer Conventions." *differences* 26.1 (2015): 1–25. Print.

Wilson, Jason, Christine McCrea, and Glen Fuller. "CFP – Special Issue for the Fibreculture Journal: The Politics of Trolling and the Negative Space of the Internet." Web. 1 June 2017. <http://fibreculturejournal.org/cfp-special-issue-for-the-fibreculture-journal-the-politics-of-trolling-and-the-negative-space-of-the-internet>.

Since Jennifer Doyle, Jonathan Flatley, and José Esteban Muñoz's landmark publication of *Pop Out: Queer Warhol* (1996), Pop's narratives about race and sexuality have begun to shift. In *Pop Out*, Muñoz could still write: "next to no people of color populate the world of Pop Art, as either producers or subjects. Representations of people of color are scarce and, more often than not, worn-out stereotypes [...] Pop Art's racial iconography is racist" (Muñoz, "Famous" 146).[1] His important work traces Jean-Michel Basquiat as a singularity, redressing these injustices. This narrative of Pop Art's deafness to the contemporaneous Civil Rights Movement has given way to a more nuanced position in recent years. Flatley's important unpublished manuscript, "Like Andy Warhol," asserts that "not only in the Race Riot canvases, but throughout Warhol's career, one can see an ongoing preoccupation with the color-line [...] even though the relative lack of critical work on the topic might give one a different impression" (Flatley, "Skin Problems").[2] This new narrative of Pop increasingly includes non-white figures in its annals, notably Leon Wainwright's work on Guyana-born Frank Bowling and "part-Iranian" Pauline Boty, and Kobena Mercer's work on Faith Ringghold, Keith Piper, and Donald Rodney (Wainwright, "Varieties" 451. See also idem, "Frank Bowling"; and Mercer).

Similarly, the narratives of sexuality and Pop have shifted. While for many years Pop criticism closeted its subject, much recent criticism presumes the significance of homosexuality to its aesthetics. For example, in a foundational essay on the sexual politics of Pop Art, Kenneth E. Silver asserts:

benjamin kahan

RAY JOHNSON'S ANTI-ARCHIVE
blackface, sadomasochism, and the racial and sexual imagination of pop art

Early Pop, or proto-Pop, is closely allied with the burgeoning gay identity in the art worlds of New York and London. In the waning years of the Abstract Expressionist hegemony homosexuality began to acquire a visual language with the vocabulary provided by the gay artists themselves. (Silver 179)[3]

In a series of influential essays, Jonathan D. Katz has referred to this process as the "homosexualization of American Art." Similarly, Richard Meyer, Douglas Crimp, and a number of other commentators have mapped the mutually constitutive construction of Pop Art and homosexuality. In the Introduction to a 2014 Special Issue of *Criticism* on Warhol, Flatley and Anthony E. Grudin write:

Almost twenty years after the editors of *Pop Out: Queer Warhol* (1996) decried "the degaying of Warhol that places whatever is queer outside the realm of critical consideration," the spell now seems to be broken. It is taken for granted [...] that Warhol is not only gay, but a key queer icon [...] (Flatley and Grudin 421)

My essay builds on the momentum of these narrative shifts, contending that while not enough attention has been paid to what Madoka Kishi calls "the high-contrast" binary of black and white, too much has been lavished on Kishi's other high-contrast binary homo and heterosexuality, overshadowing alternative narratives of Pop sexual imaginary (Kishi). I offer one such alternative to the "homosexualization of American Art" thesis in *Celibacies: American Modernism and Sexual Life* (2013), thinking about how reading Warhol as gay might prematurely foreclose the complexity of his relationship to celibacy, virginity, asexuality, and cockblocking (Kahan).[4] This essay continues that project by turning to Ray Johnson's work on sadomasochism. I understand Johnson's complex relationship to sadomasochism as providing a key switch point for Pop's racial and sexual imaginary. In the register of race, sadomasochism enables Johnson to articulate a monochrome world, attempting to void the binarized color-line's fissuring force.[5] While this strategy from our contemporary vantage point feels politically suspect, I contend it is part of a larger project of political and social reparation. In the register of sex, Johnson's sadomasochism contests the stability of the relationship between homosexuality and Pop and theorizes new models of collaborative artistic production.

In spite of the fact that almost none of his work is displayed, published, or publicly available and that he has received little scholarly attention (the first peer-reviewed articles about him appeared in 2011), we do know some things about Johnson. Born in Detroit in 1927, Johnson studied painting at Black Mountain College as a young man and was influenced by Josef and Anni Albers, Bill and Elaine de Kooning, Richard Lippold, John Cage, and Merce Cunningham. Johnson moved to New York in 1948 and began to experiment with collage art in 1951. Throughout the 1950s and 1960s, Johnson began to develop what would come to be known as "mail art," founding the New York Correspondance [*sic*] School.[6] Johnson's School was composed of a vast network of correspondents who received an enormous number and variety of mailings from Johnson and from each other. These collaborative correspondents were regularly instructed by Johnson either to transform what he sent and mail it to someone else or to send it back to him. While Johnson is also widely considered an important performance artist and collagist, his Correspondance School is his most lasting legacy. He has been the subject of several major exhibits and retrospectives at the Whitney Museum of American Art, the Wexner Center for the Arts, and Norway's National Museum of Contemporary Art.

Nicknamed "New York's most famous unknown artist," Ray Johnson strove to be unarchivable (Glueck).[7] The terms "famous" and "unknown" in this sobriquet suggest a tension not just between the public sphere of the art world and an underground counterpublic but also between the immediately recognizable and the fundamentally unknowable (Warner). That is, Johnson's work aims to be "unknown," baffling, outplaying, outsmarting, parrying, and dodging systems of classification and value.[8] This unknowability is, in part, a question of art historical classification. While I think it is important to understand Johnson in relation to (at least) mail art, Fluxus, Conceptual Art, and Neo-Dada, in this essay, I understand Johnson primarily as a Pop artist. A January 1958 *ARTnews* article makes Johnson's centrality to Pop's history clear when it describes Jasper Johns in the following manner: "Johns' first solo show [...] places him with such better-known colleagues as Rauschenberg, Twombly, Kaprow, and Ray Johnson" (Levy 15). Similarly, Warhol named Johnson one of the most important living artists (Warhol 238). His work has always included representations from popular culture, cartoons, and other typical Pop materials. His most famous work, *Oedipus (Elvis #1)* (1956–57), for example, pre-dates Warhol's *Double Elvis* (1963) and Peter Blake's *Self-Portrait with Badges* (1961), which features a prominent depiction of Elvis. I focus on Johnson's engagement with popular culture and with Mickey Mouse in particular because it is through the everydayness of these materials that his racial and sexual imaginary is most evident.

Johnson's sadomasochism practice is an integral part of what I will call his anti-archival poetics; it refuses classification by the hetero/homo binary (much as Gore Vidal famously did) and instead enables movement between a series of positions rather than fixed identities (Vidal). In an unpublished letter to Nam June Paik, Johnson illustrates just such a refusal of classification: "Someone once asked me if I was S. or M. I replied 'I was J.'"[9] Here, "J" stands for Johnson (particularly as the phrase "I was J" plays on the historical inextricability between the letters "I" and "J" at the level of typography and, as I am suggesting, subjectivity). Sadomasochism provides Johnson with an imaginary for dodging the taxonomies of sexuality. In the first part of this essay I will argue that Johnson playfully motivates these processes to disrupt the museum/gallery system. In the second and third parts I argue that recovering Johnson's archive – particularly his representations of blackface which wed the racial (part two) and the sexual (part three) – and his practice of reading (with especial attention to the "letter") enables us to reconfigure some of our most closely held narratives of Pop Art.

cataloguing ray johnson

After the show at the Whitney in 1970, Johnson began his project: *Dear Whitney Museum, i hate you. Love, Ray Johnson* (Fig. 1).[10] While such aggression against the archive re-enacts

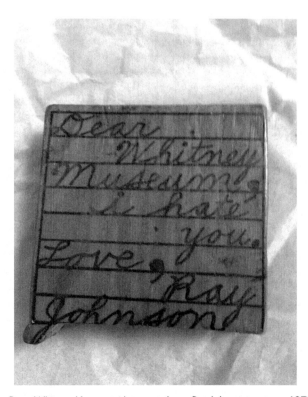

Fig. 1. Ray Johnson, *Dear Whitney Museum, i hate you. Love, Ray Johnson* stamp, c.1970. © The Ray Johnson Estate.

similar modernist gestures (for example, F.T. Marinetti's call to "destroy museums, libraries, academies of any sort" (Marinetti 14) or Marianne Moore's shocking "dislike" of poetry (Moore 36)), the form of Johnson's work constructs itself against the archive.[11] In Jacques Derrida's *Archive Fever* (1996) he describes the archive as demanding a *"domiciliation"* rooted in "consignation, that is [the] gathering together" of the archive (Derrida 2, 3). The constitutive aesthetic principles of the Correspondance School – its sheer profusion and dissemination of material – strategically thwart the archive's imperative of consignation.[12] Moreover, Johnson's creation of such a massive supply – so large as to be of uncertain scale – seems to have the aim of depressing the value of his own work.[13] I will contend that his anti-archival poetics draws attention to the complicity of the archive and capitalism.

In order to chart the dimensions of this anti-archival practice, I want to suggest some of the difficulties that constructing a *catalogue raisonné* – a key tool in the conversion of art into capital – for Johnson would pose. Theorizing and describing the *catalogue raisonné*, Griselda Pollock defines it as: "the collection of the complete *oeuvre* of the artist whose coherence as an individual creator is produced by assembling all of his or (rarely) her work in an expressive totality" (Pollock 58). Johnson's work foils such a project of compilation and collation in many registers. In addition to the aforementioned problem of dissemination, collecting the complete oeuvre seems impossible since the conceptualization of an oeuvre demands discrete objects. Several of Johnson's anti-archival practices undermine this discreteness, but his practice of disseminating photocopied material seems like a particularly strong assault on the idea of the originality and uniqueness of artistic production. Like Emily Dickinson's work which refuses to distinguish between letters and poems, Johnson's work similarly refuses distinction between letters and works of art.[14] Such a problem is exacerbated across media. His performances, often called "Nothings" – like "Happenings" to which they were nominally opposed – share a resistance to commodification and sale. But the name "Nothings" also calls into question their ontological status as works of art (or anything at all) (see Anderson).

As Pollock's definition makes evident, the "individual creator" organizes the oeuvre. Given the collaborative quiddity of the Correspondance School, Johnson's work sets itself against individual artistic biography. Beginning in 1962, he sends letters with instructions to "PLEASE ADD TO AND SEND TO [...]" and "PLEASE ADD TO AND RETURN TO RAY JOHNSON" (Fig. 2).[15] The transfiguration of his work by others and the multiplicity

Fig. 2.   Ray Johnson,   PLEASE ADD TO AND RETURN TO RAY JOHNSON" stamp, c.1962. © The Ray Johnson Estate.

of creators profoundly unsettles the idea of an individually created oeuvre, calling into question the signification of the possessive in "his works." Moreover, such individuality is further undercut by Johnson, as he stamped material with stamps such as: "COLLAGE BY U.S. POST OFFICE," "COLLAGE BY TOBY SPISELMAN," "COLLAGE BY BILL MAULDIN," "COLLAGE BY A MAJOR ARTIST" or even "Fake RAY JOHNSON."[16] These stamps suggest that even if Johnson's works are by him, they often perform disavowal of authorial attribution or, in the case of his "TOILET PAPER" stamp, of their value (echoed in the "MAJOR ARTIST" and again the "Fake RAY JOHNSON" stamps).[17]

The last part of Pollock's definition calls for the *catalogue raisonné* to represent "an expressive totality." Warhol Superstar Billy Name, who was also a friend of Johnson's, makes clear how untenable capturing and archiving such a totality is in Johnson's case:

> Andy [Warhol]'s performance is totally in his works. Where, like, Ray's performance is like half Ray and half his work. He didn't really disconnect from his work. Where Andy was still like a person too. Ray wasn't a person. He was a collage or a sculpture, a living sculpture – Ray Johnson's creation. (*How to Draw a Bunny*)

While one might dispute Name's claim that Warhol's performance is "totally in his works," the more important point for our purposes is that much of Johnson's expressive totality exists outside his work.[18] Moreover, as Diana Bowers has pointed out, Johnson's practice of burning much of his work and circulating narratives of its destruction emphasizes his work's unyielding incompleteness, further imperiling a Johnsonian "expressive totality" (Bowers 2).[19]

In case the imagined project of a Johnson *catalogue raisonné* were not doomed enough in the face of the techniques of his unarchivability that I have already elaborated, Pollock's description of such a catalogue as "a chronological ordering" which "performs an economic function," supplying "the main means by which art history services the art market through authentication, dating, and providing provenances" (63) proves fatal.[20] Johnson's practice of "recycling his works as raw material for other works" – what he called "Chop Art" in opposition to "Pop Art" – led him to date his works multiple times (Levy 15). Many collages bear three or more dates of composition or bear compositional dates spanning many years. To give a representative example, *Buddha Urinating on Antonio* is listed on the Feigen Gallery fact sheet with the following dates: "1972–8?–85–89–90–911 [sic], 11.14.90, 4.15.94, 2.14.89, 1982, 1.9.93, 6.17.91, 8.6.91, 1985, c. 1972–1993 [sic]." This dating practice, featuring chronological inscriptions spanning several decades as well as specific days, undermines both the chronology, which is essential to a *catalogue raisonné*, and the discreteness of individual works that I described above (as different elements of the collage bear different dates). The practice of collage for Johnson is thus both temporal and spatial, diachronic and synchronic.[21]

Johnson's anti-archival corpus thus contains no stable oeuvre, no stable artist, no expressive narrative, and no stable chronology. While his work, of course, can be archived – this essay draws on a number of existent Johnson archives – I am claiming that he strives to resist the systems of taxonomy and classification which are the precondition for art historical narrative and the extraordinary monetary sums that the art market often achieves. The remainder of this essay will contend that exploring this resistant archive will recast our understandings of the interlocking racial and sexual economies of Pop Art.

inking up

Johnson's most iconic and famous works are the "bunny" portraits that feature identical crudely rendered rabbit heads with individual's names on them. The racial underpinnings of these portraits emerge in a filming session with Nicholas Maravell. Maravell is shooting in black and white; Johnson and Maravell are playing with the camera and shift the colors into a "negative" mode so that the color scale is reversed, transforming black into white and white into black.

Johnson comments that: "The negative gets into a whole aspect of what I am doing which is the fact that all these rabbits and portraits – that everybody comes out in blackface. It's a kind of Howard Beach situation" (*The Ray Johnson Videos*). Here, Johnson explains that the portraits of art luminaries (which resemble inkbottles as well as rabbits) like William De Kooning, Christo, Paloma Picasso, Roy Lichtenstein, and Johnson himself are actually portraits in blackface. I use the term "inking up" to refer to the practice of using cork to create the effect of blackface minstrelsy, but foreground the shift in materials (from cork to ink) as a shift in affect. The donning of an ink costume highlights rather than enacts the particular racism and discrimination of the art establishment.[22] While it would, of course, be possible to read Johnson as participating in the asymmetrical forms of power and racial appropriation that are one of the most disturbing and unjust legacies of minstrelsy, I instead see Johnson's silhouettes performing racial critique shot through with the kind of ambivalence evident in Kara Walker's work.[23]

In suggesting that this practice of inking up these figures is a "Howard Beach situation," Johnson refers to an infamous 1986 racially charged incident in which three African American teenagers were attacked after their car broke down in a predominately white neighborhood. A gang of white youths hurled racial slurs and demanded that the African Americans leave. Ignoring the threats, the tired teens decided to have some pizza and rest. When they left the parlor, they were assaulted, one was badly beaten and another was murdered. The third escaped relatively unharmed. Johnson's analogizing of the de facto segregation of the white art world to the white neighborhood of Howard Beach lends his anti-archive a racial inflection. The space of the "negative" suggests that Johnson's black art cannot be archived by the white spaces of the art establishment and gallery system. Strikingly, the ink bottle – a tool of the artist's trade – is understood to be complicit in the segregating process. With this modification of Johnson's assault on the modes of production in the art world in mind, I understand Johnson's portraiture as engaged in a process of racial reparation, one which imagines a separatist utopia in which all of the artists, museum curators, gallery owners, and other members of the art establishment are black and producing images of blackness. In short, Johnson's compulsory blackface transforms a uniformly white art world into a world of uniform blackness.

In *AN ADVENTURE IN HIGH FIDELITY SOUND* (Fig. 3), for example, one of Johnson's many drawings which represent the art world (as well as the rarified world of celebrity), Johnson foregrounds the whiteness of the art world.[24] The piece features a number of identical stick figure-esque heads with names under them: Andy Warhol, Larry Poons, Elvis Presley, and, of course, Ray Johnson. The viewer's eye is immediately drawn to one figure in particular: Leslie Uggams. Uggams is an award-winning African American actress and singer who starred in *Roots* (1977). In Johnson's piece, Uggams' face is shaded in to suggest her blackness and her features bear the characterization of minstrelsy, particularly her mouth which features oversized minstrel lips. Upon closer examination, the viewer sees that some of the faces repeat (Larry Poons and Andy Warhol appear twice) and that there is one set of twins with an interconnected head. While Muñoz might suggest that we read this work as offering another grotesque depiction of African Americans, I think an alternative reading is possible. I see Uggams' depiction as highlighting the exclusivity and whiteness of the art world. I understand the homogeneousness of the figures (with the exception of Uggams and the twins) to be a statement of the desire for anti-exclusivity. The twins, rather than marking difference, emphasize sameness and foreground the uniformity of all the figures.[25] Similarly, Poons' and Warhol's double appearance suggests that some figures are so alike that they appear multiple times. The humor of the piece's title – *AN ADVENTURE IN HIGH FIDELITY SOUND* – registers how unadventurous the similitude of the depicted art establishment figures is, faithfully reproducing them not in "High Fidelity" but

Fig. 3. Ray Johnson, *AN ADVENTURE IN HIGH FIDELITY SOUND*, c.1963–65. Courtesy Harry Ransom Center, The University of Texas at Austin. © The Ray Johnson Estate.

with that most rudimentary technique of visual reproduction: the stick figure.[26] Johnson's searing critique is emphasized by positioning Uggams on the edges of the drawing, highlighting the marginalizing racism of the art establishment and the ways in which its techniques of reproduction always produce white figures.[27] Uggams' location seems to caption the rest of the work with the text that Johnson scrawled in large capital letters over a country club brochure: "NOT ONE BLACK IN THE BUNCH."[28]

Johnson helps us to see that the racial politics of Pop are far more complex than the narrative that Muñoz offers. Johnson's identity and his body in particular became a laboratory for such a reimagining of Pop's racial politics. In an unpublished letter to Clive Phillpot, the Director of the Library of the Museum of Modern Art, Johnson writes:

> Does your library have "Afro-American Artists". A Bio-bibliographical Directory. Compiled and edited by Theresa Dickason Cederholm. Boston Public Library, 1973?
>
> My biography appears on page 150. I mention this in reference to Nick Maravell's video, in which (unless he has deleted it) I make a remark about Romare Bearden.[29]

In drawing Phillpot's attention to Cederholm's misclassification of him as an Afro-American artist, Johnson is not only highlighting how little is known about him but also engaging in a project of racial reimagination.[30] His letter is an invitation to ask how such a mistake could have occurred, begging the question, what did Cederholm see in Johnson's work that made her think it was that of an Afro-American artist? Or was it something in his biography? His "black" name? Or the fact that Johnson was from Detroit? Johnson redirects such essentialist questions by pointing to the work of "another" African American artist: Romare Bearden. Bearden, though, was light skinned enough that he could "pass" as white (and was asked to do so in order to play in Major League baseball as a young man). Bearden refused, became an artist, and instead went on to found the Spiral Group. For Johnson, Bearden's gesture is inspirational, as he rebuffed systems of racial limitation. Rather than understand Cederholm's abbreviated bio-bibliographical entry as a license for Johnson to understand his art as a racialized production, I contend that this mistake fits into a program of racialized artistic production that he was already engaged in. For example, an untitled photograph features Johnson in blackface (Fig. 4).[31]

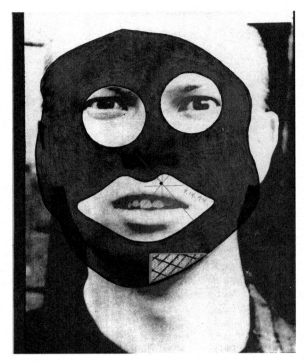

Fig. 4. Ray Johnson, untitled (Ray Johnson in blackface), 14 April 1994. © The Ray Johnson Estate.

This is far from the only example of Johnson's fashioning of a black identity for himself. In two writings from 1968, for example, he signs one "Ray Charles" and suggests in the other that there is "a Ray Johnson negro dancer," implicitly imagining his confusion with the dancer (Johnson, *Not Nothing* Plates 82, 73). Similarly, Johnson's work often depicted Mickey Mouse and he owned (at least) two Mickey Mouse jackets, one of which he made and wore during a performance (Fig. 5).[32] I highlight this proclivity for Mickey Mouse because Mickey's well-known origins in the traditions of minstrelsy suggest that we read Johnson's envelopment in and embodiment of Mickey Mouse as a kind of blackface performance.[33] Moreover, Nicholas Sammond has recently argued that Mickey is not just a figure of minstrelsy, but of sadomasochism: "the vibrancy and magic associated with the [Mickey Mouse] cartoons [...] depend on a sadomasochistic racial fantasy of encounter and resistance that is played out again and again" (Sammond 166).

Following Sammond in reading the logics of black identification and embodiment in relation to sexuality, we must attend to the sexual as well as racial overtones of Johnson's bunny portraits (reading them in dialogue with *Playboy*'s bunny logo) (Stuckey 3).[34] Almost every aspect of Johnson's bunnies can become sexual – the mouth can be replaced by a vagina or a butt crack (Figs 6, 7).[35] The ears can become penises as can the nose (Fig. 8).[36] The mutating shapes of these mail art bunnies invoke sadomasochism's non-genitally organized eroticization of the body and its resistance to sexuality's classificatory seizure. Moreover, I understand Johnson's racialization of the bunnies itself as erotic. This, in part, stems from the homoerotics of blackface (its clothing and unclothing of black male bodies, its spectatorship of and phantasmatic inhabitation of them) that Eric Lott has taught us to read in *Love and Theft* (1995).

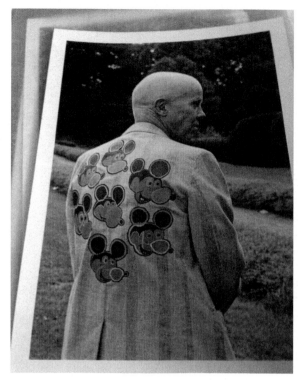

Fig. 5. Unknown artist, untitled (Ray Johnson in hand-painted Mickey Mouse jacket), c.1987. © The Ray Johnson Estate.

But for Johnson it is more than homoeroticism; Johnson's arresting portrait of the founder of Fluxus, George F. Maciunas (Fig. 9), makes clear that the sexual realm of Johnson's work foregrounds sadomasochism. While leather is not typically made of the hides of rabbits, Johnson's piece leaves no doubt that Maciunas dons a rabbit skin leather mask; the placement of the mask's eye, nose, and mouth openings are those characteristic of sadomasochistic play. For Johnson, black bodies and bodies in blackface carry a particularly eroticized charge and one which I think is central to our recasting of the racial politics of Pop Art.

lessons from ray

Johnson is particularly interested in the racial components of sadomasochistic culture and discourse and its possibilities as a mode of blackface in the donning of leather masks. Elizabeth Freeman argues that sadomasochism is a highly racialized discourse; she contends that it draws much of its iconography from US slavery (whips, chains, the popularity of black dildos, etc.). Attending to the relationship between leather and skin that Freeman calls "skinplay" and summoned in the colloquial name for sadomasochism "leathersex," I read Johnson's avowed interest in and descriptions of his experiences with sadomasochistic cultures as an extension of his blackface portraiture practices (Freeman 59). Following Freeman, who argues that sadomasochism's historical consciousness opens a space for reworking historical trauma, I understand the explicitly sadomasochistic themes of Johnson's work as a rebuttal to and reconfiguration of the racist exclusionary forces of the art world (Freeman). That is, the relay between sadomasochistic and blackface representation places racial justice at the center of Johnson's work.

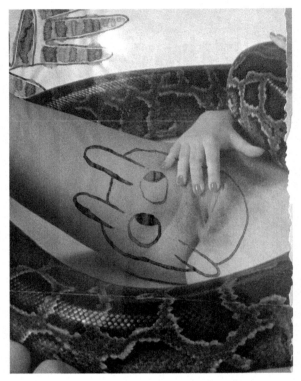

Fig. 6. Ray Johnson, untitled (Bunny head with vagina mouth), n.d. © The Ray Johnson Estate.

The intersection between race and sadomasochism is often explicitly flagged in Johnson's work as in the collage "untitled (*Mickey Snake*)" (Fig. 10) and a mail art piece of the Marcel Duchamp Fan Club which features Mickey Mouse astride a rendering of Allen Jones's *Table* (1969) (Fig. 11).[37] Thus, I will contend that even when Johnson's sadomasochistic works do not explicitly carry a racialized content, they are racially coded. Johnson demands that his viewer is able to recall all of the prior meanings of a related image. Every subsequent work is also a continuous one – forging racial meanings in sadomasochistic texts in which there is no explicit racial content. Moreover, the structure of the sadomasochistic scene provides Johnson with a tableau for imagining new modes of artistic collaboration and production. To put this differently, we must read the delay and mediation of the postal system in relation to that of sadomasochistic cultures in order to understand the formal features of Johnson's mail art. Thus, I understand the processes that Sherri Geldin describes as "Johnson's transgressive strategies" which "revel in the gesture and the transaction as much as the work of art itself" as a sadomasochistic practice (7). That is, since the gesture and transaction are repeatedly not completed or are simply impossible, we might read the sexualization of these transactions and the delay built into the use of the mail system as a kind of sadomasochistic form. In reading the form and content of sadomasochism in Johnson's work in relation to Pop, I take up where Jonathan Weinberg's excellent essay "Ray Johnson Fan Club" (1999) left off (Weinberg). Fearing that he has exaggerated the "gay content" of Johnson's work, Weinberg gestures towards "questions of sadomasochism" and expresses the (as yet unrealized) hope that he will have the chance to "explore the role of S-

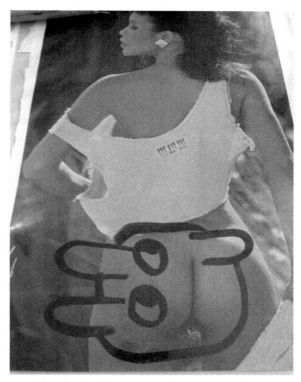

Fig. 7. Ray Johnson, untitled (Bunny head with butt crack mouth), n.d. © The Ray Johnson Estate.

M in Johnson's work in another essay" (Weinberg 108 and 109 fn. 31).[38]

To read Johnson under the sign of sadomasochism instead of homosexuality is, however, not to obviate Johnson's importance to gay history and the queerness of Pop. Johnson may, in fact, supply the earliest known usage of the term "closet" as part of a homosexual vocabulary. George Chauncey explains that: "Nowhere does it [the concept of the 'closet'] appear before the 1960s in the records of the gay movement or in the novels, diaries, or letters of gay men and lesbians" (6). Elaborating the point, Chauncey suggests that it also doesn't appear in glossaries of homosexual argot, including Will Finch's of 1963 (375). Concurring with Chauncey's findings, Craig Loftin explains that "The contemporary concept of the closet as a metaphor for hiding one's homosexual identity from others or one's self did not emerge until the late 1960s and early 1970s"

(10). In a one-sentence letter dated 15 March 1962, Johnson writes to William S. Wilson: "Bill, / I'm back in the closet again, / Out where a friend is a friend, R."[39] The text of the letter rewrites the opening lines of Gene Autry's "Back in the Saddle Again" (1939) by replacing the word "saddle" with the word "closet." The letter animates the now familiar dichotomy of closetedness and outness, suggesting its homosexual content. Fascinatingly, Wilson has also told me that when he received the letter he understood it to have meant that Johnson had resumed his relationship with Richard Lippold, suggesting that the word "closet" carries the valence of "saddle" in addition to replacing it. While there is much more to say about this letter, I want to suggest that even if Johnson's usage proves not to be the first usage – it provides crucial evidence of the closet in the process of formation.[40]

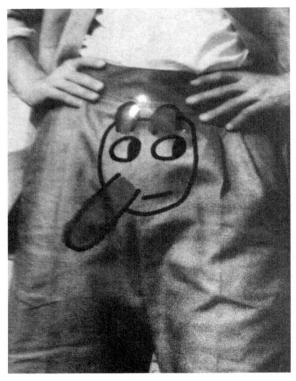

Fig. 8. Ray Johnson, untitled (Bunny head with penis nose), n.d. © The Ray Johnson Estate.

With the queerness of Johnson's Pop in mind, I understand sadomasochism to provide a crucial optic for exploring the dynamics of Johnson's life and work. Several accounts of Johnson's visits to s/m clubs survive. Peter Schuyff describes a visit with Johnson to the Mineshaft in *How to Draw a Bunny* (2002).[41] Johnson himself describes a visit to The Hellfire Club with Diane Arbus which lasted "about 24 [hours]" (*The Ray Johnson Videos*). He also mentions several visits to The Anvil with a correspondent known only as "Cowboy Bart" (quoted in Weinberg 99–101). His work often features sadomasochistic iconography – butt plugs, fisting, chains, blindfolds, masks, snakes which look like whips, and belts (Fig. 12).[42] In an interview with Henry Martin at a point where he is discussing Gertrude Stein's *The Making of Americans* (1925), Johnson mentions the role of sadomasochism in his work: "Yes, and my portrait work is subtitled 'The Snaking of Americans,' which is a very oblique S & M reference, Sade in Japan. Made in Japan. Making and Snaking, S & M, and M & S" (Martin 49). Johnson was fascinated by the name Mike Belt and sent many mailings to him, conjuring both the Belt Club, the Spam Belt Club, and many more iterations and permutations (51). Similarly, his reading "Beat It Eat It" at Coco Gordon's gallery features Johnson attempting to "cough" a single word "Kafka" (playing on Kaf/cough) while he ritually beats a cardboard box with his belt. At one point, the box is placed over his knee so that he is flagellating himself as he is whipping it in act of sadism and of masochism (Figs 13, 14, 15).[43] He also inscribes the word "Kafka" on the box as if he is sentencing it like the machine from *In the Penal Colony* (1919).[44]

In addition to the sadomasochistic content of much of Johnson's work, sadomasochism

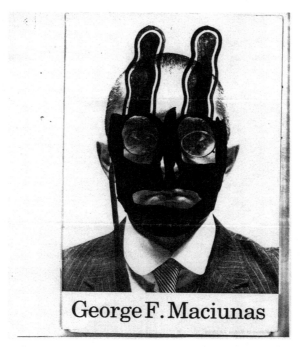

Fig. 9. Ray Johnson, untitled (George F. Maciunas in blackface), 18 July 1990, Courtesy Museum of Modern Art. © The Ray Johnson Estate.

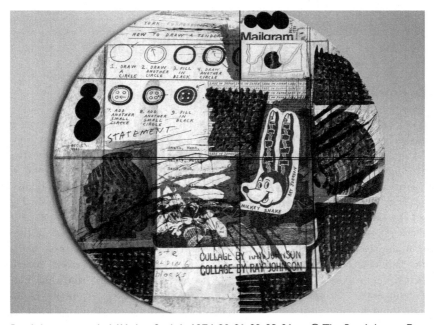

Fig. 10. Ray Johnson, untitled (*Mickey Snake*), 1974-80-81-82-83-91 + . © The Ray Johnson Estate.

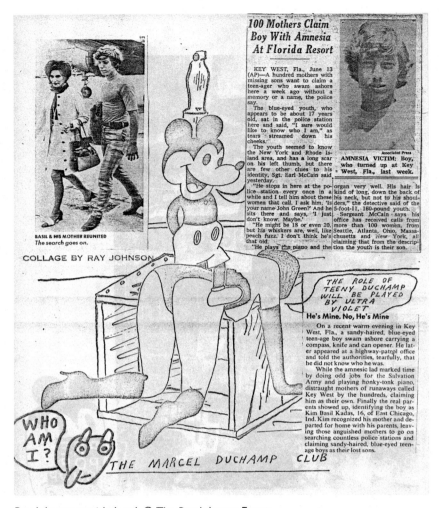

Fig. 11. Ray Johnson, untitled, n.d. © The Ray Johnson Estate.

organizes its form. Homologous logics govern the Marquis de Sade's oeuvre and the collaborations of the Correspondance School. Brilliantly describing Sadian practice as "being ruled by a great notion of order," Roland Barthes explains: "Sadian combinativity is determined by an ordinator (a director)" (*Sade, Fourier, Loyola* 27). This is the role that Johnson plays, positioned within the Correspondance School as a kind of (post)master. In *How to Draw a Bunny*, the artist Buster Cleveland comments: "I think that's how a lot of people thought about him as a guru or a Zen master." On the other side of the emotional coin, the artist Peter Schuyff describes a different affective valence to a scene of instruction with Johnson. A work of Johnson's had been inadvertently attributed to Schuyff; over the course of the next year when Schuyff would call Johnson, Johnson would put the receiver down on his desk (Fig. 16).[45]

After a year, Johnson proceeds as if nothing had transpired and won't speak of the incident. In Schuyff's words, "I'd been punished and time to move on." Likewise, Morris Graves accuses Johnson of "'whipping him'" when Johnson attempts to obtain Graves' baby photo (Johnson, *Not Nothing* Plate 35).

I see all of his Correspondance work – whether it has a recognizable sexual content or

Fig. 12. Ray Johnson, untitled, n.d. © The Ray Johnson Estate.

not – as routed through what Barthes has taught us to see as the Sadian aesthetics of totality, reciprocity, and exhaustiveness (Barthes, *Sade, Fourier, Loyola* 17, 29, 30). Johnson's 1967 New York Correspondance School Report makes clear that he also understands the School in these terms, describing how it has "strangled itself" and "mutilated itself," but that "[t]he fetish has to be fed" (Johnson, *Not Nothing* Plate 61). Rather than achieving totality through enclosure as Sade does, Johnson achieves it through dissemination and assimilation. He writes: "I consider everyone on Earth alive or dead, past and future to be or have been or are members of my [Correspondance] School participating whether they know it or not" (Plate 119). Here, Johnson imagines an astoundingly broad unity across time and space, enacted through his notion of Correspondance. The non-separation between Johnson and everything else is hauntingly performed in his elaborately staged suicide. Such non-differentiation – in its vastness – overloads and overcomes the archivable. Name's description of Johnson as not "a person" but "a living sculpture – Ray Johnson's creation," suggests the all-encompassing nature of the s/m "lifestyle." To put this differently, in s/m culture the sphere of the sexual pervades all aspects of life. There is no category of the non-sexual. Barthes describes the Sadian "erotic code" as consisting of units, the "minimal unit" of which is "the posture" (*Sade, Fourier, Loyola* 28). For Johnson, the minimal unit is the letter. I mean "letter" here to signify both an epistle (with its associations of reciprocity and courtship) and also a single alphabetic letter. Johnson can change individual alphabetic letters, anagrammatically rearranging them, the way "osmotic" becomes "moticos" or "Made in Japan" becomes "Sade in Japan." The permutations are endless: Nam June Paik becomes Nam Jan Paik, Nam Feb Paik, and all of the other months. It is mathematical and

Fig. 13. Artist unknown, untitled, c.1987–88. © The Ray Johnson Estate.

Fig. 14. Artist unknown, untitled, c.1987–88. © The Ray Johnson Estate.

Fig. 15. Artist unknown, untitled, c.1987–88. © The Ray Johnson Estate.

combinative and imaginative like Sadian pleasure.

These sadomasochistic aesthetics and their concomitant erotic saturation of "every part of the body" provide crucial strategies for disrupting the established conditions of capitalism, which similarly aspires to totality (Barthes, *Sade, Fourier, Loyola* 30). These totalities (sadomasochism and capitalism) compete in Johnson's practices of negotiation and sale of his works. Describing this practice, Jeanne Claude says: "He enjoyed discussing the price [...] [it was] a continuation of the creative process, not only written but spoken" (*How to Draw a Bunny*). These negotiations would often occur (some might say drag out) over many years. Frances Beatty describes "14 years of trying to do a Ray Johnson show" (ibid.). Morton Janklow provides one of the most vivid records of this prolonged negotiation in *How to Draw a Bunny*. Johnson made a group of twenty-six portraits of Janklow and offered them to him for $42,400. Narrating the events, Janklow says:

> He [Johnson] was always telling me, "what do you want to do? What do you want to do?" And every time I told him what I wanted to do, it was not acceptable. He came back with some kind of other proposal. (Ibid.)

Jeanne Claude's description of Johnson's enjoyment in the negotiations (which his interlocutors often found frustrating and painful) suggests the sadomasochistic nature of the pleasure (both the "exhaustiveness" and the "reciprocity" which Barthes sees its hallmark). The sadomasochistic transaction – with its seemingly endless deferral – short circuits the

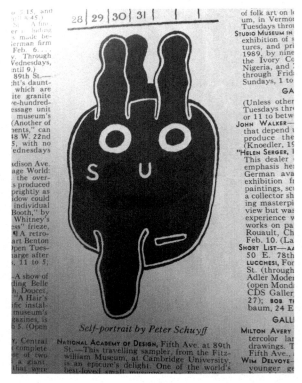

Fig. 16. Ray Johnson (misattributed to Peter Schuyff in *The New Yorker* 29 Jan. 1990, 10). © The Ray Johnson Estate.

capitalist enterprise of having gallery shows and selling works of art and thus is of a piece with his anti-archival poetics. His negotiating is transactional without the transaction ever taking place.

That this negotiation often carried the signification of sadism is evident in William S. Wilson's nickname for Johnson, "the meanest man in Manhattan" (Wilson 58 n. 12).[46] When Janklow does not purchase the portraits, they are "Polamized," combining Janklow's "head with Paloma Picasso's 26 times." Johnson's wordplay here on "pulverized" suggests the destructiveness of his collaborative creativity. Such destructiveness is also evident in an encounter where Chuck Close asked for "an artist's discount" while purchasing a portrait of himself from Johnson. "Ray said, 'Of course.' Then he cut the upper right-hand corner to match the price break."[47] Similarly, when Schuyff offers Johnson $1,500 for a portrait that Johnson wanted to sell for $2,000 – Johnson cuts out a quarter, making a new work of art in collaboration with Schuyff. Describing the incident, Schuyff says: "It was like a lesson [...] a lot of lessons from Ray. They were not all good times between Ray and I."[48] We might understand Johnson and his "students" in the Correspondance School as engaged in a sadomasochistic scene of instruction, one where there are severe consequences (the work is partially destroyed) and pleasures (Schuyff gets the work for $1,500 after all) in obeying and disobeying Johnson's "lessons." The totalities of capitalism and sadomasochism are competing inasmuch as Johnson must give up money in order to maintain artistic, emotional, and sexual control. As these examples suggest, however, creativity and reimagination come out of every collaborative transaction.

While Wayne Koestenbaum and Jeffrey Masten have written collaboration under the signs of homosexuality and homoerotic friendship respectively, Johnson enables us to theorize sadomasochism as a modality of collaboration. Where Masten beautifully reads early modern collaboration in relation to the egalitarian ideal of masculine friendship, Johnson posits an alternative collaborative imaginary in which the severe power differentials of s/m culture endow reciprocity with a negative affective valence. Rather than understanding the Correspondance School as a kind of gay coterie (akin to those of W.H. Auden, C.P. Cavafy, or Frank O'Hara), we might understand sadomasochism as opening a new avenue for understanding Pop's eponymous relation to the popular, the mass, and even, as I have been suggesting, the totality.

In Andy Warhol and Pat Hackett's *POPism: The Warhol Sixties*, for example, Warhol describes Pop as imbuing everything, as a mode of totality:

> The farther west we drove, the more Pop everything looked on the highways. Suddenly we all felt like insiders because even though Pop was everywhere – that was the thing about it, most people still took it for granted, whereas we were dazzled by it – to us it was the new Art. Once you "got" Pop, you could never see a sign the same way again. And once you thought Pop, you could never see America the same way again. (Warhol and Hackett 39)

Here, Pop is a way of seeing things (sights on the western highway, for instance) and a way of experiencing them (something "you 'got'" or "thought"), but it is also the way things are, a mode of being ("Pop was everywhere").[49] Pop's conflation of modes of perception and modes of existence is homologous with what Billy Name describes as Johnson's refusal to "really disconnect from his work." If this totalizing vision is understood as emanating from a coterie, it is a coterie which is fundamentally incorporative and which recasts the closeness of such social formations. This recasting of social structures is a crucial component of the expanded racial and sexual narratives that I have been arguing electrify Pop. But I also mean to suggest that Johnson's limitlessly incorporative networks of meaning might be said to provide something like a civil rights counterpublic.[50]

Johnson's counterpublic is not just central to Pop Art but retrains us to see and understand Pop differently. Looking at Rauschenberg's *Canyon* (1959) – one of the Rauschenberg's most famous Combines and one of the most iconic pieces of Pop Art – through Johnson's eyes we see new racial and sexual currents. Johnson has sensitized us, as I have been arguing to the "letter," as the minimal unit of meaning. With this reading practice in mind, when we look at the only visible letters ("ocra") in "Democracy," we can begin to see it as "okra." Here, this traditional southern food, with its associations with Africa and with African Americans, lends democracy a new meaning. Its cropping suggests a full-throated support (contra Muñoz) of the civil rights struggle, of the forging of democracy in the South. The bald eagle and the Statue of Liberty in the painting suddenly look different (as does the nationalism of Larry Rivers' *George Washington Crossing the Delaware* (1953) and Jasper Johns' frayed flags and ragged maps of the United States). Might we understand Jim Dine's *Crow* (2001) and Jean-Michel Basquiat's *Jim Crow* (1986) as haunting attacks on Jim Crow? Amplifying Flatley's contention about Warhol's preoccupation with the color-line, I see Pop as profoundly preoccupied with race. The construction of Combines themselves – with their amalgamation of elements – starts to look like a racial politics, especially given that the first Combine was finished in 1954, the year of *Brown* v. *The Board of Education*. Similarly, *Canyon* disrupts the "homosexualization of American Art" thesis (exemplified by Rauschenberg's *Bed* (1955), as the bed was shared with Johns) instead offering a multiplicity of sexual and affective currents. Kenneth Bendiner argues that *Canyon* and its imposing bald eagle reference the Ganymede myth (Bendiner). Given that the work features a photograph of Rauschenberg's son Christopher, we might understand it as possessing an incestuous as well as a pederastic content. Or perhaps, we might understand it less salaciously as a father's desire for nearness with his son? Or perhaps the eagle is a tribute to Rauschenberg's close friendship with Ileana Sonnabend, who found the eagle and championed Rauschenberg's work. I wouldn't want to decide between these interpretations, but rather keep them open, in permutation and combination, the way Johnson does. These new ways of seeing Pop are Johnson's gifts to us, his invitations, his letters in the mail.

disclosure statement

No potential conflict of interest was reported by the author.

notes

1 While it is certainly possible to see Basquiat as a Pop artist as Muñoz does, it is worth mentioning that he is more traditionally classified as a Neo-Expressionist. Taro Nettleton concurs with Muñoz, asserting that "it might very well be that those who were not white were marginalized even within Warhol's counterpublic space" (Nettleton 77).

2 I am grateful to Jonathan for sharing his work with me.

3 On the association of Ray Johnson in particular with a homosexual Pop coterie, see Ellen Levy's *What's in a Name? Ray Johnson's Free Associations*, which describes Ray as "landing smack in the midst of a generational cohort of gay male artists like Jasper Johns, Robert Rauschenberg, and Andy Warhol" (Levy 5).

4 Warhol studies strikes me as being more attuned to what Eve Sedgwick calls the "slip-slidy effects" of queerness than other scholarship on Pop Art (Sedgwick 2).

5 Johnson's relationship to Asianness suggests one possible direction for moving Pop's focus outside the high-contrast binary of black and white.

6 I retain Johnson's spelling throughout.

7 For a different view of Johnson's relation to the archive, see Pistell.

8 This sentence borrows many of its descriptors from Roland Barthes's *The Neutral*.

9 © The Ray Johnson Estate, Box 150. Hereafter, other archival citations to the Estate will be abbreviated RJE. Ray Johnson to Nam June Paik, 30 Nov. 1968, RJE Box 48 Folder 25 (1968).

10 RJE Box 150.

11 Johnson would often describe destroying his own archive either by burning things (most famously in Cy Twombly's fireplace) or by disposing of them, as described in this letter of 4 May 1981: "Last month, I threw out boxes and boxes and boxes and boxes and boxes and bags and bags and bags and bags of the Correspondance School Archive" (RJE Box 119 Binder 39 Number 22). On Twombly's fireplace, see Johnson, *Not Nothing* Plate 139.

12 Johnson's decision to submit his work to the Museum of Modern Art through the museum's library (because he knew the library's policy was to keep everything), which is recounted in *How to Draw a Bunny*, seems characteristic of his ability to circumvent the exclusivity of museum culture and routinized modes of collecting and archiving.

13 Diana Bowers, Assistant Archivist at the Ray Johnson Estate Archive, estimates that the archive is "779 cubic feet, of which only 130 cubic feet has been processed and is available to researchers" (Bowers). Ray Johnson's collages start selling for around $25,000, as opposed to the multi-million-dollar price tags of his contemporary Pop artists.

14 Johnson's work often makes reference to Emily Dickinson. The Feigen Gallery has records of at least twenty-three collages referencing Dickinson. Also, Johnson had an "EMILY DICKINSON UNIVERSITY" stamp (Box 150) and often referenced "Emily Dickinson's underwear" (RJE Box 4 Binder 2 Number 43).

15 RJE Box 154. An earlier form of this practice, one which instructed his correspondents to "Please Send To," dates at least as early as 1958.

16 These first three are in RJE Box 152. "COLLAGE BY A MAJOR ARTIST" is in RJE Box 151, and "Fake RAY JOHNSON" is in RJE Box 150.

17 "TOILET PAPER" is in RJE Box 154.

18 Frances Beatty echoes this sentiment: "everything that Ray did [...] was like a work of art. Everything he wore, everything he touched, everything he said" (*How to Draw a Bunny*). While Jonathan Flatley has taught us to attend to what it means for two things to be "like" each other, Beatty's suggestion simultaneously multiplies the objects in Johnson's oeuvre and underlines the impossibility of archiving them.

19 For another example of such destruction, see Spodarek and Delbeke 7.

20 As if to foreground the impossibility of putting together a *Ray Johnson Catalogue Raisonné*, Karma Gallery has recently published a mock *catalogue raisonné* under the title *Ray Johnson: Taoist Pop Heart School* (Johnson, *Ray Johnson*).

21 These difficulties of dating are highlighted by the fact sheet's seeming inability to put the dates in sequence and to encapsulate the dates "correctly," leaving out the collage's own "4.15.94" in the summary date range of "1972–1993." In one collage, Johnson refuses chronology outright writing "No Chrology" in large letters ("United (No Chrology / Chronology)," RJE Collage Number 11569). Similarly, Johnson marks another letter/essay "(undated)" (RJE Box 48 Folder 19 (1964)). In a 1975 letter, Johnson declares that "The New York Correspondance School has no history – only a present" (Johnson, *Not Nothing* Plate 143).

22 While I think one must recognize a degree of self-consciousness in nineteenth- and twentieth-century practices of minstrelsy, Johnson intensifies these processes enormously and his practice is far less ambivalent.

23 This racial history is also tied to the colonial history with which Primitivism is associated. See, for example, an image of Picasso with his *Tête de Femme* (1951) in blackface from 13 Feb. 1989 (RJE Box 110 Binder 4 Number 14).

24 Charles Henri Ford Papers, Harry Ransom Center, The University of Texas at Austin, Box 14 Folder 2.

25 Ray was fascinated by twins – particularly William S. Wilson's twins – since they represented sameness and difference simultaneously.

26 The image is cross modal and cross sensory, translating "high fidelity" from the world of sound to that of sight. More accurately, they are the heads of stick figures since the "figures" don't have bodies.

27 Edges are often important in Johnson's work. A similar use of racialized margins is evident in a Buddha University Meeting invitation which features a field of bunny heads of which only two in the corner are labeled. These bunnies sit atop a black field, while all the others sit on a white field and are labeled "Abraham" and "Lincoln" respectively, summoning Lincoln's popular reputation as the president who ended slavery (RJE Box 110 Binder 4 Number 112).

28 Private archive of William S. Wilson. Letter to William S. Wilson, Feb. 1984.

29 9 July 1990, Ray Johnson to Clive Phillpot, in Ray Johnson, *Book about Modern Art* (1990) 1: 12, Museum of Modern Art Library. The book Johnson refers to is Cederholm.

30 Johnson was sometimes mistaken for Raymond Jonson (1891–1982), who is famous for his southwestern landscapes.

31 RJE 13420.

32 The performance took place at the Nassau County Museum of Fine Art in 1987.

33 For more on Johnson's relationship to Mickey Mouse, see Phillpot 236–38. See also RJE Box 119 Binder 3 Number 94.

34 In the case of the untitled image 13420, we might note how the mask frames Johnson's lips as cartoonishly sexualized into the shape of women's lipstick. Because the first black Playmate did not appear until 1965, Johnson's bunnies racialize an image of white sexuality.

35 Figure 6 is RJE Box 110 Binder 4 Number 68; and Fig. 7 is Binder 3 Number 101. See also RJE Box 110 Binder 4 Number 86.

36 Figure 8 is RJE Binder 4 Number 77. For other sexualized bunny heads, see RJE Box 5 Binder 3 Number 30; RJE Binder 3 Number 91; and RJE Binder 3 Number 102.

37 Figure 10 is RJE Collage 11622 and Fig. 11 is in RJE Box 123 Binder 6 Number 16.

38 See also Elizabeth Zuba's brief mention of sadomasochism in Johnson's work (Zuba 12).

39 Private archive of William S. Wilson. Letter to William S. Wilson, 15 Mar. 1962.

40 There are several candidates for earlier usages of the concept of the "closet." Loftin has found a letter from a man named Dwayne dating from 1960: "Perhaps if everyone would take sex out of the dark closet into which the word [sic] has flung it, we would all be better human beings." Loftin discounts this letter, however, suggesting that it refers "to sex in general, not homosexuality in particular, suggesting that his usage of 'closet' lacked the specific meaning and implications that the term later assumed" (Loftin 10). Similarly, Chauncey draws attention to the "similar spatial" logic of James Baldwin's *Giovanni's Room* (1956), even as that novel doesn't use the term "closet" (Chauncey 375). Henry Abelove has found the most compelling precursor in Frank O'Hara's poem "Ode: Salute to the French Negro Poets" (1958) which contains the lines: "nothing / inspires us but the love we want upon the frozen face of earth / and utter disparagement turns into praise as generations read the message / of our hearts in adolescent closets who once shot at us in doorways / or kept us from living freely [...]" While I remain convincible that this poem refers to the concept of the closet as Abelove suggests, the adjective "adolescent" means that I am not yet convinced that this usage bears a homosexual inflection (even as "adolescent" might refer to the supposed arrested development of the homosexual) (Abelove).

41 Gayle Rubin describes New York's Mineshaft as "the preeminent on-going leather sex establishment from the time it opened in 1976 until it was closed in 1985" (Rubin 226).

42 Sometimes Johnson's work is connected to sadomasochism without explicitly containing sadomasochistic iconography. See, for example, S & M (Shirley Temple) in *Correspondences* 112.

43 RJE Box 77 2i, 2j, 2l.

44 *How to Draw a Bunny*. Muñoz also offers a reading of this performance (Muñoz, "Utopia's Seating Chart" 118).

45 *The New Yorker* 29 Jan. 1990, 10. RJE Box 5 Binder 3 Number 27.

46 See also Box 125 Binder 1 Number 12.

47 "An Artist Finds the Perfect Red," *Wall Street Journal* 6 Mar. 2014.

48 William S. Wilson also describes Ray as a "lesson" (though one taught by Norman Solomon) (Wilson 3).

49 My reading here is indebted to Jonathan Flatley ("Warhol Gives Good Face" 101).

50 Warhol has a similarly incorporative network (see Kahan 121–41).

bibliography

Abelove, Henry. "How Stonewall Obscures the Real History of Gay Liberation." *The Chronicle of Higher Education* 26 June 2015: B14. Print.

Anderson, Fiona. "'A Trail of Drift and Debris': Traces of Whitman in the Correspondence Art of Ray Johnson." *Journal of American Studies* 49 (2015): 55–75. Print.

Barthes, Roland. *The Neutral*. Trans. Rosalind E. Krauss and Denis Hollier. New York: Columbia UP, 2005. Print.

Barthes, Roland. *Sade, Fourier, Loyola*. Trans. Richard Miller. Berkeley and Los Angeles: U of California P, 1989. Print.

Bendiner, Kenneth. "Rauschenberg's Canyon." *Arts Magazine* 56.10 (June 1982): 57–59. Print.

Bowers, Diana. "Affecting the Art Historical Narrative: Discoveries at the Ray Johnson Estate Archive." MS.

Cederholm, Theresa Dickason. *Afro-American Artists: A Bio-bibliographical Directory*. Boston: Trustees of the Boston Public Library, 1973. Print.

Chauncey, George. *Gay New York: Gender, Urban Culture, and the Making of the Gay Male World, 1890–1940*. New York: Basic, 1994. Print.

Derrida, Jacques. *Archive Fever: A Freudian Impression*. Chicago: U of Chicago P, 1996. Print.

De Salvo, Donna, and Catherine Gudis, eds. *Ray Johnson: Correspondences*. Columbus, OH: Wexner Center for the Arts, Ohio State U, 1999. Print.

Doyle, Jennifer, Jonathan Flatley, and José Esteban Muñoz, eds. *Pop Out: Queer Warhol*. Durham, NC: Duke UP, 1996. Print.

Flatley, Jonathan. "Skin Problems." MS.

Flatley, Jonathan. "Warhol Gives Good Face: Publicity and the Politics of Prosopopoeia." Doyle, Flatley, and Muñoz 101–33. Print.

Flatley, Jonathan, and Anthony E. Grudin. "Introduction: Warhol's Aesthetics." *Criticism* 56.3 (2014): 419–25. Print.

Freeman, Elizabeth. "Turn the Beat Around: Sadomasochism, Temporality, History." *differences* 19.1 (2008): 32–70. Print.

Geldin, Sherri. "Foreword." De Salvo and Gudis 7–10. Print.

Glueck, Grace. "What Happened? Nothing." *New York Times* 11 Apr. 1965: X18. Print.

How to Draw a Bunny. Dir. John Walter and Andrew Moore. Palm Pictures/Mr. Mudd, 2002. Film.

Johnson, Ray. *Not Nothing: Selected Writings by Ray Johnson, 1954–1994*. Los Angeles: Siglio, 2014. Print.

Johnson, Ray. *Ray Johnson: Taoist Pop Heart School*. New York: Karma, 2014. Print.

Kahan, Benjamin. *Celibacies: American Modernism and Sexual Life*. Durham, NC: Duke UP, 2013. Print.

Kishi, Madoka. "The Erotics of Race Suicide: Undoing the Social Body in the Progressive Era." Diss. Louisiana State U, 2015. Print.

Levy, Ellen. *What's in a Name? Ray Johnson's Free Associations*. New York: Feigen, 2011. Print.

Loftin, Craig. *Masked Voices: Gay Men and Lesbians in Cold War America*. Albany: State U of New York P, 2012. Print.

Marinetti, Filippo Tommaso. "The Foundation and Manifesto of Futurism." *Critical Writings*. New ed. Ed. Gunter Berghaus. Trans. Doug Thompson. New York: FSG, 2006. 11–17. Print.

Martin, Henry. "Should an Eyelash Last Forever? An Interview with Ray Johnson." *Lightworks* 22 (2000): 3–24. Print.

Mercer, Kobena. "Introduction." *Pop Art and Vernacular Cultures*. Cambridge, MA: MIT P, 2007. 6–35. Print.

Moore, Marianne. *Complete Poems*. New York: Macmillan/Viking, 1981. Print.

Muñoz, José Esteban. "Famous and Dandy Like B. 'n' Andy: Race, Pop, and Basquiat." Doyle, Flatley, and Muñoz 144–79. Print.

Muñoz, José Esteban. "Utopia's Seating Chart: Ray Johnson, Jill Johnston, and Queer Intermedia as System." *Cruising Utopia: The Then and There of Queer Futurity*. New York: New York UP, 2009. 115–30. Print.

Nettleton, Taro. "White-on-White: The Overbearing Whiteness of Warhol Being." *Gay Shame*. Ed. David M. Halperin and Valerie Traub. Chicago: U of Chicago P, 2009. 76–87. Print.

Phillpot, Clive. *Booktrek: Selected Essays on Artists' Books (1972–2010)*. Zurich: JRP/Ringier, 2013. Print.

Pistell, Gillian. "Ray Johnson: Artist as Archivist." MS.

Pollock, Griselda. "Artists Mythologies and Media Genius, Madness and Art History." *Screen* 21.3 (1980): 57–96. Print.

The Ray Johnson Videos. Dir. Nicholas Maravell. DVD. 2007. Film.

Rubin, Gayle. *Deviations: A Gayle Rubin Reader*. Durham, NC: Duke UP, 2011. Print.

Sammond, Nicholas. "'Gentleman, Please be Seated': Racial Masquerade and Sadomasochism in 1930s Animation." *Burnt Cork: Traditions and Legacies of Blackface Minstrelsy*. Ed. Stephen Johnson. Amherst: U of Massachusetts P, 2012. 164–90. Print.

Sedgwick, Eve Kosofsky. *Touching Feeling: Affect, Pedagogy, Performativity*. Durham, NC: Duke UP, 2003. Print.

Silver, Kenneth E. "Modes of Disclosure: The Construction of Gay Identity and the Rise of Pop Art." *Hand-Painted Pop: American Art in Transition, 1955–1962*. Ed. Russell Ferguson. New York: Rizzoli, 1992. 179–203. Print.

Spodarek, Diane, and Randy Delbeke. "Ray Johnson Interview." *Detroit Monthly* Feb. 1978: 3–9. Print.

Stuckey, Charles. "Dear Ray Johnson." *Dear Ray Johnson*. Ed. Frances F.L. Beatty. New York: Feigen, 2010. 2–10. Print.

Vidal, Gore. *Sexually Speaking: Collected Sex Writings*. Jersey City, NJ: Cleis, 2001. Print.

Wainwright, Leon. "Frank Bowling and the Appetite for British Pop." *Third Text* 22.2 (2008): 195–208. Print.

Wainwright, Leon. "Varieties of Provincialism and Belatedness: Decolonisation and British Pop." *Art History* 35.2 (2012): 451. Print.

Warhol, Andy. *I'll be Your Mirror: The Selected Andy Warhol Interviews*. Ed. Kenneth Goldsmith. New York: Carroll, 2004. Print.

Warhol, Andy, and Pat Hackett. *POPism: The Warhol Sixties*. New York: Mariner, 2006. Print.

Warner, Michael. *Publics and Counterpublics*. New York: Zone, 2002. Print.

Weinberg, Jonathan. "Ray Johnson Fan Club." De Salvo and Gudis 95–120. Print.

Wilson, William S. "With Ray: The Art of Friendship." *Black Mountain College Dossiers* 4 (1997): 2–57 (58 n. 12). Print.

Zuba, Elizabeth. "Ray Johnson's Art World." *Ray Johnson's Art World*. Ed. Frances F.L. Beatty and Diana Bowers. New York: Feigen, 2014. 3–29. Print.

This interview was conducted over three days (30 September 2011, 15 October 2011, and 18 October 2011) and many hours with almost two dozen e-mails traded in the intervening days. Anyone who knew Bill Wilson knows that he was an unusual talker – encyclopedic, brilliant, circuitous, poetic, and marvelous; he would say "Senecan." Because of this highly idiosyncratic style, this interview is synthetic inasmuch as I have formed and shaped Bill's words into answers to my imagined questions. (I have done my best to retain his movements of thought and sentence structure.) He told me the stories and information recorded here several times over several days and often in e-mails. I believe my transcription is as accurate and faithful as possible under the circumstances.

Benjamin Kahan: Could you tell me about Ray Johnson's early sexual experiences?

William S. Wilson: Ray's first sexual experience was blowing a black boy in a rowboat in Detroit. There was not much reciprocity. His name was Pete, and Ray was sixteen. This would get complicated later when Ray had a cat named Pete. He would stroke the pussy and say, "I love you Pete." At Black Mountain College, I think that it is very clear that he had intercourse with Frances X. Profumo (probably in 1948). She was a Southern Catholic; they are rare breed. She loved Ray for the rest of her life. He was also excited about an event – not intercourse, but something that he had on the beach with Isabelle Fisher in the summer of 1953.

benjamin kahan

ON RAY JOHNSON'S SEXUALITY, LOVES, AND FRIENDSHIPS

an interview between william s. wilson and benjamin kahan

BK: Did Ray have other relationships with women?

WSW: He thought about getting married to Ruth Asawa. They were engaged after a sweet walk in the woods. I never thought of them in a male/female way. Ray was a 99 and 44/100ths percent active gay man, but did not want the category closed down over him. In Paul Valery's work Madame Teste says, "I'm free, but classified." Ray had read everything by Valery and was trying to elude this sense of classification. He never said, "I am a gay man." Ray was not lying, he was not hypocritical or insincere, he refused the system of classification that sees heterosexuality as the opposite of homosexuality. Ray never concealed his sexuality; there was no closet to hold him.

Returning to your theme, there is a principle that I can state roughly. Ray had in his life at least five special women with whom he had more than ordinary intensities. These are women who design for themselves rules of their own behavior. In her anger Malka Safro shits on Ray's threshold. Ray sends a sculpture to my mother [May Wilson] who sits on it. Marie Tavroges steals something from Claes Oldenburg's Store, Dorothy Podber shoots Warhol's paintings. Toby Spiselman and Ray are in Washington, DC. They see a work of art with a blinking light. As they are exiting, Toby pulls a string and turns off the light. These are all women who interfere with works of art. They are special to Ray. I'm not sure Frances X. Profumo fits into this, but she was earlier, when Ray was younger.

BK: Could you tell me a little about Ray's relationship with Richard Lippold?

WSW: Ray met Richard, who is a brilliant bisexual man, in the summer of 1948. Richard married Louise and had two daughters. He drove up to Black Mountain College in a hearse he used to transport sculpture and was planning to live in the hearse. Josef Albers offered them a place to stay and they moved out of the hearse. According to Richard, Ray would come howling, scratching his ass on the rug, trying to seduce Richard. I have a strong feeling that this story is an old man's story, but it's Richard's story and he is sticking to it. In any case, Ray and Richard fell in love in the summer of 1948.

When I met Ray, he was on his way to drowning. Ray and Richard worked a sexual ritual which saved Ray's life. The symbolism of the hearse that they had sex in is important, as you'll see. You know the story of the troll under the bridge who insisted on exacting a toll from the boy who crossed. When Ray would walk by Richard, he had to pay the toll and the toll was a very specific kind of kiss. Richard would squeeze the air out of Ray and then breathe air back into him often in a vehicle [the hearse] which carries those who don't breathe. These kisses occurred at least between 1948 and 1974. In 1974, Ray found out that Richard had a very delicious waiter named Gianni stashed away and that is when Ray writes the letter to George Ashley describing his "romantic problems."

It is Queequeg's coffin that saves Ishmael. In 1990, Ray would go to provincial art openings on Long Island. He met there a young lifeguard and artist named Christopher Coffin. Incidentally, Ray always called Salvador Dali's bodyguard at Studio 54 his lifeguard. Christopher gathers flotsam from the beach and calls it sculpture. When Christopher was sixteen, he came home from school and his mother said, "Your father died today." What is the relation between Ray's values as a sixty-year-old man and this lifeguard and artist at twenty-two? I think it is a vision of non-possession or non-attachment. When a woman asked Oscar Wilde how he experienced his time in prison, he replied, "Madam, I was buoyed up by a sense of my own guilt." A coffin saved Queequeg's life, a coffin saved Ray's life, and in 1948 a hearse saved Ray's life.

BK: This kind of erotic asphyxiation seems like a sort of s/m practice. Ray describes going to s/m clubs with Peter Schuyff and with Diane Arbus. What do you know about his trips there?

WSW: Ray was often pedagogical. With Peter Schuyff, Ray took him to the Anvil and I think he showed him fist fucking. This is going to seem like one of my tangents that doesn't go anywhere, but I haven't lost the thread. I had a bathtub painted with flowers. One day when I came home it was gone. I found it on the sidewalk on 9th Avenue filled with dirt and planted with flowers, which made me happy as it was refunctioned and reused. Then one night Ray comes over late and says he wants to take me somewhere. We go to the Anvil and there is a bathtub with a young man sitting in it, getting pissed on, there is a second young man in another bathtub getting pissed on, and then there is a third bathtub with flowers on it – my bathtub – with a young man getting pissed on. Ray would take you to Hell for a reference.

BK: Did Ray identify with this asphyxiational practice in any way?

WSW: There is a photograph that Ray took of himself next to a horseshoe crab with a juxtaposition that says unambiguously, "I'm the horseshoe crab." A horseshoe crab is a creature that beats like hell to get back in the water before its lungs dry out. Ray couldn't believe that Marianne Moore misspelled octopus – a creature that squeezes the breath out of him and takes him – Ray was on his way home when I met him.

BK: Did Ray have any other emotionally significant lovers other than Richard Lippold?

WSW: At the time, a blowjob wasn't as frequent as a handshake, but probably half as frequent. Ray had a lot of puppy experience. Karl Schenzer, the actor for the Living Theater, who went to the entirety of the John Cage performance *Vexations*, was at a party with Ray. Intriguingly, Karl, like Ray, was very close with the younger Richard Lippold. Karl leveled a steady gaze upon Ray, never taking his eyes off Ray. Were they lovers? Was I overreading? I don't know. Was he keeping his eyes on Ray because not his every movement but his every third movement was a visual poem? Perhaps, but I don't think so. There wasn't the least affection in his gaze. It wasn't an era for that.

BK: Is this affectionlessness connected to Ray's nickname as "the meanest man in Manhattan"?

WSW: I gave him that nickname. Man hat tan. Tan Man. This led to endless variation. Ten tan guys. He was very difficult. Ray had a marvelous way of doing something destructive that would be constructive. One night Henry Geldzahler wants Ray to sign *Oedipus* (it would later be called *Elvis*) because it was being sent to Australia. I said "as long as you're in a signing mood – would you sign this collage?" He was angry with Henry so he gouged his name into it, really gouged it. He did horrible things. Things that others would regard as cruel – he didn't care about the consequences. My daughter would say, "that is, as inhuman as Ray was."

disclosure statement

No potential conflict of interest was reported by the author.

jackson moore

THE SHAMELESS PERFORMATIVITY OF CAMP IN PATRICK WHITE'S *THE TWYBORN AFFAIR*

Camp might be said to be a queer object to the extent that it resists any attempt to define it in language. Camp is both extravagantly flamboyant and subtly mannered; it is both flaunting histrionics and a closeted code. In its flitting between different conceptual registers – sensibility, style, taste, aesthetics – camp performs a love of semiotic excess. In his comprehensive survey of the various attempts to define and conceptualize camp, Fabio Cleto argues that

> the state of the art, and the whole tradition of critical writings [on camp], can in fact be summarised in a series of oppositions, enacting the binary logic that is at once *challenged* and *invoked* by camp as a queer, transversal, "across" issue. (Cleto 23; original emphasis)

Cleto goes on to list some of the binaries through which camp has been conceptualized, including, but in no way limited to: "camp as sensibility vs. camp style and taste"; "camp as fully modern vs. camp as metahistorical"; "camp as a sign of homosexuality vs. camp as an aesthetical dimension"; "camp as private, seclusive vs. camp as community experience"; "camp as aristocratic vs. camp as democratic"; "camp as ironic mode vs. camp as parody" (ibid.). In light of the fact that eminently plausible cases can be (and have been) made for both sides of each binary listed above, Cleto concludes that

> camp won't be traceable on one of these polarities, the one that should be taken as the originary and real deployment of camp: it will be in the *movement* across, in the mobile and transversal relation of the two polarities. (Ibid.; original emphasis)

This essay reads Patrick White's *The Twyborn Affair* as a demonstration of the more performative and affective understanding of camp that is needed to overcome the conceptual impossibility of camp's existence in language alone. This essay reconceptualizes camp as a performative and affective social phenomenon by reading the protagonist of White's text as an exemplary figure who resists the disciplinary identity and legibility that history demands through a series of camp performances. E. Twyborn registers in this essay as a figure of shame on account of her/his refusal to cohere within a single gendered and sexual identity. For Eve Sedgwick, shame is an intriguingly queer affect in that it attunes the self to the vagaries of social, cultural and historical contingency, whilst reinforcing a discrete (albeit painful) individuation and separation from these historical forces. Sedgwick's affective conceptualization of shame is a useful way of approaching the protagonist of *Twyborn* in that it gives us a means of fleshing out E.'s refusal to submit to historically contingent categories of identity. Camp emerges at the conclusion of this essay as a mediation of a particular subject–object relation, and its emblem, its *thing*, is the bandaid.

For if shame appears to tyrannize the life of Eadith Trist, that subjugation is not total: shame's very performativity gives birth to a defiantly camp persona that re-routes shame as a defiant shamelessness. For Guy Davidson, the camp aesthetic of *Twyborn* functions in response to apprehensions surrounding the author's actual and literary "coming out":

> in coming out, White did not simply offer himself up in naked vulnerability to the public gaze [...] the camp aesthetic that he adopted as he came out, with its emphasis on masking, parody and play, enabled control as well as revelation. (17)

This essay argues that affect comprises an important dimension to the camp literary style that White adopts in *Twyborn*. White's camp sensibility emerges here as a means of coping with the shame, with the "naked vulnerability," that inevitably attends queer, performative or Butlerian conceptualizations of identity. If the performance of identity is always shadowed by the threat of misrecognition and shame, then camp advertises itself as a means of living in and living through performances of gender and sexuality. Shame is thus an important resource for both understanding the protagonist of White's text and understanding the camp politics of queer critique that (s)he embodies. Camp is the bandaid that facilitates the healing of the shameful wound afflicting performative identities.

The urgency of the argument this essay makes is derived from the paucity of queer objects that haunts queer theory's academic existence. This essay proposes that we think about camp in terms of the political quandary that faces queer theory, an impasse that Robyn Wiegman articulates in *Object Lessons* as "the vertigo of critique" (301). Wiegman argues that "*queer inquiry cannot have the sex it wants without losing what it wants most from having had it*" (343; original emphasis). The thrust of Wiegman's contention is that the more queer theory talks about sex, about the increasingly variegated inflections and articulations of sex, the more it produces ever more thoroughly and precisely the coercive disciplinary monolith identified (and decried) as sexuality by Foucault in the first volume of his *History of Sexuality*. This incitement to discourse that attends queer inquiry is of interest to Wiegman primarily on account of the warping effect it has on the goals, or the "affective investments," of queer theory. Politically speaking, queer inquiry has tended to express its critique of identity through the rhetoric of antinormativity. But for Wiegman, this rhetoric of antinormativity is problematic in that it is always haunted by its failure to live up to its promise of lasting emancipation. Wiegman asks us despairingly: "how can the field cultivate the antinormative without being committed to the normative?" (341). Or, posing the question slightly more provocatively: "Fist-fucking, BDSM, polyamory, sex with friends, erotic vomiting, stone femininity. What kind of critical attention can avoid the slide into analytic normativity that description and referentiality entail?" (340). The more we talk about sex, the more we layer it with description, reference and analysis, the more we begin to define it, to delimit it, to discipline it and ultimately to normalize it. This incitement to discourse is the crux of Wiegman's disquiet, where "sex, sexual difference, and sexuality comprise the fraught terrain in which political desires have come to live":

> This terrain is constituted not just by talk of sex or by the social or analytic force of sex, or even by the incommensurabilities of the domains in which the meaning of sex is lived, but by the kinds of contradictions and evasions that attention to sex provokes, including the sheer impossibility of getting

a grip on anything so dense and disconcerting, so ephemeral and material, so intrinsically related and decidedly abstract as an antinormative account of "sex itself." (342)

This "vertigo of critique" (301) animates Wiegman's argument: a sense that language, representation and referentiality betray the antinormative promise of queer theory's so-ardently-longed-for sexual revolution. Wiegman presents us with a symmetrical image of, on the one hand, a theoretical queer enterprise that is betrayed continuously by its marriage to language, and, on the other, a terrain of identity politics that is similarly betrayed by the exclusionary effects that necessarily entail any codification of political action or representation.

By coming to terms with the affective dimension of camp, and its relationship to shame specifically, we can begin to turn camp into a material and effective resource in the political struggle to live queer. Camp proffers itself as a means of coping with the shame that is the inevitable consequence of queer effacements of identity. But it can only do so if we begin to conceptualize camp affectively. Only then can camp become an enduringly queer object, something that is, in Wiegman's words, a "target of study that reflect[s] a seemingly material existence in the world" (20), or an object over which "social life, critical practice, and political commitment" can converge (21). Therefore, this essay concludes by proposing that we think about camp in terms of Lauren Berlant and Michael Warner's notion of queer world making. The affective reconceptualization of camp that this essay undertakes can be read as an attempt to come to grips with the conundrum identified by Wiegman. If Wiegman worries that "*queer inquiry cannot have the sex it wants*" (343), this essay suggests we look beyond mere sexual practices and expand the scope of our inquiry. As a resolutely non-sexual yet irrepressibly queer practice, camp advertises itself as a form of queer world making to the extent that it subsists not in the disciplinary language of identity but rather to the extent that, to quote Berlant and Warner,

it "indexes a virtual social order" (558). The affective account of camp sketched by this essay emerges ultimately as a modest example of "the concretisation of a queer counterpublic" (ibid.).

Affect theory insists on thinking about fluidity and on the distortions inherent in a purely linguistic conceptualization of the real. As such, it is arguably the best means of coming to terms with the material and political resources that camp has to offer. As Brian Massumi argues in *Parables for the Virtual*:

> If passage is primary in relation to position, processual indeterminacy is primary in relation to social determination. Social and cultural determinations on the model of positionality are also secondary and derived. Gender, race, and sexual orientation also emerge and back-form their reality. Passage precedes construction. But construction does effectively back-form its reality. Grids happen. So social and cultural determinations feed back into the process from which they arose. Indeterminacy and determination, change and freeze-framing, go together. (8)

If camp is best understood as a fluid movement between cultural signifiers, it makes sense to examine it as a process under a conceptual rubric of qualitative transformation. This essay examines camp as a field, placing to one side attempts to classify and codify it (as language, as meaning) while foregrounding its performative, ontogenetic dimensions. In this context, we can take our cue from Susan Sontag's famous asseveration that "to talk about camp is therefore to betray it" (53): it is arguably more useful to examine the ways in which camp is felt, sensed and expressed. Indeed, approaches to camp will be

> incomplete if they operate only on the semantic or semiotic level, however that level is defined (linguistically, logically, narratologically, ideologically, or all of these in combination, as a Symbolic). What they lose, precisely, is the expression *event* – in favour of structure [...] For structure is the place where nothing ever happens, that

explanatory heaven in which all eventual permutations are prefigured in a self-consistent set of invariant generative rules. (Massumi 26–27)

It may be a penetrating glimpse into the obvious, but performativity – the *event* – is the place where camp happens, and this is why it so consistently resists enclosure within any "explanatory heaven" that seeks to pin it down. And Sedgwick herself recognized this when she suggested, if only "parenthetically," that "shame/performativity may get us a lot further with the cluster of phenomena generally called 'camp' than the notion of parody will, and more too than will any opposition between 'depth' and 'surface'" (*Touching* 64). Above all, this essay is an attempt to more fully adumbrate Sedgwick's "parenthetical" notion of an affective account of camp so as to invoke a new queer object; something that will, in the words of Berlant and Warner, "support forms of affective, erotic and personal living that are […] available to memory and sustained through collective activity" (562).

the shamelessness of eadith trist

As the first Australian to win the Nobel Prize for literature (he won it in 1973), Patrick White's position in the canon of Australian literature is seemingly assured; yet his position in any putative canon of queer literature is less so. This essay seeks, *inter alia*, to redress this situation by showcasing the archive of queer objects and resources that White's texts contain. In this respect, *The Twyborn Affair* can be taken as a useful staging ground. Coming at the end of White's career as a writer, *Twyborn* represents something of a queer departure from the rest of his oeuvre. In his survey of the critical reception of White's oeuvre, Brian Kiernan observes that, for most of his career as a writer, White was read as "a traditional novelist with a religious or theosophical view of life" (291). However, since the turn of the twenty-first century, Kiernan notes that a shift has occurred in White scholarship, with critics increasingly characterizing White as "a sophisticated, ironical modern mistrustful of language" (ibid.). Kiernan places *Twyborn* at the centre of this shift: for critics engaged in the reappraisal of White as a playful, ironic, and postmodern writer, *Twyborn* represents "the winning card in your pack" (298).

Twyborn tells the story of E., a genderqueer performance of three different characters. The novel is divided into three parts, the first of which details E.'s life as the cross-dressing mistress of a senile Greek aristocrat in the south of France. In Part II of *Twyborn* the story moves to the Snowy Mountains of Australia, where E. lives as Eddie, the closeted jackaroo (cowboy) on a sheep and cattle station in the highlands of New South Wales. Part III sees the protagonist emerging as Eadith Trist, the madam of a brothel in 1930s London.

Though Davidson argues that *Twyborn* represents White's "coming out" as a novelist through the centrality that queer sexuality obtains in this text, the queer resonances and implications of this novel are still yet to be fully explored. Dean Kiley, for example, argues that despite the novel's overtly queer thematics, critics have struggled to come to grips with an out-and-proud White:

> [White's] 1979 novel *The Twyborn Affair* has to be the novel Judith Butler would write if she wanted to dramatise queer theory – it's an astonishing bravura play with volatile and mobile gender identities and sex and sexualities, the protagonist lives as a young wife, a closeted gay/bi man and a middleaged female bawd, it features a male rape scene and a male-to-female passing tranny in a lesbian scene – yet Dame Leonie Kramer, in her [Dame Edna] Everage phase, managed to conclude that it was REALLY all about "the problem and mystery of family relationships" and that White was just being "evasive." (Kiley)

Invoking a wonderful turn of phrase, Kiley goes on to note that

> other critics clearly had no idea what the genderfuck was going on and characterised White as an existential ventriloquist, a genital mannequin, a Jungian rubik's cube, a stylistic dollmaker, a metaphysical

puppeteer and a chi-chi second-rate stage magician of sexuality. (Kiley)

If critics of this text have for the most part been confused by *Twyborn*'s polysemous articulations of sexuality, this essay argues that it is this very fluidity, this thematics of performativity, that makes *Twyborn* such a wealth of queer objects.

In reading White's text as an archive of a camp sensibility rooted in affect, this essay builds upon the argument of Mark Williams, who reads *Twyborn* as that novel where "White no longer sees language and life as separate orders" (141). For Williams, fluidity and performativity are at the heart of *Twyborn*'s representation of selfhood; Williams takes what we might call a proto-affective approach in the close attention he pays to the "sensual" in this text (ibid.), and in the role that textiles, touch and clothing in particular assume in the text's construction of the self. Williams argues that clothing in *Twyborn* "is representative of the inescapable inauthenticity of human beings, our need to dress up our personalities and the lack of any essence behind the disguises we adopt" (142). To this performative dimension of self-representation Williams adds that *Twyborn* espouses a fluid conception of the subject: "the reality behind the fictive masks we adopt is always shifting and elusive" (143). Williams's reading of *Twyborn* thus gestures towards the more thoroughgoing and theoretically rigorous account of affect in this text that this essay aims to provide.

More recent analyses of *Twyborn* have sought to bring out the queer resonances of White's text by looking specifically at the "coming out" gesture effectuated by his late texts, and by emphasizing the porous ambivalence of this gesture's significance. This essay seeks to elaborate on this queering of White's oeuvre by arguing that the gesture of "coming out" that *Twyborn* performs is shamefully incomplete. Davidson argues that the public and literary confession of White's sexuality did not inaugurate an immediate flowering of critical attention to this aspect of White's work. On the contrary, Davidson argues that "White's uncloseting has generally been met in the scholarly context with assiduous reclosetting" (5). This is because "White's compulsion to tell the 'truth' by coming out was also related to his attempts to control his public image" (6); the truth of White's sexuality in fact served as a central component of a literary project whose aim is to unsettle and problematize the notion of truth itself:

> White's "display" of his sexuality [...] in his memoir [*Flaws*] is most productively read not as the revelation of a pre-existing stable identity – as the popular discourse of coming out would have it, whereby a hidden identity is salvifically brought to light – but a kind of performance, in keeping with White's longstanding devotion to theatricality. (Ibid.)

While it is true that White speaks openly and publicly about his sexuality for the first time in his autobiography, the self that emerges from this confession is far from clear. This is because, as Davidson so amply demonstrates, the expression of White's "true" feelings in fact enacts a form of "grammatical distance" between White the man and White the literary celebrity: the portrait that emerges from White's autobiography is one of "the dividedness within the self that theatricality necessarily involves" (ibid.). In projecting and performing his queer selfhood through language, White articulates a selfhood that is othered from itself. As Davidson suggests, "White harnessed his sexual identity to his claimed ability to engage empathetically with various kinds of otherness" (ibid.). And this unsettled conception of identity, this continuous dynamic of uncloseting and reclosetting, is central to any understanding of White's literary project. Moreover, it is this ambivalence which prompts Elizabeth McMahon to argue that the implications of *Twyborn*'s "coming out" gesture are not simply apprehended.

McMahon argues that a close analysis of White's prose reveals a dynamic interaction between secrecy and disclosure that belies any easy narrative of a clear and distinct gay identity unveiled by disclosure of sexual preferences:

Seemingly blunt and unornamented statements may be just as illegible or opaque as so called closeted statements, which, we imagine, operate by more veiled means such as innuendo, euphemism, and metonymy. And if *The Twyborn Affair* is the most explicit in regard to a lived practice of sexuality, it is simultaneously the most veiled and the most figurative on this subject. The line between the inside and outside of the closet is not, in White's fiction, or elsewhere, clear, easily defined, or stable. (87)

As we shall see below, this essay argues, then, that White's camp style serves to underline the shamefully incomplete nature of the "coming out" gesture that *Twyborn* performs by underlining that it is a mobile and reiterative performance of queer subjectivity, rather than a more socially acceptable and stable gay identity, that *Twyborn*'s coming out inaugurates.

The opening passages of Part III of *Twyborn*, where the novel's protagonist emerges in her final guise as Eadith Trist, are executed such that they illustrate precisely how shame informs the novel's thematics of identity as performance. Indeed, shame and the performance of heterosexual femininity are tightly bound in the final part of this text. And it is this nexus of shame and performativity that Sedgwick identifies as its most conceptually generous quality:

> Shame interests me politically, then, because it generates and legitimates the place of identity – the question of identity – at the origin of the impulse to the performative, but does so without giving that identity space the standing of an essence. It constitutes it as to-be-constituted, which is also to say, as already there for the (necessary, productive) misconstrual and misrecognition. Shame – living, as it does, on and in the muscles and capillaries of the face – seems to be uniquely contagious from one person to another. And the contagiousness of shame is only facilitated by its anamorphic, protean susceptibility to new expressive grammars. (*Touching* 64)

The somewhat incongruous opening of Part III of *Twyborn* signposts both the contagiousness of shame and the question of identity at the origin of the performative. Part III begins with a sketch of Kitty and Maud: two characters who thereafter make no further appearance in the text. That these two characters should be afforded such prominence is arguably because they illustrate a relational, contagious and above all affective dynamic of identification. These two maiden aunts draw whatever identity they have from their proximity to Eadith Trist's brothel across the road:

> Even Maud was given to smearing a trace of lipstick over the cracks in pale, rather tremulous lips, while Kitty went the whole hog, and blossomed like a tuberous begonia. If she no longer enjoyed sleep, and teeth made eating a difficulty, she could toy with the thought of shocking. But whom? Most of the shockable were dead. Unless, under their lipstick, Kitty and Maud themselves, who were intermittently shocked by what Kitty visualised, and the timorous Maud only dared suspect was going on at Eighty-Four. (305–06)

Both Kitty and Maud are constituted, brought to life even, by the contagious shame of Eadith Trist: the intermittent shocks of shame inject an affective intensity and even play "the most considerable part in their otherwise withering, insomniac lives" (307).

Importantly, however, the shame of Kitty and Maud passes through their beings and gets re-expressed in a very specific camp performativity. Shame's contagion manifests itself in the application of "lipstick over the cracks in pale, rather tremulous lips" and in Kitty going "the whole hog, and blossom[ing] like a tuberous begonia." It is the ministrations of Eadith and her whores across the road that effect in Kitty the "thought of shocking" the "shockable." The shame of these maiden aunts takes on a specular relation to the activities of Eadith's brothel in that shame passes back and forth between these two social poles, is internalized, re-routed and released again as a camp performance of femininity: Kitty and Maud are "roused by disgust for overt immorality" (306) at first, but "after an oblique fashion, the sisters [begin] shedding their opposition to the establishment across the street," and even derive "a voluptuous pleasure in associating themselves with imagined rituals of a sexual nature" (ibid.). And it is this dynamic of shame and camp performativity that captures, in a nutshell, the radically queer politics of identity that White's text expresses.

Meanwhile, the same process is mirrored across the street, with Eadith taking to "waving a long arm, and smiling out of a chalky face" in response to the silent remonstrance of the Bellasis girls, "by more blatant light," "looking out from their separate bedrooms" (307). Eadith herself embodies the anamorphic, protean susceptibility to new expressive grammars of shame in the camp, theatrical manner with which she is introduced in the text by Evadne, Kitty and Maud's maid:

> Mrs *Eadith* Trist.
> It was Evadne who came up with what one could hardly refer to as the woman's "Christian" name, together with the unsolicited detail that you spelt it with an "a." (308)

This very contrived, very camp entrance – and the bitchy rejoinder with which that "Christian" name is freighted – is executed in pursuit of obscuring the more "shameful" aspects of her character and behaviour. Drag here is a means of concealing the homosexual Eddie underneath, but it is also true that the camp performance of identity re-animates this shame, the experience of which is perhaps reserved for those who see – who enjoy! – the performance of Eadith Trist in light of all its exuberant and communicable shamelessness.

The elaborate attention paid to manners in Part III of *Twyborn* is a camp disposition deployed as a means of coping with the flashes of shame that are, for Eadith Trist, the inevitable companions of knowledge of the self. Anatomically male, though living outwardly as a woman in interwar London, Eadith embodies the potential for misrecognition that is the inevitable accompaniment of (gender) identity. Nowhere is this exhibited more prominently than in the passages of *Twyborn* that depict Eadith's friendship with Ursula, that paragon of aristocratic femininity. Here, the imperative to maintain a convincing performance of femininity gives rise to a camp fixation on ornament and gesture. However, this preoccupation with the surfaces of society does not thereby delineate an inner depth or essence, in opposition to a putative exterior, but rather it advertises the deep imbrication of affective (inner) and social (outer) realities, or the collapse of this binary altogether towards which shame so often gestures.

It is primarily through this process of aestheticization that camp operates as a means of coping with the shame that motors the performance of gender in *Twyborn*. During her visit to Ursula's mansion, before "the 'things' were arranged" (358) for tea and crumpets, the hostess leads her new friend through a tour of her stately home, which turns out to be a veritable gallery of portraits of Ursula herself. At this point there is a slippage in perspective between that of a more or less objective narrative voice and that of Eadith herself. Where once the text fetishized Eadith as something of a camp bitch-goddess – "mauve was her colour when in full panoply"; "she dressed with extravagant thought"; "the more baroque aspects of her self indulgence"; "the encrustations of amethysts and diamonds, the swanning plumes, her make-up poetic as opposed to fashionable or naturalistic"; "for the more normal perspectives of life she could not lay it on too thick" (310) – it is now the figure of Ursula that comes under the gaudy spotlight. Halting in front of one of the more prominent of Ursula's portraits, the image is thus described from Eadith's perspective:

> [S]he noticed a larger, more formal portrait of the mistress of the house in white satin and long, white gloves, the highlights and the blue shadows in satin, kid, and diamonds suggesting a noble icicle. Beneath the golden urn of unswept hair the face might have looked warmer if the painter had been interested as well as paid, or perhaps he had not detected warmth, or perhaps his subject was unfeeling. The cheeks of a young Ursula looked like crisp apples which had not been bitten into. (356)

In the noble icicles of jewellery, the golden urn of unswept hair we see an echo of Art Nouveau's tendency, noted by Sontag, to "convert one thing into something else: the lighting fixtures in the form of flowering plants, the living room which is really a grotto" (56). And in those apple cheeks we see the invocation of an Aubrey Beardsley etching: a blend of the grotesque, the decadent and the (frankly) erotic. Eadith's barbed appraisal of Ursula's image perhaps betrays a note of shame on the part of the former, owing to her own sense of feminine inadequacy, which is expressed in an aestheticization – a transformation – of an admittedly mediocre painting into an image full of style, wit and incident. And if this gallery of portrait upon portrait upon portrait of a lady serves to underline the shame of the Bawd, the arena of the salon into which the party of two proceeds for tea heightens further still the stakes upon which Eadith's performance of femininity rests.

Eadith's use of camp in response to her gender-shame is not necessarily bound to her own personal (or genital) circumstances, but rather stems from the performative nature of gender generally. While it is true that, from its inception, camp has functioned at the nexus of shame and gender, this has really only ever been clearly articulated from within a distinctly male-homosexual context. Philip Core, in *Camp: The Lie that Tells the Truth*, compiles a list of what he calls "Camp Rules," in another quixotic, albeit perhaps typical, attempt to get at the essence of camp. The following is a representative selection from this list:

> CAMP depends on where you pitch it.
> CAMP is not necessarily homosexual. Anyone or anything can be camp. But it takes one to know one.
> CAMP is a lifeboat for men at sea.
> CAMP is an ephemeral fundamental.
> CAMP is cross-dressing in a Freudian slip.
> CAMP is behaving illegally with impunity; Hemingway defined it perfectly as "grace under pressure."
> CAMP is embarrassment without cowardice.
> CAMP is gender without genitals. (80–81)

If camp is gender without genitals, then well might we ask: what does camp mean to women? Or to put it another way: what might drive a (straight) woman to affect a camp disposition? Such questions seem pertinent in light of the very prominent prospect that femininity obtains within Core's camping-ground. In *Twyborn*, as we saw earlier with Kitty and Maud, camp performance, shame and gender identity are intimately, even contagiously, linked. Thus, it becomes clear during tea that the spectre of gender-shaming looms large over both parties on account of shame's infectiousness. We see a circuit of feeling running between these two women in the following passage:

> She sniggered inexplicably. It made Ursula glance at this grotesque creature with cream and raspberry smeared over magenta lipstick. Because of all she had been taught, Ursula was quick to ask, "That lipstick, Eadith – tell me the shade, and where you get it."
> Only then Eadith came out with, "I hate it! It makes me look old, ugly and common." She visualised her tongue sticking out from between her lips like that of some frilly lizard baited by a terrier bitch.
> "Oh, but *darling*!"
> "No, it's true."
> Ursula sat tossing her ankle in Alice-in-Wonderland style. She was reared an expert at ignoring. Eadith knew by now that Ursula would never refer to Dulcie's amateurish abortion. (359)

In this exchange we can see Eadith's shame literally flare up like a frill-necked lizard, before it gets transferred to Ursula and re-articulated as the camp performance of a woman who administers the word "*darling*" in italics. We also see camp doubling back onto Eadith as she mentally anoints her interlocutor as a "terrier bitch." Crucially, this affective dynamic is generated by a tube of lipstick, by a moment of misrecognition of the parameters – or the correct "shade" – of feminine performance. Therefore, we might think of the shame generated by gender's performativity as an explanation for a straight woman's foray into camp. Camp, shame and gender assume a looping, circuitous figuration. It is on account of Ursula's camp disposition, her "Alice-in-

Wonderland style," that Eadith comes to the conclusion that the former would never refer to the botched abortion she witnessed on her previous visit to the latter's brothel, a conclusion that may seem arbitrary if we were not able to grasp the manner in which camp encloses, or covers up like make-up, an abortion which stands, however unfairly, as a prominent cultural signifier of a woman's ostensible shame. Moreover, this tea party, with its lashings of "high-treble" laughter, "charitable non-kisses" (356) and "mock-apologetic coughs" (357), turns into a parade of effete femininity, wherein any pretence to a feminine essence is worn out, through gesture and stylization, leaving a hollow, yet – as Eadith's own genital situation attests – infinitely reiterative and endlessly fabulous performance.

But if, as Kiley suggests, *Twyborn* is a novel of gender performativity par excellence – "the novel Judith Butler would write if she wanted to dramatise queer theory" (Kiley) – it must be stressed, again, that the cross-dressing protagonist of this text is not the sine qua non of said performativity. Ursula's use of camp also advertises the fact that affect, specifically shame, is an inevitable component of Butler's fundamental conceptualization in *Gender Trouble* of gender as a performance and a routine. Because gender is a performance that is continuous, is something that must be maintained as a performative event, is, in Butler's phrasing, an "apparatus of production" (*Gender Trouble* 10), it becomes susceptible to precisely the ruptures in the circuit of mirroring expressions, gestures and assumptions that Sedgwick incorporates into her affective conceptualization of shame.

The temporality and repetitiousness of Butler's conceptualization of gender is in contrast to what she terms the "stasis" of "heterosexist structuralism" (*Bodies* 90). If gender is a continuous performance it is attended by the same shame that haunts an actor who has forgotten her lines: if the circuit of expectations between the performer and her audience is broken, shame is the result. And it is on this basis – through the spectre of shame that hunts the performance of gender – that we can begin to incorporate femininity into our understanding of camp. Butler herself gives us our cues here: "*in imitating gender, drag implicitly reveals the imitative structure of gender itself – as well as its contingency*" (*Trouble* 187; original emphasis). The camp sensibility's penchant for repartee is analogous to this "imitative structure of gender" while at the same time underscoring the necessity of a turn to affect in any conceptualization of gender as performative. Indeed, Butler's definition of the performative itself is precisely analogous to camp in its relation to shame:

> Performativity describes [a] relation of being implicated in that which one opposes, [a] turning of power against itself to produce alternative modalities of power, to establish a kind of political contestation that is not a "pure" opposition, a "transcendence" of contemporary relations of power, but a difficult labor of forging a future from resources inevitably impure. (*Bodies* 184)

In their utilization of camp as a means of coping with the shame of gender, Eadith and Ursula are not unlike the jonquils in the windy garden outside, "blowing but recovering themselves, like frail but erect Englishwomen" (355) – a foppishly floral image which is telling in its expansive reference to a womanhood that must be performed over and over before a tough audience.

The camp sensibility with which the shame of gender performativity is re-articulated in *Twyborn* is a subtle, mannered and aestheticizing affectation; this is in contrast to the more intense shame that is attached to performances of sexuality, which elicits another mode of camp that is altogether more histrionic and flamboyant. Of course, it comes as no surprise that gender and sexuality should be bound to shame in similar configurations, as Butler attests:

> Precisely because homophobia often operates through the attribution of a damaged, failed, or otherwise abject gender to homosexuals, that is, calling gay men "feminine" or calling lesbians "masculine," and because the homophobic terror over performing

homosexual acts, where it exists, is often also a terror over losing proper gender ("no longer being a real or proper man" or "no longer being a real and proper woman"), it seems crucial to retain a theoretical apparatus that will account for how sexuality is regulated through the policing and the shaming of gender. (*Bodies* 182)

Butler argues that shame operates to curtail aberrant sexuality *through* gender; but the argument put forth by this essay is slightly different. It might be better to suggest that the shame of sexuality operates *parallel to* that of gender, and that the foundations of this shame are to be found in the typifying gesture of this affect: the sense of misrecognition. It is not simply through the gender of object-choice that shame colours sexuality, but rather sexuality, as Sedgwick notes, carrying as it does "far greater potential for rearrangement, ambiguity, and representational doubleness" than gender (*Epistemology* 34), also carries far greater potential for, and perhaps even deeper registers of, shame. Indeed, as Sedgwick argues, the fact that "no one person can take control over all the multiple, often contradictory codes by which information about sexual identity and activity can seem to be conveyed" (79) opens up an incredibly volatile social space in which the misrecognitions that presage shame are given a wide latitude indeed.

We see this very phenomenon in *Twyborn* when one of Eadith's whores calls in sick – "Bridie was the worse for an orgy of Guinness and oysters" (339) – and another of Eadith's aristocratic friends, Diana Siderous, volunteers to cover Bridie's shift. But Diana fails to recognize exactly what it is she is getting herself into. We are told, with delicious relish, that "though Diana's repertoire was extensive and included the game of whips and chains, she hadn't bargained for what she got: she had never been on the receiving end" (ibid.). Emerging from Bridie's filthy room afterwards, exposed in her folly, "disgust rattl[ing] at the back of her throat as she restored her lips at Eadith's rococo glass" (ibid.), Diana – in a manoeuvre which should by now be familiar to us – marshals all her powers of theatrics for an exercise in deflection and coping with shame:

> Not until Madame Siderous had got herself back into the paste bracelets, her cabuchons and pearls again nestling at her ears and throat, and doctored her nerves with a powerful slug of Armagnac, could she consider translating this gross physical outrage into an anecdote to amaze a dinner party of intimate friends.
> She tried a little of it on the bawd. "My poor hands, martyrised by oyster shells! My knees, crucified on the lust – of some little – civil *servant* – or mingy *professor! Mon Dieu*, my sweet, what these girls consent to! Does it excite their bodies? Does it stimulate their minds? Do you think they can enjoy an *orgasm?*" (340)

In this passage we have a different aesthetic range of camp to that which we have associated with gender. Here we see camp in its more over-the-top manifestation: here we have the outrageous sacrilege of the martyr to bad taste; the jewellery no longer a chic diamond-icicle but more redolent of kitsch and something altogether warmer, more flamboyant, nestling at the neck; there is something even a little coarse and guttural in that "powerful slug of Armagnac" and the exclamation marks which repeatedly arouse this scene. And the doubts expressed by Diana at the end of her monologue only serve to underline the degree of "ambiguity" and "representational doubleness," and hence the scope for misunderstanding and shame, to which sexual expression is susceptible. Sontag distinguishes between the two competing camp aesthetics according to class and history, but rather than posit a conceptual rupture between the two, an understanding of camp as a spectrum of affective intensity could more easily accommodate both:

> The old-style dandy hated vulgarity. The new-style dandy, the lover of Camp, appreciates vulgarity. Where the dandy would be continually offended or bored, the connoisseur of Camp is continually amused, delighted. The dandy held a perfumed handkerchief to his nostrils and was liable to swoon; the connoisseur of Camp sniffs the

stink and prides himself on his strong nerves. (63)

It is most apt that Diana's ordeal should conclude with Eadith offering her a small souvenir, a "memento of what I underwent one afternoon as a professional whore" (340). This ring "on which an ancient black scarab was rolling in perpetuity a ball of agate dung" (ibid.) stands as an eloquent metaphorical articulation of the more flagrant reiterations of sexuality's shame.

It is worth emphasizing that Diana's shame is not necessarily rooted in any moral condemnation, self-inflicted or externally imposed, but is rather associated in this instance with her misapprehension of the nature or quality of the sex to which she had committed herself. This is an important affective facet of sexuality that is often occluded by an over-eager (and distorting) fixation on the deconstruction of homo/heterosexual definition. In *Epistemology*, Sedgwick distils this shameful aspect of the sexual in the following entry of her list of possible differences that frustrate a single, monolithic understanding of sexuality as the difference between gay and straight: "For some people, the possibility of bad sex is aversive enough that their lives are strongly marked by its avoidance; for others, it isn't" (*Epistemology* 25). Conceptually speaking, what is most interesting about this dimension of the sexual is the potential generosity that inheres in the word "bad": it covers both an understanding of "bad" as in awkward or uncomfortable and therefore liable to provoke shame; at the same time it can be taken to mean "bad" as in *outré* or seedy or the things in respect of which you would prefer your mother remained blissfully ignorant.

Twyborn thematizes this axis of sexuality in its representation of "bad" sexuality as a vector of shame. When a man appears in the lobby at Ninety-Four Beckwith Street, Ada, Eadith's assistant, informs her mistress of his presence, warning that he "could be one of the big-time cops" (332). In the event it transpires that what Hugh is actually after is sex with Eadith herself; she declines, but not before being told "we [the police] all know you're running a house of a pretty corrupt kind" (334). Eadith fires back with the following defiant peroration:

> "Do you think a brothel will corrupt those who are already corrupted – or who'll corrupt themselves somewhere else – in their own homes – in a dark street – if overtaken by lust, in a parked car, or corner of a public park? All of us – even those you consider corrupt – I'd like to think of as human beings." (334)

Twyborn consistently advertises the universality of bad sex through its consistent, even at times oppressive, focus on shame. The possibility of bad sex, and hence the shame that attaches itself to sexuality, is as much a feature of heterosexuality as it is a feature of queer sexuality. When Gravenor walks in on Eadith and the policeman, he recognizes the latter and offers a friendly greeting. Hugh's reaction is thus described: "a visible melting had started in her inquisitor" (335). Having been sprung soliciting "bad" sex in a brothel, a straight man is here filled with shame. And further, burdened by the straight man's allergy to camp, Hugh is bereft of any resources for coping with shame; he slinks away, laughing "somewhat frenetically" and with "the least possible exchange of routine masculine geniality" (ibid.). Arguably, without the jewel-encrusted armour of camp theatrics, the straight man is even more vulnerable to the shame of bad sex, possessing none of the *élan* displayed by *Twyborn*'s cast of female characters. And when even straight men are afflicted with the burning shame of bad sex, the suffrage of sexuality is expanded into something all too human.

camp, shame and queer world making

This essay has argued that an affective understanding of camp renders an enduringly queer object, a material resource to draw upon in attempting to live through the reiterative potentials of a performative conception of identity. Camp takes the shame that attends the performative re-articulations of identity and flaunts them, throwing these shameful performances back in the face of its audience and dragging everyone – gay, straight, queer, whatever – into a community defined by its shameful inability to ever definitively arrive at identity. This self-effacing facet of camp, motored by the contagious self-extensions of shame's affective dynamics, is a hallmark of the queer politics that *Twyborn* posits. White's novel illustrates precisely how the affective currents of shame inform the performance of gender and sexuality, and how camp acts as a salve, as a daring and continuously mobile re-articulation of shamelessness. An affective conceptualization of camp is therefore an embodied and extra-linguistic utility in queer theory's attempt to find objects sufficiently antinormative and queer enough for its politics of critique.

The task that falls upon us now is to situate this affective reconceptualization of camp into a broader politics of queer struggle. That such an endeavour has barely begun should come as no surprise: the political utility of a persistently under-theorized notion of camp has often been denigrated and dismissed by queer theorists suspicious of something so shameful and seemingly frivolous. Camp has come under attack from no less a figure of queer stature than Leo Bersani, who argues that camp is "largely a parody of women" that is "a way of giving vent to the hostility toward women that probably afflicts every male" (14). Bersani is deeply suspicious of a camp sensibility that he finds laced with passive-aggressions routed both internally and externally:

> The gay male bitch desublimates and desexualizes a type of femininity glamorized by movie stars, whom he thus lovingly assassinates with his style, even though the campy parodist may himself be quite stimulated by the hateful impulses inevitably included in his performance. (Ibid.)

And Bersani goes even further in dismissing camp from the battlefield of queer struggle, ruling the camp sensibility almost inadmissible on the grounds that it is not sexy enough: "parody is an erotic turn-off and all gay men know this. Much campy talk is parodistic, and while that may be fun at a dinner party, if you're out to make someone you turn off the camp" (ibid.).

However, it is arguably camp's very unsexiness, its proximity to shame, and its very ephemerality that endows this sensibility with its radically disruptive potential as a queer object. Berlant and Warner's landmark essay "Sex in Public" is notable for the broad scope it envisions for queer political inquiry. Berlant and Warner argue that "heterosexuality involves so many practices that are not sex that a world in which this hegemonic cluster would not be dominant is, at this point, unimaginable. We are trying to bring that world into being" (557). Camp is not sex, yet we might characterize it as a queer object precisely to the extent that it undermines the "hegemonic cluster" of heterosexual identity through its insistence that any identity – sexual, gendered – is mere performance in dynamic interaction with the flowing currents of affect. Not only does this reconceptualization of camp sidestep the conundrum outlined earlier by Wiegman, proffering as it does a means of thinking about queer objects outside the purview of normative sex-practices and linguistic disciplinarity, but camp shamelessness also articulates, indeed performs, an ambitious labour of "queer world making," by inhabiting what Berlant and Warner term those "incommensurable registers, by definition *unrealisable* as community life or identity" (558; original emphasis).

For Berlant and Warner, the enterprise of world making is much broader than community or identity: it "necessarily includes more people than can be identified, more spaces than can be mapped [...] modes of feeling that can be learned rather than experienced as a birthright" (ibid.). Central to Berlant and Warner's conceptualization of queer world making is the notion of counterintimacies, and it is as a form of counterintimacy that an affective understanding of camp makes most sense as a queer object. Counterintimacies involve "the development of kinds of intimacy that bear no necessary relation to domestic space, to kinds of kinship, to the couple form, to property, or to the nation" (ibid.); they are instead "a context for witnessing intense and personal affect while elaborating a public world of belonging and transformation" (ibid.). As has been demonstrated throughout this essay, camp is a form of self-expression with little to no investment in the notion of identity; it is invested instead in a series of endlessly reiterable performances and transformations. In this sense it is a gesture of counterintimacy, advertising as it does the impossibility of normal or stable identities. If, according to Berlant and Warner, "affective life slops over onto work and political life" (560), an affective understanding of camp situates this performativity at the site of a struggle between queer attempts at world making and the forces of history so determined to abject them. If camp is a coping mechanism for dealing with shame, it exists as a resistance to disciplinary identity; it is a form of endearment that posits the shifting, transformational performance of multiple and conflicting identities as a queer object of value.

Berlant and Warner readily admit that social phenomena such as camp might be "hard to recognise as world making because they are so fragile and ephemeral" (561), and it is ultimately this fragility that *Twyborn* advertises in its final camp performance. The tragic curtain call for *Twyborn*'s protagonist comes in the final pages of this text in the form of bombs bursting in air. As E. Twyborn lies mangled and dying on a street in London during the Blitz, the final incarnation of camp's affective resistance to the forces of history is made manifest. But what is most striking about this passage are the counterintimacies it generates. When the bomb blast "heave[s]" E. and an anonymous soldier "up almost above the parapet" (398), both characters are transformed by a certain camp poignancy, with the process of dying rendered as a "melting into the worn stone, the smile congealing, the tin hat no more than a cabaret prop" (ibid.). The final passage of E. Twyborn's life is, characteristically, a very camp affair:

> A detached hand was lying in a stream of blood nor'-nor'-west of Eddie Twyborn's left cheek. It was neither of the soldier's hands he began to realise, for these were arranged on the pavement, a dog's obedient paws had it not been for blunt fingers with nails in mourning, still attached to bristling wrists.
> It was his own hand he saw as he ebbed, incredibly, away from it.
> "Fetch me a bandaid, Ada," he croaked over his shoulder, while flowing onward, on to wherever the crimson current might carry him. (Ibid.)

We could say that the death of E. Twyborn is here represented, in the words of Berlant and Warner, as the visceral dramatization of the "material and ideological conditions that divide intimacy from history, politics and publics" (562). Camp here attains the figuration of a counterintimate bandaid in the face of the crushing, of the shameful demand that history makes of us to conform to the discipline of identity. And if this very queer object, this camp bandaid, can only be imagined in the final pages of *Twyborn* as an encounter with mortality, White's text stands as a reminder of the enormous labour of queer world making that stands before us.

But perhaps more fundamentally, what the final passage of E. Twyborn's life advertises is a certain thingness that pertains to camp. The semantic ambiguity of camp that this essay has detailed, in addition to the fluid affective dynamics in which camp is implicated, might also be thought of as symptomatic of a deeper ambiguity, or that which Bill Brown calls "a more audacious ambiguity" (4). For Brown, a thing "denotes a massive generality as well as particularities [...] the word designates the concrete yet ambiguous within the everyday [...] an amorphous characteristic or a frankly irresolvable enigma" (ibid.). Following Brown's conceptualization, it is more than easy, as we have seen throughout this essay, to point to the thingness of camp. To say nothing of camp's love of actual things in the Brownian sense, which is to say objects that are "badly encountered" (ibid.), things that are just a little bit *off* (Last Supper T.V. trays, inflatable furniture), when we think about the affective dynamics of camp and shame, what more appropriately ambiguous thing might there be to describe the particular subject–object relations that camp mediates than E. Twyborn's bandaid? A bandaid is undeniably a thing, in the sense that almost anything can be a bandaid: a bottle of wine; a drag queen's make-up; a strip of sterilized plastic. If this essay has argued that camp is a material resource to live and love the labour of building a queer new world, it might also be thought of as a bandaid that covers the wound of the performing subject's own belatedness. The wound of shame that afflicts the ceaseless reiterations of the subject's many and varied identities is what camp is here to help us with. And that such help might be needed is clearly stated in *Twyborn*'s epigraph, coming from Diane Arbus: "sometimes you'll see someone with nothing on but a bandaid."

disclosure statement

No potential conflict of interest was reported by the author.

bibliography

Berlant, Lauren, and Michael Warner. "Sex in Public." *Critical Inquiry* 24.2 (1998): 547–66. Print.

Bersani, Leo. "Is the Rectum a Grave?" *Is the Rectum a Grave? and Other Essays*. Chicago: U of Chicago P, 2010. 3–30. Print.

Brown, Bill. "Thing Theory." *Critical Inquiry* 28.1 (2001): 1–22. Print.

Butler, Judith. *Bodies that Matter: On the Discursive Limits of "Sex."* London: Routledge, 1993. Print.

Butler, Judith. *Gender Trouble: Feminism and the Subversion of Identity*. New York and London: Routledge, 1990. Print.

Cleto, Fabio, ed. *Camp: Queer Aesthetics and the Performing Subject (A Reader)*. Ann Arbor: U of Michigan P, 1999. Print.

Cleto, Fabio. "Introduction: Queering the Camp." Cleto, *Camp* 1–43. Print.

Core, Philip. "From *Camp: The Lie that Tells the Truth*." Cleto, *Camp* 80–86. Print.

Davidson, Guy. "Displaying the Monster: Patrick White, Sexuality, Celebrity." *Australian Literary Studies* 25.1 (2010): 1–18. Print.

Kiernan, Brian. "Patrick White: Twyborn Moments of Grace." *Patrick White Centenary: The Legacy of a Prodigal Son*. Ed. Cynthia vanden Driesen and Bill Ashcroft. Newcastle upon Tyne: Cambridge Scholars, 2014. 291–99. Print.

Kiley, Dean. "Un-Queer Anti-Theory." *Australian Humanities Review* 9 (1998). Web. 16 Feb. 2017. <http://www.australianhumanitiesreview.org/archive/Issue-February-1998/kiley.html>.

Massumi, Brian. *Parables for the Virtual: Movement, Affect, Sensation*. Durham, NC: Duke UP, 2002. Print.

McMahon, Elizabeth. "The Lateness and Queerness of *The Twyborn Affair*: White's Farewell to the Novel." *Remembering Patrick White: Contemporary Critical Essays*. Ed. Elizabeth McMahon and Brigitta Olubas. Amsterdam: Rodopi, 2010. 77–91. Print.

Sedgwick, Eve Kosofsky. *Epistemology of the Closet*. Berkeley: U of California P, 1990. Print.

Sedgwick, Eve Kosofsky. *Touching Feeling: Affect, Pedagogy, Performativity*. Durham, NC: Duke UP, 2003. Print.

Sontag, Susan. "Notes on 'Camp.'" Cleto, *Camp* 53–65. Print.

White, Patrick. *The Twyborn Affair*. North Sydney: Random, 2011. Print.

Wiegman, Robyn. *Object Lessons*. Durham, NC: Duke UP, 2012. Print.

Williams, Mark. *Patrick White*. Basingstoke: Macmillan, 1993. Print.

Life has no meaning unless there [is] a crime in it.[1]

It was strange to feel so alone, and yet so much a part of things.[2]

The American suspense writer Patricia Highsmith is a difficult author to claim for queer studies. As Michael Trask has argued, her macabre enjoyment of various forms of social prejudice, along with her fondness for stereotype, makes her work hard to place in an archive, or canon, of queer literary texts (584–85). The most noticeable attempt to claim Tom Ripley, her best-known character, as a queer figure – Anthony Minghella's 1999 film *The Talented Mr Ripley* – exemplifies the problem. In this movie the explanation for Tom's sociopathic propensity for murder, a propensity that enables him to acquire money, social status and, eventually, a mostly satisfying bourgeois life in provincial France, is found in the very American, very mid-twentieth-century, melodramatics of ego psychology: Tom is bad because society is bad for not accepting him for the queer little boy he really is. The difficulty, in other words, of trying to claim Highsmith as a queer writer lies in the impossibility of reading her novels as political in the conventional or ideological sense of being interested in locating the distinction between what is and what could or should be, or in advocating a repudiation of a powerful majority on behalf of a marginalized minority. Nor can they be read as offering – as with, say, Proust – a subject-centered queer aesthetic of being. Highsmith's novels do not really do stories or subjects. Instead they offer a fantasy in which her central characters are provided scenes of

victoria hesford

TOM RIPLEY, QUEER EXCEPTIONALISM, AND THE ANXIETY OF BEING CLOSE TO NORMAL

proximity – to a social norm, a way of life – that in their repetition and accompanying sense of impending threat reveal both the attraction and also the precariousness of that world or way of life. To be close to normal in a Highsmith novel – and Tom Ripley more than any other of her characters figures this closeness – is to simultaneously reveal the pleasures and dangers of not being normal, of not being if that means having a psyche, a history, a sexual orientation, a conscience.[3]

In this essay I engage with the work of Patricia Highsmith in order to open up the question of queerness as a historically locatable theory and practice of antinormativity in the post-identitarian, post-new-social-movement United

States. More particularly, I argue that Patricia Highsmith's Ripley novels offer a discomfitingly intimate counter-fantasy to the politically radical ambitions of both gay liberation and queer studies, one that reminds us of the constitutive power of commodification in the making of social fantasies of gendered and sexual subversion in the United States in the second half of the twentieth century. In offering her readers scenes that become situations in their reliance on repetition in order to create and then alleviate tension, Highsmith's Ripley novels enact a relation of attachment (to excitement, distraction, danger, the illicit, etc.) indicative of the momentary and addictive pleasures of consumer capitalism. It is this structuring relation of attachment to something that goes wrong or awry in Highsmith's work that, in its formal regularity, suggests an underlying meaninglessness in her work that is better captured by the term "perversion" than by the term "antinormativity." Through this formal signature, I argue, Highsmith's work offers us access to a different affective history of queerness in the United States, one that pre-dates the new social movements of the late 1960s and can be located in the "dramaturgic approach" to social identity and interaction in the postwar era (Trask 588), as well as in the related and newly powerful assertion of consumerist nationalism that characterized domestic Cold War politics: a world in which the ease and glamour of modern appliances and personal consumer products were posited against the perceived drudgery of soviet scarcity and ideological fanaticism.[4]

Through their aesthetic rendering of a post-1945 US social world, Highsmith's novels reveal rather than protest the pervasive power of norms and their constitutive relation to commodities in late capitalism. In Highsmith's fictional world, norms and things mutually reaffirm each other in such a way that the fantasy on offer is one in which bodies and history disappear in favor of their re-presentation – as a performance, a forgery, or a commodity. What matters in a Highsmith novel, in other words, is not the origin or cause of a crime (the essence or truth of an event or person) but the details of its accomplishment – how it is enacted. Through this kind of fictional positivism Highsmith's work offers a restaging of the fantasy of pure objectification that a normative social world encourages and through which its power operates. Highsmith's queerness, as a result, is not to be found in an opposition to or critique of norms but in her ability to illuminate their power. Her fiction reflects back to her world its logics of exchange, comparison, and commodification, and as such she gives us an exceptional version of that world – she makes it strange.

Most broadly this essay is about thinking queer paradoxically rather than oppositionally, and in relation to the power of fantasy – as that which sets the scene for desire – in queer studies as well as in Patricia Highsmith's fiction. Here I join literary critics such as Mary Esteve, Michael Trask, and, more recently, Jonathan Goldberg, who have all turned to Highsmith in order to extend and complicate the conceptual appeal of queerness. But whereas for these critics Highsmith's queerness is always ultimately located in her artistry as a writer (a conclusion I don't dispute), my reading of the Ripley novels focuses more narrowly on their reinscription of the so-called normal world. That is, for the purposes of this essay I am less interested in exploring the queer aesthetics of Highsmith's writing. Instead, I am interested in how her work helps us to think through the impasse of queer theory's simultaneous attachment to an assumed political radicality and a radical anti-identitarianism. My argument is that Highsmith's Ripley novels – with their repetitive fantasies of objectification located in a historical moment prior to the emergence of gay liberation – provide a way to explore the tension within queer studies between the aspiration for a politics that seeks to bring a queerer world into existence – one in which more peoples and their desires and pleasures can flourish without threat of violence or oppression – and one that, at the very same time, depends upon the existence of a normal world in order to be queer in the first place.

the fantasy of queer studies

Within the context of US academia and its relatively powerful publishing platforms, queer studies has recently been the subject of a cluster of conversations and disagreements concerning its continued validity as an "animating" and/or radical field of critique. One beginning point for this ongoing assessment of the field is the 2005 *Social Text* special issue on the state of queer studies, "What's Queer about Queer Studies Now?," in which the co-editors, David Eng, Judith Halberstam, and José Muñoz, argue for a queer studies that is "vigilant to the fact that sexuality is intersectional, not extraneous to other modes of difference, and calibrated to a firm understanding of queer as a political metaphor without a fixed referent" (1). Two years later, Elizabeth Freeman, in the introduction to her *GLQ* special issue on "Queer Temporalities," argues for a queer studies oriented towards an understanding of queer "as a set of possibilities produced out of temporal and historical difference" (159). While Jasbir Puar, in *Terrorist Assemblages*, calls queer an assemblage – a constellation of multiple varied components that, in its contingency, can be both complicit with, and resistant to, "dominant formations" (205). Queer, in other words, for these and other critics, is a term that doesn't necessarily mean anything except in the specificity and contingency of its deployment – it is a term that mobilizes, for a particular time and place, a certain set of critical and political possibilities.

This emphasis on the productivity of queerness as a critical practice has, as Eng, Halberstam, and Muñoz note, opened up queer studies to a "broad range of social critique," including critical race theory, postcolonial studies, the political economy, the nonhuman, health, disability, war, and terrorism (4). But for the most part, this turn to a more expansive notion of queerness in the 2000s still retains, as part of its often unstated or under-theorized political project, the assumption of non-normativity and anti-identitarianism as political ideals. Even Puar, whose critique of the sexual exceptionalism of US gay and lesbian/queer politics offers one of the more sustained problematizations of the equation of queerness-as-resistance, ends *Terrorist Assemblages* with a return to queer as a political and critical ideal, albeit this time as a term, or name, for a political project that "scrambles" national and racial "sides" as well as sexual ones.

In their introduction to the recent special issue of *differences*, "Antinormativity's Queer Conventions," Robyn Wiegman and Elizabeth Wilson query the continuing attachment to the non-normative and anti-identitarianism as assumed rather than explicitly theorized political ideals in queer studies. They identify antinormativity not as a coherent theoretical or methodological approach that brands the field but as a "sensibility" that shapes its "political imaginary and analytic vocabulary" (2). While trying to decipher the thought-style of an academic field is a somewhat treacherous exercise – especially for academics who, as Bourdieu noted wryly in *Homo Academicus*, do not particularly welcome their own objectification – the direction of their inquiry is towards the political and critical aspirations that have incited the field forming investments in and alignments with the terms queer/theory/studies. That they raise the question – can you have queer studies without antinormativity? – is, in my reading, not only an attempt to historicize what has become the disciplinary imperatives of an academic field in a particular location and time (queer studies in the United States from approximately 1990 to 2015) but also, at the same time, symptomatic of a field that is becoming less US-centric and less orchestrated through its founding impulses. Rather than read Wiegman and Wilson's "Antinormativity's Queer Conventions" as an indictment of the field – a reading that performs rejection in the name of a queer "we" that is always somehow free of disciplinarity – it seems to me more productive to read it as a reckoning with the residual claims of a queer studies that is increasingly less animated by the same political and critical ambitions that saw it erupt into life in the United States in the early 1990s.

The residual claims of an earlier queer studies moment are most apparent in the posture of opposition and repudiation that queer studies scholarship assumes in relation to normativity. For Wiegman and Wilson, this posture of opposition and resistance mischaracterizes how norms actually work and tends, as a result, to misrecognize our capacity to resist or defuse them, never mind actually confront the notion that we might unconsciously or even consciously desire them. Or, as Heather Love in her essay for the issue argues, by always asking the implicit question – "whose side are we [you] on?" – queer studies reproduces an oppositionality between a queer "us" and a straight "them" that not only lets its practitioners off the hook of a self-reflective assessment of queer studies' implication in systems of "power, management, and control," but also maintains rather than disturbs the political and affective appeal of the repressive hypothesis (Love 91). The provocation for queer studies of Wiegman and Wilson's turn to the question of what, exactly, a norm is, and of Love's turn to observation and description as useful methods for queer studies, is to challenge a prevailing assumption in the field that there is a binding relation between its theoretical mode of inquiry and its status as a politically radical field of critique.

The questioning of the assumption of a binding relationship between the political and the theoretical in queer studies, of course, is not new to current debates in the field. Indeed, Love ends her essay in the *differences* special issue with Biddy Martin's 1993 in/famous querying of queer theory's antinormativity, "Extraordinary Homosexuals and the Fear of Being Ordinary," in which Martin expresses the concern that what is implicit in queer theory's radical antinormativity is an "enormous fear of ordinariness." Rather than a careful attention to the complex lives and everyday "dilemmas of the average people [queers] also are," queer theory has fallen for "the lure of an existence without limit, without bodies or psyches, and certainly without mothers" (Martin 70). Here, ordinariness signals the web of social and economic relations that both produce and constrain subjects. On the one hand, then, the lure of limitlessness that Martin identifies in queer theory is that of a radical subjectivity somehow able to free itself of these constraints. As such, her complaint is directed towards a queer theory that traffics in an antisocial thesis that would refuse the implicatedness of any theoretical position in relations of social and historical inequality. On the other hand, the terms of Martin's critique, her slippage from ordinary to average, suggest the structuring pervasiveness of normalization as something that underwrites both Martin's (liberal humanist) thought *and* that of the queer theorists she critiques.[5] To be ordinary, after all, is not the same thing as being average.

More particularly, to be average, as François Ewald argues, is to be an effect of a process of comparison and equivalence that is without limit: to be without bodies, psyches, or even mothers, in Ewald's terms, is to be measurable. The average man "is not an individual whose place in society is indeterminate or uncertain; rather, he is society itself as it sees itself objectified in the mirror of probability and statistics" (145–46). The lure of an existence without limit, then, can also be understood as the lure of becoming objectified – that is, knowable within a distributive logic of comparison "with no recourse to any kind of external reference point, either in the form of an idea or an object" (154). For Wiegman and Wilson, whose argument "against" antinormativity depends largely on Foucault's and Ewald's detailed excavations of the production and effects of norms in modernity, this lack of recourse to an outside or limit is precisely the point about norms that queer studies tends to forget: in "that strict Foucaultian sense of normative as engendering, there is no place from which to take an oppositional stance and no locale that would constitute an exclusion" (Wiegman and Wilson 17). To occupy an antinormative position in the disciplinary societies of late capitalism therefore is, strictly speaking, impossible.

Rather than a position to be occupied, Wiegman and Wilson infer that the antinormative operates in queer studies as a fantasy that sets the scene for its political aspirations. As such, they raise the question of how and where to locate the political in queer studies. Instead of assuming a binding relation between the political and queer – queer as a "political metaphor without a fixed referent" – their reflection on the complexity and power of norms provides an opening for thinking about the distinction between queer as a form, a method, or relation, and the range of its possible political effects. In addition, by arguing that queer studies' "against, against, against" stance towards a static and always already oppressive straight or normal world might just as easily suggest a closeness to or drawing towards what it wants to reject, as the multiple meanings of against would imply, Wiegman and Wilson remind us that the power of a queer approach to its objects lies in its capacity to disturb and thwart – to operate in and through paradox and proximity rather than rejection or repudiation.

the fantasy of objectification

Patricia Highsmith's Tom Ripley novels make uncomfortable reading for those who want to be sure of their outsiderness. For Ripley is in effect a reinscription of the dominant and the normal, but not in order to be against the world as it is – the socio-historical present that the Ripley novels only tangentially and sporadically acknowledge – rather, Ripley's reinscriptions take place wholly within a fantasy world arranged in relation to commodities and through the scenes they inhabit and organize. There is no outside to this fantasy world, which is why the Ripley novels can span 1955 to 1990 and take no account of the passage of time except in the odd reference to a current event or figure and detailed descriptions of stuff: the clothes, cars, and furniture might change in a Highsmith novel (and even then, not so much) but the situations in which they appear, the affects they produce, and the feelings attached to them, tend to stay the same. As a number of her critics and readers have argued, most notably Slavoj Žižek, Highsmith's fictional world demonstrates, from her first published novel, "an uncanny completeness: everything in place, no further growth needed" ("Not a Desire" 13).[6] This completeness can be attributed to the continuity of the fantasy across the range of Highsmith's work, a fantasy that is, at the same time, both irreducibly Highsmith's and also general in the details of its social reinscriptions.

The fantasy at work in Highsmith's Ripley novels, and perhaps in all her novels, is the fantasy of objectification – a becoming object that locates pleasure in commodities and norms and the way of life they signal and organize for their consumers and subjects. Rather than have characters with histories who act in a narrative that gives meaning to their actions, Highsmith's novels create situations that are full of stuff, a feature that, as Russell Harrison writes, "both creates and reflects the objectified quality of her characters" and "their strangely dissociated personalities" (x). In a Highsmith novel, characters are not so much complicated human beings burdened by the materiality of their historically produced bodies and identities but objectified entities to be possessed, played with, and discarded. But whereas Harrison finds the cause of this flight into objects in a psychoanalytic interpretation of Highsmith's "suppression" of the politics of the Cold War period and as a "displacement" of the true object of her emotions (ibid.), an interpretation that relies on the distinction between inside and outside and between the authentic and the artificial (between the psyche and the social and/or aesthetic), I want to maintain the focus of my reading on the fantasy itself – on the setting of desire and the language of its reinscriptions – for it is in the fantasy of a Highsmith novel that, for queer studies, her perversity is to be found.

Towards the end of Highsmith's second Tom Ripley novel, *Ripley Underground*, we find our antihero returning to his hotel in Salzburg after literally following a man to his death. As Ripley enters the hotel, the Goldener Hirsch, he "breathed suddenly the pleasant scent of furniture wax, the aroma of comfort and tranquility." The chapter ends with the porter saying "Good evening, sir" and handing Ripley his key (265). A few pages later, after performing the gruesome task of first burning the dead man's body and then scooping some of the remains into a suitcase and dropping more over the side of a bridge, Ripley prepares to return to his home in Villeperce, France by doing what he usually does in these moments, shopping: "He bought a green waistcoat for [Heloise, his wife] and a Wolljanker of clear blue like the colour of the Gauloise packet, a white ruffled blouse, and for himself a darker green waistcoat and a couple of hunting knives" (278). Scenes like these are repeated throughout Highsmith's Ripley novels: the contrast between the anxiety of the situation Tom finds himself in – having to anticipate and plot a series of actions in order to ward off the intrusion of an outside world (stranger curiosity, neighbor nosiness, amateur and professional detectives, etc.), and the "comfort and tranquility" of clean, orderly, attractive, and categorizable spaces and things. The colors of green (waistcoat), white (blouse), and blue (like a Gauloise packet) offer a pleasurable arrangement, like the Derwatt paintings hanging on Tom's living room walls, and become the affectless alternative to the messiness of bodies and history and the powerful, encroaching mystery of other people's desires, fears, and demands. On his return to Villeperce and "delighted to be home," Tom takes a shower "rinsing the soap off" before putting on silk pajamas (281). Returning home, for Tom, is a return to the pleasures of clean, shiny, smooth, stuff – to the pleasure of things in all their glamorous appeal: the silk pajamas signaling Tom's at-home-ness.

In the recent turn to a re-engagement with Marxism in queer studies, the body often figures as a material excess or stumbling block to commodification. The body, collective and singular, tends to mediate and absorb the contradictions of neoliberal capitalism through its affective and debilitating capacities – bodies break down, spread out, or merge and divide through the energies or force of affect. The body, or "life," is both inside and outside capitalism: it is its limit as well as the source of its regeneration. The usefulness of Foucault's notion of biopower in this regard can be located in the way it tries to account for the relation between bodies, modes of production, and techniques of administration and management in terms other than inside/outside. In a different theoretical register, Žižek, following Sohn-Rethel, defines reality as "the ideological fantasy" presupposed by an exchange economy, thereby inverting orthodox Marxism which would have economic relations determining ideology (*Sublime Object* 21), while Agamben, following Foucault, names "the impossibility of distinguishing between outside and inside, nature and exception, physis and nomos" that marks the modern state as the primary administrative mode for the expansion of capital, the "state of exception" of sovereign power (*Homo Sacer* 37). What all three theorists have in common, despite their varying commitments to Marxism, is their search for a concept that could illuminate the contradiction of bodies and life as origin and effect of capitalist expansion.

For Foucault especially, this contradiction lies at the heart of his investigations into the histories of madness, incarceration, and sexuality in the modern period. Common to all these histories is a desire to historicize modernity through the tracking of the emergence of increasingly sophisticated techniques for the management and control of bodies. Rather than begin with "a" contradiction – the economic interests of the capitalist vs. those of labor – that then becomes "the" explanation for a progressive, totalizing history of modernity as class struggle, Foucault begins tangentially by looking not at the economy or an abstracted relation between worker and capitalist but at specific forms of institutionalization and the techniques through which their administration of power and management of people radiated: the madhouse, the penitentiary, the school, and the clinic. By beginning tangentially to the explanatory account that Marxism offered him, Foucault was able to map not simply the process of immiseration for most people under capitalism but the practices and techniques of interpellation that made workers, capitalists, couples, pederasts, and madmen, for example, social subjects with distinct, if interrelated, ways of life in a complex world. That is,

Foucault's archeological method and genealogical approach to modernity allowed him to access capitalism at the level of its historicity – its productive and generative capacities, rather than through an ahistorical law of its emergence and development.

It is this tangential approach to the rise of capitalism that enables Foucault to historicize the contradiction of bodies being both the origin and limit of capitalist expansion, in that it provides him with the means to chart the rise of discourse as coextensive with the dematerialization of bodies. For Foucault modernity is marked not by the bifurcation of corporeality and mentality, or nature and culture but, as with Agamben, through the increasing indistinction between the two. This indistinction does not mean that bodies literally disappear into discourse – that "everything becomes discourse" – but that bodies no longer exist in and for themselves. The death of man is, for Foucault, a phrase that signals the end of a certain kind of vitality – the vitality of a life not captured by the administrative reach of modern state capitalism. Or, as Ed Cohen writes, the individualism that marks modernity is, for Foucault, "neither an ideological subjectification, nor a class-based phenomenon predicated on the extraction of surplus value," but rather a "new form of life that plots human existence within a quantifiable time that concomitantly constitutes 'the body' as our most vital resource" (Cohen). By turning bodies into resources and life into quantifiable time, capitalism enacts the abstraction of bodies and their conversion into commodities. It is through this process of abstraction and conversion that "man" comes to hate, deny, or strive to overcome the limits of his corporeality. In a perfect capitalist world, an ideal suggested in the corporation-as-person reality of contemporary US law – bodies would cease to matter – except as resources for exploitation.

In Highsmith's Ripley novels the contradiction of bodies as both the origin and limit of capitalist expansion is less the source of a struggle to resist or transform the desensitizing and decorporalizing relentlessness of capitalist expansion, and more the source of the pleasure to be taken in the fantasy offered: a world that is indifferent to the distinction between bodies and things and the techniques used to measure and compare them. In Highsmith's novels, bodies recede or are violently expelled from the scene of becoming objectified – of becoming the clothes we wear rather than the bodies that feel. That Ripley is a man, and a white man, makes the pleasure Highsmith takes in his becoming object notable in the sense that he occupies a subject position which liberal capitalism has marked out as privileged in relation to his Others. The becoming object I'm tracking here is not, then, the objectification of capitalism's "Others" into abstractions for misuse but that of liberal capitalist man becoming the things that he covets and by which he measures himself in relation to others. In having her bodies cathect to commodities, Highsmith reinscribes the ideological fantasy of a capitalist economy by inverting its subject/object dichotomy: Ripley's (and Highsmith's) pleasure lies in his ability to make his corporeal substantiveness and social historicity seem irrelevant or unnecessary to the success of his life. This is also the pleasure of being sexually indifferent and indifferent to sex: a pleasure without relationality, without affect. In a Highsmith novel, objectification is no longer the scene of capitalism's crime against the living world but a sign of the fantasy of freedom it offers: the freedom to be without limit – to exist without bodies and without history.

queer (american) exceptionalism

Just under half-way through *The Talented Mr Ripley*, the first and best known of the Ripley novels, Tom Ripley, having killed the man he both wants and wants to be, travels to Paris a new man:

> He walked out into the darkness and turned in the direction of the illuminated, bone-white Arc de Triomphe. It was strange to feel so alone, and yet so much a part of things, as he had felt at the party. He felt it again, standing on the outskirts of the crowd that filled the square in Notre Dame

[...] Frenchmen near him removed their hats. Tom removed his. He stood tall, straight, sober-faced, yet ready to smile if anyone had addressed him. He felt as he had felt on the ship, only more intensely, full of good will, a gentleman, with nothing in his past to blemish his character. He was Dickie, good-natured, naïve Dickie, with a smile for everyone and a thousand francs for anyone who asked him. An old man did ask him for money as Tom was leaving the cathedral square, and he gave him a crisp blue thousand-franc bill. The old man's face exploded in a smile, and he tipped his hat. (111)

Tom had decided to kill Dickie Greenleaf out of a sense of anger and "disappointment" at Dickie's rejection, not just of Tom but of the kind of life Tom imagined them living together as Americans abroad in ambiguously homoerotic coupledom. Killing Greenleaf ends Tom's exile from the things he covets but it also ends the burden of his authenticity: it sets him apart – from his past, from the demands of others, and from the impossible ambivalence of sexual desire. This scene is key for the Ripley novels because it frees Tom from the "vicissitudes of intersubjectvity," as Fiona Peters makes clear in her reading of the novel: it is the decisive act through which Tom refuses any dyadic relation with an Other (170). No longer a subject, Tom becomes an actor who, through the third-person estrangement of the narrative voice, is also able to witness and enjoy the skilled artifice of his performance. Drawing upon a widespread cultural interest in the dramaturgical in postwar American society,[7] Highsmith locates Ripley's ability to manage the situations he finds himself in, in his talent as an actor. Acting becomes the means through which Ripley is able not only to produce the social scenes he wants to inhabit but, as a result of occupying those scenes, become somebody else. The *mise-en-scène* creates the legibility of Tom's impersonations – this is the process of depersonalization that allows Ripley to become something other than himself. The focus of the pleasure – for Highsmith and her readers as well as for Ripley – lies less in his capacity to pretend and to dupe his audience (although he does take pleasure in this on occasion), and more on his ability to literally have the performance become something more real than his past, "authentic" self.

We witness this pleasure in performing in the above passage, in which Tom's transition into inauthenticity is narrativized as a triumphant journey from darkness towards the "illuminated, bone-white Arc de Triomphe." The double-entendre of bone-white invokes both the virility and whiteness of Tom's newly acquired upper-middle-class masculinity. And as Tom self-consciously mimics the Frenchmen surrounding him, his proximate apartness becomes both a source of power and knowledge: he sees himself acting the part, and for that reason his actions towards the old man are both calculating and agentic in a way that those of the surrounding, "authentic," Frenchmen cannot be. Ripley's enjoyment of his newly acquired agency is unambiguous. Immediately after the murder, Tom takes an overnight train to Mongibello, the Italian village in which Dickie Greenleaf had been living, and has an "ecstatic moment" thinking of "all the pleasures that lay before him now with Dickie's money, other beds, tables, seas, ships, suitcases, shirts, years of freedom, years of pleasure." It was a thought that left him "happy, content, and utterly confident, as he had never been before in his life" (97). And later, while in Paris, he reflects with deep satisfaction upon the success of his impersonation of Dickie:

> He had done so little artificially to change his appearance, but his very expression, Tom thought, was like Dickie's now [...] Tom was in a good humour. It was Paris. *Wonderful* to sit in a famous café, and to think of tomorrow and tomorrow and tomorrow being Dickie Greenleaf! (109; emphasis in original)

The enjoyment Tom feels here lies precisely in the vicariousness of both being and not being Dickie – of being proximate to the things he covets and the scenes he wants to inhabit rather than having to be "authentically" either Tom or Dickie.

The Talented Mr Ripley was first published in 1955, after Highsmith had traveled widely in Europe on two separate occasions. As a story about a young unattached American going to Europe to find himself, or more precisely, lose himself, the novel participates in a common theme of American writing at the time. In the postwar years, "Europe" acted as a performative space for privileged Americans and American artists trying to work out a way of doing Americanness in a world that had, in the aftermath of the Second World War, shifted on its axis.[8] The stranger-relationality of this kind of narcissism – a narcissism common to tourism in general – enabled performances of Americanness that were, in their fictionalization, both false and within the context of America's rapid rise to geopolitical and economic world dominance in this period, enormously empowering.

In this sense, Highsmith's Ripley novels can be understood as participating in the enactment of American exceptionalism more generally in the postwar years, rather than just simply providing a fictional domain for reflecting upon it.[9] Using Jasbir Puar's understanding of American exceptionalism as referring "both to particular discourses that repetitively produce the United States as an exceptional nation-state" and Giorgio Agamben's "theorization of the sanctioned and naturalized disregard of the limits of state juridical and political power through times of state crisis" (Puar 3), I want to suggest here that Tom Ripley figures an exceptionalism understood as both a distinction from the normal or the conventional, as well as an "excellence (imminence and superiority)" in relation to it – the "real" Frenchmen but also the "real," i.e., Dickie Greenleaf, white upper-middle-class nominally heterosexual American men. That is, Tom Ripley, in his desubjectified performativity, figures the contradiction of being neither inside nor outside the normative, his becoming Dickie Greenleaf suggesting the paradoxical pleasures of a normative world – the lure of an existence without limit.

For Puar, of course, the paradox of American exceptionalism becomes the problem of homonationalism as the incorporation of a particular – homonormative – form of homosexuality into the externalization – the "coming out" – of American Empire (2). Reading Ripley through Puar, then, would make him a figure of American sexual exceptionalism: he would stand as an example of a certain kind of homo performativity that extends the dominion of American power and influence. But the problem that Ripley poses for this account of homonationalism lies in his refusal to take sides – he neither takes up the appropriate identity category (homosexual) nor does he validate the (heteronormative) "reproductive valorization of living" that would, in Puar's reading, suture homosexuality to the progressive temporality of American empire (3).

Take, for example, Ripley's relationship with his wife, Heloise:

> Heloise existed. It was odd for Tom. He could not make out her objectives in life. She was like a picture on the wall. She might want children, some time, she said. Meanwhile, she existed. Not that Tom could boast of having any objectives himself, now that he had attained the life he had now, but Tom had a certain zest in seizing the pleasures he was now able to seize, and this zest seemed lacking in Heloise, maybe because she had had everything she wished since birth. Tom felt odd sometimes making love with her, because he felt detached half the time, and as if he derived pleasure from something inanimate, unreal, from a body without an identity. Or was this some shyness or Puritanism on his part? Or some fear of (mentally) giving himself, "If I should not have, if I should lose Heloise, I couldn't exist any longer." Tom knew he was capable of believing that, even in regard to Heloise, but he did not like to admit it to himself, did not permit it, and had certainly never said it to Heloise, because it would (as things were now) be a lie. The condition of utter dependence on her he sensed merely as a possibility. It had little to do with sex, Tom thought, with any dependence on that. Usually Heloise was disrespectful of the same things he was. She was a partner, in a way, though a passive one. With a boy or a man, Tom would have laughed more – maybe that was the main difference. (*Ripley Underground* 163–64)

This is Ripley at his most self-reflective. But even here, his reflections are those of an actor puzzling over the relationship of his character to a stranger. Heloise existed – she was a fact to be deciphered, not the subject of his fantasies or desires. Utter dependence is a possibility not an aspiration and certainly not a felt feeling. And the closest Ripley comes to explaining his attachment to Heloise is that they were "disrespectful" about the same things. If, to borrow from Lauren Berlant, love is a "binding relation to time" – a commitment to some future fulfillment of a promise to be faithful to a stated ideal or chosen object – then Ripley's idea of love works in reverse: he is an accumulator of things (including Heloise and the boys he might laugh more with) that are acquired for the pleasure they give now rather than the promise they offer for the future (Berlant 14). Ripley experiences pleasure – lots of different kinds of pleasure – but he doesn't feel love.

Ripley's failure to feel love could be read within the context of queer critiques of American national affect as an effect of "normative whiteness." In "Feeling Brown: Ethnicity and Affect in Ricardo Bracho's *The Sweetest Hangover (and Other STDs)*" José Muñoz writes that "Citizenship is negotiated within a contested national sphere in which performances of affect counter each other in a contest that can be described as 'official' national affect versus emergent immigrant" (69). Muñoz goes on to define the national affect of the United States as "minimalist to the point of emotional impoverishment" (70). The minimalism of white affect, of course, is dependent on context and is an effect, as Muñoz notes, of its relation to other performances of affect. Muñoz's notion of white affect as minimalist resonates with feminist accounts of the gendered as well as racialized association of successful citizenship with reason and control. But Muñoz's emphasis on the performative highlights the artifice – the doingness – of citizenship, an approach that echoes Highsmith's interest in the dramaturgical as dissociative affect. He helps us to notice its strangeness as a set of affective, emotional, and social expectations that requires us to keep watch over our and others' performances of them. Muñoz's counter-example to white affect is the nightclub life-world of Bracho's play in which the relative excess of "brown" affect helps to "map out cultural spectacles that represent and are symbolically connected to alternative economies, like the economies of recreational drugs and homoeroticism" (74). That is, the feeling brown of Bracho's play becomes, for Muñoz, the queerness of inappropriate or excessive affect, which in turn provides the spectacles for imagining other worlds – ones organized through drugs and other "nightlife" commodities. In Muñoz's reading of Bracho's play, whiteness as affective minimalism cannot be queer – it is the norm against which excessive affect becomes inappropriate and "wrong."

The critical charge of Muñoz's reading of Bracho's play is produced through a spatial and identificatory dichotomization of brown and white that depends on the binary of antinorm/norm. In contrast, Highsmith's novel, in its indifference to difference, does not easily allow us to read Ripley's lack of passion through a contrast between norm and antinorm. Instead, we might read his lack of passion proximally, as both evidence of his exemplary status as a representative of "normative whiteness" and also as a subversion of bourgeois heteronormativity from within the open display of its comforts and reward. The pleasures Ripley takes in the stuff of a bourgeois life – the tailored shirts, Liberty dressing gowns, antique chests, wine cellars, paintings, wife, country house – are the pleasures of the now, rather than those that anticipate a future secured through the accumulation of wealth and social capital. Rather than a homonationalist, Ripley acts against the futuritial scripts of American exceptionalism: he kills to secure an advantage, as part of a game, to help someone else, or out of a sense of frustration. Although he plans many of his murders, they are never strategic, and sometimes he kills simply for the thrill of it. And while Ripley enjoys the pleasures of his wealthy bourgeois existence in Villeperce, he risks it all in every book simply for the adventure of doing something wrong. Ripley's queerness, in other words, does not lie in his resistance to or exclusion from the American

Dream of white heteronormativity but in his ability to perform it exceptionally well. To return to Agamben:

> The state of exception is neither external nor internal to the juridical order, and the problem of defining it concerns precisely a threshold, or a zone of indifference, where inside and outside do not exclude each other but rather blur with each other. (*State of Exception* 23)

Ripley acts in just such a zone of indifference – *in the moment* when it becomes difficult to define exactly what he is and where his distinction from and superiority over the normal and the conventional blurs into his performances of them. This is the state of exception as the "paradoxical perverse," and as such Ripley figures the pleasure of deviation – not as an inherently resistant or necessarily political act but as something that inheres from within the generative capacities of normativity.[10]

conclusion: fantasy and politics

The fantasy on offer in Patricia Highsmith's Tom Ripley novels, as I have attempted to argue in this essay, is one in which the *mise-en-scènes* of consumption and performance repeatedly take precedence over the encroaching messiness of bodies and history. As a figuring of the pleasure to be taken in a life lived without limit whereby actions have no meaning or consequence beyond their immediate satisfaction or end, Ripley invokes the contradictory appeal of a world in which the promise of the good life lies in the things one can buy and the strangers one can meet – in a bar, at an art gallery, or party. This is the liberal capitalist world of addictive consumerism in which the haunting presence of the past is repeatedly denied in favor of always seeking the next moment of distraction, excitement, or danger. It is also the world of an expansive normativity in which the comparative equivalences between things and people orchestrate the scenes of consumption and evaluation that shape the differentiated social field of a disciplinary society. Ripley is in his element in such a world – he exemplifies its logics and its promise – and in so doing he also reveals its meaninglessness.

As a political project that wants to open up possibilities for what Deleuze and Guattari call a non-fascistic life, queerness needs a sense of collectivity that is both imagined and enacted. This sense of collectivity is vehemently rejected by Ripley (and Highsmith), who acts alone and for his own pleasure and within a fantasy world that, in repeating the same scenes over and over again, keeps history in abeyance. But in that rejection Ripley also reveals something of the complicity of a queer desire for exception from social convention and norms. As a counter-fantasy figure to the political aspirations of both Gay Liberation and queer studies, Tom Ripley exhibits a family resemblance to the characteristics of queer critique most often used to identify its specificity – mobility, adaptability, performance, disassociation, and negativity – that are indicative of the historical context from which they both emerge. In other words, if we can say that Highsmith's work is specific to its historical moment, that its singularity is, paradoxically, evidence of her historicality, then we might also say that queer studies similarly provides evidence of its historicality in the investments it makes in particular forms of critical engagement. By using Ripley as a counter-image to the fantasy of queer studies, I hope to suggest that what is queer about queer studies and what is political about its project are not one and the same thing. In this, I echo arguments within the field that call for queer to be understood as a process, or analytic device, that can illuminate the contradictions through which regimes of domination are produced and maintained in the historical present.[11] In echoing this call, I also wish to emphasize that to illuminate contradiction is not to resolve it – for that you need a politics that would destroy what we are most attached to.

disclosure statement

No potential conflict of interest was reported by the author.

notes

1 Patricia Highsmith, as quoted in Schenkar (327).

2 Highsmith, *The Talented Mr Ripley* 111.

3 Ripley, more than any other of Highsmith's characters, figures this closeness to normal quite simply because he is the character she returns to again and again in her work. Other Highsmith novels also feature psychopathic characters: see, for example, Walter Stackhouse in *The Blunderer* (1954), or Bruno in *Strangers on a Train* (1950). Similarly, the attachment to the conventions of bourgeois respectability and consumerist agency exhibited by the central characters of Highsmith's "lesbian novel," *The Price of Salt* (1952), can also be read as figuring a closeness to normality that is also, in their expression of desire for each other, a deviation from it. For a subtle reading of the relationship between liberalism and consumerism in *The Price of Salt*, see Esteve. For a discussion of *The Blunderer* and its reflection of Cold War national and social norms, see Hesford.

4 Both Michael Trask and Mary Esteve locate Highsmith's aesthetic in a 1950s that can be characterized on the one hand by social interaction theories of social performance and self-management, and on the other with widespread social and political anxiety concerning the legitimacy of both same-sex desire and consumer society.

5 On the structuring pervasiveness of normalization in the modern, disciplinary society, François Ewald writes:

> The norm is also the means through which the disciplinary society communicates with itself. The norm relates the disciplinary institutions of production – knowledge, wealth, and finance – to one another in such a way that they become truly *interdisciplinary*; it provides a common language for these various disciplines and makes it possible to translate from one disciplinary idiom into another. (141)

6 Another critic, Christa Maerker, writes: "Her books are written in a manner that one needs little of one's own fantasy when reading them" (as quoted and translated by Russell Harrison

152. Originally "Ich Liebe, Klarheit" in *Horen* 4 (1993) 38). Žižek finds an explanation for Highsmith's early completeness as a writer in the Lacanian notion of the sinthome – the trace of the singularity of a subject's enjoyment of their unconscious in their artistic production. Like Hitchcock, Žižek argues, Highsmith was an artist whose work was "literally" the "knot that tied her universe together." That is, for Highsmith, writing was not simply a displacement or escape from her biography, nor an interpretation or rewriting of the world around her. Instead it was the purest expression of Highsmith – the presentation of her irreducible particularity ("Not a Desire" 13).

7 As Michael Trask has argued, the importance of acting in the Tom Ripley novels reflects the fascination in postwar American culture with performance. From the social interactionist school of sociology and its dramaturgic understanding of social relations, to the Stanislavski-inspired "method" of the Actors Studio, acting had a cultural and sociological importance in Cold War American culture (587–88).

8 In the interests of space, I cannot go into detail about the economic and geopolitical transformation of the postwar years, but would include the rise of nationalist/anti-colonial movements in Africa and Asia; the institution of American dominance through the formation of the Bretton Woods Agreement (1944) and subsequent formation of the International Monetary Fund and International Bank for Reconstruction and Development (1945); as well as the rise of the Cold War between the Soviet Union and the United States.

9 To add to this reading of the Ripley novels: Joan Schenkar notes that Highsmith read Alexis de Tocqueville's *Democracy in America* in preparation for writing *The Talented Mr Ripley* (see Schenkar 340 fn. 16).

10 This is Jonathan Dollimore's term. For Dollimore, the perverse dynamic and the paradoxical perverse are two concepts that take us "to the heart of a fierce dialectic between domination and deviation" in the history of sexuality as it spans the early modern to the late twentieth century (see Dollimore 103–30).

11 See, for example, Jordana Rosenberg and Amy Villarejo's 2012 special issue of *GLQ*, "Queerness, Norms, Utopia."

bibliography

Agamben, Giorgio. *Homo Sacer: Sovereign Power and Bare Life*. Trans. Daniel Heller-Roazen. Stanford: Stanford UP, 1998. Print.

Agamben, Giorgio. *The State of Exception*. Trans. Kevin Attell. Chicago: U of Chicago P, 2005. Print.

Berlant, Lauren. *The Female Complaint: The Unfinished Business of Sentimentality in American Culture*. Durham, NC: Duke UP, 2008. Print.

Cohen, Ed. "Capitalizing on 'The Body': The Productive Body and La Société punitive: Cours au Collège de France (1972–1973)." *LA Review of Books* 25 July 2014. Web. 19 Dec. 2017. <https://lareviewofbooks.org/article/capitalizing-body>.

Deleuze, Gilles, and Félix Guattari. *Anti-Oedipus: Capitalism and Schizophrenia*. Trans. Robert Hurley, Mark Seem, and Helen R. Lane. London: Continuum, 2004. Print.

Dollimore, Jonathan. *Sexual Dissidence: Augustine to Wilde, Freud to Foucault*. Oxford: Oxford UP, 1991. Print.

Eng, David L., Judith Halberstam, and José Esteban Muñoz. "What's Queer about Queer Studies Now?" *Social Text* 23.3/4 (Fall/Winter 2005): 1–17. Print.

Esteve, Mary. "Queer Consumerism, Straight Happiness: Highsmith's Right Economy." *Post45* 18 Dec. 2012. Web. 19 Dec. 2017. <http://post45.research.yale.edu/2012/12/queer-consumerism-straight-happiness-highsmiths-right-economy/>.

Ewald, François. "Norms, Discipline, and the Law." *Law and the Order of Culture*. Spec. issue of *Representations* 30 (Spring 1990): 138–61. Print.

Foucault, Michel. *The History of Sexuality, Volume One: An Introduction*. 1978. Trans. Robert Hurley. New York: Vintage, 1990. Print.

Freeman, Elizabeth. "Queer Temporalities." *GLQ* 13.2/3 (2007): 159–76. Print.

Goldberg, Jonathan. *Melodrama: An Aesthetics of Impossibility*. Durham, NC: Duke UP, 2016. Print.

Harrison, Russell. *Patricia Highsmith*. New York: Twayne, 1997. Print.

Hesford, Victoria. "Patriotic Perversions: Patricia Highsmith's Queer Vision of Cold War America in *The Price of Salt*, *The Blunderer*, and *Deep Water*." *Women's Studies Quarterly* 33 (Fall/Winter 2005): 215–33. Print.

Highsmith, Patricia. *Ripley Underground*. 1970. New York: Vintage, 1992. Print.

Highsmith, Patricia. *The Talented Mr Ripley*. 1955. Harmondsworth: Penguin, 1987. Print.

Love, Heather. "Doing Being Deviant: Deviance Studies, Description, and the Queer Ordinary." *differences: A Journal of Feminist Cultural Studies* 26.1 (2015): 74–95. Print.

Martin, Biddy. "Extraordinary Homosexuals and the Fear of Being Ordinary." *Femininity Played Straight: The Significance of Being Lesbian*. New York: Routledge, 1996. 45–70. Print.

Muñoz, José Esteban. "Feeling Brown: Ethnicity and Affect in Ricardo Bracho's *The Sweetest Hangover (and Other STDS)*." *Theatre Journal* 52.1 (2000): 67–79. Print.

Peters, Fiona. *Anxiety and Evil in the Writings of Patricia Highsmith*. Burlington, VT: Ashgate, 2011. Print.

Puar, Jasbir K. *Terrorist Assemblages: Homonationalism in Queer Times*. Durham, NC: Duke UP, 2007. Print.

Rosenberg, Jordana, and Amy Villarejo. "Queerness, Norms, Utopia." *GLQ* 18.1 (2012): 1–18. Print.

Schenkar, Joan. *The Talented Miss Highsmith: The Secret Life and Serious Art of Patricia Highsmith*. New York: St. Martin's, 2009. Print.

Trask, Michael. "Patricia Highsmith's Method." *American Literary History* 22.3 (2010): 584–614. Print.

Wiegman, Robyn, and Elizabeth A. Wilson. "Antinormativity's Queer Conventions." *differences: A Journal of Feminist Cultural Studies* 26.1 (2015): 1–25. Print.

Žižek, Slavoj. "Not a Desire to Have Him But to be Like Him: *Beautiful Shadow: A Life of Patricia Highsmith*." *London Review of Books* 25.16 (2003). 13–15, 21. Print.

Žižek, Slavoj. *The Sublime Object of Ideology.* London: Verso, 1989. Print.

How can an old woman who lives alone with her cats be a figure of comfort and acceptance to all of humanity? This is the question Truman Capote leaves us with at the end of his story "A Lamp in a Window," collected in his last book, *Music for Chameleons*, in 1980.[1] The answer lies in the nature of the woman's unusual love for her cats, for, as we learn at the end of the story, not only is Mrs Kelly's "cheerful place occupied by six or seven cats of varying alley-cat colors" but she also keeps the bodies of all her deceased cats in a freezer in the kitchen: "stacks of frozen, perfectly preserved cats – dozens of them" (17, 20). Mrs Kelly confesses that these are "All my old friends. Gone to rest. It's just that I couldn't bear to lose them. *Completely*" (20). Then she laughingly admits, "I guess you think I'm a bit dotty" (ibid.). The unnamed narrator agrees to himself but adds that her way of being "a bit dotty" also makes her "radiant: a lamp in a window" (ibid.). His phrase recalls how he encountered Mrs Kelly in the first place, for she lives a hermit's existence deep in the Connecticut woods where the narrator finds himself late one night after jumping out of a car driven by a dangerously drunk acquaintance. After walking for "half an hour without sighting a habitation," he sees Mrs Kelly's "small frame cottage with a porch and a window lighted by a lamp," and Mrs Kelly gladly takes him in for the night (17). But the repetition of the symbol "a lamp in a window" in the story's final sentence and the title suggests that the inspirational aspect of her character stems from more than simply her act of hospitality or her touching inability to cope with the loss of her pets. Rather, what leads

michael p. bibler

CAPOTE'S FROZEN CATS
sexuality, hospitality, civil rights

the narrator to offer Mrs Kelly as a larger symbol of welcoming and accommodation to anyone – whether we actually visit her home or not – is the profound love that binds her to her cats in the first place.

Putting a lamp in a window is a both literal and symbolic gesture to help absent kin and loved ones find their way home; it also signals to traveling strangers that they can find shelter and safety in that abode. Although Mrs Kelly lives with no other humans, has no transportation or telephone, and never ventures out of her home for any reason – the narrator learns that "her good friend, the mailman, [takes] care of all her shopping needs" (18) – she is always prepared in case a stranger should visit.

She tells the narrator, "I have a nice little guest room that's been waiting such a long time for a guest" (ibid.), and he eventually finds himself "comfortably arranged in a double bed under a blissful load of pretty scrap quilts" (19). Moreover, since Mrs Kelly lives "so isolatedly" in the woods (18), her lamp in the window also evokes the symbol of a light in the wilderness, signifying not only shelter and hospitality but also notions of civilization and order. The story supports this interpretation of Mrs Kelly as a beacon of cultural refinement when the narrator notes that "she was a woman with a good and varied mind; intelligence illuminated her hazel eyes like the small lamp shining on the table beside her" (ibid.).

However, the "radiant" part of her character that sets the terms by which we *all* might find inclusion in her world is her profound emotional relationship with her animal companions, both dead and alive. The story suggests that because Mrs Kelly does not hide, but rather happily admits to her "dotty" affection for her cats even after their deaths, we can take comfort in knowing that we, like the narrator, will never be turned away from her world on account of *our own* peculiar object-choices. In this way, I read Capote's story not just as a quaint vignette about an eccentric character, as it is often read, but as a story that can help us rethink both the nature of sexuality and the ethics of community. The key to this re-evaluation lies in the non-symbolic literalism of Mrs Kelly's unique and uncategorizable connection to her feline "friends." The intensity and specificity of Mrs Kelly's love for her non-human, non-living companions expands the possibilities for recognizing a much broader range of intimacies and attachments as belonging within the "domain of sexuality."[2] And, by decentering the human within the domain of sexuality, the story further enables a more political reconsideration of the notion of belonging itself. The literalism of Mrs Kelly's unusual bond with her cats opens a space for reimagining the assemblages of objects and identities, and of civil rights and obligations, through which we humans seek to organize and understand the world(s) we inhabit.

Despite its short length, "A Lamp in a Window" pushes us toward this new way of thinking about love, companionship, sexuality, and sociality by shrewdly manipulating our preconceptions about character and plot and then shattering those preconceptions with the unexpected presence of the frozen cats. The first parts of this essay examine these narrative manipulations along two trajectories. In one, Mrs Kelly's dottiness invites us to understand her as what we often call the "crazy cat-lady," with an accompanying medical diagnosis of animal hoarding disorder. In the other, a cluster of tropes, allusions, and figures pertaining to marriage invite us to read the cats as compensatory substitutes for the isolated widow's absent husband and (presumably) nonexistent children. But, as I go on to show, the revelation of frozen feline bodies punctures these symbolic frameworks, because the obstinate literalism of those bodies refuses the additional layers of signification that we are prepared to project onto them. As the freezer preserves the dead cats' bodies, it also preserves their catness, hardening their material corporeality to prevent them from being rendered into other matter through decomposition, *and* locking them into a tight representational system to prevent them from being symbolically rendered into something else through metaphor. The frozen cats refuse to be representative of anything other than frozen cats, making it hard to classify Mrs Kelly's attachment to them within any familiar taxonomy of affection or desire, even zoophilia. Instead, Mrs Kelly's bond with her cats must be understood *literally*: as a uniquely rich, idiosyncratic, and otherwise unaccountable love for her feline companions specifically *as such*, as cats.

Put another way, the story prepares us to read with certain assumptions about love and identity so that the literalism of frozen cats can then shock us out of those assumptions and change how we think about sexuality, sociality, hospitality, and civil rights. More than when she opens the front door to her late-night visitor, it is when Mrs Kelly opens her *freezer* door that she invites both him and us into the shelter of a world of queer assemblages, where the literalism of non-human love-objects implicitly validates every other kind of love and attachment, no matter how "dotty" or "deviant" it may seem – including, of course, but certainly not limited to, the homosexuality of the story's famous author. Capote's use of animals to think about affiliations and attachments beyond the normativizing, human-centered structures of sexuality and kinship situates the story within a longer tradition of homoerotic literature in which, as Ruth Vanita writes, animals sometimes "facilitated explorations and defenses of homosexual experience" (216). More like J.R. Ackerley's 1956 memoir *My Dog Tulip*, however, "A Lamp in a Window" does not present Mrs Kelly's love for her cats simply as a metaphor of same-gender love that cannot be expressed directly. Rather, by presenting this love as something more literal, Capote's story asserts a powerful, if strangely counterintuitive claim for the need to expand sexual freedoms and civil rights for everyone and everything, human and otherwise. Historically, this claim strikes at the ongoing codification of the homosexual/heterosexual binary in the transition period between gay liberation and the antigay conservatism of the Reagan era. But as I will show, the story also seeks to change how we think about sexual politics itself by expressing this claim in terms of hospitality and welcoming instead of a more didactic discourse of political opposition. As a dotty woman who loves her frozen cats, Mrs Kelly is a lamp in a window whose hospitality resets the terms for social inclusion by inviting us to be equally dotty – to love whomever or whatever we want without fear of being shunned or excluded.

crazy cat-ladies

As a kind of character sketch, the story initially lures us to give more consideration to Mrs Kelly's psychological state than to the literal significance of the cats themselves. But what does it actually mean to call her "dotty"? "Dotty" is a diminutive form of "crazy." We typically reserve the word for elderly people whom we view as feeble in mind as well as body because they speak and act in eccentric, even antisocial ways with no show of shame, embarrassment, or apology. Usually viewed as harmless, dotty people are only somewhat mad, ridiculous, or amusingly absurd; they are not fully "crazy" in the pathological sense of lacking reason, control, or awareness. To be dotty can also mean to be infatuated about someone or something, but never to the point of being obsessive-compulsive. A dotty person is more silly than sick. Thus, while Mrs Kelly's freezer full of cats might seem a sign of mental illness, she is not exactly your typical "crazy cat-lady." The most familiar example of that figure today would be Eleanor Abernathy, the cat-lady who made her first appearance in 1998 on the animated sitcom *The Simpsons* (1989–present). Eleanor lives alone in apparent squalor with endless numbers of cats, haunting the streets of Springfield, shouting gibberish at anyone who crosses her path, and often literally bombarding them with one of the many cats she carries on her person. Sylvia Plath offered a similar image of the cat-lady in her 1956 poem "Ella Mason and Her Eleven Cats." Like Eleanor, Ella lives in a "ramshackle house" (line 2) with a kitchen "paved with saucers" (20) and cats crowding every surface. Also like Eleanor, she has a disheveled appearance: she is "Rum and red-faced as a water-melon" (7), she "shamble[s]" down the street (32), and she grows "More mammoth and blowsy with every season" (34). Finally, while Eleanor shouts gibberish, Ella's voice has "Long gone to wheeze and seed" (8). The messiness and muteness of these characters obviously suggest a more extreme state of mind than we see in Mrs Kelly. Yet Capote's use of the word "dotty" introduces a way to look past the supposed craziness of *any* cat-lady and pay more attention to her relationship with the cats themselves. That is, when we stop fixating on the cat-lady's mental condition, we see more clearly the inviting and empowering potential of her queer unsociability, where her non-human companions help liberate her from the constraints of conventional gender roles, identity categories, and human-centered structures of kinship and intimacy.

Of course we cannot deny that Eleanor and Ella exhibit many of the characteristics associated with what is now called animal hoarding.

Although the figure of the cat-lady has a long history in literature and culture (no doubt longer than these three examples), the clinical diagnosis of animal hoarding was not formally named until 1997 (Herring 15), and there remains some debate about it as a disorder. The authors of the article "The Hoarding of Animals: An Update" note that animal hoarding "technically fits the criteria" for a larger diagnosis of hoarding disorder, but they also lament that the American Psychiatric Association "fell short of listing it as an official subtype" of hoarding disorder in the 2013 revision of the *Diagnostic and Statistical Manual of Mental Disorders* (DSM-5) (Frost et al.). Nevertheless, DSM-5 still identifies animal hoarding as

> the accumulation of a large number of animals and a failure to provide minimal standards of nutrition, sanitation, and veterinary care and to act on the deteriorating condition of the animals (including disease, starvation, or death) and the environment (e.g., severe overcrowding, extremely unsanitary conditions). (249)

"The Hoarding of Animals: An Update" identifies other features and demographics of animal hoarding that correspond neatly with Eleanor and Ella. Most cases involve women over fifty years old who are single, widowed, or divorced – although interestingly, over half live with "other individuals, including children and elders," instead of living alone (Frost et al.). Squalid and unsanitary living conditions are more common with animal hoarders than with hoarders who collect only inanimate objects (although animal hoarders usually hoard other objects as well). Cats are the most commonly hoarded animal. And animal hoarders "often exhibit delusional beliefs about special abilities to communicate with, understand, and care for animals," even when it is clear that they are not caring for the animals very well at all (ibid.).[3]

"The Hoarding of Animals: An Update" further explains that "individuals who hoard animals show difficulty in letting go of them, even after they are dead" (ibid.). In this respect, the "dozens" of cats in Mrs Kelly's freezer would seem to support a diagnosis of animal hoarding. Yet the lack of any other symptoms shows the inadequacy of such a diagnosis. Unlike her cat-lady sisters Eleanor and Ella, for example, Mrs Kelly does not lack (or surrender) the ability to speak or carry on a sophisticated conversation. As the narrator quickly learns, Mrs Kelly's "good and varied mind" makes her a delightful conversationalist on a variety of subjects (18–19), suggesting that she also does not suffer with dementia. Furthermore, Mrs Kelly's home is neat, "cheerful," and "cozy" (17), not at all unsanitary, messy, or cluttered. Even with a full freezer, Mrs Kelly does not exhibit what Scott Herring describes as the *"material deviance"* commonly assumed to go with hoarding: "the social construction of an aberrant relationship with your things," often exhibited through what is regarded as "extreme" and/or "inappropriate" accumulation (6). Nor does Capote's story convey or participate in what Herring calls "object panic" (13); it rehearses none of the moral or medical anxieties usually expressed around hoarding disorder and animal hoarding, such as we see in the neighborhood gossip about Ella in Plath's poem. Instead, Capote's narrator almost idealizes Mrs Kelly as pleasant, friendly, and altogether quite rational. Through these discrepancies, the story thus shifts our attention away from Mrs Kelly's mental state and prompts us to pay closer attention to the unusual nature of her relationship with her cats. Sociologist Tora Holmberg argues that "animal hoarding can be understood as a verminizing phenomenon: a process through which explanatory models, law, and sensuous governance shape and reshape human/animal relations in a particular setting" (96). Consequently, she warns that observers should try to avoid working from stereotype and preconception and instead untangle "the messiness of emplaced relationships involved in urban animal hoarding, in order to understand [specific dynamics of] love, neglect and abuse" within them (ibid.). This imperative is no less true for interpreting a work of literature. Capote refuses to pathologize Mrs Kelly as having any kind of disorder; and, when the narrator celebrates her as both harmlessly "dotty" and a "radiant" example to us all, he further prevents the readers from pathologizing her as well. As readers we must look closer at the "emplaced relationships" within Mrs Kelly's household to understand them better.

Suppressing the suggestion of mental illness allows the queerness of the figure of the cat-lady to shine out more clearly – a queerness that is tied partly to her existence outside the sexual and gender norms of mainstream society. The psychiatric research indicates that most people who become animal hoarders have experienced some kind of extreme instability or trauma as children, such as "sexual abuse or assault, parental abandonment, or death or unexpected loss of loved ones" (Frost et al.). And as Holmberg explains, a "recurring theme" in both medical and popular culture representations of cat-ladies is that they "are portrayed as lonely and childless, (hetero)sexually inactive, often middle-aged or older, and are sometimes represented as ill" (103). But the imaginary characters Eleanor and Ella suggest that a key feature in the figure of the cat-lady is also that she has experienced specifically *gendered* traumas under patriarchy and heterosexism. In *The Simpsons*, Eleanor was a successful doctor and lawyer who succumbed to the dissipating effects of alcoholism mainly due to the stress of being a woman in such a high-powered career, or, as her fan page on the *Simpsons Wiki* website explains, "burnout" ("Eleanor Abernathy"). A strong advocate for women's rights, Eleanor ultimately slipped into hoarding and addiction as a result of the difficulties of that struggle. In Plath's poem, Ella's hoarding similarly appears to be part of a refusal to define herself through conventional femininity and marriage, for she is "a spinster whose door shuts / On all but cats" (17–18), and she stares, "Blinking green-eyed and solitary / At girls who marry" (38–39). Although Ella was once "A fashionable beauty, / slaying the dandies with her emerald eyes" (15–16), she has since traded what we might call the domestication of women within marriage for a very different domestic arrangement as "hostess" (10) to her cats (note that she does not "own" them). This new role as "idol" (28) and "Sphinx-queen" (30) to her cats suggests a human–animal hybridity that oddly empowers Ella and positions her outside of normal human society, even if Plath's primitivist imagery remains somewhat problematic. The "girls who marry" confirm Ella's outsider status when they gaze back at her with the wrongful belief that her eyes, like her improperly domesticated self, look "Accurst as wildcats" (42); that is, the girls who actively *want* marriage cannot imagine another woman living in a "wild" or even semi-domesticated state except as a kind of curse. But the poem itself suggests a more radical idea: by foregrounding the girls' narrowly subjective viewpoint, the poem implies that what makes some women "accurst" is not the untetheredness of being single, but rather the constraining demands of compulsory heterosexuality.

Ultimately, whether out of failure, outright repudiation, or some combination of the two, both Eleanor and Ella have chosen to "marry" their cats instead of acceding to the heterosexist requirements of feminine decorum and restrictive gender roles. Even their voicelessness is an indictment against the traumas inflicted on women who cannot or will not conform to a heteropatriarchal system, as well as perhaps a conscious refusal to communicate in a sexist language not their own. Thus, while psychiatrists see animal hoarding strictly as a disorder, in popular culture the figure of the cat-lady also incorporates an element of feminist (or at least quasi-feminist) critique and empowerment. Along with the widespread affection for cats themselves, the cat-lady's dotty rejection of heteropatriarchal norms and expectations may therefore explain why this figure enjoys so much popularity not only in literature and television but also in internet memes, Halloween costumes, and even toys and action figures. For all her apparent craziness, the cat-lady is an attractive, even enviable figure of queer liberation. She is a "lamp in a window" because she and her cats exemplify an alternative way of living and being at the edges of human society. And in Capote's story, the slightly atypical, merely "dotty" character of Mrs Kelly helps us see that queerness in an even brighter light.

marriage plots

In addition to living outside society *physically* in the Connecticut woods, it is clear that Mrs Kelly lives outside society's heteropatriarchal *ideological* boundaries just as Eleanor and Ella do, even though we only know Mrs Kelly through her married name and her status as a widow. The story indicates this through a series of closely related tropes and allusions about marriage, romance, and romantic conflict that help propel the movement of the narrative and build a conceptual framework in which the literal difference of Mrs Kelly's attachment to her cats stands apart. The story begins with the narrator catching a ride home from a wedding with a married couple, Mr and Mrs Roberts, whom he has only just met. The Robertses have consumed "a great deal of liquor" at the wedding reception, and the car ride is terrifying: "We had driven about twenty miles, the car weaving considerably, and Mr and Mrs Roberts insulting each other in the most extraordinary language (really it was a moment out of *Who's Afraid of Virginia Woolf?*)" (16–17). As the fight escalates, Mr Roberts swipes a tree, and the narrator manages to jump out of the car when it is temporarily stopped. After he walks half an hour and finds Mrs Kelly's house, she offers him some "whiskey my husband left" (17), and he notices that she is reading another literary work about marriage that is tonally very different from Edward Albee's 1962 play: Jane Austen's *Emma* (1815). Then, when the narrator explains how he wound up stranded in the woods, she praises him for escaping the car: "I wouldn't set foot in a car with a man who had sniffed a glass of sherry. That's how I lost my husband. Married forty years, forty happy years, and I lost him because a drunken driver ran him down" (18). The actual plot of this very short story seems random and pointless: the narrator escapes a dangerous car ride and finds a delightful widow living as a hermit in the woods. But the tropes of marriage, romance, and the failures of both, as well as of alcoholism and drunken driving, are interwoven with the plot in a way that sets the stage for the strange revelation of the cats in the freezer – or rather, that *does not* set the stage for it. In the conceptual framework given to us, even the cold body of her dead husband would be easier for us to accommodate. But what we actually discover through the narrator's eyes – the frozen evidence of her profound devotion to her animal companions – is not what we were prepared to discover at all.

We can only assume that the wedding where the narrator begins is a joyous celebration, but the dysfunctional Robertses and the reference to Albee's play cast a harsh light on the myth that marriage is always emotionally fulfilling. In the play, Martha and George entertain a younger heterosexual couple in their house. Over the course of the evening George mocks the younger woman, Honey, for having a hysterical pregnancy, and the older couple fight violently about (among other things) a son they claim to have raised, but who is actually an elaborate fiction. These recurring tropes of fights fueled by alcohol and the dangers of drunken driving create the expectation that Mrs Kelly's marriage could have been equally dysfunctional. We might even wonder if the bottle of whiskey could be a sign that Mr Kelly was an abusive alcoholic like George or Mr Roberts, or if Mr Kelly was himself the drunken driver and not the victim. But in the end, we can only speculate without evidence. Furthermore, the psychological conflicts in Albee's play about the hysterical pregnancy and made-up son also prepare us to speculate about whether Mrs Kelly's frozen cats could be filling the place of a missing child, or even of her absent husband. Indeed, the story sets us up to read the cats as compensatory love-objects when Mrs Kelly tells the narrator that she was "Married forty years, forty happy years," until he was killed (18). She trails off by saying "If it wasn't for my cats ... " as she "stroke[s] an orange tabby purring in her lap" (ibid.). Her cats do provide needed company, and this passage even blatantly eroticizes them. But her hoarding of her dead cats is most likely not rooted in the trauma of her loss, for it is improbable that "dozens" of cats would have all died in the six-year span after her husband's death. If Mrs Kelly is an animal hoarder, she was evidently already one during the time of her marriage – a marriage we have no concrete reason to believe was not actually "happy" – thus weakening the notion that her cats are just replacements for her husband. Also, the narrator offers no useful evidence that Mrs Kelly's cats are surrogates for the children we can only assume she never had. In her essay "Critical Pet Studies?" Heidi Nast writes that "Pets have in many ways become more salient as love objects in post-industrial contexts where fewer children are available. Their bodies and lives have become major loci of investment in these settings [...] In very practical ways, pets are easier to love and more suitable to transient lives than are children [...] [P]ets have not become substitutes for children; they supersede them" (900). But this story once again undermines this potential line of interpretation. As a hermit without even a telephone, Mrs Kelly is largely disconnected from the "post-industrial" world. The story also makes no mention of children and presents Mrs Kelly strictly in terms of widowhood, not motherhood. And finally, she describes her cats through a very non-maternal (and now also de-eroticized, if still deeply emotional) paradigm as "old friends" (20).

The story further challenges these pathologizing readings by balancing the tropes of bad marriages, deviance, and loss with tropes of good marriages and romantic love. The initial wedding and the allusion to Austen's *Emma* allow us to imagine that Mrs Kelly's marriage of forty years actually *was* as happy as she claims, for although *Emma* follows Emma's missteps as she tries to arrange marriages for incompatible couples, the novel ends with the promise of marital bliss and order for all the major characters. Moreover, Capote's narrator explicitly validates the pleasures of Austen's romantic plots when he describes her as "a favorite writer of mine" (18); and Mrs Kelly shares this sentiment, for she laments, "Ah, Jane. My tragedy is that I've read all her books so often I have them memorized" (ibid.). We might again interpret the allusion to *Emma* as Mrs Kelly's compensatory wish for a happy ending of her own. But the story's pairing of *Emma* with contradictory tropes of bad romance (not to mention the failed and bad romances within the novel itself) ultimately produces a queerer, more unsettling effect: the tensions produced by these opposing tropes destabilize and denaturalize heterosexuality itself as an identity and a structure of relation. The connections between alcohol and the failure of marriage rupture the fantasy that heterosexual love is always natural and ideal, while the positive tropes of marriage, romance, and love hold the story back from flatly demonizing heterosexuality. Poised between fantasy and deviance, happiness and tragedy, "heterosexuality" becomes an incoherent term that loses its power to explain every opposite-sex object-choice adequately because of the radical differences between every individual couple.

Read in the contexts of both her cat-lady rejection of gender norms and this further denaturalization of sexual categories, Mrs Kelly's bond to her cats thus comes into focus as a form of attachment that can only be understood in its own terms, not as a sublimation or distortion of heteronormative desires. The story leaves us with no choice but to understand Mrs Kelly's dotty kind of object-choice *literally*: as a human attachment to cats literally *as cats*. This literalism thus positions Mrs Kelly's feline connection outside the larger binary opposition between deviance and normality by which we typically define all forms of erotic and emotional affiliation. And in this way the literalism of Mrs Kelly's bond functions as what Jay Watson, writing about William Faulkner's *Light in August* (1932), calls "noise" (138). Watson argues that Faulkner emphasizes the literalism of human blood as a way to short-circuit the symbolic conflation of blood with race. Whereas Joe Christmas's alleged embodiment of both "white" and "black" blood drives him to lash out against the racist ideologies that mandate racial segregation – and that ultimately fuel the townspeople's violent murder of Christmas – Watson argues that Christmas's literal blood, the blood that moves through and pours out of his body, refuses the symbols and ideologies projected onto it. Watson writes:

> By repeatedly bringing blood to the surface of the human body, cutting in *Light in August* mobilizes the power of literal meaning and the natural world as a rejoinder to the discursive system that puts blood in the service of racial exploitation and violence. (Ibid.)

Thus, literalism is a "noise" that serves "to disturb reigning social fictions rather than to corroborate them" (ibid.). It "disrupts [the] information system" of tropes and allusions, and it "jams the interpretive circuitry, [and] takes one aback" (137), just as the revelation of the frozen cats takes Capote's narrator aback.

As a story about an elderly woman living in almost total isolation with the bodies of her deceased love-objects close beside her in the house, "A Lamp in a Window" is more similar to Faulkner's famous story "A Rose for Emily" (1930) than to *Light in August*. By replacing the decomposed corpse of Emily's male suitor with the frozen bodies of Mrs Kelly's cats, Capote's quiet allusion to Faulkner's story thus denaturalizes heterosexuality even further. But "A Lamp in a Window" also differs from Faulkner's work – and, importantly, from many of the other pieces collected in *Music for Chameleons*, as well – because it does not directly address matters of race. It might be the case that Capote wanted to leave the implicit whiteness of his characters unexamined in this story in order to bring the subject of sexuality into greater relief. Neutralizing race also makes story's queer engagement with the politics of hospitality easier to recognize, for it might feel improbable that Mrs Kelly would interact with a stranger in exactly the same way if she perceived a racial difference between them. Nevertheless, I believe the story ultimately offers a wider reimagining of the ethics of community and civil rights that includes race as well as sexuality, for the image of the lamp in the window suggests a model of social inclusion that welcomes all individuals regardless of their identities and attachments, including racial ones. Or, to put it another way, like Joe Christmas's bleeding body, the unassimilable literalism of Mrs Kelly's frozen cats refuses to "corroborate" the "reigning social fictions" that bolster both whiteness *and* heteronormativity. The cats' literalism simply challenges the social fictions of sexuality more overtly – especially the enduring myths that heterosexual marriage is the only natural and ideal structure of the human family; that women's lives are empty without their husbands; that heterosexuality is or should be a human being's default identity; that other forms of erotic and emotional attachment implicitly deviate from heterosexuality; and even that sexuality is or should be exclusively a matter of one human being's desire for, or attachment to, another human being – that sexuality cannot also be a matter of a person's love for a non-human object.

This disruption of the discursive system is also what I understand Elaine Freedgood and Cannon Schmitt as describing in their introduction to the *representations* special issue, "Denotatively, Technically, Literally," in which they argue that to read literally "is to restore obscurity to the apparently clear, to stop language from working" (4). That is, the "noise" of literal meaning is not exactly obtuse or inaccessible, but simply refuses to let us "see through" it, as it were, to some other meaning than what we see on the surface. As Freedgood and Schmitt write, "Reading literally, denotatively, and technically seeks to make us self-conscious about and to overcome such reflexive reading, to stop us from gliding rapidly and hazily from words to concepts" (10). The reader must learn to stop and listen to literal meaning as such, resisting the urge to glide past it and make it conform to the rules of some larger, or other, discursive system. Thus, I read Mrs Kelly's love for her cats literally because it is a love that invites comparison both to other forms of love (e.g., marriage) and to certain pathological behaviors (e.g., animal hoarding), yet never adequately satisfies those comparisons. We cannot look at her attachment to her frozen cats and "glide rapidly and hazily" past it to an already reified "concept" of sexuality or identity. Moreover, Mrs Kelly's literalism has nothing to do with the closet; it can't "come out" as something that we initially failed to notice or acknowledge because it was hidden in code. She announces her love for her cats freely and clearly, and if we have trouble understanding it, that is our problem as readers, not hers or the narrator's. Literalism is what it is. And it is this conceptual stubbornness, this noisy semantic eccentricity bordering on recalcitrance, that makes literalism "dotty." Not unlike the gibberish of the cat ladies Eleanor and Ella, literalism is a silly refusal to speak in any other terms than its own.

assemblages, identities, hospitality

But what terms? Donna Haraway tries to give a useful name to the bonds between humans and companion animals by adopting the term "significant otherness." In *The Companion Species Manifesto: Dogs, People, and Significant Otherness*, Haraway argues that the "significant otherness" of companion animals is a matter of "cohabitation, coevolution, and embodied cross-species sociality" (96). Companion animals are not screens that reflect back the humanity and/or mastery of the pet "owner": "They are not a projection, nor a realization, nor the telos of anything" (103). Rather, companion species retain their own specificity and individuality as "species in obligatory, historical, protean relationship with human beings" (ibid.). Thus, Haraway meditates on the ways in which the literalism of this human–animal sociality creates a semantic noise that interferes with the symbolic framework of even her own term "significant otherness":

> My multispecies family is not about surrogacy and substitutes; we are trying to live other tropes, other metaplasms. We need other nouns and pronouns for the kin genres of companion species, just as we did (and still do) for the spectrum of genders. Except in a party invitation or a philosophical discussion, *significant other* won't do for human sexual partners; and the term performs little better to house the daily meanings of cobbled-together kin relations in dogland [or in Mrs Kelly's case, catland]. (187)

In combination with Haraway's work, then, Capote's story usefully reminds us that understanding the literalism of a particular human–animal bond is more complex than simply finding a single representative name for it. In this case, "other nouns and pronouns" risk bringing us back into the domain of symbolic categories, the very thing the noise of literalism works to disrupt. This is the insufficiency of using *Who's Afraid of Virginia Woolf?* or even *Emma* to talk about "heterosexuality" *tout court*. Categories, especially identity categories, once more set us on a course to glide "rapidly and hazily from words to concepts" and perhaps misinterpret a particular bond or relation as something other than what we actually see before us: something like, in Mrs Kelly's case, the cat-lady's "material deviance" or the lonely widow's psychological transference. Literalism is more than a simplistic denotation of a noun. Indeed, if any word in Capote's story helps us hear the noise of literalism most, it is the word "dotty," because dottiness hovers between normality and craziness and can never become one or the other without losing its meaning.

In this way, Capote's story turns away from Haraway's initial impulse to name the relationship between humans and companion animals and instead extends her impulse to recognize that relationship as an irreducible assemblage of specific components whose literalism never fully dissolves away even in their interconnections to each other. I adapt the term "assemblage" from both Jasbir Puar's and Jane Bennett's readings of Deleuze and Guattari, with a further nod to Haraway's spirited rebuttal to Deleuze and Guattari in her book *When Species Meet*. Puar uses the concept of assemblages to challenge the common understanding of queerness as an ontological totality, whether as the coherent embodiment of a single identity or as an utterly incoherent anti-identity that blows epistemologies apart. Instead, Puar's theory of assemblages rearticulates queerness as a complex confluence of social, ideological, political, and material vectors that construct and define individuals in a particular place and time. Her use of the term resists "intersectional and identitarian paradigms [...] in favor of spatial, temporal, and corporeal convergences, implosions, and rearrangements" (205). Thus, for her,

> Queerness as an assemblage [...] deprivileges a binary opposition between queer and not-queer subjects, and, instead of retaining queerness exclusively as dissenting, resistant, and alternative (all of which queerness importantly is and does), it underscores contingency and complicity with dominant formations. (Ibid.)

Whereas identity categories falsely imply a stable singularity of being, queer assemblages take shape within the multiple, constantly shifting layers where normativities (including homonormativity), the *failures* of norms, and other, competing structures of being intersect, push away each other, and overlap. Mrs Kelly's bond with her cats is not the embodiment of a ready taxonomy of desire – even zoophilia, which, at best, tells us that she somehow loves her cats more than the average pet owner. Nor is it an anti-identity whose utter unknowability sets in motion the undoing of all identities. Rather, Mrs Kelly's love for her cats takes her out of a binary opposition "between queer and not-queer subjects" by foregrounding all the converging, colliding, and competing ideologies – especially competing narratives of marriage – that make the noisy, dotty literalism of her human–animal bond stand out clearly. Indeed, there seems no better evidence that the difference of Mrs Kelly's queerness still remains partly "complicit" with, rather than wholly opposed to, "dominant formations" of sociality than the fact that her closest friend is the mailman, a civil servant who preserves her tie to society and the state while also sustaining her in her isolation with groceries, news, supplies, and maybe at one point a freezer.

The prominence of non-human objects within the queer assemblages of Mrs Kelly's life – her books, her husband's whiskey, the lamp, and of course especially her cats, the freezer, and the frozen bodies *in* the freezer – helps break down the limiting structures of binary opposition even further. As Jane Bennett argues, assemblages foreground the "shared materiality" of all their constituent parts (13): "Assemblages are ad hoc groupings of diverse elements, of vibrant materials of all sorts. Assemblages are living, throbbing confederations [...] [in which] each member and protomember has a certain vital force" (23–24). Even the most seemingly inanimate object possesses a "vital materialism" that asserts the thing's fundamental commonality with the materialism of human bodies and plays an active role in defining the assemblage as a loosely affiliated whole (13). Thus, while "the states of the shared materiality of all things is elevated," Bennett writes, "the difference between subjects and objects [is] minimized" because "all bodies become more than mere objects" (ibid.). However, the shared materiality of members within the assemblage does not *erase* the differences that still make those members distinct from each other. This is the crux of Haraway's critique of Deleuze and Guattari in *When Species Meet*. She argues that when Deleuze and Guattari offer a rhizomatic pack of wolves as one example of the assemblage, their theory ultimately tells us nothing about wolves as animals. Haraway agrees that theories of the decentralized pack and assemblage usefully challenge the notion of the "individuated Oedipal subject" (28) by gesturing toward "the rich multiplicities and topologies of a heterogeneously and nonteleologically connected world" (27). But she bristles at the way animals function for Deleuze and Guattari only at the level of the sublime, showing the philosophers' utter "disdain for the daily, the ordinary, [and] the affectional" (29). "I don't think it needs comment that we will learn nothing about actual wolves in all this," she writes (ibid.). Something crucial is lost when we celebrate the shared materiality of the assemblage but ignore the everyday, *literal* specificities of bodies and relations that link human and non-human animals and objects within the assemblage.

In Mrs Kelly's case, the way to understand this relationship between the assemblage and the individual parts of the assemblage is to recognize how the literalism of the frozen cats turns both their bodies and the bodies of their living cousins into, if you'll pardon the pun, *catalysts*. As crucial parts of the queer assemblages that define Mrs Kelly's dotty character, the cats become larger than themselves, but they never become different from themselves. The bodies are frozen, but they are hardly inert, because their literal catness, preserved in the permafrost, actively works to constitute and arrange the assemblages of sexuality, hospitality, and ethics that the narrator discovers in Mrs Kelly's home. The frozen bodies are objects that Mrs Kelly refuses to let go of physically or emotionally, and the freezer further prevents the bodies from transforming into something else through decomposition; yet the cats' noisy literalism still *acts*. Like all catalysts, the frozen bodies transform the elements around them without undergoing any substantial transformation in and of themselves, whether chemical or symbolic. They change the meanings of marriage and significant otherness by opening a space for (non-pathological) human–non-human bonds, and, in the process, their bodies hold onto their catness by refusing to become surrogates for a human spouse or some other kind of love-object.

This reformulation of sexuality not as an identity (or anti-identity), but as an assemblage that includes inanimate and non-human objects as well as human ones, thus reshapes the ethics of sexuality. Bennett writes that a philosophy that recognizes the "vital materialism" of assemblages would

> set up a kind of safety net for those humans who are [...] routinely made to suffer because they do not belong to a particular (Euro-American, bourgeois, theocentric, or other) model of personhood. The ethical aim [of this philosophy] becomes to distribute value more generously, to bodies as such. (13)

The specific literalism of each part of the assemblage and the affective bonds that link those parts create a different, less hierarchical value system in which each part is equally important to the structure and vibrancy of the larger confederation. And so, by extension, these queer assemblages remind us that our ethical aim should be not to exclude people from being members of any larger *social* assemblages – to turn them away from our doorstep and deny them their civil rights – just because they are queerly bonded to non-normative and/or non-human love objects. Mel Chen also theorizes this ethical reorientation of value in her discussion of the tenacious "animacy" – the "sentience" and "liveness" – of animals and other objects (2). She writes that while humans are situated "at the very top" of the normative hierarchies of the "relative sentience" of life and materiality (89), closer attention to "the persistent ways in which animals [and other objects] are overdetermined within human imaginaries" reveals alternative structures of interconnectivity and value (90). For example, she explains that when the language philosopher J.L. Austin used the idea of a marriage to a monkey to demonstrate "a failed pronouncement of marriage" because the monkey is not human (Chen 14), the very idea of this "monkey marriage" implicitly makes us recognize the contrary construction of "fields of [sexual and social] impropriety, including the claim or right of nonhuman animals to enjoy civil liberties" (127). In turn, acknowledging these "fields of impropriety" – as well as the animacies of humans marked as racial others, of non-human animals, and of objects typically assigned to the bottom of this hierarchy – can then enable us to challenge those inequalities and align ourselves with the claim for greater civil liberties.

This rethinking of social hierarchies, rights, and human and non-human animality is at the center of the radical arguments for the "Freedom to Marry Our Pets," posted on the Bully Bloggers website in 2009. Simultaneously sarcastic and serious, the page voices a ludic protest against the fact that legalizing gay marriage would extend rights to certain gay and lesbian couples who acquiesced to "state legitimated monogamy," yet continue to withhold those rights from queers involved in less conventional relationships. In her playful epistolary exchange with José Esteban Muñoz, Lisa Duggan asks,

> why enshrine the couple form at the top of the gay agenda, when we used to want to mix things up in the world of possible significant intimacies[?] [...] [I]f we want the state to legitimate our deepest love and intimate relationships, I'm with you on Freedom to Marry Our Pets! (Muñoz and Duggan)

While certainly not an organized political platform, the call for the Freedom to Marry Our Pets takes the bold step of imagining a world of social justice where rights were no longer bound to an individual's identity – where all forms of intimacy, even the intimacy between a human and her cats, would have equal validity in the eyes of the state. "Freedom to Marry Our Pets" gives space to the very notion of human–non-human love that Austin, according to Chen, dismisses as absurd, and that Capote *validates* in "A Lamp in a Window."

Unlike "Freedom to Marry Our Pets," however, "A Lamp in a Window" does not express a direct challenge to the *legal* dimensions of marriage and queer rights. But it does prompt its readers to recognize Mrs Kelly as the paragon of "mix[ing] things up in the world of possible significant intimacies" (Muñoz and Duggan). The disruption of symbolic and discursive heteronormativities; the breakdown of hierarchies of value attached to bodies and lives; the decentering of the human and the opening up of multiple forms of affiliation that include non-human love-objects: these are what make Mrs Kelly's love for her cats "a lamp in the window." She may live like a hermit, but Capote's portrait of her invites the reader, just as Mrs Kelly invites the narrator, to inhabit a world where no one is excluded because of the love-objects and affiliations shaping their own queer assemblages. This imagining of a world of infinite queer possibility thus resembles, in a certain way, the celebration of what Peter Coviello calls "a wider sociability" (94) in Sarah Orne Jewett's *Country of the Pointed Firs* (1896). Coviello brilliantly explains how Jewett "narrates [...] the proliferation of affect into unpredicted precincts and often unnamable combinations" (93) by describing all kinds of queer affiliation at "the margins of the marriage plot" (81). These include "the unloosing of possibilities for intimacy between women," "queer affinities between unaccompanied women and strayaway men" (much like the widow Mrs Kelly and the presumably gay, Capote-esque narrator), and "impassioned investments in the nonhuman object world" (much like Mrs Kelly's love for her cats) (101). Unlike the cheerfulness of Capote's story, however, Coviello also reads Jewett's novel as infused with feelings of loss stemming from her sense that the "homogenizing drive of modernity" (97) threatens "the loss of a social world capacious enough to include errancy, variety, the curious, and the queer" (100) – a world being increasingly squeezed into "the hard taxonomies of hetero and homo that would grow only more prominent" after the trial of Oscar Wilde in 1895 (101). Published in 1980 – at the transition point between gay liberation, the rise of antigay Reagan conservatism, and the AIDS crisis – "A Lamp in a Window" takes a similar interest in queer assemblages, but with a slightly different twist. Whereas Jewett's novel tries to capture a world of queer sociability that was disappearing with the advent of the homo/hetero binary, Capote's story tries to imagine a world of queer sociability that might be opened back up and expanded *beyond* that binary.

Again, this attempt to think beyond the homo/hetero binary is echoed by "Freedom to Marry Our Pets," but Capote's story does not express this attempt as an explicitly *political* challenge. Instead, the story enlists the power structures of hospitality as a different model for imagining social change, inclusion, and civil rights. Political discourse works mainly through opposition, but, as Derrida explains, hospitality "is opposed to what is nothing other than opposition itself, namely, hostility" (4). Derrida goes on to show that hostility is actually embedded within hospitality, for by inviting the guest into the home, the host becomes obligated to the guest, while the guest remains obligated to make the host feel "assured of his sovereignty over the space and goods he offers or opens to the other as stranger" (14). Nevertheless, these paradoxical obligations establish hospitality as a mode of welcoming instead of opposition, of inclusion instead of conflict. And this is the exchange that Capote's story imagines. The narrator (and by implication, the reader) cannot judge or challenge Mrs Kelly's dotty love for her frozen cats because she is his host and has the right to be honored in her own house. At the same time, Mrs Kelly is obliged to reciprocate the honor of refusing to judge or challenge the narrator for his own object-choices, whatever they may be. In fact, it is important that we never learn about the narrator's own peculiar love objects, for they are irrelevant to his status as guest. If we believe the narrator is Capote himself, or if we focus on his status as (apparently) single, we might assume the narrator is gay. But, while the explicit literalism of Mrs Kelly's love matters, the hypothetical nature of the narrator's love does not, because her acceptance of him ought to be unconditional. The story clearly uses hospitality to imagine much more expansive models of sexual freedom, social inclusion, and civil rights that include homosexuality, but not at the expense of other queer assemblages. As a lamp in a window, Mrs Kelly invites everyone to come into her home – and thus, as Derrida writes, into "the circles of conditionality that are family, nation, state, and citizenship" (8). And those visitors, as part of this community, should be allowed, like Mrs Kelly, to love whatever objects they prefer, whether they be male or female, human or non-human, or some other thing entirely.

This effort to rethink hospitality as a way to imagine sexual freedom and civil rights is in keeping with Capote's other writing, especially his 1967 short story "The Thanksgiving Visitor," as I have discussed elsewhere (see Bibler). But where that story considered the hostilities and obligations of hospitality as a way to stop the violence of queerphobic bullying, this story focuses on the ways in which hospitality can change the structures of community and society by stressing the importance of welcoming and including those who are typically pushed (or beaten) to the margins. In the field of actual political struggles, focusing on hospitality might seem a truly dotty strategy. But in our own time, when many local, state, and federal legislatures are seeking to curtail free speech, public protest, and the civil rights of minorities, embracing a counterdiscourse of compassion and welcoming is desperately needed, and can be remarkably empowering. For example, as conservatives seek to enshrine LGBTQ discrimination in the form of "religious freedom" laws, strategic efforts to expose how those laws violate the basic social contract of hospitality can be effective in exposing and condemning bigotry without resorting to the strictly oppositional posture of political discourse or to *ad hominem* attacks. This was essentially the strategy of the "If You're Buying, We're Selling" campaign launched in Mississippi in 2014, in which merchants publicly displayed their objections to the state's oppressive "religious freedom" law by reminding their customers that no one will be denied service, no matter whom they may be or whom they may love.[4] Turning inclusiveness into a model of moral resistance, this strategy became a successful complement to concurrent legal and political challenges to the law, and it gained international attention for doing so.

Furthermore, as Capote's story shows us, there is also a certain power in just being dotty. By foregrounding the literalism of Mrs Kelly's attachments to non-human and non-living objects *as such*, Capote's story opens the possibility of setting aside restrictive, psychological models of desire and identity and rethinking the very domain of sexuality. Although it might take us aback when we see the bodies of her beloved cats in the freezer, Mrs Kelly's open acknowledgment of her own dottiness defuses any reactive impulse to discredit her love for the cats as something more pathological. She is not a "crazy cat-lady" whose animal companions are signs of a supposedly failed human connection, and she is even less a dangerous sexual "deviant" whose erotic attachment to her cats results from some supposed failure at heterosexuality in the past. Instead, the literalism of the frozen feline bodies demands that we try to understand her dottiness for exactly what it is. Recognizing the open inclusion of frozen cats in the queer assemblage of Mrs Kelly's household can help us let go of any inhospitable expectation that her life should fit a narrow – and false – preconception of marriage, heteronormative gender roles, and even mental health. And in this way, Mrs Kelly's queerness becomes a "radiant" example to us all. Her hospitality reminds us that if we give the host her due by allowing and accepting *her* queerness, that same hospitality implicitly validates and protects *our own* queerness, whatever form that may take. As a structure of power that restricts opposition and conflict, hospitality pushes us toward a more ethical aim of, in Jane Bennett's words, "distribut[ing] value more generously, to bodies as such" (13). Thus, Mrs Kelly and her frozen cats – as dotty as they may seem – become the brightest kind of "lamp in a window," precisely because they call us to join them in a queerer, more generous ethical world of comfort, safety, and inclusion.

disclosure statement

No potential conflict of interest was reported by the author.

notes

I thank Chris Barrett, Benjy Kahan, Pallavi Rastogi, and Isiah Lavender III for their help with this essay.

1 Although the story has been collected in *Portraits and Observations: The Essays of Truman Capote*, thus marking it as a piece of non-fiction, I choose to call it a short story rather than an essay in order to focus more intently on the text itself and not on the question of whether the encounter ever actually happened – the most common, and boring, approach to most of Capote's writing.

2 I am borrowing this term "domain of sexuality" from Peter Coviello, who argues for a more expansive understanding of sexuality that extends beyond erotic "acts and practices" and encompasses all of the "habitable forms and dimensions" that "may seem extravagant, naïve, oblique, or even scarcely legible as 'sex'" (4).

3 Tora Holmberg offers a more developed critique of the research and policies devoted to identifying, addressing, and policing animal hoarding. This research, she argues, may partially obscure other dynamics about human–animal crowding in urban spaces beyond discourses of mental health and social and biological transgression.

4 For news about the program, see Serwer; Associated Press. For discussion about how anti-LGBTQ conservatives reacted to this program, see Duffy.

bibliography

American Psychiatric Association. *Diagnostic and Statistical Manual of Mental Disorders*. 5th ed. Arlington, VA: American Psychiatric Publishing, 2013. Print.

Associated Press. "'We Don't Discriminate': Mississippi Business Owners Resist Anti-gay Law." *The Guardian* 25 Apr. 2014. Web. 20 Dec. 2017. <https://www.theguardian.com/world/2014/apr/25/mississippi-business-owners-law-gay-discrimination>.

Bennett, Jane. *Vibrant Matter: A Political Ecology of Things*. Durham, NC: Duke UP, 2010. Print.

Bibler, Michael P. "How to Love Your Local Homophobe: Southern Hospitality and the Unremarkable Queerness of Truman Capote's 'The Thanksgiving Visitor.'" *MFS: Modern Fiction Studies* 58.2 (2012): 284–307. Print.

Capote, Truman. "A Lamp in a Window." *Music for Chameleons*. 1980. New York: Vintage, 1994. 16–20. Print.

Chen, Mel Y. *Animacies: Biopolitics, Racial Mattering, and Queer Affect*. Durham, NC: Duke UP, 2012. Print.

Coviello, Peter. *Tomorrow's Parties: Sex and the Untimely in Nineteenth-Century America*. New York: New York UP, 2013. Print.

Derrida, Jacques. "Hostipitality." *Angelaki: Journal of the Theoretical Humanities* 5.3 (2000): 3–18. Print.

Duffy, Nick. "AFA: Shops Who Display 'We Don't Discriminate' Stickers are Bullying Christians." *PinkNews* 28 Apr. 2014. Web. 20 Dec. 2017. <http://www.pinknews.co.uk/2014/04/28/afa-shops-who-display-we-dont-discriminate-stickers-are-bullying-christians/>.

"Eleanor Abernathy." *Simpsons Wiki*. N.d. Web. 20 Dec. 2017. <http://simpsons.wikia.com/wiki/Eleanor_Abernathy>.

Freedgood, Elaine, and Cannon Schmitt. "Denotatively, Technically, Literally." *Denotatively, Technically, Literally*. Spec. issue of *representations* 125.1 (2014): 1–14. Print.

Frost, Randy O., Gary Patronkek, Arnold Arluke, and Gail Steketee. "The Hoarding of Animals: An Update." *Psychiatric Times* 30 Apr. 2015. Web. 20 Dec. 2017. <http://www.psychiatrictimes.com/addiction/hoarding-animals-update>.

Haraway, Donna. *The Companion Species Manifesto: Dogs, People, and Significant Otherness*. 2003. *Manifestly Haraway*. Minneapolis: U of Minnesota P, 2016. 91–198. Print.

Haraway, Donna. *When Species Meet*. Minneapolis: U of Minnesota P, 2008. Print.

Herring, Scott. *The Hoarders: Material Deviance in Modern American Culture*. Chicago: U of Chicago P, 2014. Print.

Holmberg, Tora. *Urban Animals: Crowding in Zoocities*. New York: Routledge, 2015. Print.

Muñoz, José Esteban, and Lisa Duggan. "Freedom to Marry Our Pets." *Bully Bloggers*. 2009. Web. 20 Dec. 2017. <https://bullybloggers.wordpress.com/2009/07/04/freedom-to-marry-our-pets/>.

Nast, Heidi. "Critical Pet Studies?" *Antipode* 38.5 (2006): 894–906. Print.

Plath, Sylvia. "Ella Mason and Her Eleven Cats." 1956. *The Collected Poems*. New York: Harper, 2008. 53–54. Print.

Puar, Jasbir K. *Terrorist Assemblages: Homonationalism in Queer Times*. Durham, NC: Duke UP, 2007. Print.

Serwer, Adam. "Mississippi 'Religious Freedom' Law Faces Business Backlash." *MSNBC* 16 Apr. 2014. Web. 20 Dec. 2017. http://www.msnbc.com/msnbc/mississippi-religious-freedom-faces-business-backlash>.

Vanita, Ruth. *Sappho and the Virgin Mary: Same-Sex Love and the English Literary Imagination*. New York: Columbia UP, 1996. Print.

Watson, Jay. *Reading for the Body: The Recalcitrant Materiality of Southern Fiction, 1893–1985*. Athens: U of Georgia P, 2012. Print.

marcie frank

COOPER'S QUEER OBJECTS

Frisk (1991), Dennis Cooper's formally perfect novel, uses a first-person narrator named Dennis, also a writer, to explore violent sexual obsession in the age of AIDS. Dennis desires to penetrate and possess the bodies of his lovers whose contents – blood, guts, shit, and bone – are equated with their essence. Repetition is critical to *Frisk*, as it is both within and across the four other novels of the George Miles cycle that Cooper, inspired by the severely bipolar young man with whom he was obsessed, published between 1989 and 2000.[1] He characterizes Dennis's sexuality not by his selection of particular partners or pleasures from amongst a range of others not chosen, not, that is, by opportunity costs but instead by marginal costs: a calculation made visible by repetition of the costs of one more iteration of his desire exposed at all levels of production, including that of the novel itself. Applying the most radical empiricism to sex, and cataloguing the range of looks, temperatures, feels, and smells of Dennis's fascination with sexual death, Cooper provides an exhaustive inventory of what it means to have (in all senses) a sexual type.

Marginal costs turn bodies into objects in Cooper, a status the narrative extends to Dennis as well, especially as the fantasy of murderous penetration and dismemberment, initially spurred by an encounter with a magazine spread of snuff photos, is repeated. The novel returns at its end to another snuff sequence, and the reader is kept in the dark up until then about whether the scenes of sexual murder it records, as Dennis has moved from imagining to writing fiction about to reporting them, have actually occurred.

Cooper exploits this uncertainty to suggest both that it is never possible to capture the elusive object of desire and that its repeated pursuit itself objectifies, because it automates, the desiring subject. The reader is also objectified because continuing to read means seeing, most of the time, through Dennis's objectifying and self-objectifying eyes.

As this characterization suggests, Cooper is a more abstract writer than others associated with the "Blank Generation" such as Jay McInerney and Bret Easton Ellis. Although he squeezed Cooper into his materialist account of consumerism and the contemporary American novel of the 1980s and 1990s, James Annesley had to concede, "*Frisk* needs to be interpreted, not as a self-reflexive text about the representation of the body, but as a novel which actually concerns itself with the relationship between writing and materiality" (Annesley 34). The desires that Dennis relentlessly pursues fail when the limit experiences he describes in gruesome realistic detail are revealed all along to have been fantasies. *Frisk* thereby both invites a realistic reading and exposes the limits of novelistic realism, but its recursive narration is only one element of the novel's structure: it also exploits the discontinuity between fiction and autobiography.

Although the novel is ultimately about the nature of fantasy, its subject matter of violent sexual death ratchets up the stakes for distinguishing fiction from autobiography by injecting this question of literary form with such deeply disturbing content.[2] Indeed, the list of greatest influences that Cooper consistently cites – Bataille, de Sade, Rimbaud, Blanchot and Bresson – could include Proust.[3] In David Ellison's account of *A la recherche du temps perdu*, the difference between autobiography and fiction is not to be found in the degree of resemblance between the text and existential reality, for such an account does not properly understand the dialogic, shifting, indeed indexical, nature of the pronouns "I" and "you" theorized by French linguist Emile Benveniste. Nor is it only to be found in Gerard Genette's distinction, derived from his own reading of Proust, between *discours* and *récit* (Ellison 133). Rather, the semi-identity of "Marcel" and Marcel Proust signals a modal transgression: one name designates two separate literary functions, fiction and autobiography, that negotiate differing temporalities (*discours* and *récit*) as well as representational modes (symbol and allegory), to bring together the problem of the name and the problem of reading.

As Ellison points out, in Proust, "the saying of *je* when one may or may not, may and may not, mean what one says" is perverse (139); Proust, moreover, explicitly links art to homosexuality, especially in *The Fugitive* in which Marcel's sadistic obsession with Albertine provides a template of sorts for Cooper. Describing the "duty of the theoretician" to describe in Proust the "conflict between the desire of a subject to penetrate and possess the essence of the symbol and the allegorical-hypothetical narration of the failure of this desire" (ibid.), Ellison could as easily be describing *Frisk*. Cooper distils Proust's narrative mode and makes him sexually explicit – indeed, rated XXX. Cooper's work, moreover, demands to be understood *as* theory, for it melds queer content with its own narrative practice to produce a queer sort of queer theory.

In "What Does Queer Theory Teach Us About X?" Lauren Berlant and Michael Warner called into question the usefulness of considering queer theory a thing because they were interested in its capacity to capture diverse queer practices, including AIDS activism and community building (Berlant and Warner). Queer theory is certainly not one thing, but certain things in Cooper permit his narrative to cross the divide from practice to theory. As the bodies that Dennis desires become objects, Dennis himself becomes an object; but some of these objects also become media, including, perhaps, Dennis himself, and certainly the novel in which his writing appears. This essay analyses *Frisk*'s narrative recursions and repetitions as they transform some objects of desire into media. These objects-cum-media are queer not just because they reflect, direct, and/or express perverse desires, but also because they skew the status of the desiring subject. Cooper's queer objects, I propose, illustrate a queer narrative theory whose absence in current writing across fiction and autobiography by Ben Lerner, Maggie Nelson, and Sheila Heti is instructive for its disclosure of their problematic over-investment in the authenticities of subjectivity.

I fantasy's objects and narrative's recursions

The opening sequences of *Frisk* are designed to disorient. Dennis does not actually appear until page 13 in an introduction that encapsulates both the formal structure of Cooper's narration and its thematic concerns. The first short description of the magazine spread of snuff photos seems to belong to an omniscient narrator, but the next chapter, "Wild (1974)," treats a party scene from a limited third-person perspective filtered through Henry's point of view. It begins,

> "Wild." Henry *knew* it. His feelings, thoughts, etc., were the work of people around him. Men particularly. The first made a weirdly detached person out of his body and mind when he was thirteen or something. The next man corrected his predecessor's mistakes. The next changed other stuff. The last few had only tinkered because Henry was perfect, aside from some bad habits.
>
> He raised his glass, sipped, and tried to think about one particular "ex." (5)

After Henry's first anonymous sexual encounter, the focus quickly shifts to Julian, who gets Henry's phone number, and finally to Dennis, who waits the next day with Julian at his parents' house for Henry to arrive. This sequence orchestrates a rapid series of revisions. When Henry gets there, he

> remembered the party. It seemed to revolve in his mind around Julian hugging him. The guy seemed so sensitive then. He glanced over his shoulder, saw a pale, blurry face. Then he squinted and looked at the other guy, me. I was still too far away, badly lit. (20)

The expectations that the introduction of Henry has elicited are deflected when he turns out to be a minor character who does not appear in the novel again. Yet his drug-addled thoughts explicitly lay out the basic assumptions of the novel — or at least, its narrator: that people, or at least gay men, are in some fundamental way constituted by their sexual experiences and, therefore, by the fantasies of others. The perspective of the description of the snuff photos with which the novel begins comes to be reassigned to Dennis in the next chapter, "Tense 1969–1986," in which Dennis narrates his encounter with them at the age of thirteen, but not before the encounter with Henry comes to a climax of sorts with the disclosure that Henry was their model.

Henry, moreover, is given a tic that Cooper sticks with in subsequent writings: after every sexual encounter, he asks, "If you could change one thing about me, what would it be?" *The Sluts* (2004), for example, which consists almost entirely of users' entries on the weblog of an escort service site, includes comically various descriptions of "Brad" that assess his services. Though his clients all want to do him grievous bodily harm, and even kill him, "Brad" may not exist, as is implied when their reports cannot agree on his height, weight, hair color, or even if he is circumcised. Henry is here replaced by a format, as each entry culminates in the following questions: "Did he live up to his physical description?" "Did he live up to what he promised?" "Hire again?"

In *The Sluts*, the weblog comes to occupy a similar status to the one occupied by snuff photos in *Frisk*: as alternative platforms for individual and collective fantasy. As companion forms to the novel, they disclose the darkly comic nature of violent – indeed, murderous – sexual fantasy, which is linked, through repetition and perspectival play, to the act of writing itself. The comparison becomes possible because, in displaying the capacity of certain objects, the snuff photos or the escort service, to mediate fantasy, Cooper pushes them to stand in for their media: photography and the weblog, respectively. The contrast between the two companion forms then permits the specific aesthetic powers of writing to emerge.

Frisk's opening, with its vertiginous revisions in perspective, puts on display Cooper's virtuoso descriptions of the altered states of perception induced by drugs, music, and fandom in general. Although these experiences might seem to be important only for the contributions they make to, or the ways they enable, the violent sex acts that the novel describes, closer examination reveals that distorted perception and its objects are critical in and of themselves: the snuff photos are only the most outré of the other objects in the novel that elicit the fantasies that shape characters' experiences and identities. Describing these operations as precisely as possible is as central to Cooper as describing sex – even when the fantasies that the objects elicit are not sexual per se but pop-cultural or even literary. Perceptual distortions mesh these objects with their media, which links them, in turn, to Cooper's materialization of writing.

2 objects and media

Objects associated with Art Rock of the 1970s shape porn-star and occasional hustler Pierre's experiences of the sex industry, as detailed in "Spaced 1987–1989." When Warren, a porn-film director, pays him to stay on after the shoot for sex, Pierre associates the "glary sheen" in Warren's eyes, which "might or might not be imploding emotion" (82), with the "metallic-hued" contact lenses "Peter Gabriel wore to look mechanical when he was in Genesis" (ibid.). Or again, preparing to shower before he heads out on a sequence of dates, including one with Dennis, Pierre listens to Brian Eno's *Here Come the Warm Jets*. Pierre may not be able to articulate his love for Eno, but this only makes the way the record functions more fascinating:

> It has this cool, deconstructive, self-conscious pop sound typical of the '70s Art Rock Pierre loves. He doesn't know why it's fantastic exactly. If he were articulate, and not just nosy, he'd write an essay about it [...] Instead he stomps around yelling the twisted lyrics [...] Pierre covers his ears, beams, snorts wildly. (71)

Pierre's investment in 1970s Art Rock is more identity-forming and identity-sustaining than the sex acts he performs for money. Pierre's association of Warren with a Peter Gabriel robot, for example, seems to give him the wherewithal to go through with their encounter.

Pierre is also the recipient of letters from Dennis that describe his murderous pursuits. These letters do not function the way they usually do in novels: instead of delivering readers their contents, they are received as objects, placed, say, in the pocket of Pierre's jeans, to give access to scenes in which Dennis does not otherwise appear. Moreover, although Pierre does not really seem capable of writing an essay about Eno, this idea posits him, however fleetingly, as Dennis's alter-ego. Indeed, insofar as they are prompts for writing, the objects that Pierre loves function as the narrative equivalent of the snuff photos and the violent fantasies they induce Dennis to entertain and write about. Cooper makes Pierre's objects compelling for the places they take him: they're fantastic. Just like Dennis's letters.

It is significant that the only one to perceive the fictional status of the murders in a Dutch windmill that Dennis elaborately describes in letters sent separately to Pierre and Julian is Kevin, Julian's younger brother, and the George Miles character of *Frisk*. Kevin is confident that Dennis's letters report fantasy and not fact because he recognizes that rooms like the bell-shaped one at the top of the windmill, the supposed site of the murder of the Dutch junkie punk, "exist only in books" (122). His experience as a reader comes mainly from J.R.R. Tolkien's fantasy trilogy, *The Lord of the Rings*. Kevin is described reading Book One on the train to Amsterdam to meet Dennis: "This was the fifth time he'd read it. Its narrative felt like his ulterior life" (108). Immersion in the novel makes him "extremely lost, happy, etc." (109). Having acknowledged he is nervous about meeting Dennis after years of not seeing each other, Julian says to him, "You look sort of ... I don't know, carefree or something."

> Kevin sniffed. "It's this book," he said, opening, reentering it. "I'm ... half with you, half ... in here." Tolkien's language began to affect him again. " ... uh ... " He forgot the train. Actually a fraction of his eyes still registered it in a way, because he could sense his brother staring off, then watching him, then glancing around the compartment. But most of his thoughts trailed a handful of tiny humanesque men around a sinister forest. (Ibid.)

Kevin may be as inarticulate as Pierre about the objects he loves, but Cooper is not: his descriptions capture their appeal to characters whose inarticulacy Cooper also loves.[4]

Kevin reminds Dennis "of something I felt before I stopped feeling anything. Pre-desire, pre-violence" (114): perhaps the productivity of an imaginative immersion associated with but not reducible to erotic fantasy. When Dennis appears at the train station to greet them, Kevin

> feel[s] the small, fat rectangle of *The Lord of the Rings*, Book One, through the *plasticesque* fabric of the knapsack. " ... because you won't believe how I can ... " He gripped the rectangle like it was J. R. R. Tolkien's hand. (112; my emphasis)

"Plasticesque" echoes "humanesque" in an inventive and comical bleeding of a strange Tolkienesque diction into the novel that thereby enacts what it describes. Cooper's special talent is to capture the power of some objects to provide an "ulterior life": especially those of obsessive fans in whom they inspire fantasy, erotic and other, and a DIY creativity. These objects, and the fantasies they inspire, serve as analogues for Dennis's violent obsessions and his writing about them, which together provide both subject matter and form for Cooper's own. They do so both because these objects mediate fantasy and because Cooper's descriptions push them from objects to media. Silvan Tomkins observes that, "any affect may have any 'object.'"[5] When an affect saturates its object and that object is made to communicate its affect across two or more vectors, the object can then be said to become a medium.

3 recursion, revision and the limits of realism

The novel ends with Kevin orchestrating a post-sex production of another snuff photo sequence in order to exorcise the morbid hold the initial photos had on Dennis, this time with Chretien, a Dutch boy they have picked up. The final section of the novel describes the photos, thereby looping back to the description of the initial photo-spread. The crater on Henry's ass is now a "wound" made by "a glop of paint, ink, makeup, tape, cotton, tissue, and papermaché sculpted to suggest the inside of a human body" (128):

> It sits on the ass, crushed and deflated. In the central indentation there's a smaller notch maybe one-half-inch deep. It's a bit out of focus. Still, you can see the fingerprints of the person or persons who made it. (Ibid.)

Reproducing the first photo sequence revises it. The infinity signs that title both the first and last segments of the novel raise the possibility that the first sequence was no more realistic or fingerprint-free than the second. The final sequence of photos not only revises the way the first sequence was understood by the young Dennis; now revealed as the product of a happy post-coital collaboration of Dennis, Julian, Chretien and Kevin, the second sequence puts quotation marks around "snuff" for the reader as well.

Reflecting on the train after he has left Kevin with Dennis to return to his boyfriend in Paris, Julian observes, "Kevin and/or his camera would have to be God to transform a mud pie on someone's ass into the sort of nightmarish image one spends one's adult life obsessing about" (126). The order of the descriptions of the photos, including Julian's thoughts about them, the sleight of hand by which their first description is delivered (ostensibly from an omniscient perspective only slightly later revealed to be Dennis's point of view), and the tendency of intensely cathected objects, including the photos, to turn into media, together force an analogy between reading the photos and reading the novel itself that presses the reader into revising her own readings. Though we have been invited to take the erotic violence Dennis's descriptions depict as transcriptions of real events within the world of the novel, this revision produces the understanding that they refer instead to the process of writing itself.

The novel first invites and then deflects a realist reading in order to expose both the limits of realism and the aesthetic powers of fiction. The escalation of violent sexual episodes solicits and encourages fast and excited reading.

But re-reading reveals the careful placement of signs that call the realness of each episode into question. The last paragraph of the section before "Torn 1986 (1987)," for example, introduces it as the "salvageable fragments" of Dennis's "artsy murder-mystery novel" (40), thereby announcing its fictional status. Cooper exploits us by both inviting our shock and then showing it to have no basis in order to expose and deflate the seriousness with which matters of sex must be treated when they are brought into the domain of high culture, especially if they are to be distinguished from pornography. In addition to its narrative functions, then, the snuff photos both accomplish this inclusion and deliver this critique.

It is tempting to situate Cooper, especially insofar as he explores fantasy's marginal costs, within the genealogy of American post-war economic fiction that literary critic Michael Clune has developed (Clune, *American Literature*). Clune proposes that in literary works by William Burroughs and Kathy Acker, "the aesthetic disembeds the economic from social relations grounded in recognition" (149); by transforming the economic into aesthetic terms, this work discovers the market as non-social (163). For Clune, this work demands a departure from the sort of criticism that treats literature as a reflection of the social. Cooper, too, demands such a departure, but his work also proposes a modification to the articulation of social relations as grounded in recognition in the real world that Clune borrows from Hannah Arendt. In Cooper's depiction of fantasy, the objects that elicit it enable relationships (in *Frisk*) and communities (in *The Sluts*) by means of their circulation, even if those relationships and communities can be more fantasmatic or virtual than actual. Cooper's queer relationships and communities, with their possible status as fantasmatic, put pressure on the kinds of recognition required for social relations.

4 visual and verbal objects and media and the limits of realism

Others, including controversial photographer Sally Mann and aesthetic theorist Elaine Scarry, upon whose work Clune relies, have proposed accounts of the relations between photography and memory, between the visual and the verbal, that sharply contrast with Cooper. His treatment of the verbal and visual both leans on and exposes the limits of the applicability of the concept of marginal costs to the aesthetics of realism by exploiting the transformation of objects into media that repetition enables. Like Robert Mapplethorpe, Mann was subject to intense critique during the Culture Wars of the early 1990s, around the same time that Cooper produced *Frisk*. Mapplethorpe offended those who thought his gorgeous photography of gay male subjects was an abomination; Mann offended those who imagined that the evocative nude pictures of her own children constituted some form of child abuse. In her memoir, *Hold Still*, Mann responded, insisting that her photos' status as art flows from their distance from life, though this does not deny their mimetic power. She describes her children's contributions to her creative process, proposing that their collaboration maintains their dignity. She points out, further, that her children agreed to the initial display and that, where the memoir contains pictures they originally had requested not to be shown, they have now given their consent (Mann 140–41).

Mann discusses her preoccupation with "the treachery of memory" more than once in *Hold Still*:

> I tend to agree with the theory that if you want to keep a memory pristine, you must not call upon it too often, for each time it is revisited, you alter it irrevocably, remembering not the original impression left by experience but the last time you recalled it. (xii–xiii)

Although the idea that revisiting memories changes them would apply to the revisionary aspect of the photos in *Frisk*, Mann, unlike Cooper, considers this revision under the sign of loss. The passage cited above continues: "With tiny differences creeping in at each cycle, the exercise of our memory does not bring us closer to the past but draws us further away" (xiii). For Mann, moreover, just as memories, once familiarized, move us further from past realities, so "photographs actually rob us of our memory" (137). Cooper's narrative, by contrast, calls into question the differences between "closer" and "further" of both memory and photography to reality; his infinity signs, moreover, convey the photos' timeless power to both produce and exemplify creative production.

Mann relates photography to memory in order to address the status of photography as art, but her conception of memory is one in which its impression upon awareness is associated with sensory vividness, a process canonically described by Proust with his madeleine. As Proust makes clear, however, the fading of memory's vivacity under the pressure of investigation reflects its involuntary nature; voluntary memory, which may lack this capacity to surprise or produce sensory vividness, resembles perhaps more closely Mann's idea that using memories uses them up. Mann, moreover, conflates the experience of the involuntary with that of novelty, a confusion that Cooper exploits by making Dennis's early encounter with the snuff photo-spread something he did not seek out, practically an involuntary experience by which he was surprised and overwhelmed. For Proust, as for Cooper, and presumably also for Mann, who, after all, has written a memoir, narrative can recuperate the past. Yet Mann remains more suspicious than the two novelists of the proximity of narrative to fiction; for Cooper, as for Proust, the novel makes it possible for writing to recuperate the powers of memory, both voluntary and involuntary.[6]

Cooper's use of repetition as revision in his treatment of the photos also indexes a key difference between the powers of narrative and visual media. Scarry has provocatively described the different kinds of vivacity that can be achieved by the visual arts, music and the verbal arts, especially since the first two depend upon sensory perception, an element that remains entirely imaginary in the third (Scarry). She is interested in the ways in which realist narrative can depict the solidity of objects in volumetric space, an effect achieved, as she brilliantly observes, when authors issue a set of instructions for visualizing the passage of one object, often transparent, across the surface of another. This sleight of hand, as it were, tricks the mental eye into imagining as vivid and experiencing emotionally as real the events of fiction.

Scarry knows, however, that this is not the only means for producing what Roland Barthes called "the effect of the real"; nor, despite her implications, is the overlay of a moving object on the surface of another object to solicit the believability of a fictional world exclusive to realist texts, as her own example of clouds moving across the sky in Hayao Miyazaki's animated films betrays (Scarry 6–7). Cooper, by describing the effects of intensely cathected objects in a narrative that also takes the narrating self as an object, discloses a different way the verbal arts construct and probe the limits of realism.

In the first place, vivacity in Cooper relies as much on the verbal as the visual, if not more so, and not as a set of instructions. Dennis acknowledges this early on, during a conversation with Henry about his past as a model. Henry has asked Dennis to describe the original snuff spread so he can confirm which photos Dennis is referring to. Dennis does so, "very colorfully, the way I'd describe the images to myself while jerking off" (30). The verbal elements of description, here revealed as central to Dennis's arousal and satisfaction, take on a life of their own. Dennis reflects: "Spoken aloud, the descriptions seemed much more pretentious, ridiculous, amoral... something, than they'd never been in the secret uncritical world of my fantasies (ibid.). For Cooper, moreover, the vivacity of the verbal is brought out in the erotic context by its divergence from the visual. The effect is comically deflationary, something other than orgasmic, but *something* nonetheless.

Although Cooper is fascinated by the interactions between the verbal and the visual, the contrast between them is crucial in a second way as well. To use Scarry's terms, the drawing of one object across the surface of another is writ large in *Frisk*: it structures the narrative as a whole and the objects thus positioned are differentiated not only by texture but because they are in different media. When we "see the fingerprints of the person or persons who made" the snuff photos at the end of the novel, their artifactual manufactured nature immediately forces us to see differently what they had initially appeared to present. Moreover, seeing Cooper's fingerprints, the authorial hand, as it were, works less instantaneously than does seeing the fingerprints on the mud pie in the photos. The temporal retrospection of the whole, induced not just by self-referentiality but by the ending of the novel's mirroring its beginning, returns us back to the beginning even if we don't actually read the novel again. More than one medium is required to produce the narrative effects that Cooper, like Proust, uses to capture the effects of memory; both, moreover, exploit the different temporalities of each.[7] As Cooper's visceral representations of viscera suggest, he is just about as much of a literalist as Dennis is, but Cooper's literalizations pull away from Dennis's at the interface of object and medium, and as they do so, Dennis's relentless pursuit of sex to the point of death is disclosed as fantasy.

Frisk thus traces a double logic: it becomes increasingly intense, violent, and destructive in an escalation driven by the idea that (sexual) experience is the most significant site of personal authenticity; but it also circles back upon itself, recursively framing its relentless trajectory forward to comically deflate this idea by exposing its absurdly high costs. Narrative's capacity to fix objects in space and time, which makes it a precondition to fantasy, associates it, on the one hand, with novelty and disposability; narrative, that is to say, invests in the notion that using memories, or erotic fantasies for that matter, uses them up. On the other hand, its capacity for self-referential revision makes it endlessly productive. Cooper uses the photos to queer this contradiction, which is shown not to be reducible to the purely formal difference between the actions described (*discours*) and the frame of the telling (*récit*) because he treats it at both the conceptual and the formal levels. In demonstrating the productivity of erotic fantasy even when it is obsessed with death, Cooper both exploits and calls into question the idea that the self is defined by its investment in and pursuit of one particular fantasy at the expense of any other fantasy as well as any other people. By pursuing this idea to the extreme, he exposes the relations between marginal costs and the concepts that cluster around it, including those of narrative theory.

5 autofiction

In the epigraph that Cooper takes from Jean Genet, images and language are deeply bound up together: "Put all the images from language in a place of safety and make use of them, for they are in the desert, and it's in the desert we must go and look for them." In taking Genet up on his call for a search, Cooper sends Dennis off into the desert of the realist novel; he comes back with two sets of snuff photos. Cooper's novel not only stages the "I" prospectively and retrospectively according to the double temporality that Ellison, Genette and others have analyzed in Proust, but also turns the narrating subject into an object. Cooper, in other words, writes a post-Proustian autofiction in which the status of the narrating subject as object is easiest to see in the dictionary definition of autofiction.

Though now pervasive, the earliest use of "autofiction," according to the *OED*, occurred in 1976 in pages of the academic journal *New Literary History*.[8] Reflecting the significance of Proust to its genealogy, autofiction was mainly French: exponents included Nathalie Sarraute, through whose *Enfance* (1983) it intersected with the concerns of the Nouveaux Romanciers to decenter character and plot. Curiously the *OED* entry signals the ascendancy of autofiction in the Anglo-American world by citing a 2005 *N. Y. Magazine* essay about JT LeRoy: "More illuminating is the case of JT LeRoy, onetime prostitute and drug addict, whose auto-fictions have garnered legions of fans." Although LeRoy was a celebrated producer of autofiction, LeRoy himself was exposed as a wholly fictional character in 2006. His creator, Laura Albert, was successfully sued for fraud in 2007 by Antidote films. In fact, the essay cited by the dictionary was one of the earliest print sources to call into question LeRoy's existence (Beachy).

LeRoy may exemplify autofiction's popularity, but because the autobiographical subject of his fictions is itself a fiction, he also demonstrates its problematic status. The dictionary definition thus discloses, perhaps inadvertently, the status of the narrating subject of autofiction as fictional object. Encouraged to write as therapy to process the sexual and physical abuse he had suffered as a child, by the time LeRoy was fifteen, in 1999, he had published the novel *Sarah*, and the short story cycle *The Heart is Deceitful Above All Things*. A drug-addicted young hustler who had once lived on the streets, not only was LeRoy a character ripped from the pages of a Cooper novel; he also dedicated *Sarah* to Cooper (and Dr. Terrence Owens, Albert's therapist), and modeled the linked stories of *The Heart is Deceitful Above All Things* on Cooper's *Closer* (1989).

The celebrity LeRoy achieved is truly remarkable. Nominally too shy to appear at art gallery readings in San Francisco, Los Angeles and New York, LeRoy was able to involve A- and B-list celebrities, including Sharon Olds, Sandra Bernhard, Michael Musto, Carrie Fisher, Mathew Modine, Lou Reed, Nancy Sinatra, Shirley Manson and Rufus Wainwright, to preface their readings with personal anecdotes about him, thereby augmenting and cementing his celebrity status. Testimonies about LeRoy's betrayal given by Cooper and other well-known figures of the queer writing scene of the 1990s, including Ira Silverberg and Bruce Benderson, to documentary filmmaker Marjorie Sturm in interviews support the film's presentation of their involvement in a cult (Sturm). The terrible experiences he was supposed to have survived, and his astonishing transformation of them into the materials of art, garnered the recognition of the cognoscenti as well as all the trappings of celebrity. "JT LeRoy" reflected back to people what they wanted to believe about the redemptive powers of therapy – and literature.

The ironies for contemporary autofiction abound. Sturm's documentary ends with individual reflections of LeRoy's many supporters who do not agree on whether the work can stand on its own once it was revealed not to have been written by a fifteen year old and not to reflect any one real's actual experiences. Recent practitioners of autofiction, in extending the novel further into the domain of creative non-fiction, have embraced more closely the sincerity that LeRoy so spectacularly failed to deliver. Their narrators do not acquire the status of objects; instead, they cling to subjecthood, skirting the potential charges of fraud or impersonation by demanding the identification of the narrator with the author, even if they do so with an indeterminate amount of irony. But perhaps the authors of the new autofiction would do better to return to LeRoy's inspiration: Cooper. We never mistake Cooper's narrator for himself. Matthew Stadler has even proposed that critics' tendency to identify the "perversely named" Dennis with Cooper miss the crucial ways in which Cooper instead is "with the boys" Dennis desires (Stadler 238).

Ben Lerner's *10:04* (2014), for example, which examines the prelude to and aftermath of the sperm donation of a New York-based creative writing teacher to a friend with whom he afterwards has a sexual relationship, is an extended and self-conscious exploration of the pathetic fallacy especially insofar as Hurricane Sandy provides the narrative's overarching structure. The specter of natural disaster raises the possibility that the behavior of the self-absorbed narrator is organized by a force beyond his, or the author's, or indeed anyone's, control. Highly self-conscious about his own narcissism, Lerner explores the powers and limits of writing to reproduce the world, and the relationships it thereby forecloses and/or enables, but the identification of the narrator with the author, though coyly ironized, is never repudiated.

Reflecting on the unexpected success of an earlier novel, the narrator describes the foundering of his blind dates. The women that his friends have set him up with

> had invariably read his book, or had at least glanced, in advance of their meeting, at those preview pages available on Amazon. This meant that instead of the conventional conversations about work, favourite neighborhoods, and so on, he'd likely be asked what parts of the book were autobiographical. Even if those questions weren't posed explicitly, he could see, or thought he saw, his interlocutor testing whatever he said and did against the text. And because his narrator was characterized above all by his anxiety regarding the disconnect between his internal experience and his social self-presentation, the more intensely the author worried about distinguishing himself from the narrator, the more he felt he had become him. (Lerner 66)

The identification of narrator and author that the fiction demands when it references the earlier novel is here anxiously reproduced within the narrative, a feature that may disclose the fictional nature of the narrative but does so by adhering to the identification, its unavoidability now redoubled.

Maggie Nelson's *Argonauts* (2015) identifies itself as non-fiction but, as a second-person narrative, "I – you," it borrows from the venerable tradition of the novel as a found cache of letters, latterly revived by David Foster Wallace, among others. Its audacious "I" addresses a "you" throughout to put the reader into the position of Harry, her interlocutor and lover, as he undergoes transsexual transition. The story of their relationship is delivered in paragraphs among which the continuity is variable, the tone frequently cemented by interpolated passages of dialogue, the use of italics, and quotations from academic texts. The whole is accompanied by periodic sidebars: names are produced in the margins that oblige the reader to imagine the narrator's associations with and forge her own connections to what is being narrated. Nelson thus straddles the boundaries of memoir and autofiction.

Like Lerner's, Nelson's narrative fluctuates easily between personal experience and the state of the world, pivoting on inserted materials (quotations in Nelson, photos in Lerner), with section breaks, headings, and allusions to news items, both local and global, that cue spatio-temporal orientation. Both narratives are premised on the perception that the narrating self is both fragile and resilient, the only safe haven in a world with no guarantees. In both, narrative is a ballast against external threats of disaster on every scale: personal, social, economic, national, global, and ecological; it can ward off, guard against, or recuperate loss because it is grounded in an identification of its author with the narrating subject. Lerner's fiction and Nelson's memoir intersect where the old suspicion about memoir, that it was fiction, like the old fear about the realist novel, that it was fake, meets the new desire: that fiction, like memoir, be true. An unfortunate corollary seems to be that what's great about them is not just that they're real but that they're about voice.

For both Lerner and Nelson, fictionalization is one technique among others that serve not to queer narrative but to assert its truth. There is nothing queer about Lerner; Nelson's narrative, by contrast, is queer at the levels of content and citationality. But, like his, her inventive and stylish text places its faith in narrative voice, in the narrating subject rather than its objects; it promises access to the truths of the self rather than disclosing the self's status as another object. Nelson does not produce a queer narrative practice, notwithstanding all of the self-conscious referencing of queer theory.

6 the new sincerity[9]

Long ago, Lionel Trilling identified two sets of narrative strategies that organized the integration of the individual into society particularly, though not exclusively, prominent in the history of the novel: sincerity and authenticity (Trilling). Curiously enough, Trilling identified Jane Austen, notwithstanding her complex ironies, as sincere. "Jane Austen," Trilling claimed, "is concerned with teaching her readers how they are not to be if they really wish to *be*" (104). When Sheila Heti called her non-fiction novel *How Should a Person Be* (2010), she signaled the sincerity of the new autofiction.

The positive imperative mood of her title, even though syntactically it is also a question, announced its own contribution: the relation of the individual to the social world was in need of reinvention, and Heti turned to female friendship to re-narrate the portrait of the artist as a young woman. Like the autofiction of Lerner and Nelson, and unlike that of Proust and Cooper, Heti's demands, rather than both demanding and refusing, the identification of its narrating subject with the authorial self. Cooper, like Proust, executes the simultaneous demand and refusal by means of his treatments of aesthetic or aestheticized objects, including snuff photos, music, and the bodies of their lovers that approach the status of media. In Cooper, as in Proust, the aesthetic powers of narrative are accessed not just through self-referentiality or voice but also through a sustained examination of the capacities of narrative to capture its objects, and the fantasies and senses of self it can deliver in comparison with those available in another medium.

Of authenticity, Trilling observed one of its Greek roots: "*Authentes*: not only a master and a doer, but also a perpetrator, a murderer, even a self-murderer, a suicide" (131), a description singularly appropriate to Cooper, with his fascination by the proximity of sexual desire to murder. Lerner, Nelson, Heti, and other practitioners of contemporary autofiction extend novelistic narrative's realist program under the sign of sincere irony rather than authentic impossibility. For Trilling, however, ultimately the relation between sincerity and authenticity was dialectical, both as a driver of literary history and as a dynamic within some literary texts. And *Frisk*, for all its formal ingenuity and shocking subject matter, exhibits this dialectic in its penultimate treatment of memory in terms of photography.

On the train leaving Amsterdam, Julian mentally reviews his relationship to Dennis in a series of imaginary photos. He recalls when Dennis was a "teenager gazing purposefully into the holes in boys' bodies" (126).

Back in those days my compulsions were de rigueur, business as usual, part and parcel of sex, as far as Julian knew. I, he seemed like each other's reflections in every way. Smart, cold, curious, horny, drugged. So why was I "out there" and he relatively okay?... *clack, clack, clack*... He pictured the upper two-thirds of my sweaty face across a skinny white back, circa '74, then circa this afternoon... *clack, clack*... The former picture was fuzzy, unfocused. The latter picture was eerie and sad, as though I and he were the last survivors of some fringe master race. (Ibid.)

This last picture of Dennis comes from Julian's point of view. In this formal counterpart to our first view of Dennis on page 13, remediated photographically by Julian's memory, Cooper sounds an elegiac note that skirts bathos. The strange and almost sci-fi formulation "last survivors of some fringe master race" reflects that which was lost to AIDS even as it remains characteristically tongue-in-cheek. "Fringe" here does double duty: both emphasizing the inescapably neo-Nazi overtones of "master race" and recalling that some skinhead punks rejected the ideology though they took up the look. For Julian, punk, and the Dennis of "circa '74," were "no more than mildly amusing, in retrospect" (ibid.), which offers, perhaps, another distance on the novel's dehumanizing sexual violence.

Significantly, neither Julian nor Cooper is able to fix any certain value to being "the last survivors." Julian's response thus recalls the dual intersection of photography and memory with the exhaustive tally of the marginal costs of one particular fantasy, the ultimate penetration, and its recuperation by means of repetition. Together with the final description of the second snuff sequence, Cooper thereby discloses that the novel's aesthetic power to invent, preserve, and destroy comes from its descriptions of the queer objects of a world whose fictional status is acknowledged. With its inventive first-person, taut prose style, and extreme formalism, *Frisk* gives narrative form to the mobility and transitivity of objects, including bodies, in fantasy. For Wayne Koestenbaum, part of Cooper's power comes from putting sex first: "Putting sex first is a good way to achieve *concentration*, a pitch of intensified, compacted consciousness" (189). The rest, as I have argued, comes from exposing the transformation of objects into media when they communicate the affects with which they are charged to more than two people, and working with relations across more than one medium. These are the means by which Cooper can reveal the stakes for literature in the queer sexual imagination.

disclosure statement

No potential conflict of interest was reported by the author.

notes

1 See Dennis Cooper's blog for the author's account of the genesis and structure of this cycle of novels: <http://www.dennis-cooper.net/georgemiles.htm> (accessed 6 Jan. 2018).

2 Alan Sinfield explored the novel's investment in fantasy in *On Sexuality and Power* (Sinfield).

3 In his introduction to *Dennis Cooper: Writing at the Edge*, Danny Kennedy argues that Cooper should be understood in the context of European avant-garde literature and theory (Kennedy, "Introduction" 1). The collection includes two such discussions of *Frisk*: Matias Viegener, "Philosophy in the Bedroom: Pornography and Philosophy in Dennis Cooper's Writing" (Viegener), and Paul Hegarty, "The Self Contained and its Emptying in *Frisk*" (Hegarty).

4 As Wayne Koestenbaum puts it, "He exhibits a taste for inarticulateness – not for silence, but for unresolved, unformed communication" (Koestenbaum 188).

5 Silvan Tomkins cited in Sedgwick and Frank 5.

6 It is worth considering the possibility that the idea that using memories uses them up emerges historically alongside the development of photography.

7 On Proust's use of music to this effect, see Clune, *Writing Against Time*. Scarry is important to Clune's characterization of Proust's vividness.

8 Wikipedia offers a slightly different though related genealogy, crediting the term to Serge Dubrovsky, who used it in 1977 to describe his own novel, *Fils*.

9 Adam Kelly uses the term to characterize a different set of writing in "The New Sincerity" (Kelly).

bibliography

Annesley, James. *Blank Fictions: Consumerism, Culture and the Contemporary American Novel*. New York: St. Martin's, 1998. Print.

Beachy, Stephen. "Who is the Real JT Leroy? The Search for the Real Identity of a Great Literary Hustler." *New York Magazine* 7 Feb. 2005. Print.

Berlant, Lauren, and Michael Warner. "What Does Queer Theory Teach us about X?" *PMLA* 110.3 (1995): 343–49. Print.

Clune, Michael. *American Literature and the Free Market 1945–2000*. London: Cambridge UP, 2010. Print.

Clune, Michael. *Writing Against Time*. Palo Alto: Stanford UP, 2013. Print.

Ellison, David R. *The Reading of Proust*. Baltimore: Johns Hopkins UP, 1984. Print.

Hegarty, Paul. "The Self Contained and its Emptying in *Frisk*." Kennedy and Hegarty 175–86. Print.

Kelly, Adam. "The New Sincerity." *Postmodern/Postwar and After*. Ed. Jason Gladstone, Andrew Hoberek, and Daniel Worden. Iowa City: U of Iowa P, 2016. 197–208. Print.

Kennedy, Danny. "Introduction." Kennedy and Hegarty 1–12. Print.

Kennedy, Danny, and Paul Hegarty, eds. *Dennis Cooper: Writing at the Edge*. Portland, OR: Sussex Academic P, 2008. Print.

Koestenbaum, Wayne. "32 Cardinal Virtues of Dennis Cooper." Kennedy and Hegarty 187–90. Print.

Lerner, Ben. *10:04*. New York: Picador, 2014. Print.

Mann, Sally. *Hold Still: A Memoir with Photographs.* New York: Little, 2015. Print.

Scarry, Elaine. "On Vivacity: The Difference between Daydreaming and Imagining-under-Authorial Instruction." *Representations* 52 (Autumn 1995): 1–26. Print.

Sedgwick, Eve Kosofky, and Adam Frank. *Shame and its Sisters: A Silvan Tomkins Reader.* Durham, NC: Duke UP, 1995. Print.

Sinfield, Alan. *On Sexuality and Power.* New York: Columbia UP, 2004. Print.

Stadler, Matthew. "An Exacting Laxness." *Enter at Your Own Risk: The Dangerous Art of Dennis Cooper.* Ed. Leora Lev. Madison, NJ: Fairleigh Dickinson UP, 2006. 238–40. Print.

Sturm, Marjorie, dir. *The Cult of JT LeRoy.* Purplemaze, 2014. Film.

Trilling, Lionel. *Sincerity and Authenticity: The Charles Eliot Norton Lectures, 1969–1970.* Cambridge, MA: Harvard UP, 1971. Print.

Viegener, Matias. "Philosophy in the Bedroom: Pornography and Philosophy in Dennis Cooper's Writing." Kennedy and Hegarty 130–43. Print.

introduction

The genre of "lad lit" comes on the heels of postfeminism and, more specifically, the genre of "chick lit." Rosalind Gill characterizes these literary phenomena as a place where genre meets gender, with lad lit in particular featuring "heterosexual men in their late 20s or early 30s who are 'on the make' – pursuing women, alcohol and football, looking back nostalgically upon childhood and youth and forward apprehensively to commitment, marriage and children" (51). The great success of the genre, with such authors as Tony Parsons, Mike Gayle and David Nicholls achieving international recognition and popularity, is explained by Andrea Ochsner as rooted in its "mix between sophistication and obsession, on the one hand, and the high potential for reader identification, on the other" (91).

English novelist and screenwriter Nick Hornby is considered to have fathered lad lit with his publication of the memoir *Fever Pitch: A Fan's Life* in 1992, which was followed by the novels *High Fidelity* in 1995 and *About a Boy* in 1998. While Hornby has written seven novels to date, the three works he published in the 1990s encapsulate the concerns of lad lit fiction most compactly. The plot of *High Fidelity* follows Rob, a record shop owner, as he re-evaluates his love life through the vernacular of popular music after his girlfriend has left him. *About a Boy* is about the parallel stories of thirty-six-year-old Will and twelve-year-old Marcus, two strangers whose lives serendipitously intersect and who forge an unlikely friendship as they both struggle with the responsibilities of growing up.

While much critical attention has been given to lad lit in terms of its gender politics and

nikola stepić

OBJECTS OF DESIRE
masculinity, homosociality and foppishness in nick hornby's high fidelity *and* about a boy

intersections with popular culture, the relative foppishness of the characters, which represents a key clue to the genre's ideological makeup, has not been accounted for. Characterized by an overinvestment in style, the fop serves as a response to a crisis in masculinity at a particular point in time, and perennially as a register of these anxieties as they develop over time. In order to deepen the understanding of the connections between gender and genre, and the lads of lad lit as cultural constructions arising from particular, and often contradictory, ideologies of masculinity, this paper draws a line across literary history and across genres to locate in foppishness a genealogical marker for the ways in which gender, social deviancy and attitudes towards style continue to be embodied in late twentieth-century literature.

lad lit as interface of masculinity and homosociality

Ochsner dubs lad lit the "male confessional novel" and describes the genre as a postmodern *Bildungsroman*. In order to define lad lit's main preoccupations in terms of the novel of development, she borrows from Ortrud Gutjahr, who writes that the genre represents

> [...] the maturation process of a protagonist who in virulent confrontation with social norms and the natural environment aims at finding an adequate, socially accepted lifestyle that is also in compliance with his talents and desires. (Gutjahr quoted in Ochsner 92)

Unpacking lad lit through the language of the *Bildungsroman* is helpful, as the development of the protagonist in this tradition mirrors the larger genealogy of masculinity and its types, particularly in the accelerated twentieth century. As Raewyn Connell writes, gender represents "a way in which social practice is ordered" (71), as well as a practice unto itself, one that is configured according to different parameters and historical trajectories. Masculinity has been analyzed from a variety of perspectives, outlined by Connell as essentialist, positivist, normative and semiotic (68–71), and in this light, contemporary masculinity, "like femininity, is always liable to internal contradiction and historical disruption" (73).

I outline Connell's genealogy of masculinity because I believe it cuts to the core of what the genre of lad lit is preoccupied with. While lad lit indeed assumes the conventions of the *Bildungsroman*, it also crucially recognizes that it is precisely these internal contradictions of gender construction that cause what Gutjahr calls the protagonist's "virulent confrontation with social norms," as the male protagonist finds himself suspended between various models of masculinity at a moment when (hetero)masculinity is undergoing a crisis "attendant on broader cultural changes," such as the wearing away of masculine privilege and the commodification and objectification of masculinity (Shugart 281). The different models of masculinity may include at least two or more of Connell's definitions, including Freudian promises of masculine activity vs. feminine passivity (the essentialist definition), the notion that what men most commonly do makes up an observable truth of the gender (the positivist definition, or what Connell calls "common sense typology"), a reliance on given models of behavior of what manhood "should" be (the normative definition), and finally the idea of gender as an embodiment of "a set of symbolic differences" (the semiotic definition) (Connell 68–71). Finally, male development as seen in lad lit comes not only as a result of these various traditions but it also serves the purpose of signaling the artifice of masculinity, denaturalizing it and transforming it into a "marked gender" (Ochsner 92), the genre in turn becoming a rhetorical vehicle for the deconstruction of masculinity.

In lad lit, proper socialization into what Gutjahr calls "an adequate, socially accepted lifestyle" hinges on the protagonist successfully achieving a romantic relationship. In this sense, the genre follows the mandates of romantic commitment, ritualized through coupledom either in the form of marriage or what might be called a long-term relationship, and is thus comparable to the comedy of manners from *The Man of Mode* to Jane Austen, with its interest in marriage as an institution that responds to the development of civil society. An early scene in *About a Boy* juxtaposes Will to his married friends John and Christine, to whose family life Will feels a physical aversion. Hornby writes: "These two were beginning to make him feel physically ill. It was bad enough that they had children in the first place; why did they wish to compound their original error by encouraging their friends to do the same?" (8). In turn, John and Christine see Will's status as singleton as a character flaw. When he refuses their offer to be their daughter's godfather, John disappointedly states, "We've always thought you have hidden depths" (9). A strikingly similar conversation occurs in *High Fidelity* between Rob, his ex-girlfriend Jackie and her current husband. The couple's insistence on the necessity of commitment and the centrality of marriage agitates Rob:

> But they're ... *evangelical* about what they have, as if I've come up from north London to arrest them for being monogamous. I haven't, but they're right in thinking that it's a crime where I come from: it's against the law because we're all cynics and romantics, sometimes simultaneously, and marriage, with its clichés and its steady low-watt glow, is as unwelcome to us as garlic is to a vampire. (*High Fidelity* 179; emphasis in the original)

Hornby's insistence on the characters' physical reactions to marriage serves as an extreme metaphor for their inability to negotiate the mandates of romantic love. It also serves as the first discursive link between the lads of lad lit and the stock character of the fop as he emerges in the seventeenth-century comedy of manners. In her novel *The Fair Jilt* (1688), Aphra Behn characterizes the fop as immune to the transformative powers of love: he is "harden'd, incorrigible," "conducted by vast Opinionatreism, and a greater portion of Self-Love, than the rest of the Race of Man" (4). Finally, Behn opines that, "since no Metamorphosis can be made in a Fop by *Love*, you must consider him one of those that only talks of *Love*, and thinks himself that happy thing, *a Lover*" (5; emphasis in the original). Similarly, in her study on Colley Cibber, the emblematic author and performer of such fops as Sir Novelty Fashion in *Love's Last Shift* (1696) and Lord Foppington in *The Careless Husband* (1704), Elaine M. McGirr writes that "the lisping fop also defined himself both physically and aurally in opposition to his rival, here the forceful, the harmonious, round and 'swelling' lover" (33). Indeed, *The Careless Husband*'s Lord Foppington is a particularly egregious example of the fop's skepticism of love, which he not only states in typically affected fashion, "stap my Breath, if ever I lov'd One in my life," but immediately after proclaims that "a Man shou'd no more give up his Heart to a Woman, than his Sword to a Bully, They are Both as Insolent as the Devil after it" (20). The fop's and the lad's shared distrust in love (and conversely, their marginal position in relation to marital norms) puts them at odds with other characters who populate their respective milieus.

In "A Few Kind Words for the Fop," Susan Staves writes that "though fops are in various ways effeminate, they are rarely presented as homosexual," but instead lean towards asexuality (414); however, it is important to note that Restoration comedies in particular insist on homosocial relationships between men, fostering an affinity ultimately in service of marital mandates. McGirr stresses the early period of Restoration comedy as a moment when the fop and the rake share "traits of narcissism and misogyny: both see women as possessions that soon become encumbrances, both seek to please the self, largely at the expense of others" (37). Moreover, the fop's defining traits, such as narcissism and overzealous consumerism, are still seen as masculine (ibid.).

Hornby similarly stages his male characters' relationships within the bonds of homosociality in order to account for their narcissism and for their transformation in line with the directives of the *Bildungsroman*. As Will Straw notes, Rob's "successful passage into middle age is marked by his renouncing the secure refuge of his record shop and the system of values and homosocial relations which has taken form around it" (10), which in turn recalls the transformation of the foppish rake Dorimant in George Etherege's *The Man of Mode* (1676), who goes off to court Harriet in the countryside at the play's end.

About a Boy stages homosociality between Will and Marcus, the former's unlikely twelve-year-old protégé, in more complex ways. The relationship between the two comes to be organized as one of ritualized intimacy similar to the one observable in *High Fidelity*'s record shop setting. Will and Marcus bond primarily over watching television, which in itself represents a refuge from the world they are unable or unwilling to participate in. For Will, unburdened by duties related to either romance or the workplace, the daily watching of programs *Home and Away* and *Countdown* exemplifies his dubious "ability to stay afloat in the enormous ocean of time he had at his disposal; a less resourceful man, he felt, might have gone under and drowned" (*About a Boy* 71). This practice is reminiscent of what Fiona Buckland calls the "club time frame," a queer way of being that she traces in gay club culture to explain the creation of an alternative temporality with peak hours between 1 a.m. and midday, characterized by antisociality, unproductiveness, and insularity vis-à-vis the heteronormative world (43). Will's alternative lifestyle as an unemployed singleton who is not actively looking for either work or a committed relationship, and spends his daytime exclusively in leisure, is a symptom of a queer relationship with the normative world.

On the other hand, Marcus struggles both at home, due to his inability to distance himself from the value systems of (and the responsibility for) his suicidal New Age mother, and school, where he is being bullied:

> If he tried to tell Lee Hartley – the biggest and loudest and nastiest of the kids he'd met yesterday – that he didn't approve of Snoop Doggy Dogg because Snoop Doggy Dogg had a bad attitude to women, Lee Hartley would thump him, or call him something that he didn't want to be called. It wasn't so bad in Cambridge, because there were loads of kids who weren't right for school, and loads of mums who had made them that way, but in London it was different. The kids were harder and meaner and less understanding, and it seemed to him that if his mum had made him change schools just because she had found a better job, then she should at least have the decency to stop all that let's-talk-about-this stuff. (*About a Boy* 14)

The unconventional feminine influence of Marcus' single mother Fiona, which has a ripple effect on his outlook on both musical taste and gender roles, and in turn his social life, is understood in the novel as the biggest obstacle in overcoming social problems (the mysterious slur Lee Hartley calls him is ostensibly homophobic, suggesting that Marcus is read as overtly feminine by his peers). It is through his relationship with Will, which crucially also includes discussions about sex, that the influence of the mother must be banished for normative masculinity to be recuperated.

Hornby's treatment of the relationship between Will and Marcus strongly follows the three dynamics of homosociality that Helene Shugart outlines as (1) "the eradication of the feminine," (2) "strategic civility," or the understanding that the relationship serves a higher purpose and is not an end unto itself, and (3) "acknowledging the spectre of homosexuality and cordoning it off from homosociality" (287). I have discussed the first two elements but it is important to mention that the acknowledgment of the risk of a homosexual relationship between Will and Marcus is swiftly dealt with in the scene where Fiona learns of their friendship and obliquely raises this concern, and is in turn met with indignation on Will's part, and cruelty on that of Marcus', who, in order to "shut her up" (122), tells her the reason he needs Will in his life is because he needs a father. The negotiation of the feminine through strategic thinking laced with misogyny is present on both Marcus' and Will's ends, bringing to mind Eve Kosofsky Sedgwick's discussion of mentorship as a transhistorical institution of homosociality (207), and is in turn what connects Hornby's darkly humorous lad lit to the particular kind of humor associated with the fop as discussed by McGirr, who writes that "the fop is not a popinjay or jester, rather he is the libertine who thinks himself above the law, [...] who advises for his own advancement, not the greater good" (41).

Cruelty towards women as a symptom of homosociality holds a central place in both *High Fidelity* and *About a Boy*, pointing to what Benjamin A. Brabon outlines as the problem of what he dubs the "Postfeminist Male Singleton," who is "unable to fulfil his patriarchal duties due to the incapacitating social and economic topography of late capitalism [...] and thereby relinquishes his long-held position of power and independence"

(117). Brabon's theorization of the Postfeminist Male Singleton, based on "lad flicks," or the cinematic equivalents of lad lit, is in line with Gill's discussion of the figure of the "new lad," a far more ubiquitous theoretical conception of masculinity, emblematic of the 1990s, and one that represents a reactionary move against the sensitive, feminist "new man" of the 1980s. In short, Gill understands the new lad as "hedonistic, post- (if not anti) feminist" and "anti-aspirational" (36). The relative antisociality of Hornby's characters fits the bill, as both Will and Rob struggle with aspiring to either professional or romantic successes, while Marcus' youthful aspirations in the arenas of social life and romance cannot proceed without the introduction of cynicism and pessimism.

Like the fops seen in both Restoration comedies and their later iterations (the violent fop of Frances Burney's *Evelina*, the criminal dandy as the fop's adjacent type in Oscar Wilde's *The Picture of Dorian Gray*, and even the deranged titular character of Bret Easton Ellis' *American Psycho*, Patrick Bateman), the protagonists of *High Fidelity* and *About a Boy* register as socially deviant (if relatively mildly). Rob, who compulsively makes lists inspired by music magazines, outlines the top four ways he hurt his main romantic interest, Laura: cheating while she was pregnant, which in turn resulted in her getting an abortion, borrowing money from her and not repaying it, and treating her with apathy and disinterest throughout the ordeal (*High Fidelity* 92). On the other hand, a large section of *About a Boy* concerns Will's misrepresentation to a group of single mothers, whom he deceives into thinking he is a single father himself in order to obtain casual sex based on the premise that they are emotionally and sexually starved but ultimately focused primarily on their children, in turn making the inevitable break-up easier – "women who would start off by thinking that they wanted a regular fuck, and end up deciding that a quiet life was worth any number of noisy orgasms" (*About a Boy* 24).

The development of the protagonist in lad lit depends on his negotiation of two models of masculinity: the new lad, who can be traced back to what Connell calls the "biological-reductionist theory of masculinity," or the understanding of men as "hunting species" or the "bearers of natural masculinity," an outlook previously popularized in the 1970s by Lionel Tiger, who also coined the term "male bonding" (Connell 46); and the 1980s' new man, who preceded the new lad by a decade and was a concept greatly influenced by the development of feminism. Although the novels' resolutions (the creation of a chosen family and successful romantic couplings for both Will and Marcus in *About a Boy*, the committed relationship between the now-responsible, grown-up Rob and his girlfriend Laura in *High Fidelity*) certainly endorse the values of the new man, it should be noted that Hornby treats his characters' laddism with a softness that brings to mind both the magnetism and the charm of the rake, and the gentle treatment of toxic masculinity in late twentieth-century chick lit. In other words, there is a questionable redemption at play in lad lit, which points to the protagonists' shortcomings while at the same time being enamored with them. Certainly, the respective casting of two sheepish, charismatic actors well-known for their work in the romantic comedy genre, John Cusack and Hugh Grant, in the filmic adaptations of *High Fidelity* and *About a Boy*, buttresses this point, and at the same time normalizes the inherent social deviancy of the lad lit protagonists.

Hornby's lads thus occupy an uneasy position somewhere between sensitivity and brutish masculinity. As much as lad lit makes use of humor in order to register masculinity as a construct by trading in its porosity, its satire mirrors that of the eighteenth-century attitude towards the fop. As Staves writes, "Satire on fops, like most good satire, is conservative, indeed, reactionary, longing for the good old days when men were men, simple and strong, brave soldiers and hunters" (420). Thus, when Rob defends his actions by addressing the reader and challenging them to put their worst offences on paper – "who's the arsehole now?," he asks smugly (*High Fidelity* 93) – or when Will assumes the mask of the loving, engaged single father he dubs "Will the Redeemer" (*About a Boy* 20), the novels trade in humor rooted in the backwards charm of laddism. The lads' exoneration is made possible through their confessional self-reflexivity, bringing to mind McGirr's discussion on the way fops were received by their contemporary audiences: "Foppish spectacle is not decried because it was obviously ridiculous, but because even though its pious critics felt that it should be despised, the majority still found it attractive, even compelling" (41).

the vinyl closet: style, spectacle and the conspiratorial impulse

The notion of foppish spectacle as attractive and compelling is aligned with Ochsner's stance that "Identities are constructed discursively, and whether this process is achieved in a novel or in so-called 'real' life does not change the material implications [for identity formation]" (90). In this sense, the confessional, realist, self-reflexive mode of the lad lit novel, whose aim is to "draw the reader into a conspiratorial relationship with the main character" (92), shares its project with that of the Restoration comedy by producing new fantasies of normative masculinity. As Staves observes, "the specific affectations of particular fops represented current fashion [...], thus affording the audience a certain pleasure of self-recognition," even if that self-recognition registered as repentant to the more alert part of the audience (417).

Indeed, Hornby's confessional writing continually attempts to build a conspiratorial relationship with the reader no matter how dark or serious the subject matter might be – for example, he opens one of his later novels, *A Long Way Down*, with the premise that suicide can be made fully comprehensible for his imagined readership, male and female, as long as a line is delivered in the pithy, recognizable tone of the male protagonist: "Can I explain why I wanted to jump off the top of a tower block? Of course I can explain why I wanted to jump off the top of a tower block" (3).

Chick lit relies on similar attempts at relatability through spontaneity and candor, its heroines employing "self-deprecating humour that not only entertains but also leads readers to believe they are fallible – like them" (Ferriss and Young 4). Moreover, the recognizable trappings of modern life were made standard in such representative novels as Helen Fielding's *Bridget Jones's Diary* and Candace Bushnell's *Sex and the City*; notably, Fielding's novel is based on Austen's *Pride and Prejudice*, itself a novelistic apotheosis of the comedy of manners. As Ferriss and Young claim, "Invoking the 'physical stuff of everyday life', chick lit's often criticized investment in fashion and cocktails, from this perspective, is not simply superficial but a reflection of consumer culture" (4). Much like the "single girl" of chick lit, the "male singleton" of lad lit who combines traits of the new man and the new lad should be understood less as a fixed identity and more as a discourse- and identity-producing creation; indeed, Gill prefers the terms "interpretive repertoires" (38) and "'regimes of representation' or practices in advertising, fashion and photography" (39).

In tracing the male singleton's relationship to the stock character of the fop, the notion of regimes of representation becomes particularly helpful in light of Staves' insistence that the fop is "an historical phenomenon, [and] not simply a theatrical convention," and that his development over time was "significantly affected by changing English attitudes towards foppery itself and also by deeper shifts in attitudes about what ideal masculine behaviour should be" (414). Much like Cibber's fops, whose treatment and fashions altered as the spirit of the time shifted (Davies quoted in Staves 417), the intermediality of Hornby's work, evident in his novels' self-conscious, intertextual relationship with the popular culture of the "real world," points to an endless adaptability of lad lit's foppish singletons.

The very form of *High Fidelity* resembles the top lists commonly found in music publications. Early on in the novel, Rob lists his favorite songs and attempts to calculate how many times he has heard them, to which he adds:

> How could that not leave you bruised somewhere? How can that not turn you into the sort of person liable to break into little bits when your first love goes all wrong? What came first – the music or the misery? Did I listen to music because I was miserable? Or was I miserable because I listened to music? Do all those records turn you into a melancholy person? (*High Fidelity* 25)

In other words, the lad is inextricable from the culture that produces him, and vice versa, even if he struggles with this co-dependency in witty first-person narration. Similarly, *About a Boy* not only utilizes taste in music as shorthand for creating character, as evident in the Snoop Doggy Dogg paragraph included in the previous section, but also organizes the novel's dénouement around the suicide of Kurt Cobain. Moreover, the intermediality of the texts can be observed in their filmic adaptations, particularly when locating the changes these texts have undergone in the process.

High Fidelity was adapted for film in 2000 and directed by Stephen Frears, notably exchanging the novel's London setting for Chicago; as Barbara Antonucci notes, the canon of "good" and "bad" music the characters refer to was updated in order to reflect the tastes of American audiences (180). Similarly, the filmic adaptation of *About a Boy* (2002, directed by Chris and Paul Weitz) jettisons all references to Nirvana, including the entirety of the book's ending as it pertains to Cobain's suicide, and instead shifts its focus onto the centrality of hip-hop in youth culture. Whereas the culminating addition of a talent show sequence at Marcus' school where he and Will perform a rendition of "Killing Me Softly" can easily be read as a way of softening the source material for a more family-friendly effect (not to mention marketability), the film is still concerned with questions of style, as the performance references and redeems Marcus and Fiona's un-hipness. The lad lit novel in general, and Hornby's output in particular, thus become fluid texts, "'offered' [...] to other media to be prismatically *re-used*, deconstructed and reassembled, thus producing stratal configurations of [Hornby's] written discourse" (Antonucci 181; emphasis in the original). Antonucci's concept of "stratal configurations" not only brings to mind the remix culture already present in lad lit and chick lit as part of the genres' postmodern leanings, but also realigns the male singletons with fops in their capacity to transform based on the needs of particular audiences, ideologies and time periods so that the satirical "mirror" of the text remains effective.

Much like *The Man of Mode*, which opens with the rakish Dorimant getting dressed and sets up the acceptable level of interest in style as one of the play's concerns – that level, of course, represented by Sir Foppling Futter who, in true foppish fashion, cannot deduce the threshold of uncritical engagement with fashion – Hornby stages his protagonists within a wide variety of consumerist trappings. Perhaps the most emblematic statement which demonstrates Hornby's interest in style is the one Rob makes in *High Fidelity*, when he states that "what really matters is what you like, not what you *are* like" (117; emphasis in the original). Vinyl records, films, clothing and entertainment venues are at the core of the singletons' identities, and thus form a key concern in the novels, the question of how a character's development may be negotiated with his obsession with material culture, the flipside of the "adequate, socially accepted lifestyle" defined by romantic partnership. In their favoring of things over people, Will and Rob represent collectors whose hedonistic existence prevents them from performing masculinity as it is defined by the contemporary ideologies of romance; moreover, their tastes are fine-tuned to the point where they have become unshakeable. As such, they overwhelm the lads' social lives and act as barriers to normative socialization. Indeed, Rob goes as far as to state that "it's no good pretending that any relationship has a future if your record collections disagree violently, or if your favourite films wouldn't even speak to each other if they met at a party" (*High Fidelity* 117). As Straw argues vis-à-vis Eric Weisbard and Lawrence Grossberg, "To collect the obscure is to refuse the mainstream, and, therefore, to participate in an ongoing fashion in [...] 'operating at and reproducing the boundary between youth culture and the dominant culture'" (Straw 11).

It should be noted that Will's taste is much less discerning than Rob's – unlike Rob, whose ritualistic production of compilation tapes signals a degree of critical insight into contemporary commodity culture, Will is only concerned with being "cool." Indeed, the very first section of the novel written from Will's point of view assigns a point system to measure his coolness according to how much he spends on a haircut, what drugs he has tried, what restaurants he has eaten at, what types of women he has slept with, etc. (*About a Boy* 5). Later, Hornby writes a scene in which Will buys Marcus his first pair of Adidas shoes, at which Marcus originally sneers, and calls the rest of the shoppers "sheep."

> "The whole idea of this expedition, Marcus, is that you learn to become a sheep."
>
> "Is it?"
>
> "Of course. You don't want anyone to notice you. You don't want to look different. Baaaa." (*About a Boy* 112)

While Will's undertaking of Marcus as a project means removing the latter's individuality and in turn carving out a place for him in a larger community through the commodification of his body, the success of this project is based on Will's discernment of what constitutes "cool." Moreover, the passage that follows describes the experience as a physical pleasure Will feels: "So this was what people meant by natural high! [...] And, unbelievably, it had only cost him sixty quid! How much would he have to pay for an equivalent unnatural high?" (112). The exhilaration Will feels at Marcus' transformation effectively objectifies Marcus, turning the boy into another piece in Will's collection of "cool," pleasurable phenomena. Michael Camille writes that collecting is not only a pleasure-producing performance, "an active, productive and shaping stimulation of all the senses," but that:

> [The] collector's desire has often seemed to strain the limits of the heterosexual matrix [...] It is not just that the unmentionable nature of same-sex desire has often meant that the subject had to communicate the "secret" in a coded language, but the fact that this language was a system of objects. (Camille 164)

In other words, as collecting objects and treating people and experiences as commodities emerge as conditions of urban life in lad lit, they come to constitute another obstacle to the protagonists' achievement of compulsory heterosexuality; collecting is thus revealed to be deeply steeped in queer vernacular and practices. As Thomas Waugh has put it, "Collecting is erotic, whether the objects are collected for the advancement of knowledge, for the purpose of private consumption, or for social interaction [...]" (Waugh, "The Underground Collector"). Another example of a fetishistic relationship to others through the mechanics of objectification can be seen in an earlier scene where Will experiences a similar bodily jolt when Fiona is taken to the hospital after her suicide attempt: "Will only just managed to restrain himself from rubbing his hands together. He was completely absorbed in all of this – absorbed almost to the point of enjoyment" (60). The repeated, uncontrollable, crypto-erotic physical sensations brought about by shopping or even another person's attempt at suicide, which Hornby likens to drug intake, are reminiscent of the affectations of Sir Novelty Fashion/Lord Foppington in John Vanbrugh's 1696 play *The Relapse* (a continuation of Cibber's *Love's Last Shift*), in which the fop continuously exclaims "Stap my vitals": an uncontrolled, even mispronounced exclamation that reiterates his eccentricity on the page as much as on the stage. In a word, the bodily reactions betray Will's fragile mastery of style and social cues, and instead suggest that his interests are impulsive, overwhelming and betray a foppish lack of self-awareness as well as a buried queer sensibility.

On the level of both plot and genre, these protagonists represent what Shugart calls "commercial masculinity," or the "objectification and commodification of men and masculinity [...], driven by relentless consumerism and attendant patterns and practices of consumption" (281). Moreover, they participate in metrosexuality, "a concentrated manifestation of commercial masculinity" (283), representative of the men's new regimen of ornamentalization and never-ending consumerism. The male gaze that is turned back on them, both through socialization with those of similar ilk (Rob and his employees at the record shop, Marcus and Will) and by the genre of lad lit itself, is relativized through a self-proclaimed sense of mastery – of culture, women's and men's bodies, both their own and each other's. Indeed, Shugart's theorization of metrosexuality as a rhetorical device for "restabilizing commercial masculinity against normative masculinity [...] by foregrounding and organizing homosociality in strategic ways" (286–87) applies to the protagonists of lad lit, as their confessions aim to relativize their adolescent overinvestment in particular fashions, not to mention the panic-inducing specter of queerness, as a way to mask the crisis of masculinity they are experiencing in the face of growing older. The city, thus, becomes less a man's playground and more his refuge, with places of entertainment and shopping providing escapism from the productive places of work, school and even the domestic sphere.

The queer dimensions of object worship and collecting are well documented. For Wayne Koestenbaum, "collecting is a code for homosexual activity and identity" (62). While my impetus here is not to queer Hornby's characters per se, it is simultaneously important to account for the queer sensibility their practices of consumption and collecting betray, particularly with the lads' status as bachelors in mind. In his study *Bachelors of a Different Sort: Queer Aesthetics, Material Culture and the Modern Interior in Britain*, John Potvin writes that the turn-of-the-century bachelor "was identified as a decidedly queer type, one whose gender performances and sexual identity were at best dubious and at worst immoral given how he reneged on his obligation to serve wife, home and nation" (2). Furthermore, Potvin claims that

> Cross-sex relationships act as socially acceptable purveyors of longevity, progeny and stability as they develop along a narratological model that sees a so-called natural progression of things which privileges genetic offspring over cultural legacy. (9)

With this in mind, the lads' resistance to marriage or long-term relationships, as well as their orientation towards objects, place them in a queer dynamic with heteronormativity. As Koestenbaum writes, "The collector hides from romance through his records; the records are a curtain, dividing the collector from human contact" (62).

The characters' foppish obsessions with consumption and objects bring to mind not only the repertoire of the metrosexual but also his ancestor, the mid-century "consuming male," who, according to Carrie Pitzulo, would have been considered either "a predictable product of the affluent times, or a result of the era's supposed 'crisis' of masculinity" (72). Pitzulo's tome, *Bachelors and Bunnies: The Sexual Politics of* Playboy, provides opportune connecting tissue between Potvin's and Hornby's bachelors in its historicization of the development of the popular men's magazine. A collectable object unto itself, *Playboy* "promoted male-centered heterosexuality and celebrated capitalism through rampant spending" (73) in what seems a mission to legitimize the status of the bachelor from the sexually ambiguous hedonist of the nineteenth and early twentieth centuries to the virile, heterosexual spender of the fifties. In her own study on the magazine titled Playboy *and the Making of the Good Life in America*, Elizabeth Fraterrigo mirrors this idea when she writes that Hugh Hefner "affirmed the centrality of consumption" when, "in the guise of the well-heeled bachelor, he made the individual, rather than the family, its centerpiece" (5).

Without a doubt, Hornby's characters emerge as products of this contested masculinity, legitimate and/or deviant at different moments in history. On the one hand, Will is happily unemployed, living off the royalties he receives for a popular song his father had written; on the other, Rob's work at his record shop allows him to spend his day submerged in his private passion, sharing it with his two employees in a homosocial environment. Thus, the lads fit Potvin's description of the turn-of-the-century bachelor who was thought to be "similar to if not the same as the connoisseur, the eccentric and free-loving globetrotter, unbound and unrestricted, unfettered by familial obligations in his search for the exotic and the novel" (1). Indeed, the transformations that Rob and Will experience vis-à-vis the objects of their identity-producing, fetishistic interests – music for Rob, fashion and entertainment for Will – bring to mind Pitzulo's claim that, with *Playboy*, "[men's] wardrobe, manners, taste in music, and bedroom décor were placed under a microscope and evaluated with a self-consciousness traditionally reserved for women" (73). This inherently queer appropriation of traditionally feminine interests speaks to the crisis in masculinity that is at the core of lad lit, the collecting impulse bringing to mind Waugh's helpful primer on the nature of queer collecting when he writes that queer collectors of the nineteenth and twentieth centuries "all indiscriminately mixed 'regimes,' shuffled the personal creation in with the impersonal appropriated image, and all recklessly interspersed the licit and the illicit" (Waugh, *Hard to Imagine* 39). As particular kinds of collections, Rob's record shop and Will's apartment thus function as metaphorical closets. Michael Lobel notes the similarity between the closet and the collection, remarking that both "provide material or spatial models for thinking the self" (47). Material culture is a way for Hornby to narrativize his protagonists, their identities derived from the objects they surround themselves with, from vinyl to Adidas. Their formal and informal collections represent the parameters of their identity, based on what they like and not what they *are* like. The impulse to self-narrate through cultural appropriation is the organizing principle of both the collection and the closet, or as Lobel puts it, "In the collection objects are accumulated, ordered, and narrativized into a coherent whole, an activity that echoes the attempt to construct a stable unity out of the heterogeneous elements that make up the self" (ibid.).

The protagonists' ultimate transformation, or rather negotiation of the disparate identities they are suspended between for the duration of the novels, forces them out of the closet and into public life that does not serve an escapist, antisocial function but precisely a social one. Rob emerges from the confines of his record shop and private collection and begins a career as a disc jockey, putting his private skills of making top lists and mixtapes to public use, and thus making his tastes and himself vulnerable to public opinion and scrutiny. Through a convoluted sequence of events, Kurt Cobain's suicide in *About a Boy* forces the disparate group of characters to come together and coexist, their differences minimized due to the suicide's symbolic import. For both Will and Marcus, the celebrity death can be read as a public tragedy in which they are obliged to participate because it provides a sense of an imagined community both global and local, a community that simultaneously gives form to and purges the fear of Marcus' mother reattempting suicide, the "smoking gun" of the novel. Hornby writes: "Will couldn't recall ever having been caught up in this sort of messy, sprawling, chaotic web before; it was almost as if he had been given a glimpse of what it was like to be a human" (264). In his discussion on *High Fidelity*, Straw notes that "these transformations are meant to signal a (belated) coming of age, and the signs of this new maturity are a declining interest in policing other's tastes and the withering of the main character's commitment to anti-commercial, connoisseurist musical tastes" (11). The mandates of lad lit call for a transformation in the figure of the lad, and while that transformation is most easily seen in their newfound capacity for romance (a utopian promise never afforded to the fop), the romantic ideology at play suggests that with romance comes a newfound relationship with commercial masculinity – if not a sharpening of one's own stylistic sense, then a tolerance for divergent tastes and, in turn, an opportunity to re-emerge from the private into the public.

conclusion

The fop has been defined throughout this paper as an interpretive repertoire signaling an obsession with style and consumer culture, a lack of self-awareness and ability to gauge the appropriate level of consumerism, a way of self-fashioning that emerges from the most immediate cultural and material circumstances, and an aversion to change. While the specificities of the multitudes of fops that have populated both the stage and the page are far too numerous to account for in this essay, the construct remains ubiquitous in works that tackle the constructions of gender, and particularly masculinity, and is central to the notions of romance, consumerism and deviancy.

In this light, the fop is aligned with the crisis of masculinity as the latter emerges in the wake of feminist progress, and is given shape by the constructions of the new man and the new lad. As a literary genre that tackles the late twentieth-century masculine identity suspended somewhere between the two models, particularly vis-à-vis commercial masculinity, the historical and literary traditions of the fop offer precedent and a critical vocabulary for understanding lads and their lit, encapsulating both the charisma and humor of these protagonists and the antisociality and arrested development they embody. The uneasy relationship that the fop has with the heteronormative milieu to which he belongs, and particularly his homosocial tendencies, comes to define the lad lit genre. The inextricability of a cultural product from its time and place (equally true of Cibber and the fop, and of Hornby and the lad) hints at the secret of the fop's continued success under different names, guises and gendered conceptions: namely, that the cultural reproductions of quotidian concerns over subjects and objects provide a "psychological and ontological security in a vastly contingent world," while their dissemination through the various avenues of popular culture, from theater, to the novel, to music, to cinema, "[offers] a way of making sense of what we already know" (Ochsner 91) – no more, but certainly no less.

disclosure statement

No potential conflict of interest was reported by the author.

bibliography

Antonucci, Barbara. "Mediatic Metamorphoses and Postmodern Novels by Chuck Palahniuk, Bret Easton Ellis and Nick Hornby." *Literary Intermediality: The Transit of Literature through the Media Circuit.* Ed. Maddalena Pennacchia Punzi. Bern: Lang, 2007. 163–82. Print.

Behn, Aphra. *The Fair Jilt: Or, the Amours of Prince Tarquin and Miranda.* 1688. George Mason U. Web. 21 Apr. 2017.

Brabon, Benjamin A. "'Chuck Flick': A Genealogy of the Postfeminist Male Singleton." *Postfeminism and Contemporary Hollywood Cinema.* Ed. Joel Gwynne and Nadine Muller. New York: Palgrave Macmillan, 2013. 116–30. Print.

Buckland, Fiona. *Impossible Dance: Club Culture and Queer World-Making.* Middletown, CT: Wesleyan UP, 2002. Print.

Camille, Michael. "Editor's Introduction." *Art History* 24.2 (2001): 163–68. Web. N.d.

Canfield, J. Douglas, and Maja-Lisa Von Sneidern, eds. *The Broadview Anthology of Restoration and Early Eighteenth-Century Drama.* Peterborough, ON: Broadview, 2005. Print.

Cibber, Colley. *The Careless Husband.* 1705. Cambridge, 1996. ProQuest Literature Online. Chadwyck-Healey. Web. N.d.

Cibber, Colley. *Love's Last Shift; Or, The Fool in Fashion.* 1696. Canfield and Von Sneidern 710–59. Print.

Connell, Raewyn. *Masculinities.* Berkeley: U of California P, 2008. Print.

Etherege, George. *The Man of Mode; Or, Sir Fopling Flutter*. 1676. Canfield and Von Sneidern 526–89. Print.

Ferriss, Suzanne, and Mallory Young. *Chick Lit: The New Woman's Fiction*. London: Routledge, 2006. Print.

Fraterrigo, Elizabeth. Playboy *and the Making of the Good Life in Modern America*. Oxford: Oxford UP, 2011. Print.

Gill, Rosalind. "Power and the Production of Subjects: A Genealogy of the New Man and the New Lad." *The Sociological Review* 51.51 (2003): 34–56. Web. 9 Apr. 2017.

Hornby, Nick. *About a Boy*. London: Penguin, 1998. Print.

Hornby, Nick. *High Fidelity*. 1995. New York: Riverhead, 2000. Print.

Hornby, Nick. *A Long Way Down*. Waterville, ME: Wheeler, 2005. Print.

Koestenbaum, Wayne. *The Queen's Throat: Opera, Homosexuality, and the Mystery of Desire*. New York: Poseidon, 1993. Print.

Lobel, Michael. "Warhol's Closet." *Art Journal* 55.4 (1996): 42–50. Web. 6 Sept. 2017.

McGirr, Elaine M. *Partial Histories: A Reappraisal of Colley Cibber*. London: Palgrave Macmillan, 2016. Print.

Ochsner, Andrea. "Fictions of Uncertainty: The Crisis of Masculinity and Fatherhood in 'Ladlit.'" *European Journal of Cultural Studies* 15.1 (2012): 89–104. Web. 11 Apr. 2017.

Pitzulo, Carrie. *Bachelors and Bunnies: The Sexual Politics of* Playboy. Chicago: U of Chicago P, 2011. Print.

Potvin, John. *Bachelors of a Different Sort: Queer Aesthetics, Material Culture and the Modern Interior in Britain*. Manchester: Manchester UP, 2015. Print.

Sedgwick, Eve Kosofsky. *Between Men: English Literature and Male Homosexual Desire*. New York: Columbia UP, 1985. Print.

Shugart, Helene. "Managing Masculinities: The Metrosexual Moment." *Communication and Critical/Cultural Studies* 5.3 (2008): 280–300. Web. 12 Apr. 2017.

Staves, Susan. "A Few Kind Words for the Fop." *Studies in English Literature, 1500–1900* 22.3 (1982): 413–28. Web. N.d.

Straw, Will. "Sizing up Record Collections: Gender and Connoisseurship in Rock Music Culture." *Sexing the Groove: Popular Music and Gender*. Ed. Sheila Whiteley. London: Routledge, 2005. 1–16. Print.

Vanbrugh, John. *The Relapse; Or, Virtue in Danger, Being the Sequel of The Fool in Fashion*. 1696. Canfield and Von Sneidern 1480–544. Print.

Waugh, Thomas. *Hard to Imagine: Gay Male Eroticism in Photography and Film from their Beginnings to Stonewall*. New York: Columbia UP, 1996. Print.

Waugh, Thomas. "The Underground Collector." Queering the Visual, CLAGS/QCA Art Conference. New York. 2004. Lecture.

S-Town (2017) is an investigative journalism podcast that centres on John B. McLemore, a clockmaker who sets in motion Brian Reed's trip to Woodstock in Bibb County, Alabama: the place that John caustically dubs "shit town" and to which the podcast's title alludes. Brian Reed, the producer and narrator of *S-Town*, is a journalist known for his work on *This American Life*, the Chicago Public Radio program hosted by Ira Glass. *S-Town* is essentially a docudrama told in seven episodes in the form of audio files. Named "chapters" on the show's website (https://stownpodcast.org), all seven audio files were released simultaneously on 28 March 2017, available free for either downloading or streaming. This mode of delivery facilitates the phenomenon of "binge-watching" (in this case "binge-listening"), the practice of viewing/listening to multiple episodes of a program in rapid succession. Early in *S-Town*'s Chapter One, and in what will become recognizable as his pessimistic and excoriating style, John denounces the practices and habits associated with the current era of readily accessible, online content when he remarks of the young people that he had employed to dig a hole on his property: "you can't get them to do nothing because they're on their cell phone [*sic*]. And they're tweeting, and they're YouTubing, and they're always on Facebook." Despite this expressed negativity about online culture, it is John's e-mail to Brian Reed concerning a murder about which he'd overhead the young hole-diggers gossiping that sets the *S-Town* story in motion.

Following their e-mail correspondence, John and Brian are soon communicating by

monique rooney

QUEER OBJECTS AND INTERMEDIAL TIMEPIECES
reading s-town (2017)

telephone. On the basis of John's claims about two local crimes (one of which is the alleged murder), Brian travels to Woodstock but, about a year after their first in-person meeting, John takes his own life. This suicide had taken place while the program was in production, displacing Brian's investigation of the crimes John had reported. In terms of narrative sequence, the suicide is revealed to listeners at the end of Chapter Two, after John has been introduced and interviews with potential suspects for the alleged murder have been heard. It becomes clear, beyond Chapter Two, that John, not the alleged crimes, is both magnetic object of Brian's investigation and enigmatic focus of the docudrama. Within the audio-form of the podcast, John's voice becomes *S-Town*'s loquacious, though relentlessly negative, presence. It is as if, despite John's passing, it speaks immediately to listeners, communicating directly through recorded telephone calls and in-person interviews.

This voice from beyond the grave structures the series, but it does so alongside an array of other communicative and/or aesthetic forms that, ranging from novels to photographs and videos embedded online, bring John to life in uncanny ways. The noun "intermedia" has emerged as a descriptor for the intricately networked arrangements that connect film to television, social media, theatre, photography and, more recently, radio.[1] Intermedia is most commonly defined as an artform that combines or incorporates other artforms or media.[2] In *S-Town*, these forms include clocks and sundials that John either made or mended, often using methods, such as fire-gilding, belonging to a much earlier time. Other forms described, referred to or evoked include: an elaborate hedge maze that John created, unrecorded conversations, letters, a novel and other print narratives, poetry, songs, film, e-mails, Google maps, theatrical rituals, tattoos and tattooing, text messages and graffiti.[3] In part prompted by the show's references to the internet (Facebook etc.), my Google searches turned up drone images of the hedge maze and a photograph of the tattoos on John's back to suggest the way in which the podcast drama can be read through the intermedia that are the World Wide Web. Some of these images appear to have been uploaded by those involved in the production of the podcast, while others (including drone photographs of the hedge maze) seem to be the result of listener interest and, perhaps, amateur investigation of information associated with the *S-Town* story. Whether as paratactical presences (it's possible to search for an image of John online while listening to his voice) or as forms incorporated within the podcast (segments of song heard throughout), these forms animate John's presence and give rise to rhythms and ways of understanding time that work both within and against the linear and arguably death-driven structure of the series

itself. These intermedia reveal how meaning and plot can be generated across and between various artforms, including the ever-proliferating network that is the internet.

In terms of narrative timing, intermedia work in a way that is somewhat at odds with the sequential form of the podcast. Users of the internet, for example, may well have read or have heard about John's suicide, before reaching the disclosure of that event at the end of Chapter Two. Likewise, Brian Reed's description, in Chapter One's opening, of the operations of an ancient clock fits with the edited and selectively timed sequence of the podcast. The full significance of this clock can only be understood belatedly, that is only once John's story is heard, his suicide revealed and his intense attachment to clocks and sundials expanded beyond Chapter Two. The opening description of the clock poetically anticipates the ongoing narrative, especially given that the forward-movement of ticking clocks is metaphorically connected, in a later chapter, to the irreversible time of one person's (John's) life. Brian's prefatory remarks about clocks are meaningful not simply in the light of John's suicide but also in terms of the ends-driven structure of the podcast narrative itself. By this I mean the sequential or episodic movement of the podcast narrative, which arguably compels appetites for narrative resolutions of the kind that Peter Brooks theorizes in *Reading for the Plot*. The aforementioned mode of "binge-listening," with its auditors who hasten, or who are driven hastily, toward a narrative end, further augments this temporality. The narrative arc episodically discloses other details about John's life, including discussion of his homosexuality. Whether or not this narrative timing is designed to incite speculation about the connection between John's sexuality and suicidal motives, the sequential structure of the podcast incites listener desire to know what it means to time one's own death.[4]

While acknowledging the power of this narrative structure, it is this essay's contention that *S-Town*'s *queerly* intermedial form counteracts its ends-driven sequential form and its death-driven themes. The phrase "queerly intermedial" refers to the dynamic, communicative structure through which homoerotic themes, practices and meanings resonate. Such meaning is transmitted not only through the podcast's various voices but also through other aesthetic modes, practices and performances. In what follows, I explore the significance of the podcast's intermedial structure for thinking about time, selfhood and the place of the South, focusing particularly on the temporally queer legacy of the Alabama clockmaker, on non-linear aspects of the grammar organizing the spoken-drama and on temporally dissonant media incorporated within the podcast.

There is a moment in the final episode that brings together the meaning of the podcast's intermedia and their queer temporality. This moment comes after a number of carefully timed revelations about John, including the transmission of sounds and voices closely connected to the suicide and the withholding of John's frank discussions about his queer sexuality until the last two chapters. Apart from the controversy that these disclosures have generated about the ethics of the series' style of investigative journalism (see, for example, Alcorn), the timing of such revelations within the sequential narrative of the podcast produced unease in this listener, in so far as it seemed to draw attention to listener complicity in the ends-driven structure of narrative itself. However, existing in tension with this linear structure is the exchange that occurs when Brian visits, as is narrated in Chapter Seven, an old friend and client of John's named Bill (last name omitted for privacy reasons) in his suburban home, which is full of clocks. In this scene, Brian realizes that clocks are not just "appliances" but works of art and "feats of engineering" and, quoting Bill, that they "make you think." He describes:

> ... a clock with a turtle that bobs in water in a dish, and the turtle floats from hour to hour to tell the time. There's a clock with a woman pulling a sheet over the face of it, covering day with night time. There's one small clock encrusted in super detailed silver and gold and green-gold, which I've never even heard of – that's shaped like the kind of chair servants used to carry royalty.[5] (*S-Town*, Chapter Seven)

Brian discovers that John has worked on these clocks in Bill's collection and that he has made others "from scratch," often by using methods "from the period the clock was made," including the dangerous method of fire-gilding whereby mercury is used to plate clocks with gold or silver. When Brian asks Bill about the specific nature of his fascination with clocks, Bill responds that their allure goes back to childhood and to watching his grandfather fix a cheap kitchen clock in the house. "[Bill] was mesmerized by how this object suddenly became alive, ticking, hands turning. And he began crying as he told me." When pressed further about the emotional appeal of clocks, Bill responds that "it was just the measure of time had something to do with me." Brian's interpretation of Bill's words: "even as a kid the clock captured the feeling of time going by, going by, and never coming back." The next words we hear are from John who, his suicide having been revealed in Chapter Two, effectively speaks from beyond the grave:

> If someone says the name John B. McLemore 25 years in the future, you'll remember exactly who that is. (Chapter Seven)

These words of John's offset the plaintive idea that the ticking of clocks both iterate and measure the passing of time and, by implication, a living being that moves from past into present and future. Against Bill's expressly unidirectional concept of time ("the feeling of time going by, going by, and never coming back"), the not there/there of John's voice communicates, on one hand, his irretrievable pastness and, on the other, the immediate presence generated by a podcast that, beyond the moment of his death, places John's voice within earshot.

Like a spiritual medium, John's intermediary voice thus offsets the clock's mechanistic ticking, its linear time and what Elizabeth Freeman calls "chrononormative" temporality. The moment in which John speaks of his future legacy is an instance of what Freeman calls "temporal lag," an undertow that pulls against heteronormative perceptions of linear time, resisting the heroic forward march of capitalism's biopolitical subject who, in succumbing to labours and other demands of the present, is rewarded with the abstract hope of a better future (Freeman 3).[6] Alternatively, what if time returns and, in doing so, drags another time along with it? This is a question that Rebecca Schneider also asks in her study of how the theatrical arts might, in her words, "inter(in)animate" the present. Repurposing a word found in John Donne's poem "The Ecstasy," which speaks of how the souls of two lovers affectively intertwine to create the sense of a third presence, Schneider turns to contemporary re-enactments of American Civil War events in an attempt to decipher the relationship between performance and time. Schneider combines Donne's concept of "inter-inanimation" with an observation of Michel de Certeau's about what kind of time inheres in the relation between monuments on a city street and the proximate flow of everyday passers-by. Temporal inter(in)animation, as Schneider re-phrases it, is analogous to de Certeau's sense of the temporal relations flowing between static and living things. This dual framework allows her to explore the multiple and sensory ways in which historical places, landmarks and performances co-constitute one another, bringing forth alternative perceptions of time in the process (Schneider 19–31).

Schneider's "inter(in)animate" is a neologism that places together the words *animate* with *inanimate*, encapsulating her concept that an ongoing temporal stream of bodies and things might be discernible in proximity to static forms (such as monuments), momentarily syncopating the past with the present in the process. Bill's collection of clocks includes one with a woman frozen in the act of "pulling a sheet over the [clock's] face, covering day with night time." The description of this clock, a photograph of which this listener found on the internet, points to a medium that is incorporated within the podcast. It is not clear whether or not John fire-gilded this golden object. Nevertheless, the clock, and its frozen woman covering time, cryptically animates a theme that *S-Town* never fully surfaces. This theme is to do with past and present representations of the American South as a place that – once upon a time the locus of gilded-age discovery, wealth and progress, the seat of the new American Republic – is now often more likely to be viewed as less-than-civil culture, including by John himself. As noted previously, the *S* of *S-Town* denotes "shit," John's pejorative phrase for his home town. In addition, *S* implies the South, particularly the American South but potentially the Global South as well. While "S-Town/shit-town" refers to John's relentlessly caustic and negative views of life in the American South, this essay's closing emphasis on his fascination with clocks and sundials draws attention to their significance as objects that register time and place not simply in terms of an individual's preoccupations or in terms of national/regional divisions but in terms of a cosmological measure of things. It is through a consideration of the podcast's intermedial structure, which opens the listener to wider networks and spheres, that John emerges as both an intermediary who facilitates non-linear conceptions of time and as a figure who, as we shall see, engages in processes of self-objectification and historical re-enactment, confounding in the process established hierarchies and conventional subject/object relations. This essay thus queers John's role both as object of investigative reportage who animates the intermedial podcast and as an intermediary who facilitates far-reaching concepts of time.

II

S-Town's focus on a white man living in the majority white town of Woodstock, Alabama has generated controversy, not least as a result of its timing. Its early 2017 release took place in the wake of the election to Presidency of Donald Trump and his divisive appeals to so-called "forgotten" Americans, a category that summons the idea of hard-working men and women (often assumed to be white) associated with the Fordist era of flourishing industry and manufacturing that is now in decline in many areas of the United States. Moreover,

S-Town's March 2017 publication places it between two violent events directly provoked by white nationalist anger over the removal of Confederate statues in the South: one armed showdown took place in New Orleans and another erupted in Charlottesville in August 2017. While the polarized reception of *S-Town*'s representation of a suicidal white man and "redneck" culture in the American South should be understood in terms of Trump-era politics, it taps into long-standing ambivalences about the South as a region that, as Jennifer Greeson argues, since the nineteenth century has played a foundational yet anomalous role in political and legal depictions of the United States as the globally dominant, enlightened nation-state. For Leigh Anne Duck, likewise, representations of the South as an exceptionally atavistic locus of race segregation have been placed in the service of depictions that run counter to the nation-state as bastion of equality, freedom and progress. For Duck, such categorizations of the South not only disavow innovative literary treatments of and from the region but also downplay the existence of race apartheid occurring in other parts of the country.

Ongoing anxiety about regional difference, and the role that perceptions of racial division play in maintaining North/South divides, can be discerned in both positive and negative reviews of *S-Town*. On one hand, there are those who have applauded *S-Town* as "quality" drama that, in transcending the ordinary true-crime genre or even producing "Aural Literature" (see, for example, Quah; Larson; Waldman), tells a sensitive and original story. On the other hand, it has been labelled "high-art" condescension that, through the perspective of its New York narrator, recycles clichés about Southern life, emphasizes regional idiosyncrasies and focuses on instances of sexism and racism within the majority white community of Woodstock, Alabama (see, for example Bady; Hooton). Brian Reed's simultaneously wide-eyed and educative approach to his experiences and encounters in Bibb County arguably reproduces social hierarchies on the basis of regional difference. From the outset, the series' narrative tone implies a naïve listener who, like the investigator himself, will be educated in the ways and manners of an othered group. This narrative structure is openly explicated in the following recorded exchange from Chapter One in which Brian tells of how John persuades him to travel to Alabama to investigate the alleged crimes:

> BRIAN REED: It felt as if, by sheer force of will, John was opening this portal between us and calling out through it, calling from his world, a world of –
> JOHN B. McLEMORE: Proleptic decay and decrepitude.
> BRIAN REED: So eventually, I decide I'll come check it out.
> JOHN B. McLEMORE: I was just dying for them to search this house without a warrant. I think they knew it.
> BRIAN REED: That's right after this.
> John says his home town is filled with "proleptic decay and decrepitude." I'm not ashamed to say I had to look up the word "proleptic." It means using a word or phrase in anticipation of it becoming true. When I go to Alabama, I don't want to cause any trouble, proleptically speaking, so John and I discuss a plan.

The enchantment that the urbane Northerner (Brian) senses when beckoned by the provincial Southerner (John) to "his world," as if a "portal" had opened, is quickly dispelled when John describes his place as one of "proleptic decay and decrepitude" and thereby encapsulates his view of the place he dubs "shit-town." To some extent, this shuttling between utopian and dystopian imaginings of the Southern place is of a piece with the "middle-brow" manner and structure of the public-radio podcast,[7] yet this narrative style is intensified by metaphorization of regional difference, which is inflected by a history of race segregation. Magical descriptions of John's nineteenth-century plantation home and awe-inspired renderings of the giant hedge-maze (comprising sixty-four "solutions") that John had built on the property with the help of his friend Tyler Goodson are countered by recordings of "hillbilly" lingo, racist slurs and acts of violence that Brian encounters in Bibb County. This part-enchanted and part-disparaging style is echoed when Brian presents himself as the intermediary who – "not ashamed" to translate foreign words for his listeners and pre-emptively preparing for the "trouble" his own foreign presence may cause – moves between the world to which John beckons him and the conventionally more sophisticated world of his implied listeners.

"It means using a word or phrase in anticipation of it becoming true," Brian reports as he decodes the word "proleptic" as well as other sights and sounds for listeners who are positioned, like Brian himself, as naïve outsiders willing to be educated in the idiosyncratic ways of provincial folk. That "proleptic" is not a word that is readily associated with folky provincialism troubles, however, the idea that *S-Town* is simply reproducing an ethnographic or investigative account of the South. John's proleptic statement, moreover, reverses and substitutes the terms of such a generic approach, through which Brian would normally be understood as investigative subject and John as investigated object. "Proleptic decay and decrepitude" introduces not only John's "high" vocabulary and wide-ranging knowledge, which itself overturns polarized metropolitan/provincial hierarchies. It also anticipates John's role as intermediary who, displacing Brian at key moments, summons a near future in which he will have died (an event bringing the ultimate "decay"), his voice effectively haunting listeners temporally positioned beyond the moment of his suicide. If we consider again the episodic frame of the narrative, with its editorially selected and carefully timed events and disclosures, then it's worth noting that the exchange above was initially recorded when Brian first met John and therefore at a moment at which Brian cannot know that John is going to die in the near future. The word "proleptic" thus operates meta-proleptically as it gestures obliquely to a narrative structure in which the object of investigation (John) tacitly plans a suicide that will later become the focus of Brian's (the investigating subject's) investigation.

Further complicating this structure, with its reversals and substitutions of conventional subject/object positions, are John's statements and ruminations about time. Before I expand on my argument concerning John's complex role as both intermediary and queer object in the podcast, it is worth dwelling on an episode that countenances the idea of linear temporality. Following his arrival in Woodstock, Brian tracks down and interviews the young man whom John had named, on first e-mailing Brian, as the murderer of another Bibb County local. John's initial claim to Brian is about Kabrahm Burt, the son of a wealthy family and the owners of a company called K3 Lumber – a name that, particularly in the current Trump era of racially divisive rhetoric and of media attention to white supremacist views, cannot be disentangled from the legacy of the Ku Klux Klan and its history of racially targeted violence. As already mentioned, John had overhead news of the murder from local kids. They had talked of how Kabrahm had brutally kicked and beaten to death another young man, named Dylan Nichols, after the latter had lashed out at Kabrahm's friend with a knife. Brian's interview with Kabrahm is heard in Chapter Two, following which Brian repeats to John details heard from Kabrahm that match John's initial reports, except for the vital information that Dylan had not died as a result of the beating. On recounting to John the important news that Dylan is still alive, Brian also tells Kabrahm's version of events, including colourful detail about having been "hiding in the woods." It is worth reproducing the following lengthy exchange, which provides a snapshot of John's complicated view of his hometown and an example of how his contrarian views frustrate the assumptions about time underpinning Brian's investigative approach:

JOHN B. McLEMORE: I'm sitting here looking out the window at the clouds going by, just in loathing disgust at the town that I live in and the fact that I didn't pack my bags and get the hell out of here decades ago. I think it's the part about hiding in the woods that did it. That's just so classic Bibb County. I don't know how many times

I've heard that expression in my life – "hiding in the woods." I think hiding in the woods in Bibb County is like having your afternoon tea in London.

[JOHN: SIGH]

BRIAN REED: You know, there is another way John could have responded to all this news. I dare call it the normal way. That sigh he let out, rather than being one of despair, could have been one of relief – relief that a young man has not been killed, that local officials have not been bought off by a powerful, rich family, and that, in fact, law enforcement has done what appears to be a competent job responding to this incident. Shittown, at least in this case, doesn't look so, so terrible to me.

[PAUSE]

BRIAN REED: I don't know. Progress, right?

BRIAN REED: But no. I've learned that sometimes you catch John in a spell of depression, sometimes you catch him in a bout of mania, and sometimes, like today, I think, you catch him in an alchemy of the two.

JOHN B. McLEMORE: I'm trying to think of a snappy comeback to that.

BRIAN REED: Because what is it, if not progress?

JOHN B. McLEMORE: Oh my God. Oh, Lord, it's just a clusterfuck of sorrow, isn't it?

BRIAN REED: A clusterfuck of sorrow.

JOHN B. McLEMORE: It's kind of like progress as in ISIS is making progress. You know, it's that type of progress.

[LAUGHTER]

It's like ISIS, is all I can come up with. Oh, shit.

[LAUGHTER]

BRIAN REED: Damn, man. I'm over here busting my ass off. When you contacted me, you wanted to know what actually happened. So it's progress in that sense, right?

JOHN B. McLEMORE: It's progress in that sense.

Having been brought to Woodstock to investigate a murder that has, as it turns out, not "happened," Brian does not so much "catch" John as he is himself caught out by a man who himself appears to be caught in an alchemy of depression and mania. The podcast form can, in this context, be understood as itself a kind of "gilding" of various elements. Further on in the series, and in an oblique repetition of the idea that bodies might be "caught" in an "alchemy" that exceeds rational agency, there is speculation about whether manic-depression (of which John shows signs) might be a result of mercury poisoning, transmitted from John's fire-gilding methods. This alchemical undertow pulls against rhetorical structures as does John's "catching out" of Brian. The mercurial exchange overturns the subject/object position of the investigative genre through John's parodying of Brian's report about Kabrahm, which, again reversing the metropole/province hierarchy, compares "hiding in the woods" with drinking tea in London. Reversal of narrative expectation also occurs through John's nihilistic insistence that such activities do not amount to the "progress" that Brian associates with investigative reportage and thus with the Northerner's take on an ostensibly backwards South. This also challenges the idea that telling about "what happened" somehow moves us forward. Here John intermediates an alternative temporality, by which I mean that his words draw attention to temporalities and modalities that exist at odds with progressive ideas of time. Such "intermediation" is enacted when John refers to Kabrahm's beating up of Dylan as a "clusterfuck of sorrow" and when he anticipates the "decay and decrepitude" of life, momentarily short-circuiting, in the process, the ends-driven compulsion of narrative sequencing itself.

In terms of the podcast's murderous and/or suicidal plots, the exchange between Brian and John above raises the question of whether John had ever believed that Kabrahm had killed Dylan. Was this merely a ruse that John concocted to bring the *This American Life* reporter to Bibb County? My concern is not so much with these questions – which have been significant to discussions about the ethics of the series (see "Gilded Souths") – but with the idea that John functions, within the Southern-town story, as both an intermediary and as a queer object within the narrative. Throughout the recording, John's voice simultaneously anticipates that which comes to pass and speaks back to the present from beyond the grave. John's role as temporally queer intermediary gains further force from the intermedial structure of the narrative. With their variously expressive forms, performances and temporalities, these intermedia upset received ideas, particularly concerning the potential for thought and transformative communication in a (Southern) time and place perceived to be socially/politically regressive or incapable of change. John's pejorative view of Woodstock as a "shit-town" is complicated, for example, by the fact that John's coming-to-life takes place posthumously and through the "muckraking" investigative drama that is *S-Town/* "shit town." "Proleptically speaking," Brian tells us toward the end of Chapter One, he wishes to discuss a "plan" with John so that his (as he later refers to it) "Yankee" presence in the South does not cause any "trouble." Yet the "decay and decrepitude" of which John speaks, and that already precedes their plan, names the death that will follow on from Brian's first journey down to Bibb County as John's proleptic decay and decrepitude become the literal "shit" of a story world in which John's disparaging expressions cannot be separated from his abiding narrative presence.

The word "shit" arises frequently throughout the series, ranging from its implied presence in the series' title, the expletive repetition of the word throughout the drama and its use in both literal and more metaphorical contexts. "Time does not give a shit" Brian says melancholically after first learning of John's death (Chapter Three). The tattooist Bubba – co-owner with Tyler Goodson of Black Sheep Ink – refers to "shit" when he ruminates on why it is that John, having previously disparaged the practice, wanted to be tattooed in the last year or so of his life. He wrote all that "shit down," Bubba tells Brian, referring to how John documented what he heard about Bubba and Tyler's financial struggle and then paid for his many tattoos thus helping them pay bills. Here it is as if Bubba knows that the medium of writing productively supplements and redeems the "shit" that is Tyler and Bubba's everyday financial struggle. Writing here becomes a medium that, in contradistinction to speech, turns wasteful "shit" into something socially useful. In a counter-moment, and one that has attracted controversy, Brian invokes shit as the equivalent of that "decay and decrepitude" that John seems to oppose to ideas of progress and social utility. This invocation of decaying "shit" takes place when Brian openly justifies his decision to disclose and further investigate details that John has confidentially reported about the queer sexuality of closeted Bibb County men. When Brian reasons about what some have since considered an unethical disclosure (see Romano), he implicitly returns to John's words about proleptic decay and decrepitude. "[S]ince John died," Brian claims, "two other people who knew him well have told me the same information on the record," before going on to state that "John was very clear that he did not believe in God or an afterlife. So John, in his own view, is worm dirt now, unaffected by this … " (Chapter Six). The idea that the posthumous John is now the equivalent of "worm dirt" resonates further when Brian, in a flash-forward to the near future, gives details of John's burial:

> Tyler will be the one who makes John's tombstone. It'll be a couple of months before he does it. But as time goes on, no one else will get John one. John loved old cemeteries and gravestones, and it'll start nagging at Tyler that John's in the ground, decomposing into worm dirt, without so much as a marker. Tyler won't have any money for it, so he'll find an old piece of gray concrete – actually a leg off one of the benches at the table in back of his granny's house – and he'll paint it a rich brown so that it looks like a carved piece of oak … (Chapter Three)

Brian's use of the future tense ("Tyler will be … ") here chimes with John's earlier anticipation of the death that has now taken place. Both Brian's and John's flash-forwards express the flexibility of language, its capacity to account for a kind of temporal loop. Grammar can simultaneously foretell time and tell of what has already taken place. A grammatical feedback and feed-forward structure is enunciated when Brian tells of what "will" come to pass when he and Tyler take care that John has a proper burial. John's anticipatory pronouncements about "decay and decrepitude" can, in this context, be associated with the "shit-town" of the podcast title, where "shit" implies a John who is not necessarily headed toward narrative closure so much as part of a living cycle. This is communicated through the association of John's body with the decomposing earth, the "worm dirt," that will surely reproduce further life. John's body is here posthumous in the etymological sense of the word: *post* (after) and *humous* (earth/burial ground), implying a state of being human or a state of being *after* human-ness that involves a return to the earth that is already associated with human/*humous* substance. Connected to these *pre-* and *post-humous* meanings is *S-Town*'s attentiveness to John's posterity. Throughout the series, John's body, and the marks on that body, are linked with the "shit" or "worm dirt" of the place in which he dwells. This suggests that *S-Town*'s John is an intermediary for a time and a way (or substance) of being that exists both prior to and beyond this life.

The intermedial form of the podcast is integral to understanding *S-Town*'s complex engagements with being and time. What, then, are the "queer" implications of this form and what do these queer traces have to do with the way *S-Town* positions itself in relation to the American South/South? Queer theory suggests that performance is key to both the intersubjective energies and intermedial dynamics animating *S-Town*'s narrative – in particular, the performative significance of tattoos and tattooing deserves attention, as does the part played by the so-called "church" rituals involving John and Tyler Goodson and, finally, the temporally queer interaction between insignia and the clocks and sundials made by John. In addition, John's fascination with past and present media (photographs and clocks) raises questions not only about the queer relation between John, Tyler and their objects but also about the role that racial difference, particularly as it pertains to the history of slavery, plays in processes of objectification that augment their bond. As we shall see, the revelation of queer intimacy between white men takes place via a performance in which John willingly subjects himself to whipping and which problematically bears witness to a violent history of slavery and of subjugation of African Americans in the South.

III

As already noted above, reception of *S-Town* registers ongoing cultural sensitivity about the politics of telling a story about the South that focuses on the pessimism of a white man and represents the views of others who, also white and male but much less well-off than John, call attention to their own disenfranchisement. Sensitive to how he might be received, that is as a cosmopolitan liberal reporter from the North, Brian Reed reflexively considers in advance his status as a New Yorker visiting Woodstock. Not wanting to make "trouble" (Chapter One), Brian notes how in preparing to visit Woodstock he attempted to conceal the fact of his marriage to an African-American woman as well as the fact of his part Russian-Jewish heritage. Such hesitancy is vindicated when the views propounded unapologetically by the tattoo artist who "goes by the name" of Bubba are heard. Openly espousing racism and sexism, Bubba rants about how "if you got a taxpaying job, you got to take care of some nigger's wife that's in jail because she's drawing a child support check." Bubba here rehearses the wounded white masculinity and anti-liberal view stereotypically associated with demographics in the South as well as other regions of the United States, particularly in the racially divisive moment of Trump-era rhetoric. At the same time, Bubba expresses awareness of hierarchical regional divisions, including widespread assumptions that associate apartheid with the South rather than the nation at large. "You're just as racist as we are," Bubba comments to Brian (Chapter Two). Cognate with Bubba's expression of ambivalence about race – or, more precisely, his ambivalence about the idea that being a white man living in the South is necessarily equivalent to being racist – are the tattooing performances and other rituals that are disclosed from Chapter Two onwards. As we shall see, further ambivalences about race emerge through queerly intimate rituals between white men, including fascination with the objectifying legacy of slavery.

The way in which Bubba and Tyler talk about tattoos and tattooing both reproduces and destabilizes stereotypes about white men in the South. Black Sheep Ink is the tattoo parlour that Tyler Goodson and Bubba co-own and that Brian Reed visits, in Chapter Two, as part of his search for information about Kabrahm Burt. Located in a room hidden at the back of a public bar, the parlour is entered through a secret door, ensuring exclusive access to white customers. Brian's narrative draws attention to the defensive racism of the subcultural group that congregates in this parlour, as he elaborates briefly on Black Sheep Ink's close and uneasy proximity to the city of Bessemer and its majority black population. Yet Brian also evinces sympathy for Black Sheep Ink's misfits, who are described as disenfranchised white men on the "wrong side of the law," possessing little sense of purpose (Chapter Two). Within this subculture, tattoos mediate a range of dispositions and experiences. There is, for example, the "feed me" that is tattooed across the distended stomach of one Black Sheep customer and the pistons, whip and other marks tattooed on John's back. A Google search of "Black Sheep Ink" brings up photographs of other tattoos associated with the parlour and posted on the business's Facebook page, including one of a buxom woman sitting, with cowboy hat on, astride a cannon.

Bubba speaks of tattooing as a social ritual, comparing the communications that take place during the ritual with "therapy" (Chapter Two). Bubba tells Brian of how, when questioning a client about his/her motivations for choosing a particular tattoo, he learns about everyday appetites and proclivities. Tattoos and the performance of tattooing here mediate states of consciousness or ways of knowing. For example, Bubba interprets John's late-stage desire to be tattooed as a kind of death drive. Having previously heard only negativity about tattoos from John as well as constant disparagement about the "failures" that are obsessed with them, an admission that links John's corrosive pessimism directly to the situation of white men of Black Sheep Ink (rather than African Americans), Bubba wonders whether the "pistons" and other "redneck ass" tattoos that John was getting "tatted up" with were in preparation to "blow his brains out" (Chapter Two). This description of a scene in which John appears to be becoming (rather than born) a redneck has implications for thinking about white masculinity, at least as it operates within Black Sheep Ink, as a performative rather than stable or authentic category. Indeed, Bubba's conception of bodily inscription is that it is essentially a performative enactment of both living desires and death drives.

On one hand, tattoos operate in the narrative as media that posthumously enable multiple interpretations of John and of his views of life and death. On the other, tattoos and tattooing are associated with performative rituals that are themselves intermedial and that speak to queer temporalities and ways of being that are, in turn, shaped by the legacy of slavery/racial hierarchies in the South. The performative rituals, involving John and Tyler, work against Bubba's reading that John's tattooing either signifies suicidal tendencies or functions as an alibi for John's tacit support of Tyler Goodson. John and Tyler's relationship is contextualized through narrative elaborations of Tyler's troubled background, including Tyler's struggle to come to terms with the sexual abuse he suffered from his biological father. Tacit interpretations of John's support as a kind of surrogate paternity for the younger man (i.e., for Tyler, in particular) feed into the "chrononormative" temporality that Freeman theorizes, whereby John's relationship with Tyler might only be understood as supplementing a wounded or absent genealogical inheritance. By contrast, and as it is described separately by John and then Tyler, the tattooing seems to provide a temporal and spatial escape from everyday social pressures and family expectations. Narrative descriptions are of tattooed timepieces (clocks, sundials) and of marks on John's body that, the result of either ritualized whipping and/or tattooed inscriptions over the whipping marks, are pictorial markers of time. This intertwining of graphic recording of time with performative process (the process of tattooing here inscribes time and is inscribed by it) is a reminder of the grammatically and narratively loop-ish order of the series. This is the structure that includes anticipations of decay along with retrospective ruminations on John's motivations. Adding to this non-linear arrangement is the intermedial form of the tattooing rituals, which include performative re-enactments of John's research into the slave history of the South. These rituals and re-enactments simultaneously give form to a white Southerner's preoccupation with racial difference and function as a holding place for the "queer timing" that, in many ways, characterizes John and Tyler's relationship. The latter temporality and the legacy of slavery intertwine, or, to use Schneider's word, become "inter(in)animated," through the rituals that take place in John's clockshop, the full description of which is left for the final chapter.

This "queer timing" has to do not only with the evocation of temporal lag (Freeman), but also with a feed-forward mechanism at work within the narrative. The first mention of tattoos and tattooing had, for instance, occurred in the first chapter, when Brian had visited John in the clockshop on one of his earliest visits to Woodstock. Echoing the temporal discontinuities that open the series, Brian's description of John's home then was of a 200-year-old place that simultaneously holds remnants of the past and already summons the future. In Chapter One, Brian remarks of the late nineteenth-century structure of the dwelling that it looks like it "hasn't changed since the Civil War" and notes the graveyards of people who had died in the 1880s, before anticipating the narrative significance of the workshop (later known as the "clockshop") that he and John wander past when John gives him a tour of the property. "I'll later learn" says Brian that "[the workshop] is filled with disassembled clocks, as well as the rare machines and tools and chemicals he uses to restore them" (Chapter One). On a later return visit, Brian finds John in the workshop and it is there that he first meets Tyler and Tyler's brother Jake Goodson. Introducing Tyler is Brian's description of his standing "shirtless and tattooed, with an anatomical heart on his chest that says '"Misery loves company.'" The men are drinking whisky while sharpening tools and at one point Brian is taken aback when John lifts his shirt and flashes his own bare chest, on which Brian catches a "glimpse" of "what's possibly a beaker and maybe a clock-type thing" (Chapter One).

There is no reference made to the (queerly) erotic mood of this scene. Nor is there any explicit link made, at this or at any other point in the series, between the respective tattoos on Tyler's and John's chests. However, the final episode's focus on the ritual that John and Tyler had called "church" – one that had involved tattooing, nipple-piercing, cutting and whipping – tacitly speaks to the connection between anatomical heart and clock. "Church" was a ritual that had taken place in John's clockshop. It had begun with the tattooing that, Brian remarks in Chapter Seven, Tyler had recommended to John as "therapy" and as "distraction" from his "tortured thoughts," intensifying in frequency and method in the weeks leading up to John's death. When John's back and chest were all but covered with tattoos, Tyler had begun tattooing over existing tattoos until he was eventually using a needle without ink so that John could continue to experience the administered pain. "Church" transforms from therapeutic distraction to intermedial performance when Tyler shows Brian a video of one of these sessions and Brian notes that the internet is full of such "cell phone" videos in which "dudes" inflict pain on one another (Chapter Seven). John and Tyler's renaming of the location and objects associated with "church" is similarly performative. John tells Brian of how the clockshop, for example, had been renamed the "sanctuary" and the tattoo needles referred to as "reliquaries." Brian defines the latter as "a container that holds a holy relic, like the bones or ashes of a saint" (Chapter Seven). No longer simply a pen-like instrument that inscribes a surface, the tattoo needle becomes here a container of a sacred substance.

Quasi-sacred ritual is intertwined with historical re-enactment when Tyler shows Brian a photograph of John's bare back. The photograph reveals the tattooed bullwhip that had stretched across John's shoulders and neck and the dozens of red lash marks that are

> ... like in a famous historic photo that John included in a collage in the 53-page manifesto he sent me documenting society's moral decline.
>
> A photo of a slave named Gordon who was believed to have escaped from a plantation in Louisiana, and whose back was photographed and distributed by abolitionists as visual proof of the terrors of slavery.
>
> ... Tyler tells me that in order to create this tattoo, John went into the woods, handpicked a tree branch, and asked Tyler and his friends to whip him with it, and then had them tattoo over the welts. (Chapter Seven)

For Roland Barthes, a photograph records a moment that is never coming back. "What the Photograph reproduces to infinity has occurred only once: the Photograph mechanically repeats what could never be repeated existentially" (Barthes 4). Punctuating passing time, Barthes's "punctum" is a trace of the past that is also a wound (a puncture), indexing the immediate context from which it was taken. For Barthes, a

> Latin word exists to designate this wound, this prick, this mark made by a pointed instrument: the word suits me all the better in that it also refers to the notion of punctuation, and because the photographs I am speaking of are in effect punctuated, sometimes even speckled with these sensitive points; precisely, these marks, these wounds are so many *points*. (Barthes 26–27; emphasis in the original)

The scene described above implies a fetishization of the photographic wound, as the punctured and punctuating marks that John has observed in the photo of the slave are performatively repeated on his own body. The use of the tattooing needle intensifies the marks left by that which Barthes calls a "pointed instrument" (26), which is the camera lens that punctuates time. In the context of John and Tyler's ritualized "church," such temporal marks and corporeal wounding should be distinguished from the "accident" and non-agential "break" through which Barthes locates the punctum, through which he separates the marks on the photograph from the intention of the photographer. By contrast, as the result of theatrical and mutually permissive role-playing, the marks left by John's whipping and tattooing are about individual will rather than accident or involuntary subjugation to punishment. Such ritualized punishment and wounding must be distinguished from the situation of the photographed slave, whose beating John has voluntarily imitated.[8] That John's requested beating is an act that had been gleaned from a photograph nevertheless speaks to the complex interactions and integration of various media (performance, bodily inscription, photography) organizing the recorded drama.

The queer meaning of John and Tyler's "church" ritual is, for example, accentuated by its placement in the final episode of the podcast's sequential narrative. My introduction notes the unsettling timing of John's suicide as it takes place in the context of the edited podcast, its "binge-listening" tempo and its cooptive appeal to narrative appetite for endings. Similarly, narrative disclosures about John's queer identity and intimacies in the last two episodes of the series play uncomfortably into plot-based drives, in so far as these disclosures are withheld until the penultimate chapter of the series, providing missing pieces to the story thus far provided of John's life. Preceding Tyler's and John's separately recorded elaborations about "church," there are the stories and impressions from John's long-term acquaintance Olin. The latter tells of how he had met John on a gay dating website, of their subsequent friendship and of stories he had heard from John about another intimate of John's who had probably broken his heart (Chapter Seven).

The temporal structure of the podcast narrative adds a complicated dimension to an already fraught structure through which intimacy between white men is enacted with reference to the objectifying oppressions of slavery. "John was actually quite good at appreciating the time he had. That wasn't his problem. His problem was a proleptic one. He saw nothing but darkness in the future. Shittown, for John, was not believing that anything good would last" (Chapter Seven). In tension with Brian's interpretation of John's "proleptic" problem and with the ostensibly deathly drive of John's sexual orientation is the "church" performance and the pivotal role that Tyler Goodson plays within a narrative that works in other than straightforwardly linear or plot-driven ways. During Brian's aforementioned visit to the Black Sheep Ink parlour (Chapter Two), there is a moment that explicitly prefigures Tyler's role in "church." He is described "crouched" on a bar, holding a business case that …

> … he carries around with him. He calls it his minister's case. It has a sticker that says "minister" slapped on the outside, and it's filled with his tattoo machines and a gun and his welder's cap and some nipple jewelry, and his Black Sheep Ink business cards, and also his minister's license, which he got online because he wanted to found a non-denominational church, where people of all backgrounds could come together and talk it out. (Chapter Two)

While there is no subsequent mention of this picture of Tyler with his "minister's case," his non-denominational administrations obviously play a key role in the final episode. The above picture, embedded in Chapter Two, anticipates the "church" ritual and communicates the recorded narrative's queerly dissonant invocations of past, present and future time. This dissonance is uncannily articulated, and can be understood in terms of Schneider's inter(in)animation, when Tyler says of the punishing re-enactment of the historical photograph: "[i]t was like he wanted to know the feeling of – wanting to know what folks went through back in that time." That John "wanted to know the feeling" separates his voluntary act from the enslavement itself that he wants to know about.

In dwelling on the significance of this re-enactment, my intention is thus not to repudiate the damaging legacy of slavery and what this history has meant for the continuing existence of white supremacist social structures in the United States. Indeed, as scholars such as Christina Sharpe and Frank B. Wilderson argue forcefully, the legacy of slavery continues to pose a grave problem for African-American civil rights, autonomy and agency. Rather, my intention is to connect John's queer fascination with processes of objectification to his interest in far-reaching temporalities. While the imitation of the photograph looks back to a fraught history, my final examples of intermedia within the podcast refer to forms that orient *S-Town*'s focus on regional/race difference beyond a specifically national context and toward a broader network/sphere.

The final chapter of *S-Town* intertwines intermedia with queer intimacies and temporalities. Following Tyler's and John's recorded versions of what took place in "church," Brian tells of how on the front of John's body there is tattooed "a sundial," and of how "John included a sundial motto there on his chest. The one he chose is *omnes vulnerant, ultima necat* – each wounds, the last kills" (Chapter Seven). Brian's translation of *omnes* as "each" here is notable, given that *omnes* is equivalent to "all" and the phrase is commonly translated as "all (hours) wound, the last kills." Brian's translation of *omnes* as "each" fits within an overall picture that the podcast has created of John. This picture emerges through the podcast's analogue of a marked and wounded object (tattooed chest, the marks left from beatings, the re-enactment of a photograph of a beating). It also emerges through descriptions of John's impressive knowledge of ancient clocks, sundials and astrolabes and of his far-reaching understanding of cosmological time and of more local history. The conclusion augments the characterization of John's rare knowledge and "saint"-like submission to punishment. After providing a brief summary of John's colourful ancestry, telling of shady types who swindled land left to John's mother, Mary Grace, the series ends with an image of her, sitting on her land, pregnant with John, and praying to God for a "genius." Such a picture potentially rarefies John's suicide, making his death more exceptional than those that came before it (including those of slaves). The recording of John's death is here analogous to Barthes's "Photograph," which creates its own worthiness as it over-determinately draws attention to "*something* or *someone* [...] [involving] Photography in the vast disorder of objects – of all the objects in the world: why choose (why photograph) this object, this moment, rather than some other?" (Barthes 6; emphasis in the original).[9]

Such questions about the worth of the putatively exceptional over the more general tell of a narrative desire for a "this" that demarcates a thing or person from the "vast disorder" (ibid.). Does Brian's (mis)translation of *omnes vulnerant* as "each wounds," rather than "all (hours) wound," suggest a similar privileging of the exception or the genius over the general? These questions return me to the queer correspondence between Tyler's anatomical heart and John's sundial as well as that between tattooed timepieces and their written inscriptions. In this context, can "each" ambiguously suggest both shared alienation/mutual wound and private experience? There is, likewise, the description of "each" of John's and Tyler's proximate but separately "established" initials and dates that, in the final chapter, Tyler tells Brian that he and John had left underneath a bridge on the day before John's suicide. That day was Father's Day (21 June 2015) and, following an argument with John over the latter having insulted Tyler's daughter, the two men had spent an afternoon walking near the Cahaba River in a National Wildlife Refuge.[10] Brian finds the graffiti on the support of a bridge that overlooks a bend in the river: "Tyler's initials on one side, with an '"Established 1991."' John's on the other, '"Established 1966."' The "established" names and dates, which perhaps resonate with the significance of "Black Sheep Ink" as a business establishment that John helped Tyler keep afloat, are placed in a spot overlooking the river. There is an evocative proximity at work here between the temporally static (the "established") dates and names of the graffiti and the flowing time of the river. Also existing amidst the incessant streaming of time are the relatively contained temporalities afforded by the graffiti as well as performance, tattooing and other discrete rituals that are intermediated by the podcast. Momentarily memorialized yet proximate to the river that flows on regardless, these insignia hold their own proleptic effacement, their eventual "decay and decrepitude." The relationship between the "each" and the "all" might thus be thought of as analogous to the proximity between the podcast and its inscribed media (graffiti, tattooing, etc.) and incorporated performances (the "church" ritual). These intermedia communicate in particular ways but they exist in proximity to an indifferent temporality (including the downloadable/streamable mode of binge-listening) that streams on, overlooking such meanings.

Proximity between intermedia and streamed recording is evoked in an earlier moment. After the meeting with the clockmaker Bill, Brian includes an interview with Tom Moore, a chemistry professor who had taught John when he was an undergraduate. During the interview, Tom shows Brian his own prized possession: a sundial that John had made especially for him. Tom is audibly moved when he recounts the time that John had taken to construct the object, which, Tom guesses, was begun in about 1984 and completed in 2012 or thereabouts. Brian describes it this way:

> In the middle there's a tiny button which flips up the gnomon – that's the centerpiece of the sundial, the one that casts the sun's shadow. Gnomon means "the one who knows." This gnomon has Tom Moore's initials in it. And the sundial is designed specifically for the latitude and longitude of Tom's home.

As Brian interprets it, the "gnomon" is the centrepiece of the sundial, the "one that casts the sun's shadow." From *gno* meaning "have power to, be able to, know to," the gnomon has played a pivotal role in the calendar time that is itself foundational to Western knowledge systems. The invention of the sundial and its gnomon prefigures the Gregorian calendar, indexing the paradigmatic connection between sun-based measuring tools and the invention of clocks and calendars. Brian's literal translation of the gnomon personifies the inanimate object, implying a "one" who knows. Alternatively, and in a reverse interpretation, his identification of the gnomon tacitly objectifies John as a gnomon-like knower of time and its complex movements. The latter interpretation echoes clock collector Bill's melancholy about the relentless mechanical ticking of clocks and of human life caught within the unidirectional movement of the calendar. The human condition, according to this view, is oriented toward a future and away from a past that is "never coming back" (Chapter Seven). Is it in view of this forward-moving time that we should understand the graffitied initials of Tyler Goodson and John B. McLemore, remaining on the bridge support, continuing to stand by the river that flows? If understood as intermedia that disrupt sequential time, both the initials engraved on Tom Moore's sundial and John and Tyler's graffitied initials momentarily suspend time. Read this way, engraved, inscribed and tattooed insignia exist at odds with and inter(in)animate the forward march of time, holding traces of past lives in abeyance. Tattoo needle and engraving pen become, in this context, more than writing implements. They instead fulfil John's "church" name "reliquary," becoming containers or keepers of relics that continue to queerly intermediate the time-measuring objects of which they are a part.

This essay's dwelling on the significance of John's queerness as it resides in spoken words, engraved initials, tattoos, clocks and sundials has run the risk of fetishizing his particular loss, of positioning him as the "gnomon," the "one," the "genius," the "saint."[11] As well as referring to "the one who knows," the gnomon refers us to the cosmological orientation or inclination of any "one" perspective. In the northern hemisphere, the gnomon is normally oriented so that it points toward the North celestial pole. Here, the inclination of the one (the gnomon) situates the object (including John as "genius") not simply within the American South but within a vast cosmology. By lingering on the flash-forwards and flash-backwards that organize the drama, and in thinking about the Latin phrase inscribed on a sundial, this essay has drawn attention to the expressive forms and media that animate the *S-Town* podcast and that are held within what might otherwise be understood purely in terms of formal dimensions (the sequential movement of the podcast) or in terms of nationally contained history (the particularity of the American South). These intermedia have told us something of the immediate contexts out of which they were born and from which they may be transported into the future. They also tell us something of the queer dispositions and inclinations of time-collectors, timekeepers and time-takers, including he who chose a sundial to mark the decay and decrepitude of a time that will be visited upon us all.

disclosure statement

No potential conflict of interest was reported by the author.

notes

1 Rémy Besson discusses the emergence of intermediality as a "strategic response" to the "hyper-specialisation of research in the humanities" (139). Much discussion of intermediality has focused on the form and function of film, including early silent film, in the context of the larger media ecology that film incorporates and to which it is inextricably connected. On the intermediality of film, see Besson; Chamarette; López; Mueller; Shail. For an intermedial reading of theatre, see Chapple and Kattenbelt's edited collection *Intermediality in Theatre and Performance*; see also Nelson; Rajewsky. Rosemary Overell writes about the intermediality of television and microblogs. See Edmond for a reading of the intermediality of

contemporary podcasting – a narrative form that simultaneously incorporates other media and is itself embedded in globalized digital networks and adds a new dimension to scholarship that has tended to focus on the intermediality of film. My conceptual approach to intermedia aligns most closely with that of Ágnes Pethő as set out in her *Cinema and Intermediality*.

2 Throughout this essay "intermedia" is a plural noun but in this instance, where I refer to how it functions as "a noun," I use the singular.

3 William Faulkner's "A Rose for Emily" is an intermedial form with which this essay doesn't engage, even though it has significance for the theme of time and for the way in which the *S-Town* episodes are structured. Apart from Brian's opening reference to Faulkner's story – it is one of a number of reading materials that John recommends to him – each episode ends with a rendition of The Zombies' song "A Rose for Emily," which is based on the story.

4 On the immense popularity of *Serial*, the *This American Life* podcast that precedes *S-Town*, and the immersive qualities of this particular form of audio-drama, see McMurty. In another essay, Richard Berry considers the popularity of *Serial* in the context of technical change and podcast histories ("A Golden Age of Podcasting?").

5 This and all subsequent quotes are taken from *S-Town*'s chapter transcripts, which can be found at <https://stownpodcast.org/>.

6 On regulatory time and the biopolitical management of bodies, see also Dana Luciano, *Arranging Grief*. In addition to work that investigates the relationship between sexual orientation and normative ideas of time, there is the important scholarship that probes the "metronormativity" (Halberstam) of urban-based queer identity. See in particular Herring; Halberstam. For studies of "queer rurality" that have been published in the wake of Halberstam's argument about metronormativity, see Colin Johnson as well as Gray, Johnson, and Gilley's edited collection *Queering the Countryside*.

7 Following Joan Shelley Rubin and Janice Radway's influential work, scholarship about middlebrow pivots on the social value (Rubin), as well as gender-inflected denigration (Radway), of literature and art ostensibly made for the purposes of broad accessibility, educative value and social/cultural distinction. That prevailing accounts of middlebrow as "reception practice" tend to focus on the role of literary/aesthetic objects in the context of the larger culture industry can create difficulties for tracking middlebrow across national "borders," raising "issues such as audience and address, genre and authorship and legibility and universality" (see Galt and Schoonover). The reading of middlebrow as both a mode of reception and a culture-industrial product also tends to overlook the distinct ways in which any given cultural form interacts with other media that, ranging from filmic, journalistic, televisual texts and radio podcasts, may contain elements that contradict the alignment of aesthetic forms with social value.

8 See Leo Bersani's argument about sado-masochistic practices in *Homos*. Elizabeth Freeman challenges Bersani's reading in her chapter "Turn the Beat Around," in which she explores what she calls the "erotohistoriographic" implications of performances in which "the individual subject's normative timing is disaggregated and denaturalized" (*Time Binds* 137).

9 Barthes's *Camera Lucida* attends to the specific properties of photography – to what Barthes refers to as the technology's "own genius" (3) – at the same time as it places photography within a broader spectrum through which the exceptional moment it privileges is questioned. My reading of photography in the context of *S-Town* as intermedia aims, similarly, to acknowledge photography's specific qualities while understanding how its elements interact with other media, such as performance/re-enactment. For an inspiring reading of photography as "ec-static visual object" that also draws on Barthes, see Cannon.

10 The date on which John took his own life (22 June 2015) also holds significance in relation to calendar and clock time. In 2015 in the United States, 21 June was the day on which Father's Day was celebrated – an occasion that signifies in a particular way within the drama, with its implications that Tyler's relationship to John is one informed by the sexual abuse he suffered at the hands of his biological father. Similarly, the persistent references to Father's Day (21 June 2015) rather than to the summer solstice (which takes place over 21/22 June each year in the northern hemisphere) uncannily displace the seasonal rhythms that undergird calendar time.

11 Through its privileging of John's peculiar perspective on death and decay, the podcast, and

this essay, may be guilty of overwriting, for example, the experience of a slave known only by the name Gordon and one whose beating John has re-enacted. Such an approach may similarly be read as fetishizing a certain kind of knowledge, including that of the supposedly knowing investigator or that of the academic scholar whose approach somehow trumps that of the plot-driven binge-listener.

bibliography

Alcorn, Gay. "S-Town Never Justifies its Voyeurism and that Makes it Morally Indefensible." *The Guardian* 22 Apr. 2017. Web. 19 Jan. 2018. <https://www.theguardian.com/commentisfree/2017/apr/22/s-town-never-justifies-its-voyeurism-and-that-makes-it-morally-indefensible>.

Bady, Aaron. "Airbrushing Shittown." *Hazlitt* 1 May 2017. Web. 19 Jan. 2018. <http://hazlitt.net/longreads/airbrushing-shittown>.

Barthes, Roland. *Camera Lucida: Reflections on Photography*. Trans. Richard Howard. London: Vintage, 1993. Print.

Berry, Richard. "A Golden Age of Podcasting? Evaluating *Serial* in the Context of Podcast Histories." *Journal of Radio and Audio Media* 22.2 (2015): 170–78. Print.

Bersani, Leo. *Homos*. Cambridge, MA: Harvard UP, 1995. Print.

Besson, Rémy. "Intermediality: Axis of Relevance." *SubStance* 44.3 (2015): 139–54. Print.

Brooks, Peter. *Reading for the Plot: Design and Intention in Narrative*. Cambridge, MA: Harvard UP, 1994. Print.

Cannon, Kristopher L. "Ecstatically Queer Images: Queering the Photographic through Fetal Photography." *Photography and Culture* 7.3 (2014): 269–84. Print.

Chamarette, Jenny. "Between Women: Gesture, Intermediary and Intersubjectivity in the Installations of Agnès Varda and Chantal Akerman." *Studies in European Cinema* 10.1 (2013): 45–57. Print.

Chapple, Freda, and Chiel Kattenbelt. eds. *Intermediality in Theatre and Performance*. Leiden: Brill, 2006. Print.

Duck, Leigh Anne. *The Nation's Region: Southern Modernism, Segregation and U.S. Nationalism*. Athens and London: U of Georgia P, 2009. Print.

Edmond, Maura. "All Platforms Considered: Contemporary Radio and Transmedia Engagement." *New Media and Society* 7.9 (2015): 1566–82. Print.

Freeman, Elizabeth. *Time Binds: Queer Temporalities, Queer Histories*. Durham, NC and London: Duke UP, 2010. Print.

Galt, Rosalind, and Karl Schoonover. "Hypotheses on the Queer Middlebrow." *Middlebrow Cinema*. Ed. Sally Faulkner. London and New York: Routledge, 2016. 200–15. Print.

"Gilded Souths & S-Towns." *About South*. Season 1, episode 2. Web. 19 Jan. 2018. <https://soundcloud.com/about-south/s02-episode-3-gilded-souths-and-s-towns>.

Gray, Mary L., Colin R. Johnson, and Brian J. Gilley, eds. *Queering the Countryside: New Frontiers in Rural Queer Studies*. New York: New York UP, 2016. Print.

Greeson, Jennifer Rae. *Our South: Geographic Fantasy and the Rise of National Literature*. Cambridge, MA: Harvard UP, 2010. Print.

Halberstam, Judith. *In Queer Time and Place: Transgender Bodies, Subcultural Lives*. New York: New York UP, 2005. Print.

Herring, Scott. *Another Country: Queer Anti-Urbanism*. New York: New York UP, 2010. Print.

Hess, Amanda. "'S-Town' Attains Podcasting Blockbuster Status." *New York Times* 5 Apr. 2017. Web. 19 Jan. 2018. <https://www.nytimes.com/2017/04/05/arts/s-town-podcast-blockbuster-status.html>.

Hooton, Christopher. "S-Town Review: The Story of John B. McLemore Makes for the Warmest Podcast I've Heard." *The Independent* 29 Mar. 2017. Web. 19 Jan. 2018. <http://www.independent.co.uk/arts-entertainment/tv/reviews/s-town-podcast-john-b-mclemore-macklemore-shit-town-review-episode-1-to-4-tyler-woodstock-alabama-a7656301.html>.

Johnson, Colin. *Just Queer Folks: Gender and Sexuality in Rural America*. Philadelphia: Temple UP, 2013. Print.

Larson, Sarah. "'S-Town' Investigates the Human Mystery." *The New Yorker* 31 Mar. 2017. Web. 19 Jan. 2018. <http://www.newyorker.com/culture/sarah-larson/s-town-investigates-the-human-mystery>.

López, Ana M. "Calling for Intermediality: Latin American Mediascapes." *Cinema Journal* 54.1 (2014): 135–41. Print.

Luciano, Dana. *Arranging Grief: Sacred Time and the Body in Nineteenth-Century America*. New York: New York UP, 2007. Print.

McMurty, Leslie Grace. "'I'm Not a Real Detective, I Only Play One on Radio'": Serial as the Future of Audio Drama." *Journal of Popular Culture* 49.2 (2016): 306–24. Print.

Mueller, Juergen E. "Intermediality in the Age of Global Media Networks – Including Eleven Theses on its Provocative Power for the Concepts of 'Convergence,' 'Transmedia Storytelling' and 'Actor Network Theory.'" *SubStance* 4.33 (2015): 19–52. Print.

Nelson, Robin. "Introduction: Prospective Mapping and Network of Terms." *MediaMatters*. Amsterdam: Amsterdam UP, 2010. 13–25. Print.

Overell, Rosemary. "Intermediality and Interventions: Applying Intermediality Frameworks to Reality Television and Microblogs." *Refractory: A Journal of Entertainment Media* 6 Aug. 2014. Web. 19 Jan. 2018. <http://refractory.unimelb.edu.au/2014/08/06/overell/>.

Pethő, Ágnes. *Cinema and Intermediality: The Passion for the In-Between*. Newcastle-upon-Tyne: Cambridge Scholars, 2011. Print.

Quah, Nicholas. "*S-Town* Transcends the True Crime of *Serial*." *Vulture* 28 Mar. 2017. Web. 19 Jan. 2018. <http://www.vulture.com/2017/03/review-s-town-podcast-serial.html>.

Radway, Janice. *A Feeling for Books: The Book-of-the-Month Club, Literary Taste, and Middle-Class Desire*. Chapel Hill: U of North Carolina P, 2000. Print.

Rajewsky, Irena O. "Intermediality, Intertextuality and Remediation: A Literary Perspective on Intermediality." *Intermédialités* 6 (2005): 43–64. Print.

Romano, Aja. "*S-Town* is a Stunning Podcast. It Probably Shouldn't Have Been Made." *Vox* 1 Apr. 2017. Web. 19 Jan. 2018. <https://www.vox.com/culture/2017/3/30/15084224/s-town-review-controversial-podcast-privacy>.

Rubin, Joan Shelley. *The Making of Middlebrow Culture*. Chapel Hill and London: U of North Carolina P, 1992. Print.

Schneider, Rebecca. *Performing Remains: Art and War in Times of Theatrical Reenactment*. London and New York: Routledge, 2011. Print.

Shail, Andrew. "Intermediality: Disciplinary Flux or Formalist Retrenchment?" *Early Popular Visual Culture* 8.1 (2010): 3–15. Print.

Sharpe, Christina. *In the Wake: On Blackness and Being*. Durham, NC: Duke UP, 2016. Print.

Waldman, Katy. "The Gorgeous New True Crime Podcast S-Town is Like *Serial* but Satisfying." *Slate* 30 Mar. 2017. Web. 19 Jan. 2018. <http://www.slate.com/blogs/browbeat/2017/03/30/s_town_the_new_true_crime_podcast_by_the_makers_of_serial_reviewed.html>.

Wilderson III, Frank B. *Red, White and Black: Cinema and the Structure of U.S. Antagonisms*. Durham, NC: Duke UP, 2010. Print.

The Department of Prints and Drawings in the British Museum, London, is located next to an exhibition gallery in room 90. To gain access to the Department you first have to make an appointment online; on arrival the visitor presses a button and is then admitted to a small ante-room guarded normally by a middle-aged woman (or two), who supervises disposal of bags and coats in a locker and the signing of a register. The attendant then escorts you to one of two large tables where you wait until one of the Department's staff is free to assist you with your inquiry: she (or sometimes he) delivers the required item to the table and is the visitor's main point of contact. Sitting at a raised desk, a superintendent keeps an eye on visitors at the two tables and the work of the study room as a whole which is lined with wooden-framed glass cases and surrounded by a gallery at an upper level. The room, constructed in an expansion of the British Museum just before the First World War, is illuminated by natural light from skylights and window at the far end, and is one of the most beautiful, if lesser known, spaces in the Museum (Griffiths 16). In contrast to the rest of the Museum, noisy with the press of tourists, the Department of Prints and Drawings seems a place apart, less obviously customer-oriented than the Museum as a whole or the equally crowded British Library. The rituals of access, though enhanced by digital gatekeeping, are reminiscent of long-lost civil service protocols of the mid-twentieth century: the Department even closes for lunch.

The scholarly disciplines most identified with the Department of Prints and Drawings are art history and connoisseurship. Among its prized

gillian russell

EPHEMERAPHILIA
a queer history

possessions are works by Michelangelo, Dürer, Rembrandt, Claude, Blake, and Hogarth. But since its establishment in 1808 as a section of the British Museum, before becoming a Department in 1837, Prints and Drawings was also a repository of less prestigious works on paper, some of which would not readily qualify as outstanding works of art (Edwards 1: 31). For example, the Department houses collections of prints and ephemera illustrating costume; theatrical portraits illustrative of the history of the theatre; topographical illustrations of London, including of amusements, ceremonial occasions, and natural phenomena such as the freezing of the Thames between the seventeenth and nineteenth centuries; prints relating to ice-skating; and collections of fans, leaves from fans, and playing cards (see Griffiths and Williams). Many of these collections were the result of donations made to the Museum in the eighteenth and nineteenth centuries rather than official collecting policy: as Antony Griffiths notes, "the scope of the mainstream of print collecting has progressively narrowed through the centuries" (Griffiths 16). Among the most significant of the eclectic collections housed in the Department are those of Sarah Sophia Banks (1744–1818), the sister of the naturalist and leading figure in British science, Sir Joseph Banks, who donated them to the British Museum after her death. The scale of Banks's collection is enormous, consisting of over 20,000 items, including a substantial coin collection, trade cards, and tickets of admission, as well as albums of cuttings and books. Her work in acquiring, organizing, and preserving these records has until recently been largely unrecognized because of the status of what she collected as "ephemera," a term to which I will return later.[1] It was in the course of researching Banks's collection of tickets in the Department of Prints and Drawings that I diverged to look at a similar if much smaller collection of tickets made by Sir Augustus Wollaston Franks (1826–97).

Described as "the second founder of the British Museum" (the first being Sir Hans Sloane (1660–1753), Franks was an independently wealthy gentleman scholar, connoisseur, networker and facilitator, who held a variety of positions at the Museum, beginning in 1851, eventually becoming a trustee and member of the Museum's standing committee (Wilson, "Franks." See also Wilson, *The Forgotten Collector*; Caygill and Cherry). Franks was a notable collector in his own right, donating much of his collections to the Museum, as well as encouraging others, through his networks and influence, to give material to the nation: he was responsible, for example, for ensuring that the collections of the banker and philanthropist Henry Christy were secured to form the basis of the Museum's ethnographic collection. Not a professional in the modern sense of the term, nor bound by a particular academic discipline, Franks's work in organizing the Museum and expanding its collections was foundational in the development of archaeology, ethnography (and ultimately anthropology). His interests were diverse, ranging from Indian sculpture to Anglo-Saxon rings and Italian Renaissance majolica (tin-glazed earthenware). Among the outstanding and beautiful pieces that he donated to the British Museum are the so-called Franks casket, a box made of carved whalebone depicting scenes that have Roman, Jewish, Christian and Germanic references, possibly made in Northumbria in Anglo-Saxon times; a delicate Chinese Ming dynasty bowl that is so translucent that the fingers of the person holding it are discernible; and a striking pre-Colombian mask from Mexico, made of mosaic of turquoise.[2] Franks also made an enormous collection of book plates, amounting to 70,000 items, going back to the sixteenth century, as part of an interest in heraldry and genealogy that was common in antiquarian circles (*Catalogue*). In a codicil to his will, he requested that his collection of book plates be deposited in the Department of Prints and Drawings and "kept together as such and not distributed under the Engravers names" (Caygill and Cherry 357). In his entry on Franks for the *Oxford Dictionary of National Biography*, David Wilson writes that "although a lifelong bachelor, Franks was a sociable – if shy – man [...] in personal terms [he] remains an enigma." A contemporary referred to him as a "grey dreamy person" with a habit of "addressing himself to his top waistcoat button" (Wilson, "Franks").

In consigning his book plates, as well as his trade cards and tickets, to the Department of Prints and Drawings, Franks would have been aware that his paper collections were joining those of Sarah Sophia Banks, who was also interested in book plates and, like Franks, was unmarried with a reputation as somewhat of an eccentric. In studies of her brother Sir Joseph Banks, Sarah Sophia is often depicted as "quaint" and "unconventional," or "an oddity. Tall and masculine in appearance [...]" (Smith 345 n. 1; Cameron 255). The

Franks collection of tickets, though much smaller in scale than Banks's, is similar in documenting the importance of paper instruments such as invitations to associational culture and the trading of goods and services in the form of trade cards (what we now know as the business card). The Georgian ticket economy, particularly as it developed in the late eighteenth century, was a highly sophisticated example of paper as a support for signification, a prosthetic or filtering mechanism capable of traversing a spectrum between what Jacques Derrida referred to as the "condition of a priceless archive" and the "abjection" of rubbish (Derrida 43; Lloyd). Tickets made the value of sociability mobile and transferable as part of a wider cultural economy comprising other micro-exchange relations – familial, sexual, political, and financial. As Sarah Lloyd argues, "an ability to recognize and use tickets had become an essential form of literacy" for all levels of eighteenth-century society (855). This "literacy," moreover, was multivalent: "tickets were [...] experienced through the eye, touch, imagination, and memory. Circulation, form and use gave tickets 'social lives,' so that their specific histories disclose the processes that created substance, feeling and value" (847). It was this elusive and affective dimension of ticket literacy, the "social life" that specific tickets were capable of disclosing, that was the focus of Sarah Sophia Banks's collecting.

Banks mainly collected tickets produced by the process of printing from copper engraving. The techniques of intaglio printing allowed for more elaborate and decorative design elements than were possible in letterpress printing, often making these tickets arresting visual artefacts that integrated the arts of word and image (Hudson 14; see also Moger). Occasional, topical and often personal, these tickets lacked the impact of forms of cheap print such as ballads or lottery advertisements that were produced in the millions, but they were no less "ephemeral." Indeed, the intaglio-printed ticket could be described as more ephemeral in its reference to a specific social encounter between individuals, an event in time and place, or, as in the case of an invitation to a funeral, a lost life.

Even an elaborately designed masquerade or ball ticket was more object-like than the book because handling and exchange were integral to its function and meaning: tickets were more contiguous with the material world than books, carried as they were in pockets and reticules from place to place, tended for scrutiny by attendants or box-keepers, or discarded on floors to be swept away as rubbish.

Franks's collection of tickets includes a number of examples of the kind of ticket amassed by Banks to which he added records of his own sociability in the form of invitations to dinners and exhibitions, making this archive, as indeed Banks's also was, cryptically autobiographical. His compilation of a collection of tickets on the same model as Banks's was not only a recognition of her achievement but also of the institutional contexts in which her collection was housed. Rather than writing about Banks (which he does not appear to have done), Franks sought to emulate her through the performance of a kind of archival sociality similar to the kind of social contingency that her collections recorded and mapped – being in the same place, speaking or not speaking to the other, perhaps being unaware that the other is even there. Franks's tribute to Banks, if it is one, was so invisible (we might also say queer) that his collection has been used as a place to which the Department of Prints and Drawings consigns similar kinds of documents. The integrity of the Banks collection is maintained but Franks's gesture in replicating or mimicking her practices has enabled Prints and Drawings to keep on adding tickets to his collection, meaning that Franks's tribute to Banks theoretically continues.

It was such an object in the Franks collection that I found particularly memorable, to the extent that I remember the circumstances in which I encountered it – a late November afternoon, when darkness was encroaching in the study room and the world was circumscribed by the desk light to me and the object I was handling. Let's describe what it was/is – a ticket for a ball at the assembly room in Clapham for Thursday November 22 1798, belonging to a Mr Pycroft. The British

Museum identification number indicates that the ticket was acquired in 1938, long after Franks's death.[3] The top left-hand corner has a hole that has worn through, indicating where Mr Pycroft would have pinned the ticket to his clothing, consistent with the often close relationship of such ephemera with the bodies who wore and carried them.[4] Made of pasteboard, the ticket is brown with age and dense with a history of human handling (indicated, for example, by folding): in contrast to many of the tickets in the Banks collection it is not artistically beautiful but a humble, battered testimony to the sociability of an individual, unrelated to an event that is historically significant (such as the impeachment trial of Warren Hastings, tickets for which were collected by Banks and also represented in the Franks collection). The Clapham assembly room exemplified the kind of suburban sociability of the minor gentry and upper middling orders that is the subject of the fiction of Frances Burney and later Jane Austen. (Mr Pycroft is perhaps the historical equivalent of the nonentity Mr Smith who invites Evelina, the heroine of Burney's 1778 novel of the same name, to an assembly at Hampstead.)

It was this ticket's battered ordinariness and its resistance to interpretation that was so arresting on that late November day, making me conscious of the circumstances in which I was handling it. The musicologist Carolyn Abbate has described such an encounter as an "aesthetic experience, having an immediate physical effect, engendered by the present object"; 79). In Abbate's case, the object producing that effect for her was a still from a 1940s German film which had retained a blurred image of an actor's hand moving, i.e., an action that was fleeting and "ephemeral." Abbate writes:

> Once within the photograph, the textures and the physicality they convey are overwhelming […] The performers assume life in defiance of physical law (since they are all dead) at the very moment when whatever characters they were impersonating fall away. There are forms of knowledge that these textures and presences convey, but is there a place in academic culture for them? And if so, how do you articulate it? (Ibid.)

Abbate's essay is concerned with how a flaw in a photograph, unnoticed by the photographer and those for whom the image was made, had the effect of suggesting the "liveness" of performance, in a way that made her, as a scholar, conscious of her own apprehension of that liveness (as possibly the only viewer to have noticed the photograph's flaw). If such an effect was produced by the photographic image, how much more powerful, then, is that produced by a different kind of materiality: the humble pasteboard, engraved ticket?[5] My encounter with Mr Pycroft's ticket was "overwhelming" in its mute loquacity, its dead liveness, produced by the sense that the pasteboard was saturated with a history of human handling; the mystery of the unknowable "Mr Pycroft"; the significance of Franks's posthumous institutional imprimatur for something he could not himself have known about; and above all, the apparent incongruity of the ticket's preservation among Dürers and Rembrandts. What has such a grubby object to do with the irreplaceable prints and drawings with which it is housed in close proximity? And, as Abbate suggests, how do we "articulate" a place in academic culture for such objects, for their arresting effects that challenge the requirement for academic self-effacement, as well as what counts as an "aesthetic experience, for I would contend that in spite of its battered qualities the ticket was nonetheless beautiful"?[6] The Clapham assembly ticket was arresting not only in making me aware of the ephemeral context in which I was encountering it – the darkening room of Prints and Drawings – but also in how I myself had been momentarily hailed or impossibly stopped in time.

At stake, then, in what happened on that November afternoon and for Abbate when she received the still of the forgotten German film is the meaning of the "ephemeral." The ephemeral and ephemerality are increasingly being invoked in a wide variety of fields – book history, literary studies, art history, digital media studies, performance studies and the "archival turn" in the humanities as a whole – but rarely are these terms examined in their own right.[7] The origin of ephemera's valency in queer and performance studies can be traced to José Esteban Muñoz's important article "Ephemera as Evidence: Introductory Notes to Queer Acts," published in 1996 (Muñoz). Muñoz highlighted how "anecdotal and ephemeral evidence," including performance and documents normally classified as "ephemera" such as photographs, tickets, posters, album covers, flyers, personal memorabilia – could "grant access to those who had been locked out of official histories," an insight subsequently and influentially elaborated by Ann Cvetkovich in *An Archive of Feelings* (Muñoz 9; Cvetkovich). Ephemera, Muñoz argued, "is always about specificity and resisting dominant systems of aesthetic and institutional classification [...] *without abstracting them outside of social experience and a larger notion of sociality*" (my emphasis): i.e., ephemera carries social, material, and thus political valency, inevitably linked with struggles over racial, ethnic, sexual, class and gender rights and identities.[8] "Ephemera," for Muñoz, also refers to an epistemology, a way of knowing the queer object that is itself "queer": "central to performance scholarship is a queer impulse that intends to discuss an object whose ontology, in its ability to 'count' as a proper 'proof,' is profoundly queer" (Muñoz 6). Writing more than twenty years before Abbate's "Overlooking the Ephemeral" (which does not refer to queer studies), Muñoz recognized, firstly, that attention to the ephemeral intensifies rather than diminishes the affect of the material object, and secondly, that the "queer impulse" inspired by the queer object of knowledge is a challenge to scholarly protocols of transparent objectivity and the scholar's professional obligation to be invisible, to stand outside time. Abbate's questioning of the implications of not overlooking the ephemeral for "academic culture" was anticipated by Muñoz's idea of scholarship itself as a performative queer act that could "*contest and rewrite the protocols of critical writing*" (Muñoz 7).

Sara Edenheim situates the work of Muñoz, but primarily that of Cvetkovich and Judith Halberstam, as exemplifying a "queer utopianism" in opposition to Lee Edelman's emphasis in *No Future* on political negativity (Edenheim; Edelman). For Edelman, as is well known, the queer is profoundly anti-social because it names the death drive, the negativity opposed to every form of social viability. The ephemeral, the fragmentary and the incoherent, Edenheim argues, are crucial to the distinction that "queer utopianism" makes between the archive of feelings and hegemonic and official archival institutions (such as, for example, the British Museum). Not only does Edenheim suggest that history is not so devoid of "feelings" and "psychic needs" as Cvetkovich and others would suggest, but the very fact of positing an archive, she argues, is inevitably oriented towards futurity or an "after," meaning that the archive of feelings shares with the public research library a desire to preserve knowledge against loss and death. Edenheim notes the paradox of the investment of the archive of feelings in the ephemeral because "this *strange colonization* of the ephemeral prevents the ephemeral from being what it is: momentary, short-lived, fleeting, always already dying" (49; my emphasis). The ephemeral thus serves, for Edenheim as much as for "the archive of feelings," as an embedded discursive signifier of the inherent problem of all archives: i.e., the imperative to preserve what cannot ultimately be preserved, firstly, because all things must die, and secondly, the fact that to preserve everything would lead to "entropy and chaos" (54). In other words, there must always be an ephemeral beyond the ephemeral. The ephemeral thus potentially stands for the archive's confrontation of the limitations of knowledge and awareness of what it cannot possibly know, a kind of archival sublime, what the media archaeologist Wolfgang Ernst describes as the "assumption that every statement forms a border against a vast emptiness, a vast field of the unsaid: the anarchive" (18). Ephemera both as a discursive category and as a categorizable phenomenon – the flotsam and jetsam of everyday lives, without obvious historical value, useful only for a day and not for all time – functions as an expression of the desire to preserve and the realization of that desire's impossibility that are inherent to the idea of the archive. As a concept and as an archival object, ephemera is thus simultaneously utopian and negative; in so far as it stretches the boundaries of knowledge as well as confronting knowledge's limitations – the deep space or vacuity of absolute ephemerality – thinking about ephemera is thus always already a queer exercise or "impulse," to use Muñoz's term.

A notable feature of the deployment of ephemera and its cognates in the work I have been citing, including that of Abbate, is its tendency to assume their meaning as given, as universal and transhistorical. But the use of ephemera to apply to "the minor transient documents of everyday life" in the widely cited definition of Maurice Rickards has a relatively recent history (13). Ephemera derives from the Greek "epi" (on, at, or around), and "hemera" (a day), via the medieval Latin "ephemera," and is used in entomology to classify insects that live for a day and in medicine to refer to a temporary fever. In astronomy the term ephemeris (plural ephemerides) refers to the position of astronomical bodies (including mechanical satellites) at a specific time of the day (or days). Beginning in the mid-eighteenth century, most notably in Samuel Johnson's description of "the papers of the day" (referring to newspapers, periodicals, and pamphlets) as the "*Ephemerae* of learning," "ephemera" gradually began to be used to distinguish between certain kinds of printed matter – newspapers, broadsides and the jobbing print that was coming to dominate print production in this period – and the codex-form book.[9] By "Ephemerae" Samuel Johnson was making an analogy between "papers" and the kinds of insects that lived only for a day, suggesting an idea of knowledge as a complex eco-system with its own evanescent life forms, part of an overarching, hierarchical order of nature. "Ephemerae" supplemented the well-established use of "grub," as in "Grub Street," signifying a class of hack writers who, maggot-like, fed on the genius of other writers: to the idea of literary "grubs" as the lowest form of life, "Ephemerae" added the idea of the transience of that life and of the "grubby" papers it was producing (see McDowell).

The use of ephemera to refer to print media was closely linked with the application of the term "diurnal." Describing the revolution of the earth that produced night and day, "diurnal" was applied in the seventeenth century to the Europe-wide circulation of daily news sheets, in both hand-written and printed forms. Stuart Sherman has argued that the late seventeenth and early eighteenth centuries are characterized by a new consciousness of diurnal time, driven by technological and media change and by the daily transactions of commerce (Sherman). Inventions such as the pocket watch and the minute hand, by which the individual could possess and monitor precisely a personalized sense of time, were aligned, according to Sherman, with the emergence of the "diurnal form" of diaries, journals, newspapers, and the novel. The concept of the diurnal assumed confidence in every day's return – the sun always sinking to rise again – a pattern exploited by new media such as the newspaper which, while "fresh" only for a limited period, was renewed in the form of the next issue. "Ephemeral" differed from "diurnal," however, in offering no consolation of the possibility of another day: a thing that was ephemeral lived for a day and quickly died. Whereas the diurnal was cosmological in scope, the ephemeral was micrological and sublunary, deriving from the empiricism of the natural sciences and the increasing awareness of both the diversity and the evanescence of myriad forms of life.

The emergence of an ephemeral/diurnal time consciousness and of printed ephemera as a category of knowledge shaped ideas of literary value, the disciplines of bibliography and philology that underpin the development of literary history and criticism, and the ordering of knowledge in libraries and museums in the Romantic period and after.[10] This development was accentuated in the wake of the French Revolution and the response to the revolution by both radicals and loyalists when printed ephemera such as handbills – small flyer-like broadsides – became potent means of rapid political communication and mobilization. After 1800, ephemera, in relation to print, increasingly replaced the alternative term "fugitive." Throughout the eighteenth century fugitive was applied to small books or pamphlets, periodical publications and newspapers, as well as to collections of occasional literary pieces, mainly poetry, originally published in newspapers or periodicals. A fugitive or flying piece of writing was one that could not be easily fixed or immobilized, in contrast to the increasingly more stable technology of leaves bound to form the spine of the codex-form book. As used in relation to print, "ephemera" increasingly supplemented the lawlessness and uncontrollability associated with "fugitive" with the characteristics of limited lifespan and debased value. The label of ephemera suggested that such texts were essentially evanescent and worthless, the work of a day that would disappear, unlike the solidity and endurance promised by the book.[11]

The importance of the ephemeral to queer theory therefore encodes within it the politics of "fugitive" – of being outside or escaping the regime of law and also, in so far as fugitive is not defined by temporality or the limits of time and space. The challenge of fugitive or ephemeral print also derives from how it tends to evade the control of the market, being distributed for free or, in the case of advertisements or tickets, designed to promote commerce indirectly. It is on account of its tangential, unpredictable relationship to something or someone else – an event, individual, a place or time – that the ephemeral document such as the ticket is capable of being everything or nothing (or simultaneously both): a discarded scrap of rubbish or an object saturated with affect. Whether this document "lives" or "dies" depends on arbitrary circumstance, accident, or the attention of an individual, whereas the fate of the book, because it is a legitimate and tradable object that circulates within recognized institutions of knowledge such as the library or the bookshop, is much more predictable. Ephemera thus tends to escape "the normal channels of [...] bibliographical control" because it is not easily assimilated to systems and institutions of knowledge based in and on the book (Clinton 15). It remains a troublesome category in library science, Timothy Young, for example, ascribing to ephemera a perverse anthropomorphic agency, a tendency to "just show up" in library collections, acting as "awkward also-rans" in contrast to the uniformity and manageability of sturdy books (12). Pamphlets have a "hard time standing up," Young writes, their "limp pages unprotected from wear" (18, 16). Even when ephemera doesn't just "show up," the librarian is always aware of the possibility of private collections existing somewhere out there, old broadsheets lining the walls of country houses, hidden but making their presence felt under layers of wallpaper: "left alone, they literally become the fabric of existence" (19). Ephemera, in other words, is queer, indeed so queer, that the extent of its constitutive role in knowledge formation in the eighteenth and nineteenth centuries has been obscured, even though, like the old broadsheets in Young's imaginary house, it is ineluctably there as part of the "fabric of existence." Queer studies, such as, in particular the work of Muñoz and Edenheim, both knows and doesn't know this.

The supplanting of fugitive by ephemera in the early nineteenth century coincides with the efflorescence of "bibliomania," the fashion for the acquisition and accumulation of rare books, mainly incunabulae, that gripped the male social elite and received extensive contemporary newspaper and periodical commentary.[12] The term "bibliomania" was coined by the main publicist of the phenomenon, Thomas Frognall Dibdin, who produced a number of books about the love of books, written in a self-consciously arch and florid style: in 1821 Dibdin was labelled as "the Typo-Dandy [...] well known in the literary world as the Beau Brummell of book-makers."[13] The bibliomania was later stigmatized in the nineteenth century as inappropriate for its homosocial mixing of aristocrats and lower middle-class nobodies, its emphasis on the pleasures and excesses of collecting, and an unscientific, possibly unhealthy, focus on books as fetishized objects rather than as transmitters of knowledge. Nonetheless, as Jon Klancher has argued, the "wild bibliography" of the bibliomaniacs, in its attention to how books might be described and classified, was formative in the development of the discipline of bibliography, while Michael Robinson has claimed that the "queerness" of the bibliomaniacs has "continuities with later forms of queer self-expression and constructions of selfhood [that speak] to the link between queerness and textuality" (Klancher; Robinson 697). If this is so, then the link between queerness and textuality is also grounded in the ephemeral, as a number of the bibliomaniacs were also collectors of printed ephemera. A notable example is Richard Heber, probably the leading bibliomaniac of the period.[14] When he died in 1834, the *Gentleman's Magazine* claimed that Heber's collecting of books had become "uncontrollable": his town house in London was filled with "books from the top to the bottom – every chair, every table, every passage containing piles of erudition." He had libraries in Paris, Antwerp, Brussels and Ghent full to bursting of books: "in short," commented the *Gentleman's Magazine*, there was "neither end nor measure to his literary stores."[15] Heber's collecting was not confined to books, however. The sale catalogue of his library indicates that he possessed "A large Selection of Scraps from Newspapers and Periodicals; together with an extensive collection of single leaves, consisting of Christmas Carols; Old Ballads; Songs; Monumental Inscriptions; Proposals for Literary Undertakings, Lectures, &c.; Exhibition Hand-bills [...] and a Variety of others, Serious, Humorous, and Political" (*Bibliotheca Heberiana* 83). Heber also owned Daniel Lysons's *Collectanea Historica*, an eight-volume collection of newspaper cuttings, prints, and portraits, covering the period 1646–1824 (*Bibliotheca Heberiana* 81). Lysons was a notable antiquarian and topographical historian, a member of Sir Joseph Banks's circle, who made a number of such collections of ephemeral material, some of which are now held in the British Library. Heber's interest in ephemera was thus not exceptional but part of a long-standing and widespread focus of antiquarians concerned to document the social world in its widest possible sense. Though the book madness of figures such as Heber has been recognized, the commensurate fascination of bibliophiles with ephemera and their transmission of ephemera collections has not. Bibliomania and its counterpart, "ephemeraphilia" (my term), can be said to bracket or "queer" what would become more normative views of book love such as the idea of books being surrogate "wives" to which Romantic-period collectors were "married" (Lynch). The importance of ephemera to queer studies in the 1990s therefore has a long history: queer studies itself is arguably impossible without the invention of the ephemeral as a zone of fugitive knowledge, indeterminate legibility, and potentially boundless affect.

This context, the long, queer history of ephemera, is relevant to the scenario I described at the beginning of this essay, because the presence of Mr Pycroft's ticket for the Clapham assembly in the Department of Prints and Drawings is indicative, in its own "queer" way, of the constitutive role of ephemera in the formation of larger systems of knowledge and of institutions. In the form of the collections of the first founder of the British Museum, Sir Hans Sloane, ephemeral literature such as pamphlets, bills, and cuttings became part of the Museum's "fabric of existence."[16] Sir Joseph Banks's depositing of the ephemera collections of his sister in 1818 integrated the kind of knowledge that her archive represented – a history of sociability as it was happening – with his own ambition to document, classify, and profit from knowledge in the service of the British empire. Print culture and increasingly sophisticated networks of information meant that the ideal of accumulating knowledge and power in the form of the British Museum was more realizable than ever. Even the smallest scrap of paper – the data of daily existence – was implicitly meaningful in its physical contiguity with other disparate curious things. Among the artefacts that Sir Joseph Banks collected and eventually distributed to the British Museum were those relating to Cook's voyages and the colonization of

Australia, articulated, handled, and exhibited in the same contexts as Sarah Sophia Banks's ephemeral tickets. The kind of ephemerology practised by Sarah Sophia Banks, and by contemporaries such as Heber and Lysons, was therefore materially and ideologically linked not only with the explosion of fugitive political information in the 1790s and after but also with the ambitions of colonialism and imperialism. Rather than being marginal or tangential to Enlightenment aspirations to knowledge, which led ultimately to the formation of the modern disciplines, an interest in the ephemeral tested just how far those aspirations could go. Ephemera was symptomatic of, on the one hand, the exhilaration and the reach of curiosity, and on the other, the fear that curiosity could lead to an encounter with entropy and chaos (or in Edelman's terms, the death drive). As Jonathan Lamb and others have pointed out in relation to the British Museum, confidence that knowledge could be organized and systematized was haunted by fear that the Museum was being overwhelmed by too much stuff, and the realization of the inability to account for the "multifariousness of nature." Sir Joseph Banks's "fascination with the singular and the inexpressible," Lamb writes, "[left] him sometimes without a system of differences or a language with which to identify or speak of them" (310, 313). Sarah Sophia Banks shared this "fascination with the singular and the inexpressible," her ephemera collecting representing not so much a subversion of or counter-archive to the work of her brother; rather, it was her own version of its ambition, a documentation of the raw "multifariousness" of sociality, its queer curiosity casting a light on the queerness of curiosity as a whole.

In the eclecticism of his interests and his amateurism, Augustus Wollaston Franks was closer to the antiquarians of the seventeenth and eighteenth centuries than to the modern museum professional or discipline-identified academic, one possible reason why he is largely forgotten today. His creation of a ticket collection emulating and supplementing Sarah Sophia Banks's much larger collection, and cryptically embedding the illegibility of his own social and affective life within the national repository of the British Museum, is a sign of his identification with that antiquarianism and, as I have been suggesting here, a "queer act," in Muñoz's terms, because it is uncertain of what or how it might "count" as a proper "proof." (The "queerness" of Franks's act of consigning his ticket collection to the Department of Prints and Drawings is that he unknowingly ensured a home for the humble Pycroft ticket forty years after his death.) While Franks's ticket collection is dwarfed by the magnificence and beauty of his other legacies to the British Museum, his tickets are nonetheless important in suggesting the investments of modern institutions and disciplines in ephemera and ephemerality – their "strange colonization," in Edenheim's terms, of what can never be rendered fixed or secure. The ephemeral both simultaneously resists and encourages inquiry, like queer, in ways that work around, within, and between the disciplines in which it figures, such as performance studies, media studies, and indeed, queer studies itself. Similarly, the queerly ephemeral is both historically conditioned – a feature since the early Enlightenment of the development of the print media and institutions of knowledge – as well as being transhistorical in its reach in so far as there was always ephemera before ephemera, as well as there is always the ephemeral beyond the ephemeral. The academic study of the ephemeral therefore needs to be conscious of its status as a "queer act" and the ephemerality of its own practices, voice, and presence in the archive, and indeed of that archive's own impermanence. Students of the ephemeral, such as Banks and Franks, have always existed, their marginality and elusiveness in the modern disciplines being a sign of what Carolyn Abbate calls their "insouciance." Insouciance, she says,

> is having made peace with the ephemeral. It is what you see in performers who know that what they are doing will not last and does not matter – which frees them to return the next day, and the next, with something even better.[17]

Abbate confuses the ephemeral with the consolations of the diurnal, i.e., that a specific day or event, though gone forever, will come again in the form of another day or another performance (analogous to the utopianism of some queer theory). The insouciance of men and women such as Banks and Franks is the realization that the work of a day, of a sociable encounter, of an act of love or of violence, is finite and unique, and no matter how often it is returned to, in the form of the queer act of research, archivization, preservation, re-enactment, that work has happened and is dead, over (a version of Edelman's death drive). Such insouciance does not necessarily make peace with the ephemeral but rather continues to worry the ephemeral in a way that can be seen as courageous, defiant, and above all, queer. Occupying a boundary between the archive and the "anarchive," the ephemeral is both there and not there (both utopian and deathly): the paradox of its non-presence (not absence) endures, if one knows where to look for it or for those, such as Franks and Banks, who may have insouciantly, queerly, noticed it before.

disclosure statement

No potential conflict of interest was reported by the author.

notes

1 Research on Banks's collections is growing: see Credland, "Sarah and Joseph Banks and Archery in the Eighteenth Century," and "Sarah and Joseph Banks contd."; Pincott; Eagleton, "Collecting African Money in Georgian London," and "Sarah Sophia Banks, Adam Afzelius and a Coin from Sierra Leone." Arlene Leis's 2013 Ph.D. represents the first significant study of the material in the Department of Prints and Drawings (Leis, "Sarah Sophia Banks"). See also Leis, "Displaying Art and Fashion," and "Ephemeral Histories."

2 British Museum no. 1867,0120.1; British Museum no. Franks.1; British Museum no. Am,St.400.a.

3 British Museum no. 1938,3.19.2.

4 The signs of wear and tear indicate that the ticket either (a) was used carelessly on the night of the ball in question, (b) may have been used on multiple occasions or (c) was subsequently used as a plaything.

5 Printed ephemera could be described as protophotographic in its capacity to document transient social experience, as indeed photography itself can be seen as imaged ephemerality. More work needs to be done on printed ephemera as part of the prehistory of photography.

6 For work in what might be called the "poetics of the archive" that draws attention to research as affective experience, see, for example, Steedman; Farge.

7 For example: Kirschenbaum; Chun; Gitelman. For a discussion of ephemera and ephemerality in performance studies, see Schneider 94–96.

8 Muñoz 10, derived from Raymond Williams' influential idea for affect theory of a "structure of feelings."

9 Johnson 11. For an excellent study of the rise of jobbing print, see Raven.

10 For a more detailed discussion of this, see Russell.

11 As Leah Price shows, the codex-form book was also prone to perishability and diverse uses, apart from reading (Price).

12 For Romantic bibliomania, see, for example, Connell; Lynch; Jensen; Klancher; Ferris.

13 *The London Literary Gazette* 26 May 1821 quoted in Ferris 17.

14 See Sherbo. Rumours and newspaper publicity concerning a sodomitical relationship between Heber and Charles Henry Hartshorne led Heber to move to the Continent between 1825 and 1831.

15 "Obituary" 109. In this respect, Heber's collecting mania can be seen as a form of "material deviance" that Scott Herring identifies as developing in the late nineteenth and early twentieth centuries (Herring).

16 For Sloane's collections of ephemera, see Mandelbrote.

17 Abbate 85.

bibliography

Abbate, Carolyn. "Overlooking the Ephemeral." *New Literary History* 48.1 (2017): 75–102. Print.

Bibliotheca Heberiana: Catalogue of the Library of the Late Richard Heber, Esq. Part the Eighth. London: Evans, 1836. Print.

Cameron, Hector Charles. *Sir Joseph Banks, K.B. P.R.S: The Autocrat of the Philosophers.* London: Batchworth, 1952. Print.

Catalogue of British and American Book Plates Bequeathed to the Trustees of the British Museum by Sir Augustus Wollaston Franks. 3 vols. London: British Museum, 1903. Print.

Caygill, Marjorie, and John Cherry, eds. *A. W. Franks: Nineteenth Century Collecting and the British Museum.* London: British Museum, 1997. Print.

Chun, Wendy Hui Kyong. "The Enduring Ephemeral, or the Future is a Memory." *Critical Inquiry* 35 (2008): 148–71. Print.

Clinton, Alan. *Printed Ephemera: Collection, Organisation and Access.* London: Bingley, 1981. Print.

Connell, Philip. "Bibliomania, Book Collecting, Cultural Politics, and the Rise of Literary Heritage in Romantic Britain." *representations* 71 (2000): 24–47. Print.

Credland, A.G. "Sarah and Joseph Banks and Archery in the Eighteenth Century." *Journal of the Society of Archer-Antiquaries* 34 (1991): 42–50. Print.

Credland, A.G. "Sarah and Joseph Banks contd." *Journal of the Society of Archer-Antiquaries* 35 (1992): 54–76. Print.

Cvetkovich, Ann. *An Archive of Feelings: Trauma, Sexuality, and Lesbian Public Cultures.* Durham, NC: Duke UP, 2003. Print.

Derrida, Jacques. *Paper Machine.* Trans. Rachel Bowlby. Stanford: Stanford UP, 2005. Print.

Eagleton, Catherine. "Collecting African Money in Georgian London: Sarah Sophia Banks and her Collection of Coins." *Museum History Journal* 6 (2013): 23–38. Print.

Eagleton, Catherine. "Sarah Sophia Banks, Adam Afzelius and a Coin from Sierra Leone." *The Material Cultures of Enlightenment Arts and Sciences.* Ed. Adriana Craciun and Simon Schaffer. London: Palgrave Macmillan, 2016. 203–05. Print.

Edelman, Lee. *No Future: Queer Theory and the Death Drive.* Durham, NC: Duke UP, 2004. Print.

Edenheim, Sara. "Lost and Never Found: The Queer Archive of Feelings and its Historical Propriety." *differences* 24.3 (2014): 36–62. Print.

Edwards, Edward. *Lives of the Founders of the British Museum.* 2 vols. London: Trubner, 1870. Print.

Ernst, Wolfgang. *Stirrings in the Archives: Order from Disorder.* Trans. Adam Siegel. Lanham, MA: Rowman, 2015. Print.

Farge, Arlette. *The Allure of the Archives.* New Haven: Yale UP, 2013. Print.

Ferris, Ina. *Book-Men, Book Clubs, and the Romantic Literary Sphere.* London: Palgrave Macmillan, 2015. Print.

Gitelman, Lisa. *Paper Knowledge: Towards a Media History of Documents.* Durham, NC: Duke UP, 2014. Print.

Griffiths, Antony. *Landmarks in Print Collecting: Connoisseurs and Donors at the British Museum since 1753.* London: British Museum, 1996. Print.

Griffiths, Antony, and Reginald Williams. *The Department of Prints and Drawings in the British Museum: User's Guide.* London: British Museum, 1987. Print.

Herring, Scott. *The Hoarders: Material Deviance in Modern American Culture.* Chicago: U of Chicago P, 2014. Print.

Hudson, Graham. *The Design and Printing of Ephemera in Britain and America 1720–1920.* London: British Library, 2008. Print.

Jensen, Kristian. *Revolution and the Antiquarian Book: Reshaping the Past, 1780–1815.* Cambridge: Cambridge UP, 2011. Print.

Johnson, Samuel. *The Rambler 145. Works.* Ed. W.J. Bate and Albrecht B. Strauss. Vol. 3. New Haven: Yale UP, 1969. Print.

Kirschenbaum, Matthew G. *Mechanisms: New Media and the Forensic Imagination.* Cambridge, MA: MIT P, 2008. Print.

Klancher, Jon. *Transfiguring the Arts and Sciences: Knowledge and Cultural Institutions in the Romantic Age.* Cambridge: Cambridge UP, 2013. Print.

Lamb, Jonathan. "Scientific Gusto versus Monsters in the Basement." *Eighteenth-Century Studies* 42.2 (2009): 309–20. Print.

Leis, Arlene. "Displaying Art and Fashion: Ladies' Pocket-Book Imagery in the Paper Collections of Sarah Sophia Banks." *Konsthistorisk tidskrift/Journal of Art History* 82.3 (2013): 252–71. Print.

Leis, Arlene. "Ephemeral Histories: Social Commemoration of the Revolutionary and Napoleonic Wars in the Paper Collections of Sarah Sophia Banks." *Visual Culture and the Revolutionary and Napoleonic Wars*. Ed. Satish Padiyar, Philip Shaw, and Phillipa Simpson. London: Routledge, 2017. 183–99. Print.

Leis, Arlene. "Sarah Sophia Banks: Femininity, Sociability and the Practice of Collecting in Late Georgian England." Ph.D. U of York, 2013. Print.

Lloyd, Sarah. "Ticketing the British Eighteenth Century: 'A thing ... never heard of before.'" *Journal of Social History* 46.4 (2013): 843–71. Print.

Lynch, Deidre. "'Wedded to Books': Bibliomania and the Romantic Essayists." *Romantic Libraries*. Ed. Ina Ferris. Spec. issue of *Praxis: An Online Journal of Romantic Circles*. Web. 24 Aug. 2017. First posted 2004. <http://www.rc.umd.edu/praxis/libraries/lynch/lynch.html>.

Mandelbrote, Giles. "Sloane and the Preservation of Printed Ephemera." *Libraries within the Library: The Origins of the British Library's Printed Collections*. Ed. Giles Mandelbrote and Barry Taylor. London: British Library, 2009. 146–68. Print.

McDowell, Paula. "Of Grubs and other Insects: Constructing the Categories of 'Ephemera' and 'Literature' in Eighteenth-Century British Writing." *Book History* 15 (2012): 48–70. Print.

Moger, Victoria. *The Favour of Your Company: Tickets and Invitations to London Events and Places of Interest c. 1750–1850*. London: Museum of London, 1980. Print.

Muñoz, José Esteban. "Ephemera as Evidence: Introductory Notes to Queer Acts." *Women & Performance: A Journal of Feminist Theory* 8.2 (1996): 5–16. Print.

"Obituary. Richard Heber Esq." *Gentleman's Magazine* new series 1 (1834): 105–09. Print.

Pincott, Anthony. "The Book Tickets of Miss Sarah Sophia Banks." *The Book Plate Journal* 2 (2004): 3–30. Print.

Price, Leah. *How to Do Things with Books in Victorian Britain*. Princeton: Princeton UP, 2012. Print.

Raven, James. *Publishing Business in Eighteenth-Century England*. Woodbridge: Boydell, 2014. Print.

Rickards, Maurice. *Collecting Printed Ephemera*. Oxford: Phaidon/Christie's, 1988. Print.

Robinson, Michael. "Ornamental Gentlemen: Thomas F. Dibdin, Romantic Bibliomania, and Romantic Sexualities." *European Romantic Review* 22.5 (2011): 685–706. Print.

Russell, Gillian. "The Ephemeral Eighteenth Century: Print, Sociability and the Cultures of Collecting." MS.

Schneider, Rebecca. *Performing Remains: Art and War in Times of Theatrical Reenactment*. London: Routledge, 2011. Print.

Sherbo, Arthur. "Heber, Richard (1774–1833)." *Oxford Dictionary of National Biography*. Ed. H.C.G. Matthew and Brian Harrison. Oxford: Oxford UP, 2004. (Online ed. Ed. David Cannadine. May 2015. Web. 25 Aug. 2017. <http://www.oxforddnb.com/view/article/12854>.)

Sherman, Stuart. *Telling Time: Clocks, Diaries, and English Diurnal Form, 1660–1785*. Chicago: U of Chicago P, 1996. Print.

Smith, Edward. *The Life of Sir Joseph Banks*. London: Lane, Bodley Head, 1911. Print.

Steedman, Carolyn. *Dust: The Archive and Cultural History*. Manchester: U of Manchester P, 2001. Print.

Young, Timothy G. "Evidence: Toward a Library Definition of Ephemera." *RBM: A Journal of Rare Books, Manuscripts and Cultural Heritage* 4 (2003): 11–26. Print.

Wilson, David M. *The Forgotten Collector: Augustus Wollaston Franks of the British Museum*. London: Thames, 1984. Print.

Wilson, David M. "Franks, Sir (Augustus) Wollaston (1826–1897)." *Oxford Dictionary of National Biography*. Ed. H.C.G. Matthew and Brian Harrison. Oxford: Oxford UP, 2004. (Online ed. Ed. David Cannadine. May 2014. Web. 24 Aug. 2017. <http://www.oxforddnb.com/view/article/10093>)

Responding to the thematic focus of this special issue on queer objects, five contemporary critics address one of the most popular queer books of the past five years: Maggie Nelson's *The Argonauts*. Exploring the memoir's genre-bending conventions, contributors assess Nelson's autotheoretical exploration of the everyday intimacies of gender, sex, love, pregnancy, motherhood, and transition.

DOSSIER

***THE ARGONAUTS* AS QUEER OBJECT**

Jason and Medea resemble each other, they are one and the same character.
   Pier Paolo Pasolini interviewed by Paul Willemen (68)

There is someone missing from Maggie Nelson's *The Argonauts*, a ghost in its machine for making sodomitical mothering: Medea. The *Argo*, the ship whose infinite capacity for change without loss of identity Nelson finds in *Roland Barthes by Roland Barthes*, was her home, too. Medea was not among the Argonauts who set out to steal the Golden Fleece from Colchis, but she returned to Corinth on the ship – unrecognized on the crew list, yet deeply influential on its journey. Following *Bluets* and *The Red Parts*, *The Argonauts* is subtly a book of gold: of the "so-called golden trimester" during which Nelson book toured with *The Art of Cruelty* (111); of the "golden, oily T" that Harry injects (52) – hints of the fleece with which Medea bought her passage from Colchis. Pasolini's observation, discussing his own adaptation of the play with Maria Callas in the title role – surely one of the "many-gendered mothers" of many queer cultural hearts – resonates subliminally with *The Argonauts*' desired slipperiness around gender, its investment in the capacity for mutability.

Medea's absence from *The Argonauts* is perhaps unsurprising, given that Euripides depicts her murdering her own children in order to punish Jason for his erotic and political infidelity; but it is also surprising, for Medea is the only Argonaut to bear a child: a difficult antecedent maybe, but a powerful one to think with. In Christa Wolf's retelling of the myth in *Medea*, the priestess Medea leaves behind

so mayer

MEDEA'S PERINEUM

the corruption of her homeland, but uncovers a cult of child sacrifice underlying the king's power in Corinth; in Wolf's hands, Medea becomes one way to approach the edge of one of Nelson's central questions:

> When or how do new kinship systems mime older nuclear-family arrangements and when or how do they radically recontextualise them in a way that constitutes a rethinking of kinship? How can you tell; or rather, who's to tell? (Quoting Judith Butler (in Kotz 83) 16)

Medea might be seen – or rather, radically recontextualized – as a limit case; not of the tropes of the obedient wife and abjectly grateful immigrant, as she was for the classical Athenians, but of the gaps and lacks in our account of parenting and kin-making, that which Nelson herself explores.

In the quotation that Nelson singles out, Butler is referring specifically to house mothers in ball culture, as seen in Jennie Livingston's documentary *Paris is Burning* (1990), which captured New York ball culture at the end of the 1980s, and included celebrated house mothers Paris Dupree, Pepper LaBeija, Willie Ninja, and Anjie Xtravaganza. Butler goes on to note that, in ball culture, a "'house' is the people you 'walk' with," emphasizing the active, rhizomatic and embodied labour, as pioneered by transwomen of colour, through which radically rearticulated kinship is produced (Kotz 83). In "m/other ourselves: a Black queer feminist genealogy for radical mothering," published a year after *The Argonauts*, Alexis Pauline Gumbs expands on this proposition:

> What if mothering is about the how of it? In 1987, Hortense Spillers wrote "Mama's Baby, Papa's Maybe: An American Grammar Book," reminding her peers that motherHOOD is a status granted by patriarchy to white middle-class women, those women whose legal rights to their children are never questioned, regardless of who does the labor (the how) of keeping them alive. MotherING is another matter, a possible action, the name for that nurturing work, that survival dance [...] worked by house mothers in ball culture who provide spaces of self-love and expression for/as queer youth of color in the street. What would it mean for us to take the word "mother" less as a gendered identity and more as a possible action, a technology of transformation that those people who do the most mothering labor are teaching us right now? (22–23)

Work – the work of motherING – weaves its own way through *The Argonauts*, perhaps a gentle reproof to Barthes for that which is absent from his account of the changing Argo: the labour that makes change and maintains relationality. As Nelson notes, "if we want to do more than claw our way into repressive structures, we have our work cut out for us" (32). For Nelson, work appears to mean the transformative, a constellation of writing and living that is summed up when she comments on how the "realization that I could incorporate the stalker into my talk about Sedgwick eventually became an incitement for me to get back to work. *Yes, get back to work*" (153). This instance, in which a traumatic individual experience is a precursor to a commitment to labour, prefigures the manner in which the complexity of MotherING Iggy will be "an incitement [...] to get back to work" as a writer (writing, in fact, *The Argonauts*).

The book is thus a queer object that anticipates its own production as it also details the labour of its own making in parallel with the labour of conception, pregnancy and parenting, and of transitioning or reshaping gender, connecting these to the work of political change, particularly around queer and cultural politics. The "work" that is "cut out for us" by Nelson's piercing intellect is that of opposition to easy assumptions of homonormativity or assimilation, in terms – or rather, actions – more complex than those of the radical call to arms in a pamphlet from an intervention into Oakland Pride 2012 that she quotes on the same page as noting the work cut out for us. Nelson notes that she does not "share in this fantasy of attack," and *The Argonauts* works through a Butlerian commitment to non-violence and complexity (32). "How to explain," Nelson asks, "in a culture frantic for resolution, that sometimes the shit stays messy?" (65)

Yet Nelson's shit is also messy, in ways that facing Medea might have been able to address: the significant genealogy – of literary and political queer feminisms in the United States – on which Gumbs draws is parenthetically hinted at by Nelson, when talking about lesbians in radical feminist circles who had children: "(Cherríe Moraga, Audre Lorde...),” and on whose "mothering labor" – like those of house mothers – Nelson implicitly draws in her own account of defining a queer kinship (93). Gumbs notes that this labour was, importantly, literary as well as literal:

While the U.S. state enacted domestic and foreign policies that required, allowed and endorsed violence against the bodies of Black women and early death for Black children, Black feminists audaciously centered an entire literary movement around the invocation of this criminal act of Black maternity, demanding not only the rights of Black women to reproductive autonomy in the biological sense, but also the imperative to create narratives, theories, contexts, collectives, publications, political ideology, and more. I read the Black feminist literary production that occurred between 1970 and 1990 as the experimental creation of a rival economy and temporality in which Black women and children would be generators of an alternative destiny. (21)

There is thus a literary genealogy for Nelson's inscription of queer kinship, and particularly of queer reproductivity, one with important alliances to labour and class politics. Significantly, the words of writers such as Lorde and Moraga reached, as Nelson does, into myth and theory as well as politics and autobiography to generate an "alternative destiny" whereby they rewrote misrepresented (colonized) histories. Moraga – challenging both Euripides' play and Spanish accounts of women such as La Malinche, who were inscribed as "traitors" to their people – wrote a play called *The Hungry Woman: A Mexican Medea*, in which Medea – a lesbian – seeks to return from prison and exile, having led an anti-colonial struggle that has made Jason a leader. Domino Renée Perez draws attention to Moraga's parallel between Medea and the Aztec goddess Coatlicue, who opens the play (99–103). For Moraga, as for Wolf – who marks her Medea as dark-skinned and thick-haired – Medea is not only a figure of gendered Otherness as the intellectual, political, and spiritually gifted woman, but of raced Otherness, a subaltern colonial subject. Gumbs notes that the "radical potential of the word 'mother' comes after the 'm.' It is the space that 'other' takes in our mouths when we say it. We are something else" (21).

The absence of Medea marks, for me, the almost complete absence – in fact, persistent erasure – of people of colour in *The Argonauts*, either as lived beings or through Nelson's citational practice of queer kinship. The lack of acknowledgement that there is a Black queer and trans feminist (literary) genealogy for the kind of mothering and/as writing that Nelson undertakes is startling given her parenthetical acknowledgement of the queer feminist parent-writers who precede her, and whose work precedes hers, particularly in the anthologies of the Kitchen Table Collective. One (token) lived being configures (in order to disappear) the indigenous and African American presence in Nelson's home city of Los Angeles, "a lactation consultant […] a member of the Pima tribe from Arizona […] married into an African American family […] in Watts" (168). The consultant, whose knowledge is implicitly embodied and essentialized by the comment that she nursed all six of her children, tells Nelson and Harry a story that legitimates their choice of a "Native American […] (tribe unknown)" name for Iggy (ibid.).

The consultant tells them, "*I don't know why I'm telling you guys so much about my family* […] I like to think she had an intuition that something about identity was loose and hot in our house, as, perhaps, it was in hers" (ibid.). This series of deductions – first, a magical intuition of "loose and hot" queer and trans identities; second, a speculative parallel between these identities and the idea that a mixed-race household would consider themselves similarly "loose and hot" – is deeply problematic, a *Last of the Mohicans* substitutional move that tacitly allows Nelson exactly the politics she rails against when she writes that "the time for blithely asserting that sleeping with whomever you want however you want is going to jam [the world's] machinery is long past" (33). Queerness is not a ticket to political solidarity or radical alterity at the start of *The Argonauts* and yet, at the moment of birth, a kind of sentimental white liberal feminism seeps in, a determination to be placed in a Black and indigenous genealogy – without having done (or cited) any of the work. In a strange (self-)erasure of this magical adoption, Nelson continues that she learned (source uncited) that Pima was a name misderived by the Spanish from the Othama phrase "*pi 'añi mac* or *pi mac*, meaning 'I don't know' – a phrase tribe members supposedly said often in response to the invading Europeans" (169). "I don't know" is what the consultant says, according to Nelson: is the author thus implicitly recognizing her inclusion among the (confusing and confused) invading Europeans; or is this, in fact, an erasure of Othama speakers past and present into a self-denial; even, a lack of an epistemology that permits Nelson's appropriation?

Perez notes that in Moraga's play the resistance fighter

> residents [led by Medea] have renamed the city [of exile] Tomoanchán, which is translated in the play as "we seek our home," but this act of naming only underscores the depth of their exclusion from the Aztlán they helped make a reality. (99)

This is at once a painful reminder of Jason's betrayal of Medea, on whom he was dependent in his quest for power, and of the displacement of indigenous, Chicanx and Latinx people in and from California, particularly in recent years due to gentrification, although their communities persist. *The Argonauts* ends with the claim that "we're still here, who knows for how long, ablaze with our care, its ongoing song": a we that is intended as both intimate and inclusive, recognizing all the book's readers in the perverse possibilities of Nelson's vision of genders and sexualities as "acts of production" (178). Yet, in its lack of an account of race, its erasure of who that we includes, *The Argonauts*' desiringly expansive vision comes up against a limit, one that could be analogized through that other (almost-)missing term, the perineum.

In the same concluding paragraph, Nelson quotes Gilles Deleuze and Félix Guattari: "*Flying anuses, speeding vaginas, there is no castration*" (32, quoted in Nelson, *Argonauts* 178), a reincorporation of the book's important account of a female anal sexuality that is cleverly connected to the idea of "sodomitical maternity" as a queer feminist stake. Yet there is, if not a castration, an erasure. Despite the book's detailed narration of labour, and its less detailed but passionate and original narration of sexual encounters, there is only one mention of the perineum, just before Iggy crowns:

> Then they suddenly tell me to stop pushing. I don't know why. Harry tells me that the doctor is stretching my perineum in circles around the baby's head, trying to keep the skin from tearing. Hold, they say, don't push, but "puff." Puff puff puff. (165)

Technically, the perineum refers to the entire surface region between the pubic symphysis and the coccyx, including (for those that have them) the vagina and the anus; it could be described as that which stops the anus flying and the vagina speeding, that which limits them to the body. What's commonly called the perineum, in the sense Nelson employs it, is the perineal body, or central tendon, common to people of all genders, where the sphincters and muscles of the genital and anal regions meet in a fibrous mass. Approximately 85 per cent of patients delivering by vaginal birth experience some extent of perineal trauma, and in about 69 per cent the trauma is so extensive that suturing is required (McCandlish et al.). Nelson makes no further comment about her perineal body after this single, transitional moment of late labour.

Earlier, Nelson quotes a letter from the Q&A section of a pregnancy magazine, and her reaction thereto:

> Q: If my husband watches me labor, how will he ever find me sexy again, now that he's seen me involuntarily defecate, and my vagina accommodate a baby's head?
>
> This question confused me; its description of labor did not strike me as exceedingly distinct from what happens during sex, or at least some sex, or at least much of the sex I had heretofore taken to be good.
>
> No one asked, *How does one submit to falling forever, to going to pieces*. A question from the inside. (104–05)

Nelson's resistance to revisiting this question later is confusing: has her perineal elasticity been increased by "sex [she] had heretofore taken to be good," sexual activities that extend beyond heteronormative reproductive categories and explore the perineal as a site of capacity? How might the perineal mass, with its convergence of muscular structures including those that are involved in the spasms of orgasm, and those that maintain the integrity of the perineal floor and prevent prolapse, answer Nelson's unasked question about "*going to pieces*" – both literally and metaphorically? Might it hold together what her account both fears and eroticizes in falling for ever and fragmentation?

As a queer object of/enabling sodomitical maternity, the perineal body would appear to be a central term to be uncovered from *The Argonauts*: like Medea, it is a limit or test case of both gendering and physical/intellectual capacity (maternal and erotic). Known colloquially in the United States as the "taint" – as in "taint one thing or the other" – the perineal body is a site whose unnameability, its lack of configuration even in a queer erotic, works to name the stain (or taint) of queerness, but also – perhaps – the taint of genocide and slavery that underlies the birth of America in, as Nelson says of vaginal birth, "shit and labor" (104). Its vulnerability to the stresses of birthing-labour, of motherING rather than motherHOOD, offers a parallel to Nelson's quotation from Eileen Myles concerning the complexity of the performative autobiographical, which she relates, laterally, to Luce Irigaray's image of the self-touching labial lips: "My dirty secret has always been that it's of course about me" (Myles 151 quoted in Nelson, *Argonauts* 75).

Myles' *about*-ness is connected imagistically and theoretically to the circularity of the labia and the auto-stimulation that Nelson tries – but fails – to feel while reading Irigaray; it is in the work of the perineal body, pulling together muscles and sphincters, that labial self-touch would be worked. So Myles' phrase might be reconceived to mean "that which is around (and/as about) me," that is, the self as a manifestation of a wider (socio-political as well as cultural) context, an *about*-ness of writing that could be analogized by the entirety of the perineum, the full muscular situation of sexual and reproductive labo(u)r, which would entail a full exploration of its raced and classed as well as gendered nature. Concerned with presenting dirty secrets, *The Argonauts* – in missing Medea and the perineum – realizes, subtextually, that it has more, of and in, and especially about, itself, to reveal.

disclosure statement

No potential conflict of interest was reported by the author.

bibliography

Deleuze, Gilles, and Félix Guattari. *A Thousand Plateaus: Capitalism and Schizophrenia*. 1980. Trans. Brian Massumi. Minneapolis: U of Minnesota P, 1987. Print.

Gumbs, Alexis Pauline. "m/other ourselves: a Black queer feminist genealogy for radical mothering." *Revolutionary Mothering: Love on the Front Lines*. Ed. Alexis Pauline Gumbs, China Martens, and Mai'a Williams. Toronto: Between the Lines, 2016. 19–31. Print.

Kotz, Liz. "The Body You Want: Liz Kotz Interviews Judith Butler." *Artforum* 82 (Nov. 1992): 82–89. Print.

McCandlish, R. et al. "A Randomised Controlled Trial of Care of the Perineum during Second Stage of Normal Labour." *British Journal of Obstetric Gynaecology* 105.12 (1998): 1262–72. Print.

Medea. Dir. Pier Paolo Pasolini. Perf. Maria Callas. San Marco S.p.A, Les Films Number One, Janus Film und Fernsehen, 1969. Film.

Moraga, Cherríe. *The Hungry Woman: A Mexican Medea*. 1995. The Hungry Woman. New York: West End, 2001. 1–100. Print.

Myles, Eileen. "Long and Social." *Biting the Error: Writers Explore Narrative*. Ed. Mary Burger, Robert Glück, Camille Roy, and Gill Scott. Toronto: Coach House, 2000. 149–51. Print.

Nelson, Maggie. *The Argonauts*. London: Melville House, 2016. Print.

Nelson, Maggie. *The Art of Cruelty*. New York: Norton, 2012. Print.

Nelson, Maggie. *Bluets*. London: Cape, 2017. Print.

Nelson, Maggie. *The Red Parts: Autobiography of a Trial*. London: Vintage, 2017. Print.

Paris is Burning. Dir. Jennie Livingston. Perf. Paris Dupree, Pepper LaBeija, Willie Ninja, and Anjie Xtravaganza. Miramax, 1990. Film.

Perez, Domino Renée. *There was a Woman: La Llorona from Folklore to Popular Culture*. Austin: U of Texas P, 2008. Print.

Spillers, Hortense. "Mama's Baby, Papa's Maybe: An American Grammar Book." *diacritics* 17.2 (1987): 64–81. Print.

Willemen, Paul, ed. *Pier Paolo Pasolini*. London: British Film Institute, 1977. Print.

Wolf, Christa. *Medea: A Modern Retelling*. Trans. John Cullen. London: Virago, 1998. Print.

kaye mitchell

"FERAL WITH VULNERABILITY"
on the argonauts

A multitude of ideas radiate outwards from the pages of Maggie Nelson's *The Argonauts*, but I want to trace the trajectory of just one: vulnerability. In doing so, I read the text as elaborating a politics and ethics of vulnerability in both its thinking and its formal qualities, thereby showing us the radical aesthetic, personal and political potential of this state of apparent unguardedness. I understand vulnerability here, as Erinn Gilson does, not as "a generalizable weakness" but rather as "a basic kind of openness to being affected and affecting in both positive and negative ways" (310). As Gilson asserts: "Vuln*erability* is not just a condition that limits us but one that can *enable* us," and Nelson's beautiful paean to love and queer kinship admirably bears this out (ibid.).

Foremost among the vulnerabilities charted by *The Argonauts* is emotional vulnerability. A couple of days after her "love pronouncement" to Harry, Nelson proclaims herself "now feral with vulnerability" (*Argonauts* 5), thus resituating vulnerability as wildness: as something that both exceeds and confirms our (supposed) humanity, that represents indiscipline, unpredictability, the animal and the undomesticated, deviant with disruptive potential – but also fearful. The text as a whole presents vulnerability as a necessary condition of both recognition and relationship – any relationship – but particularly as a necessary condition of love. If I open myself up to you, what do I gain precisely *by* what I risk, by the boundaries I demolish or disregard? Despite the "rushed" nature and tacky locale of their wedding ceremony, in the hours before Prop 8 is passed, Nelson and Dodge are "undone" (30), just as Judith Butler suggests we should be, by each other (*Undoing Gender* 30). Later, Nelson is further undone by her relationship with her new baby, Iggy, and she foresees more profound undoing to come: quoting Eula Biss, that "The mother of an adult child sees her work completed and undone at the same time," she asks "Can one prepare for one's undoing?" (174).

This openness to the point of being undone is desired and it is joyful, but it also risks either "merging" (as Nelson opines, of her relationship with Dodge: "I wasn't ready to lose sight of *my own me* yet" (58)), or "obliteration" – as Alice Notley, quoted here, describes pregnancy and motherhood: "he is born and I am undone – feel as if I will / never be, was never born. // Two years later I obliterate myself again ... "

(45). Pregnancy is an "[experiment] with my obliteration," writes Nelson. Nevertheless, she repeatedly refuses to "[hide her] dependencies in an effort to appear superior to those who are more visibly undone or aching" (127); the admission of vulnerabilities, dependencies even, is, indeed, connected to pleasure – or at least to Nelson's conclusion, fairly late on in *The Argonauts*, "that a studied evasiveness has its own limitations, its own ways of inhibiting certain forms of happiness and pleasure" (140). She refuses such an "evasiveness" and remains "ashamed, but undaunted" in her commitment to the personal and to forms of self-exposure, asking whether "ashamed, but undaunted" is "(my epithet?)," the question's parenthetical tentativeness both shield and encapsulation (75). "Ashamed but undaunted" signals both vulnerability and courage, the two not opposed but utterly interlinked. The shame, notably, is not overcome, but is rather inhabited; it is even (creatively) productive rather than paralysing, as it might at first glance seem to be.

And yet, importantly, Nelson takes issue with Kaja Silverman's account of women as, so often, "egoically wounded," so that they "bathe in the sun of [the] idealization" that they receive from their infant children. "Remnant Lacanian that she is," writes Nelson, "Silverman's aperture does not seem wide enough to include an enjoyment that doesn't derive from filling a void, or love that is not merely balm for a wound" (120). So to be vulnerable, in various ways, is not necessarily to adhere to a view of oneself as wounded – or, indeed, as (feminine) *wound* (Latin *vulnerabilis*, from *vulnerare* "to wound," from *vulnus* "wound"). Love is not simply, or not only, a response to vulnerability, nor is it a cure or compensation for it; rather, vulnerability is both condition and consequence of love; and vulnerability, like love, has its pleasures. (As an image of this, consider Nelson standing naked "in a friend's cavernous fourth-floor painting studio," while Dodge asks her "to say aloud what I wanted you to do to me"; she faces "a lifetime of unwillingness to claim what I wanted, to ask for it," but somehow finds the words anyway (87).)

In its tale of bodily transformations and transitions, *The Argonauts* also muses on physical vulnerabilities, on the sense of the body as pregnable, penetrable, defenceless, susceptible to death, decay and ageing – but also as something that is transformed by desire. The year 2011 is "the summer of our changing bodies. Me, four months pregnant, you six months on T," writes Nelson (99); and the text juxtaposes the labour of birth and the cessation of labour that is the death of Harry's mother. However planned, however anticipated these transitions may be, their precise trajectories remain uncertain, surprising, unsettling:

> On the surface, it may have seemed as though your body was becoming more and more "male," mine, more and more "female." But that's not how it felt on the inside. On the inside, we were two human animals undergoing transformations beside each other, bearing each other loose witness. In other words, we were aging. (103)

What does "bearing witness" amount to, for Nelson? *The Argonauts* is itself a kind of bearing-loose-witness (the looseness an indication of its necessarily improvisational, impressionistic, lovingly makeshift quality). We might read it as an acknowledgement of a kind of dependency – but an acknowledgement that is not an excoriation. As Shiloh Y. Whitney writes, parsing the work of Eva Kittay, "Once we admit the possibility of enabling and valuable dependencies, our norm of personhood can no longer be defined against vulnerability and dependency"; accordingly, "*dependency is not necessarily domination, nor does corporeal vulnerability necessarily signify an opportunity to wound*" (560). Catherine Opie's *Self-Portrait/Cutting*, Harry's unremovable tattoos, Harry's physical pain from binding and later surgical scars, Nelson's own body "queered" by pregnancy – in *The Argonauts* the bodies bear literal wounds as a result of their diverse histories, their surfaces vulnerable to invasion, inscription, to rewriting and reinvention but also to misreading (to pass or not to pass?). Pregnancy, as it is presented here, involves the willingness "to go to pieces"

(155). Nelson says of labour: "you will have touched death along the way. You will have realized that death will do you too, without fail and without mercy" (167). Mortality, then, is the ultimate bodily vulnerability and it makes its presence felt even – especially – in acts of birthing, in sex, in those moments when we are most open, most undone.

In a recent interview, Butler asserted that "gender assignment finds us, from the start, vulnerable to its effects," and she figures vulnerability not as a form of "pure passivity" or as an absence of will, but rather as "the condition of responsiveness" that might lead to quite productive or positive challenges to "the terms by which we are addressed" (Ahmed 485). On Butler's reckoning, we are "vulnerable" in the sense that we are *subject to* the "enormous discursive practice" of gender, and vulnerable because we require these "forms of enabling address" – what she elsewhere refers to as *recognition* (ibid.). For Butler, a refusal or denial of vulnerability is linked to "fantasies of sovereignty" (at the state level but also at a personal level); in texts such as *Excitable Speech* (1997) and *Precarious Life* (2005) she "endorses an engagement that is anchored in and arises from acknowledgement (not disavowal) of human interdependence and incompletion," an acknowledgement of our vulnerability, our susceptibility to injury at the hands of the Other (Shulman 232).

The Argonauts touches also on the vulnerability *of* gender: its "ontological indeterminacy," in Nelson's phrase (18) and thus its susceptibility to obfuscation, misreading, revision, subversion; as she quotes Denise Riley, "Gendered self-consciousness has, mercifully, a flickering nature" (ibid.), and that flickering manifests as a source of both consolation and anxiety. (Here and elsewhere, "flickering" becomes a metaphor for, a model of, the precarious and impermanent, the hard-to-pin-down: early on, Nelson describes how she "looked anew at unnameable things, or at least things whose essence is flicker, flow" (5).) The text treats also of our vulnerability *to* what Butler calls the "enormous discursive practice" of gender – our apparent need for these "forms of enabling address" (again: to pass or not to pass?), but also our perturbation when confronted by them: as Nelson asks, baffled by the terms by which she is, at one moment, required to understand herself and her relationship, "Was Harry a woman? Was I a straight lady?" (10). Nelson reveals the vulnerability of marriage to the threat of the non-normative (that "long history of queers constructing their own families" (90)), but also the vulnerability of the non-normative to assimilation, to normativity itself: "Poor marriage! Off we went to kill it (unforgivable). Or reinforce it (unforgivable)" (28).

Perhaps most strikingly, *The Argonauts* reveals the vulnerability of the writer, particularly the writer who puts herself, her personal experiences and feelings, into her work – "contaminating" that work, and making herself open to "shaming" (as Jane Gallop is by Nicole Krauss, at the event that Nelson attends) (50–52). "Part of the horror of speaking, of writing," Nelson claims, is that "there is nowhere to hide" (121). While Roland Barthes "adds to each sentence some little phrase of uncertainty, as if anything that came out of language could make language tremble," Nelson notes that: "My writing is riddled with such tics of uncertainty. I have no excuse or solution, save to allow myself the tremblings, then go back in later and slash them out. In this way I edit myself into a boldness that is neither native nor foreign to me" (122). If Barthes's uncertainty is an artificial insertion, in the service of an anti-totalizing politico-philosophical point, Nelson's "tremblings" are part of her writerly process, part of her work's admission, staging and reworking of textual and authorial vulnerability.

In writing *of* and *through* and *in* vulnerability, Nelson contributes to a heterogeneous "tradition" of feminist art that might include Chris Kraus's attempt to "handle vulnerability like philosophy, at some remove" in *I Love Dick* (207–08), Dodie Bellamy's assertion that "an in-your-face owning of one's vulnerability and fucked-upness to the point of embarrassing and offending tight-asses is a powerful feminist strategy" in *the buddhist* (34–35, 42), or Kathy

Acker's investment in "wildness" as a state of being "soft and totally hurtable," "no longer separated from other people" (*Blood and Guts* 93); we might think also of the work of visual and conceptual artists like Hannah Wilke, Ana Mendieta, Sophie Calle and Marina Abramovich. These authors and artists explore and document (rather than "confess") experiences of romantic injury and vulnerability, shame and self-abasement. In connecting these experiences to the structural conditions of gendered vulnerability by situating their work in relation to a tradition of feminine and feminist self-exposure, such works touch on a "primary vulnerability" with very particular social and cultural consequences for those gendered or addressed as women. Such a primary vulnerability also works against a kind of sovereignty at the level of the self and of the text – hence the foregrounding of a shame that both produces and undoes the self, hence the texts' formal and other incoherencies (the text itself is "undone"), hence the disruption of any kind of stable narratorial "I" – while exploring qualities of "interdependence and incompletion."

What, though, is the political potentiality of this acknowledgement of "primary vulnerability"? Its obverse has lately come in for some criticism. Thus Gilson asserts that:

> The denial of vulnerability can be understood to be motivated by the desire [...] to maintain a certain kind of subjectivity privileged in capitalist socioeconomic systems, namely, that of the prototypical, arrogantly self-sufficient, independent, invulnerable master subject. (312)

And she maintains that, "in seeking invulnerability we specifically ignore the constitutive aspect of vulnerability, the way in which we become who we are through openness to others" (319). Butler, more pertinently, views the "vanquishing" of vulnerability as "a masculinist ideal," and, in her recent work, seeks to contest this "form of thinking that models itself on mastery" ("Rethinking" 15, 17). In *The Argonauts*, Nelson muses: "Perhaps it's the word *radical* that needs rethinking. But what could we angle ourselves toward instead, or in addition? Openness? Is that good enough, strong enough?" (33). She poses the question, rather than answering it, leaving it – appropriately – vulnerable. And if vulnerability is, indeed, originary, constitutive, then perhaps we have no option but to angle ourselves towards it and to see where that angling takes us (our vulnerability is not vitiated by our agency, nor should it be). What Gilson terms "epistemic vulnerability" involves – among other qualities – "being open to not knowing," accepting "the genuine value of discomfort," and attending to "the affective and bodily dimensions of knowledge" (325). *The Argonauts*, on my reading, enacts exactly these qualities. The text itself practises a kind of radical openness as it merges Nelson's own thoughts and words with the words of others (Deleuze and Parnet, Butler, Sedgwick, Winnicott). This foregrounding of its intertextuality (and its fragmentariness) models a vulnerability of borders/boundaries, an interpenetration of words and ideas, and a refusal of the assumed sovereignty of selfhood and authorship that becomes its strength (through conversation, communion). Reading *The Argonauts*, I am reminded, too, of the transmissibility of vulnerability: I am wounded by it, but blissfully so; I surrender to it, my own "studied evasiveness" (as reader, scholar, person) thwarted; I carry it with me, still, feeling both undone and encountered.

disclosure statement

No potential conflict of interest was reported by the author.

bibliography

Acker, Kathy. *Blood and Guts in High School*. 1978. New York: Grove, 1984. Print.

Ahmed, Sara. "Interview with Judith Butler." *Sexualities* 19.4 (2016): 482–92. Print.

Bellamy, Dodie. *the buddhist*. Berkeley: Allone, 2011. Print.

Butler, Judith. "Rethinking Vulnerability and Resistance." *Vulnerability in Resistance*. Ed. Judith

Butler, Zeynep Gambetti, and Leticia Sabsay. Durham, NC: Duke UP, 2016. 12–27. Print.

Butler, Judith. *Undoing Gender*. London: Routledge, 2004. Print.

Gilson, Erinn. "Vulnerability, Ignorance, and Oppression." *Hypatia* 26.2 (2011): 308–32. Print.

Kraus, Chris. *I Love Dick*. Los Angeles: Semiotext(e), 2006. Print.

Nelson, Maggie. *The Argonauts*. London: Melville House, 2016. Print.

Shulman, George. "On Vulnerability as Judith Butler's Language of Politics: From 'Excitable Speech' to 'Precarious Life.'" *Women's Studies Quarterly* 39.1–2 (2011): 227–35. Print.

Whitney, Shiloh Y. "Dependency Relations: Corporeal Vulnerability and Norms of Personhood in Hobbes and Kittay." *Hypatia* 26.3 (2011): 554–74. Print.

monica b. pearl

THEORY AND THE EVERYDAY

What delights me about *The Argonauts* is that it does something so obvious and so rare – and so very welcome: it combines high theory and the everyday. It does – not just illustrates but actually seems to perform – what life feels like to me, with its immingling of lofty thought, the quotidian, close attention to words and ideas and stray thoughts, and desire. And it does this largely through form, the way it both (at the same time) blends and refuses genre. The way it seems to skip around from one thought or story to another – in the very way one might turn one's attention to different eventualities and possibilities (and impossibilities) in a day – and by doing one thing and then another making them connect by virtue of contiguity.

The title of the book comes from Roland Barthes's evocation of what is known philosophically as the paradox of Theseus' ship, which is a paradox of identity: can something (the ship the *Argo*) still be known and called by the same name if all its parts have changed? Nelson's book borrows this concept from Barthes and also, in many ways, its structure. For example, like *A Lover's Discourse*, *The Argonauts* performs a theoretical conversation by referring to others whose ideas one is engaging with in the text's margins. These are not exactly scholarly references ("It's a philosophical memoir with lots of ideas but zero footnotes" (Brennan 20)), but naming, making a web of the people in the room (as it were). "Intertextuality abounds in *The Argonauts*" (Gilmore, "Life of the Body"). Yet it confounds scholarly structure.

If we are thinking about how we might make sense of the "narrative" of this book, the flow of one anecdote or thought or story to another, we might look to the section called "How this Book is Constructed" in which we read that "to discourage the temptation of meaning, it was necessary to choose an *absolutely insignificant* order." This is Roland Barthes who in *A Lover's Discourse* goes on to explain where the anecdotes, thoughts, and ideas come from:

> In order to compose this amorous subject, pieces of various origin have been "put together." Some come from ordinary reading [...] Some come from insistent readings [...] Some come from occasional readings. Some come from conversations with friends. And there are some which come from my own life. (8)

The marginal mentions in *The Argonauts* do seem very much like conversations: this is whom I am in dialogue with in thinking on this point or that idea; this is who has inspired this perception, this is whom I must ventriloquize to make my thoughts clear ... "The references supplied in this fashion are not authoritative but amical" (8–9), explains Barthes about his own marginal mentions ("zero footnotes"). Nelson herself comments on the intimacy of this kind of referencing: "I also think of the names in the margin as another scene of family-making" ("Diary, Theory, Poem, Memoir").

The Argonauts confounds scholarly form not only in refusing footnotes but in (anyway) engaging the words and ideas of myriad others, and not only those whose ideas are validated by academic pedigree – some are acquaintances, friends, experts outside the realm of scholarly thought, poets, her partner – and also in not having a point: no overarching claim that is being pushed and proved. At least, not in any methodical way. It is also not a story – neither fiction nor non-fiction – that we might recognize as developing, having a trajectory; nothing so old fashioned or familiar as a beginning, middle, and end: "a horizontal discourse" is how Barthes puts it, "no transcendence, no deliverance, no novel" (7).

The Argonauts refuses form in a way that parallels how Maggie's and Harry's bodies and identities refuse taxonomy: "not on the way to anywhere," she quotes her lover Harry as saying when pressed about where he might be in his gender transition. Queer, of course, is the rubric for these refusals and resistances. In other words, it might look like the same thing – family or femininity, memoir or monograph ... but it is not the same thing, depending on who is doing it, who is doing it with whom, and how they are thinking about it. It has new parts. (But it is still the *Argo*.) And new ways of expressing. New ways of being expressed. New ways of being seen and understood.

"Nelson's *Argo* is her queer family unit, a home and way of being in relation and in the world" (Gilmore, "Life of the Body"). Maggie is pregnant at the same time that Harry is having his surgery. Although they are both having experiences of their bodies stretching beyond what they have previously known them to be, one is more normatively recognizable. Pregnancy is the more categorically fathomable shape shifting. They are mistaken as a heteronormative couple; they are also mistaken as a lesbo-normative couple. Harry is mistaken for a man, who just doesn't have a matching manly name on his driver's licence. Maggie is mistaken for a pregnant woman and a mother who, with her man, is doing it all in the same old wonted way. This is the puzzle presented in the book: the paradox of how we might understand or recognize queerness when it looks conventional.

Nearly all commentary on *The Argonauts* refers to its genre bending, for example: "Genres in this book are bent beyond recognition; boundaries are transcended and ignored" (Szalai) and: "While many critics call this book a memoir, I see it as more of a genre-bender" (Hagan 39). The term "genre bending" is a not very oblique reference to the still fairly recent, yet nevertheless now practically dated, concept of "gender bending," and some commentary refers more directly to the text as gender bending: "this gender-bending memoir" (de León). Genre and gender are the same word, "a kind" or "type," and come from the same root (the root "gen" means to give birth, beget). And: "Neither genre nor gender is as categorically stable as common usage tends to imply" (Stevens).

The book is a paradox not only of content but also of genre. The title, *The Argonauts*, in referring to a structure – a ship – is also referring to a genre. In other words, genre works in precisely this way: it has a rough structure and with it a name. Those things that fit into the rubric of that structure are called by that name; at the same time, what is claimed and named under that structure changes the category. Maggie Nelson calls *The Argonauts* "autotheory," a combination of autobiography and critical theory. But by using critical theory in her autobiographical account she is stretching the category of autobiography (and possibly also of critical theory). Like the *Argo* and its commutable parts, once we have an idea of the genre – even an innovation of a genre – it can do almost anything and still be that name. Nelson conjures Eve Sedgwick's concept of queer as "a kind of placeholder – a nominative, like *Argo*, willing to designate molten or shifting parts" (29). At the same time, naming a category transforms the contents. Of pictures in an exhibition, Nelson observes that "Some of the subjects of *Puppies and Babies* may not identify as queer, but it doesn't matter: the installation queers them" (72).

So, even if Maggie Nelson finds it "a little romantic" to let "an individual experience of desire take precedence over a categorical one," in the way that she cites both Djuna Barnes and Gertrude Stein preferred to claim their love for their particular lover (Thelma for Djuna; Alice for Gertrude) "rather than identify as a lesbian," and even if Nelson is "taken aback" at the imputation that her relationship with Harry might be a lesbian one ("Soon after we got together, we attended a dinner party at which a [...] woman who'd known Harry for some time turned to me and said, 'So, have you been with other women, before Harry?' I was taken aback" (8)), her book is nevertheless engaged in some lesbian practices. That is, there is a legacy of generic autobiographical messiness when it comes to representing lesbian lives.

Historically, women have never had a straightforward or comfortable relationship with the genre of autobiography, and even women whose proximity to the category lesbian comes from refusing it or kicking against it have had to come up with novel names and methods to do their life writing. There are some obvious historical progenitors, including the life writing of Gertrude Stein and Djuna Barnes. The genre paradox of *The Autobiography of Alice B. Toklas* is that it is written by Gertrude Stein. "For Stein," Leigh Gilmore tells us, "lesbianism is not an identity with a predictable content, and neither is autobiography. Rather, both become occasions for experimentation" ("Signature" 72). Audre Lorde invented a new category for a book that could contain the story of her life as a black lesbian: she referred to her book *Zami* as a "biomythography." There are myriad examples (see Pearl). Including Djuna Barnes' nearly inscrutable *caricature à clef*, *Ladies Almanack*.

I am aware that I am in danger of being among those blinded by the tyranny of identitarianism, whom Nelson cites dismissively when she describes how some people respond to the philosopher Judith Butler, that despite "whatever words come out of her mouth [...] certain listeners hear only one thing: *lesbian, lesbian, lesbian*" (54). Of course, what I am referring to as lesbian pressures on autobiographical form are in many ways what we would now refer to as queer. (And indeed it does now seem that Gertrude Stein was probably more queer than lesbian – or, and this anyway is what is pertinent here, that her writing was.) And that the generic messiness associated with lesbian life writing is now legible as an anticipation of a queer (or queered) genre.

Is this the same ship – here with continuous parts yet called by a different name?

Queerness, however, is not just a category or a name; it describes the undoing, the fluctuation of parts. If it is a classification that attempts to capture something shifting and subversive and untamed, then it does the work of what naming (and taming) an affect – or feeling – might do: it harnesses something wild, something that only truculently obeys boundaries and borders.

The reference to the *Argo*, the ship that is always called the *Argo*, and is recognizable as the *Argo*, even when it has none of its original components, is a metaphor that works for many of the queer collocations and conventions that Nelson interrogates and reimagines, deploying theory, poetry, and anecdote to do the reimagining; however, we might recall that it was originally introduced to defend and reanimate the most clichéd and worn-out phrase and feeling around: "I love you."

A day or two after my love pronouncement, now feral with vulnerability, I sent you the passage [...] in which Barthes describes how the subject who utters the phrase "I love you" is like "the Argonaut renewing his ship during its voyage without changing its name." (5)

I have said this book is about structure, about form, and about genre; it is also about feelings. Which are also structured, also formed. And also have an originary existence.

In seeming sagacity of the *Argo*-paradox as it pertains to language and love, Freud tells us that "Even in its caprices the usage of language remains true to some kind of reality." "Thus," he continues,

> it gives the name of "love" to a great many kinds of emotional relationship which we too group together theoretically as love; but then again it feels a doubt whether this love is real, true, actual love, and so hints at a whole scale of possibilities within the range of the phenomena of love. (141)

Is "I love you" always already a worn-out phrase? Does it have a referent: does the signifier of the phrase have a signified in a feeling? Is it old or new – the same name but obsolete parts? "I thought the [Barthes] passage was romantic," Nelson writes. "You read it as a possible retraction" (5).

Freud explains that even though we give up our formative erotic attachment to our parents, it nevertheless persists in shadow and echo in all and any adult love: "It is well known," Freud writes, "that the earlier 'sensual' tendencies remain more or less preserved in the unconscious, so that in a certain sense the whole of the original current continues to exist" (Freud 142). (Maggie and Harry themselves discover that the imprint of erstwhile attachment is not easily erased: early in their relationship they are "crestfallen" when they learn that the cost of removing "the names and images of others" tattooed on Harry's body is too dear and accept "the improbability of ever completely eradicating the ink" (6).)

We might be able to queer marriage and queer the couple and motherhood and the body, but can we queer feelings? It may be disappointing to conclude that there is no queer love – there is only that ordinary love that everyone feels and everyone expresses with the same words. It may be that we feel it differently, more deeply, more magnificently than anyone ever has felt it before, but literature (for example) tells us otherwise. That whatever intoxication we experience is just that. (Freud likens being in love to hypnosis – a kind of rudderless ensorcelled submission (Freud 144–45).)

Perhaps this is what *The Argonauts* is doing, besides exciting us with its innovative amalgam of genres and gender, something more quotidian than queer. Which anyway is what Maggie Nelson has been telling us all along, that whatever we think we are innovating or learning, we are probably telling ourselves something we already knew, again: "Sometimes one has to know something many times over. Sometimes one forgets, and then remembers. And then forgets, and then remembers. And then forgets again" (18).

Nelson reassures us, however, that this relentless repetition is "not because one is stupid or obstinate or incapable of change, but because such revisitations constitute a life" (112). Which is a relief, because if we imagine we can redo or renew or rebuild love with new parts or new names – queer the ordinary and the conventional and the universal and by doing so somehow satisfy or restructure our original frustrated yet pure and untested devotions that we have had to absorb in order to disavow and then figure out how to reattach to a new object – well: that ship has sailed.

disclosure statement

No potential conflict of interest was reported by the author.

bibliography

Barnes, Djuna. *Ladies Almanack*. 1928. Manchester: Carcanet, 2006. Print.

Barthes, Roland. *A Lover's Discourse: Fragments*. 1977. Trans. Richard Howard. New York: Farrar, 1990. Print.

Brennan, Samantha. Review. *Kennedy Institute of Ethics Journal* 26.3 (2016): 19–20. Web. 13 Sept. 2017.

de León, Concepción. "20 Years of L.G.B.T.Q. Lit: A Timeline." *The New York Times* 23 June 2017. Web. 13 Sept. 2017.

Freud, Sigmund. "Being in Love and Hypnosis." 1921. *Civilization, Society and Religion*. Ed. and trans. James Strachey. London: Penguin, 1991. Print.

Gilmore, Leigh. "The Life of the Body in American Autobiography." *Biography* 39.4 (2016). Web. 13 Sept. 2017.

Gilmore, Leigh. "A Signature of Lesbian Autobiography: 'Gertrice/Altrude.'" *Prose Studies* 14.2 (1991): 56–75. Print.

Hagan, Debbie. Review. *Pleiades: Literature in Context* 37.1 (2017): 39–40. Web. 13 Sept. 2017.

Lorde, Audre. *Zami: A New Spelling of my Name*. New York: Crossing, 1982. Print.

Nelson, Maggie. *The Argonauts*. Minneapolis: Graywolf, 2015. Print.

Nelson, Maggie. In Conversation with Adam Fitzgerald. "'The Argonauts': Diary, Theory, Poem, Memoir." *Lit Hub* 5 May 2015. Web. 13 Sept. 2017.

Pearl, Monica B. "Lesbian Autobiography and Memoir." *The Cambridge Companion to Lesbian Literature*. Ed. Jodie Medd. Cambridge: Cambridge UP, 2016. 169–87. Print.

Stevens, Dana. "Bookends." *The New York Times Book Review* 5 July 2015: 31. Print.

Szalai, Jennifer. Review. *The New York Times* 7 May 2015. Web. 13 Sept. 2017.

jackie stacey

ON BEING A GOOD-ENOUGH READER OF MAGGIE NELSON'S *THE ARGONAUTS*

In trying to articulate some of my mixed responses to this book, I had a strange uneasy feeling that I might not be a *good-enough reader*. When I first began *The Argonauts*, the marginal citations irritated me so much that I nearly gave up.[1] This elliptical style assumed a great deal of cultural capital; many readers would just not be familiar with all these names. What use is a citation without a date and page number anyway? And what was this self-alignment with Roland Barthes? Was Maggie Nelson naming her band of Argonauts in the margins to protect her on her epic journey? Would they make her the good-enough writer – secure her place alongside her muses? Just as Nelson describes the dedication to "the queerest of the queer" at the end of a porn film she has just watched feeling like "the needle zig-zagging off the record after a great song" (79), so each new marginal citation grated on me. But then I became aware of my own envy: how great not to have to bother with full references. And, I had to admit to myself, there was some satisfaction in recognizing most (though not all) of the marginal names.

Accompanied by her two favourite "Argos," Winnicott and Barthes, Nelson reconfigures the psychic dynamics between readership and the act of writing. Prompted by Nelson's attachment to Winnicott's concept of the "good-enough mother," I want to consider what it might mean to be a good-enough reader of *The Argonauts*. Winnicott offers us the figure of the good-enough mother as a way to refuse both maternal idealization and denigration – two sides of the same tendency. For Winnicott, the good-enough mother is the one who holds the baby in mind, attending to and anticipating its needs, while also failing and thereby enabling the infant to become disillusioned: the mother's "eventual task is gradually to disillusion the infant," he writes (*Playing and Reality* 15). Unlike fantasies of the perfect all-providing mother, the good-enough one simultaneously gives the infant the sense of illusion and disillusion, enabling it to begin to tolerate frustration and to access its own aggression and creativity. "*If all goes well*," he argues, "the infant can actually come to gain from the experience of frustration, since incomplete adaptation to need [by the mother] makes objects real, that is to say, hated as well as loved" (14; emphasis in original). According to Winnicott, the infant whose every need is instantly met by the mother for too long a period after its birth is likely to suffer because her "exact adaptation resembles magic and the object that behaves perfectly is no better than an hallucination" (ibid.). In Winnicottian terms, the idealizing fantasy of the perfect mother is precisely *not good-enough* because she needs to succeed enough but also simultaneously fail at containment; failure lies at the heart of the infant's experience of good-enough mothering and is necessary for separation and for the emergence of creativity.

If we take the centrality of the "good-enough" in *The Argonauts* as our guide, then we should resist the temptation to idealize both the book and its author. To extend the good-enough to the dynamics between the reader and the author is to refuse idealizing relations between writing and its reception, and to welcome ambiguity and ambivalence on both sides. But more than this, if we want to follow Winnicott we would need to value what Adam Phillips refers to as *not quite "getting it"* (34–80) or not being sufficiently *in the know*. The good-enough reader is the one expected to tolerate being on the verge of failure and welcome its creative potential. To be open to generative failure is what Nelson's good-enough pushes its readership towards.

To couple Winnicott and Barthes is to bring together a psychoanalytic critique of idealization with a deconstruction of the fantasy of the omnipotent author. Straddling her love of these two writers, Nelson's tightly woven, yet loosely connected, poetic registers combine auto-theory with anecdotes about ordinary and messy lives, and stories of bodies transformed and intimacies deepened. The pleasures of these everyday textures flow into moments of psychoanalytic and philosophical insight whose wisdoms are blended with a modesty founded in tales of commonplace frustration that collide with more ambitious longings. Nelson demands of readers that they engage with her own ambivalent (and often not always admirable) responses to everyday encounters, as she guides us through the landscapes of the good-enough queer lives, loves and losses she narrates.

Given the refusal of idealization that flows from Nelson's kinship with Winnicott, there is an irony in the swoony kind of fandom that circulated in response to the book's publication (which I experienced in the United Kingdom anyway). Olivia Laing described *The Argonauts* as a "universally beloved book,"[2] and she was right. The buzz around it was heady and intense. To love this book was to feel included in something special (*we* are the Argonauts who'll renew the ship!). Several friends and colleagues told me that, when they got to the end of it, they immediately started reading it again for a second time. Many others said that they had read it all in one sitting, as they literally could not put it down. Perhaps its reflexive address somehow invites readers to share in the exhilaration of its aura and in the pleasure of its success; or maybe its subtle and shifting modes of address allow a flattering involvement (however vicariously) in the improvised queer worlds of creativity it invokes.

Whatever the reasons, there was something in the psychic life of the book's reception that meant that I both could not wait to read it and felt a rising, perverse resistance to joining the fandom – much like Nelson's account of her desire to find the cracks in stories of George and Mary Oppen's idealized relationship of lifelong mutual devotion: "so, shamefully, I looked [...] for evidence of their unhappiness" (42). Perhaps my initial irritation with its marginalia was a defence against feeling such a strong imperative to love it? I do remember feeling relief when finally someone said to me: "*The Argonauts*: I didn't straightforwardly *love* it; does that make me a puppy strangler?"[3] This comment confirmed something about the character of the book's reception that had made me feel that to say anything critical about it at all was like being the parent who turns on the lights in the middle of a teenage party. As Barthes put it: the "horror of spoiling" is even stronger than the anxiety of losing" (*A Lover's Discourse* 25).

Given Nelson's capacity for such eloquent critical self-reflection, it felt odd to me *not* to take up the book's invitation to enter into a dialogue that could accommodate some sense of my mixed responses. But in the giddy hype, to be not entirely swooning was to be on the outside of something (an othering which itself was the focus of the book's critique, I thought). Responses to *The Argonauts* carried something of an excited (and maybe anxious) over-identification, which was in danger of idealizing the book and fetishizing its author. For me, such idealizations went against the grain of Nelson's writing, which again and again pushes us away from such impulses. Nobody in *The Argonauts* gets to be idealized – except perhaps the pure pleasure of the couple giggling on the red couch at the beginning of their passion for each other. Grandiosity is always cut down to size, as the sense of inadequacy it masks becomes the more interesting focus. Reflecting back on my first reading of the book now, I wonder if my initial irritation emerged as much in response to the book's reception as it did to the form of the writing itself.

The Argonauts extends Nelson's interest in the messiness of our affective responses to each other to the dynamics of authorship and readership. The book generates in the reader the thrill (and threat) of feeling that one's reactions have already been read and yet are never fully foreclosed. This experience of readership is one of being gently tripped up yet not fully falling, or of feeling trapped somewhere but noticing the door has been left slightly ajar. It is seductive (hard to resist) and flattering (we are keen to live up to its demands). We imagine ourselves to be co-habiting with the shifting and uncertain ground of ethical and political affiliations formed in the particularities of these lives. As Nelson follows the maxim "pluralize and specify" from another of her Argos – Eve Kosofsky Sedgwick – we stretch ourselves to meet whatever paradoxical modes and scales of readership are demanded (78). But as soon as we begin to feel the comfort of recognition, it slips away as Nelson's change in register unexpectedly demands yet more of us; and, just as the pain of others becomes unbearable, the tone opens up the potential for deeper compassion. Never the all-knowing narrator, Nelson holds us in the spaces of these transitions, in the sheer difficulty of "shifting gears," which, she reminds us, is not the same thing as an "ontological either/or" (81). This experience of being put in motion, of being Nelson's transitive readers, speaks to the opening up of the psychic dynamics of readership and authorship in Barthes's work.

When Barthes announced the death of the author ("Death of the Author"), he named a series of substitute figures, such as the scriptor, who might open up the imaginative terrain of writing as a process of unpredictable and yet reiterative collaboration with the reader. If not the all-seeing, all-knowing author, then the writer might instead be involved in a process that generates "'transitional' spaces and objects" (to use Winnicott again) between the "me" and the "not-me" and the "you" and the "not-you" ("Transitional Objects"). Like Barthes, who made the moment of spoiling inherent to processes of idealization (*A Lover's Discourse* 25), Nelson refuses to let love become self-satisfying. Instead of gratifying the reader in search of self-confirmation or narcissistic pleasure, she moves us with her sometimes fleeting, sometimes recurrent, reflections on how to live compassionately outside the prescriptive imperatives and normativities of moral high ground and knee-jerk judgementalism.

In *The Argonauts* Nelson makes "the personal public" (75) in ways that hold readers in the critical tension between judgement and compassion. Finding a register that challenges easy responses to the scenarios recounted, she requires an openness in her readers that feels thrilling but sometimes only just tolerable: we are repeatedly on the verge of being wrong-footed by shifts in allegiance and then finding ourselves held again by the compassion the writing allows us to inhabit. In rehearsing her own encounters with humility so publicly, Nelson puts our critical responses in play, only to shift the ground away from the easy pleasures of self-righteousness. The reader feels vulnerable yet never fully exposed. Ultimately, if we take the risks demanded of us, we feel gratified by the demands this book makes on its readership. We find our "selves" set in motion and shaken out of complacency and familiar loyalties, as Nelson pays "homage to the transitive"

(66), with all the implications of *moving across* that this word holds. It is flattering to feel included in these intimate stories, which require readers to sit with ambiguities instead of reaching for predictable places to settle. Any academic who has attempted to write the self "otherwise" cannot fail to feel some sense of admiration (and probably envy) when reading *The Argonauts*.[4]

When Nelson refuses her aforementioned disidentification with the "queerer than queer" at the end of the porn film (79), she catches the desire to belong to the cutting edge and then strips it of its glamour. And, when she assumes that her partner Harry Dodge will share her outrage at the story of a mother's grief for the loss of her transitioning daughter, and she encounters instead his matter-of-factness, the reader feels Nelson's shame folding back the tendency to politically condemn the emotions of others: her capacity to revisit her own shame and transform into something else demands that the reader also shift gear. These moments, when Nelson puts her private shame onto the page for us to reckon with, are those in which the reader's affective identifications are put into play most intensely. Throughout the book, our intolerance is sparked and then turned into something more interesting, as Nelson's commitment to the non-judgementalism of psychoanalysis meets the quiet compassion of Buddhism as an ethical practice. We are tripped up by our own assumptions and affinities in relation to gay marriage, anal pleasure, feminist sadism, family photographs, trans bodies, breast feeding eroticism and ageing crones, as the limits of our compassionate readership are tested over and over.

This combination of feeling challenged yet held makes us imagine we can become the best versions of ourselves and rise above our usual predictable reactive responses. As the confessional becomes the conceptual, and as the utopian accommodates the limits of historical particularity, we are thrilled to be the readers we hope might match the "grace and appetite" of Nelson's writing.[5] Capital-letter categories (Life, Death, Sex, Money) find expression in accounts of pregnancy and transitioning, illness and bereavement and caring and letting go in ways that recognize the painful demands of an unpredictable existence and celebrate happiness without sentimentality. Vulnerability is held open for us, as we enter the intimate worlds of others through a direct address that we hope might have been meant for us; and yet, as Nelson reminds us, we are always "*for* and *of* others" rather than the autonomous subjects we might imagine (118).

Bringing together the scriptor and the ship builder, Nelson begins the book with reference to Barthes's use of the Argonauts as a metaphor for the reiterative function of the statement "I love you" which is renewed by each use. Like "the Argonaut renewing his ship without changing its name" the subject who says "I love you" seeks to give it "inflections which will be forever new" (5). In Greek mythology, the *Argo* (meaning swift), named after its builder Argus, was the ship on which Jason and the Argonauts set sail to retrieve the Golden Fleece (something which represented kinship and prosperity). In Nelson's book, the omnipotent author is replaced by the wordsmith who invites her readers to inhabit affective ambivalence in the spaces between shame and compassion that hold open an invitation to share a vision of the good-enough queer life. Refusing the heroism of the memoir as quest, Nelson instead offers us glimpses, fragments, fleeting moments of how kinship and prosperity might be recast through a feminist queerness that imagines bodies and desires beyond the binary, yet never forsakes a critique of misogyny.

In the end, perhaps the book poses the question of the good-enough writer and the good-enough reader to all of us. Perhaps it invites us to reconsider whom we take with us in our minds on our creative and academic journeys and how we might give our readers a different experience of encountering these imaginary genealogies. If this book is about the yearning towards queerer (but not the queerest) ways of doing relationality and reproduction beyond heteronormative genres, then perhaps even its break with citational conventions underscores the vision of the scrambled lines of descent that belong to the new improvised kinships of queer and feminist lives in all their messy and incomplete glory.

disclosure statement

No potential conflict of interest was reported by the author.

notes

1 Nelson's marginal citations use only authors' name and are reminiscent of Roland Barthes's *A Lover's Discourse*.

2 Olivia Laing used this phrase when she introduced Maggie Nelson at their dialogue at the London Review Bookshop. Video available at <https://www.youtube.com/watch?v=s-Yxhc2nNxo> (accessed 10 Oct. 2017). Laing also published a review of *The Argonauts* in *The Guardian* (Laing).

3 Intentionally or not, this comment echoes ironically with Nelson's discussion of *Puppies and Babies* (88).

4 I am borrowing this phrase from the collection *Writing Otherwise* (Stacey and Wolff).

5 I borrow this description from Christina Crosby at "The Argonauts: A Salon in Honor of Maggie Nelson," Barnard College, New York. Video available at <https://vimeo.com/164424580> (accessed 10 Oct. 2017).

bibliography

Barthes, Roland. "The Death of the Author." *Image, Music, Text*. London: Flamingo, 1984. 142–48. Print.

Barthes, Roland. *A Lover's Discourse: Fragments*. 1977. London: Vintage, 2002. Print.

Laing, Olivia. *The Argonauts* by Maggie Nelson Review. "One of the Sharpest Thinkers of her Generation." *The Guardian* 23 Apr. 2015. Web. 10 Oct. 2017. <https://www.theguardian.com/books/2015/apr/23/the-argonauts-maggie-nelson-review-harry-dodge-transgender>.

Nelson, Maggie. *The Argonauts*. London: Melville House, 2015. Print.

Phillips, Adam. *Missing Out: In Praise of the Unlived Life*. London: Hamish Hamilton, 2012. Print.

Stacey, Jackie, and Janet Wolff, eds. *Writing Otherwise: Experiments in Cultural Criticism*. Manchester: Manchester UP, 2013. Print.

Winnicott, D.W. *Playing and Reality*. Harmondsworth: Penguin, 1971. Print.

Winnicott, D.W. "Transitional Objects and Transitional Phenomena; A Study of the First Not-Me Possession." *International Journal of Psycho-Analysis* 34.2 (1953): 89–97. Print.

robyn wiegman

IN THE MARGINS WITH *THE ARGONAUTS*

I read Maggie Nelson's *The Argonauts* for the first time on a Kindle App on my android phone and was transfixed by what publicity materials called its "genre-bending" experimentation with "autotheory." Then a friend told me that Kindle had dismembered the book by eliminating its experimental dimensions in accordance with standard Kindle conventions. Read the print version they insisted or you will miss the full force of Nelson's autotheoretical punch. I followed their instructions and am intrigued by the difference between the page and digital versions, especially if we consider that interpretative practice does not stop at the *meaning* of the words that appear on the page – or screen. The visual orchestration of the text matters, in both aesthetic and ideological terms. What, then, should I make of the fact that my Kindle eliminates the paperback's use of the outer margin of the page, that space in which Nelson quite literally drops the name of many of the theorists, cultural warriors, friends, and lovers she quotes? The names dazzle: Eve Kosofsky Sedgwick, Judith Butler, Gilles Deleuze, Michel Foucault, Jacques Lacan, Luce Irigaray, D.W. Winnicott, Lee Edelman, Sara Ahmed, Leo Bersani, Adam Phillips, Paul Preciado, Eileen Myles, Harry Dodge. Is it true – or nearly true, or significant even if not true – that I am now the reader of two different if identically titled books, one more authentic than the other? Is my friend correct that the Kindle version does a certain violence to *The Argonauts*, "assassinating" the theory side of Nelson's genre-bending investment in bringing academic discourses into a first-person memoir about sodomitical motherhood, domestic normativities, and embodied transformations and hence that its *Argonauts* is merely a poor imitation of the real thing? Or are there times when charting a difference between things, even things purportedly identical to one another, requires attention to how each thing operates on its own, without adjudication? Can something be different from *but remain itself*? Is *The Argonauts* without references in the margins *The Argonauts* nonetheless? These are my animating questions.

To be sure, such questions might strike readers of *The Argonauts*, in paperback or not, as aiming in the wrong direction. After all, the title of Nelson's book goes a long way in assuring us that she holds no warrant for dutiful replication as the key to the force or value of meaning. "A day or two after my love pronouncement," Nelson writes to her lover Harry Dodge, "I sent you the passage from *Roland Barthes by Roland Barthes* in which Barthes describes how the subject who utters the phrase 'I love you' is like 'the Argonaut renewing his ship during its route without changing its name'" (5). As Monica Pearl discusses in this issue, the use of Barthes establishes Nelson's engagement with "a paradox of identity" – an engagement that is about content and form as much as the norms attending love, family, and social attachment (this issue 199). By reading the author's work as akin to the labor required to keep the *Argo* afloat, Pearl parses the different ways in which Nelson not only deconstructs the generic conventions of memoir and academic prose but remakes them as well. Multiple voices appear and disappear as Nelson integrates words and phrases from numerous thinkers into the text, often without attribution, thereby referencing while upending the formal practice of academic legitimation. Memoir's traditional narrative arc is similarly disassembled as *The Argonauts*, properly speaking, is "not a story," as Pearl writes, at least not in the "old fashioned" sense that provides "a beginning, middle, and end" (this issue 200). Instead, *The Argonauts*' narrative desire takes shape in episodic terms, more as a performative assemblage of potentially interchangeable parts than as a commitment to a knowing destination. In her contribution here, Kaye Mitchell links such formal transgressions to the "ethics of vulnerability" that pervades the text – an ethics that arises from Nelson's risky confrontation with sovereignty as self-infatuation and protection (this issue 194). In all these ways, the performance of the text conjures the work of the title, designating the author as an Argonaut who restores and rebuilds the world beneath her feet. Love, marriage, pregnancy: yes, but not with the affective underbelly of conservative ideology and its gendered regulation; autobiography, academic criticism: yes, but demonstrably oriented toward interlocution not individual experience as the sole means and measure of queer survival and repair.

That this interlocution is crucially staked to *The Argonauts*' frequent use of quotations is not in dispute. In fact, my Kindle-without-marginal-references offers its readers ample engagement with the critical theorists, philosophers, and cultural warriors that appear in the list above. Wittgenstein comes first, in the second paragraph. "Before we met," Nelson writes in reference to Harry's counter belief in language as a primal scene of violence, "I had spent a lifetime devoted to Wittgenstein's idea that the inexpressible is contained – inexpressibly! – in the expressed" (location 32–33). Shortly thereafter, Nelson gives us Thomas Jefferson and beyond him Roland Barthes who is used to introduce the book's title before reappearing again as the segue to the fragment of a poem by Michael Ondaatje (location 44; 56; 68). Multiple swipes later we encounter Cherríe Moraga, Audre Lorde, Adrienne Rich, Karen Finley, Pussy Riot: all offered in a rush of appreciation at location 1006 for their refusal to follow Rita Mae Brown's demand that to "join the movement" feminists must "abandon their children" (location 1066). Beyond this is Adam Phillips: "*The self without sympathetic attachments is either a fiction or a lunatic*" (location 1367). And throughout the e-book, twenty-eight times by my Kindle's search count, the conversation is drawn to Eve Sedgwick, whose appetite for the simplicity of analytical reduction – as in Axiom 1: "*People are different from each another*" – is central to Nelson's claim that "the great invitation of Sedgwick's work [...] is to 'pluralize and specify'" (location 989; 835). As the typography of these quotes suggests, the Kindle duplicates the paperback's use of italics to indicate direct quotation. Here's Butler, via Nelson: "*Performativity has to do with repetition, very often with the repetition of oppressive and painful gender norms to force them to resignify*" (location 195; p. 15). Or Nelson recalling a barb she is unable to forget: "*Wow*, my friend said, filling [the cup] up. *I've never seen anything so heteronormative in my life*" (location 159; p. 13). There's even Nelson on Nelson: "*You've punctured my solitude*, I told you" (location 56; p. 5). When it comes to interlocution, then, all is not quiet on the Kindle screen, no matter its technological deficiency in replicating the paperback's marginal citations.

The e-book and paperback are most in sync when it comes to the visual performance of the paragraph, which always appears in singular form, a little island of text differentiated from the others by the unused space that surrounds it. No paragraph is indented. All are typographically justified. Some are simply one sentence long; others take up more than half of the page or screen. In every case, the blank space separating paragraphs is composed of a single unused line or two, never more. The double line enacts the deeper visual cut by indicating a transition, sometimes temporal, sometimes topical, often both. The separation of paragraphs, the justification, the lack of indentation: these formal characteristics replay the complexity of sameness and difference at stake in the story of the *Argo*, generating pages and screens that conform to compositional rules while remaining distinct from those that precede or follow. Unique but the same. To be sure, this description gives priority to the perspective of the paragraph by conceiving of the space around it as blank or, in language more ideologically weighted, as empty. Such a description prompts a question about relations of dependency within the visual order: are page and screen the background against which the *Argo*'s parts move, or are they part of the *Argo*'s moving parts? If, as we might suspect, *The Argonauts*' answer is that dependency is always a two-way street, then the paragraph, as visual unit, is at once anchored and unmoored, *embedded* in the page or *projected* onto the screen as much as floating over and above them. None of this is to say that my friend suffers from misplaced enthusiasm for the paperback – on that score I prefer not to judge. My point is rather that the e-book is no second-rate knockoff; its digital mode of reproduction has the capacity to keep visual pace with several of the key features (interlocution, narrative disassemblage) of autotheory's formal intervention.

What, then, of the main divergence – the paperback's active margins and the citations that land there? The simplest reading would engage them as mere space-saving shorthand, thereby avoiding the question of whether the reduction of reference to proper names mocks or honors the authority we grant by calling them "citations." Nowhere in the book, let's remember, are readers provided with comprehensive bibliographical information. A more celebratory reading might approach the paper margins in graphic terms, much like graffiti, which values property transgression as a practice of everyday aesthetic intervention – in this case, graffiti in minimalist form. What you see is where the meaning lives. Still other readings might traffic more fully in the psychic consequences of ambivalence, finding the use of the margins both experimental *and* pretentious. How many canonical figures does it take before readers are certain that *The Argonauts* is both learned and smart? And once readers know this, are they – are we – more firmly identified with the author's quest to make critical sense of quotidian desires or overcome by insecurity if not alienation that the reading list is too unwieldy for anyone not in graduate school? Jackie Stacey's contribution to this issue offers one fascinating encounter with these questions as she follows her own readerly resistance by attending to the book's meditations on Winnicott and maternal attachments. Her point, in the end, is that Nelson's expectations for the reader are not as deeply tied to bibliographic competency as theory devotees might like, as the psychic implications of all social relations is that they cannot *not fail*. Other readers – *"People are different from each another"* – have wondered about the exclusions that Nelson's genealogies inscribe. In this issue, Sophie Mayer identifies the two that concern her the most: the citational absence of feminist/queer of color ruminations on maternity and the excision of the story of Medea, herself a passenger on the *Argo* whose mothering, let's just say, fell far short of Winnicott's standard of being "good enough." In Mayer's analysis, these absent genealogies offer limit cases for exploring the raced and classed implications of "kin-making," demonstrating how much messier sodomitical motherhood might be if race and class were figured more centrally in the identity conundrums that *The Argonauts* inhabits and explores.

Whether cast as negotiation borne of readerly discontent or in the mode of critique as political supplement, both Stacey and Mayer demonstrate that there is more to be said about the inner logics and interpretative effects of *The Argonauts'* genre transgressions. How, then, might we discern with some kind of precision what the margins perform in the visual economy of the paperback book? To students in my queer theory course last semester, I paired this question with news of my Kindle's evacuations to encourage them to approach *The Argonauts* as budding queer theoretical detectives. Initially they took this as a command to discover the rule that governed when the space of the margin was used. Each time someone thought they "had" it – i.e., "Nelson always posts a name in the margin when she quotes without clear attribution" – another Sherlock would joyfully offer up the negating example, stoking the hunt and frustrating it at once. We were especially perplexed about the text's orientation toward Eve Sedgwick, arguably its most important queer theorist. She is the only author who appears in marginal reference at first mention without a first name – as, simply, "Sedgwick" (74). Notably, this comes forty-six pages after Nelson first discusses Sedgwick's significance in reframing the political capacity and personal force of the concept "queer" (28). "She wanted the term," Nelson writes, "to be a perpetual excitement, a kind of placeholder – a nominative, like *Argo*, willing to designate molten or shifting parts, a means of asserting while also giving the slip" (29). Everyone else who enters the margins, even those with previous appearances in the main text, are initially given full nomination: Ludwig Wittgenstein (4), Eileen Myles (11), Judith Butler (14), Leo Bersani (26), Ralph Waldo Emerson (33), D.W. Winnicott (37), Luce Irigaray (38), Lucille Clifton (53), Michel Foucault (64), Monique Wittig (98). There is only one exception: Harry Dodge, who is cited in the margins only as "Harry" and only in the final pages of the book (129; 131; 133). In addition, Eileen Myles never appears simply as "Myles" but is referenced instead with her full name (11; 97).

Are these "irregularities" or measured practices of intimacy creative instances of authorial design or a game plan gone awry? Or might it be the case that there was never a defined plan and hence that no rule has been undermined? Or perhaps we should raise our cynicism a level and consider whether disrupting the reader's desire for a rule is the operative rule? In a book that opens by foregrounding the grammar of gender rules (or should I say the rules of gendered grammar?), the quest to answer these questions may seem inconsequential, especially in light of the larger political stakes that attend *The Argonauts'* deconstructive and reparative ethics. But these questions have a certain necessary inflection when reframed by what I consider the routinely unasked question: what is the relationship between the authorial figure, Maggie Nelson, and the narrator who speaks in the book *as* her? I know this question cuts against what is widely heralded as the book's most important achievement which lies in the power and pleasure it delivers by bringing theory down to earth – an achievement that casts *The Argonauts'* experiment in form as most successful from the auto side of its genre transgressions. To be sure, there is evidence in the text to support this contention, best represented by Nelson's last-minute rejection of the universalizing presumptions of theory. Quoting Adam Phillips and Leo Bersani as preamble to the book's concluding lines, she ruminates on what it means that living, much like thinking and loving – or narrative itself – inevitably comes to an end: *"the joke of evolution is that it is a teleology without a point, that we, like all animals, are a project that issues in nothing"* (143). "But is there really such a thing as nothing?," Nelson asks as she brings everyday intimacies close: "I don't know. I know we're still here, who knows for how long, ablaze with our care, its ongoing song" (ibid.). With this use of rhyme, the only in the book, *The Argonauts* ends with a visual and aural insistence on poetic diction, transposing a confrontation with death into a celebratory emphasis on the present with the shift of a single letter: long, song. From this perspective, *The Argonauts* overrides theory's knowingness in its final gesture, underscoring the sustenance to be found in the register of a de-universalized "we," one whose bonds lie in the intimate sphere where maternity, marriage, and kinship are revalued as queer.

This reading depends, of course, on how far we are willing to go in wedding the *Argo* to its Argonaut or, in a different idiom, in conferring agency for the constitution and effect of a text on the conscious intentions of its maker. Much of the critical archive that travels into the margins of *The Argonauts* stands against this rendition of authorship, though devotees of the staunchly poststructuralist writings of Judith Butler might wonder how *performativity* can be cited for its attention to the instability of norms without any mention of Butler's accompanying concern for the representational hallucinations of the self-authenticating "I" (Butler). Still, I'm willing to second the idea that what makes *The Argonauts* compelling *to read* is Nelson's authorial navigations – her ability, as several of my students put it, to focus on the ongoing negotiations (with others, the social world, one's self) that register how queer life emerges and endures. These navigations go a long way in consolidating the author as the voice of the text, its reliable, because autobiographical, "I." After all, there is nothing in the queer theoretical archive to suggest that queer world building happens by accident; to rephrase the title from an interview with Judith Butler, "There is [Always] a Person Here" (Breen 7). To see this in context, just consider how discussions of *The Argonauts*, including my own, give the author, Maggie Nelson, far more power than Barthes would allow in his mapping of the authorial function. "Linguistically," he writes in "The Death of the Author," "the author is never more than the instance writing, just as *I* is nothing other than the instance saying *I*: language knows a 'subject,' not a 'person'" (145).

This is not to say that Nelson, as author, intends the suture that the reader's desire for identification in the figure of the person most often performs. What the writer might want from her text, what the text *does*, and how it is read are elements that mean well beyond anyone's ability to grapple with the nuances and missteps of tracking intentions. If we add to this the fact – and I do take it as a fact – that the author and the "I" she unleashes under her name are never exactly the same, there is no safe cover when it comes to discerning which version of *The Argonauts* is to be heralded as the original resource for understanding autotheory's lessons. Everything that is the same is also different. The Kindle *Argonauts* is *The Argonauts* nonetheless.

disclosure statement

No potential conflict of interest was reported by the author.

bibliography

Barthes, Roland. "The Death of the Author." *Image–Music–Text*. Trans. Stephen Heath. London: Fontana, 1977. 142–48. Print.

Breen, Margaret Soenser, and Warren J. Blumenfeld. "'There is a Person Here': An Interview with Judith Butler." *International Journal of Sexuality and Gender Studies* 6.1–2 (2001): 7–23. Print.

Butler, Judith. "Imitation and Gender Insubordination." *Inside/Out: Lesbian Theories, Gay Theories*. Ed. Diana Fuss. London and New York: Routledge, 1991. 13–31. Print.

Nelson, Maggie. *The Argonauts*. Minneapolis: Graywolf, 2015. Print.

Index

Note: Page numbers in *italic* type refer to figures
Page numbers followed by 'n' refer to notes

Abbate, Carolyn 177–9, 182–3
Abelove, Henry 82n40
About a Boy (Hornby) 144–8, 150, 153
Abramovich, Marina 196
academic culture 178
Acker, Kathy 136, 195–6
Ackerley, J.R. 118
Adventure in High Fidelity Sound, An (Johnson) 66, *67*
affect theory 90
Against Nature (Huysmans) 42
Agamben, Giorgio 107–8, 110, 112
Aguilar, Laura 19–21
AIDS crisis 22–3
Albee, Edward 121
Albert, Laura 139
American art, homosexualization of 61–2, 79
American exceptionalism 108–12
American Psychiatric Association (APA) 119
anal object relation 7
anarchive 178, 183
animal hoarding 117–23, 129n3
Annesley, James 131–2
antinormativity 59n2, 89–90, 102–5
Antinormativity's Queer Conventions (Wiegman and Wilson) 104
Antonioni, Michelangelo 48–50
Antonucci, Barbara 150
Arbus, Diane 72, 86, 101
archival turn 178
Archive of Feelings, An (Cvetkovich) 178
Archive Fever (Derrida) 64
Arendt, Hannah 136
Argonauts, The (Nelson) 140, 186–91, 193–6, 198–9, 201, 203–6, 208–12
art: American 61–2, 79; high- 160; mail 62, 68, 70; Pop 61, 63, 65, 69, 79, 80n4
Art of Cruelty, The (Nelson) 187
artistic activity 48–9
ARTnews 62
assemblages 124–9

Aston, Mark 53
Aural Literature 160
Austen, Jane 121–2, 140, 145, 149, 177
Austin, John Langshaw 5, 126–7
authenticity 140–1
autobiography 132, 199–200
Autobiography of Alice B. Toklas, The (Stein) 200
autofiction 138–40
autotheory 199, 208, 210, 212
Autry, Gene 71
Azuma, Hiroki 56–7, 59nn4&5

Bachelors and Bunnies (Pitzulo) 152
Bachelors of a Different Sort (Potvin) 152
Back in the Saddle Again (Autry) 71
Bagemihl, Bruce 24
Bailey, Paul 56
Balint, Michael 12
Banks, Joseph 175, 181–2
Banks, Sarah Sophia 175–7, 182–3
Barad, Karen 21–8, 29n2, 30n10
Barnes, Djuna 200
Barthes, Roland 74–5, 137, 167, 169, 171n9, 188, 195, 198–9, 203–6, 209, 212
Basquiat, Jean-Michel 61, 79, 80n1
Bathroom Song (Sedgwick) 8–16
Bearden, Romare 67
Beatty, Frances 77, 81n18
Because We're Queers (Shepherd) 51
Behn, Aphra 146
Bellamy, Dodie 195
Benderson, Bruce 139
Bendiner, Kenneth 79
Bennett, Jane 124–6, 129
Benveniste, Emile 132
Berlant, Lauren 14, 17n13, 111; and Edelman, Lee 13; and Warner, Michael 90–1, 99–100, 132
Berman, Marshall 34
Bersani, Leo 22–3, 35, 99, 171n8, 211
Besson, Rémy 170n1

INDEX

Bibler, Michael P. 116–30
bibliomania 180–1
Bildungsroman 145–6
binge-listening 156–7, 167
biological-reductionist theory of masculinity 148
biomythography 200
biopower 107
Biss, Eula 193
Blake, Peter 63
Blank Generation 131
Blow-Up (1966) 48–9, 52–4
Blues 42
Bluets (Nelson) 187
bonding, male 148
Book/Alphabet (Sedgwick) 13, *14*
Boone, Joseph Allen 43, 45
Booth, Mark 40
Bourdieu, Pierre 104
Bowers, Diana 65, 80n13
Brabon, Benjamin A. 147–8
breaching 24–6, 30n10
Bridget Jones's Diary (Fielding) 149
British Museum, Department of Prints and Drawings 174–7, 181–2
Brooks, Peter 157
Brown, Bill 100
Brown, Rita Mae 209
Brown v. The Board of Education (1954) 79
brutality 20
Bryant, Marsha, and Mao, Douglas 32, 37
Buckland, Fiona 147
Buddha Urinating on Antonio (Johnson) 65
Bully Bloggers 126
Burney, Frances 177
Burroughs, William S. 136
Bushnell, Candace 149
Butler, Judith 96–7, 188, 193, 195–6, 200, 209, 212

Callas, Maria 187
Calle, Sophie 196
Camille, Michael 151
camp 32, 34–8, 40, 42–5, 88–101; affective 88, 90–1, 98–100; high 43; low 43; performative 88
Camp (Core) 95
camp modernism 45
Camp Rules 95
Canyon (Rauschenberg) 79
capitalism 77–8, 103, 105, 107–8
Capote, Truman 116–24, 127–8
Careless Husband, The (Cibber) 146
Carpetbaggers, The (Robbins) 55
Carver, Beci 38
Cederholm, Theresa Dickason 67
Celibacies (Kahan) 62
Certeau, Michel de 159
Character and Anal Eroticism (Freud) 9
Chauncey, George 43, 71, 82n40

Chen, Mel Y. 28n1, 126–7; and Luciano, Dana 19–22, 26, 28
chick lit 144, 148–50
Child, Lydia Maria 8
Chop Art 65
Christy, Henry 175
chrononormative temporality 158, 165
church ritual 164, 166–70
Cibber, Colley 146, 149, 154
Civil Rights Movement 61
Claude, Jeanne 77
Cleckley, Hervey M., and Thigpen, Corbett H. 57–8
Cleto, Fabio 34, 36–7, 88
Cleveland, Buster 74
Closer (Cooper) 139
closet concept 71, 82n40
club time frame 147
Clune, Michael 136
Cohen, Ed 108
Collectanea Historica (Lysons) 181
Colsell, Ilsa 58
Come as You Are (Sedgwick) 8–13, 15
coming out 89, 91–3, 110
commercial masculinity 152–4
common sense typology 145
community, queer 45
Companion Species Manifesto, The (Haraway) 124
Connell, Alexander 53
Connell, Raewyn 145, 148
conspiratorial impulse 149
Cook, Matt 50, 54–5
Cooper, Dennis 131–9, 141–2
Core, Philip 95
Cortázar, Julio 49
counterintimacy 99–100
Country of the Pointed Firs (Jewitt) 127
Coviello, Peter 127, 129n2
Creekmur, Corey K., and Doty, Alexander 36
Crimp, Douglas 61
Critical Pet Studies? (Nast) 122
Critical Possibility-Production 12
critical theory 199
Criticism 61
critique, vertigo of 89–90
Crow (Dine) 79
culture, academic 178
Cusack, John 148
"cuts both ways" idiom 26–7
Cvetkovich, Ann 178

database animals 56–8
Davidson, Guy 89, 91–2; and Rooney, Monique 1–4
Dear Whitney Museum, i hate you. Love, Ray Johnson (Johnson) 63, *63*
Death of the Author, The (Barthes) 205, 212

INDEX

death drive 178, 182–3
Deleuze, Gilles, and Guattari, Félix 112, 124–5, 190
demystification 41
Denotatively, Technically, Literally (Freedgood and Schmitt) 123
Department of Prints and Drawings (British Museum) 174–7, 181–2
depressive position 8, 11–13
derailment 54
Derrida, Jacques 27, 30n9, 64, 127–8, 176
Descartes, René 33
Detloff, Madelyn 38
détournment 55
developmental achievement 11–12
deviance, material 6, 119, 124, 183n15
Diagnostic and Statistical Manual of Mental Disorders (DSM-5) 119
Dialogue on Love, A (Sedgwick) 5–6, 8, 16
Dibdin, Thomas Frognall 180
Dickinson, Emily 64, 80n14
différance 25, 27, 30n9
differences 104–5
Dine, Jim 79
discours 132, 138
discourse, horizontal 199
diurnal time 179, 183
Dodge, Harry 193–4, 206, 209, 211
Dollimore, Jonathan 113n10
domain of sexuality 117, 128, 129n2
Donne, John 159
Doty, Alexander, and Creekmur, Corey K. 36
Double Elvis (Warhol) 63
Douglas, Mary 15
Doyle, Jennifer, Flatley, Jonathan and Muñoz, José Esteban 61
dramaturgic approach 103
Drushel, Bruce E., and Peters, Brian M. 35–6
Duck, Leigh Anne 160
Duggan, Lisa, and Muñoz, José Esteban 127
Dyer, Richard 35
dynamism 20

Ecstasy, The (Donne) 159
Edelman, Lee 22–4, 27–8, 178, 182–3; and Berlant, Lauren 13
Edenheim, Sara 178, 180, 182
Edwards, Jason 7, 17n15
effect of the real 137
Ella Mason and Her Eleven Cats (Plath) 118
Ellis, Brett Easton 131
Ellis, Havelock 35
Ellison, David 132, 138
Emma (Austen) 121–2, 124
Enfance (Sarraute) 138
Eng, David, Halberstam, Judith and Muñoz, José Esteban 104
ephemera 174–83
Ephemera as Evidence (Muñoz) 178

ephemeraphilia 181
Epistemology of the Closet (Sedgwick) 12–13, 98
Ernst, Wolfgang 178
erotic code 75
erotohistoriography 171n8
essentialist definition of masculinity 145
Esteve, Mary 103, 113n4
Etherege, George 146
ethics of vulnerability 193, 209
Euripides 187, 189
Ewald, François 105, 113n5
exception, state of 107, 112
exceptionalism, queer (American) 108–12
Excitable Speech (Butler) 195
Extraordinary Homosexuals and the Fear of Being Ordinary (Martin) 105

Fair Jilt, The (Behn) 146
fantasy: of objectification 106–8; and politics 112; of queer studies 104–6
fantasy objects 132–4
Faulkner, William 122–3, 171n3
Feeling Brown (Muñoz) 111
Feminine Mystique, The (Friedan) 57
Ferriss, Suzanne, and Young, Mallory 149
Fever Pitch (Hornby) 144
Few Kind Words for the Fop, A (Staves) 146
fiction 132
Fielding, Helen 149
Finch, Will 71
Flatley, Jonathan 79, 81n18; and Grudin, Anthony E. 61–2; Muñoz, José Esteban and Doyle, Jennifer 61
fluidity 90, 92
Fluxus 69
foppishness 144, 146–54
Ford, Charles Henri 42; and Tyler, Parker 43–5
Foucault, Michel 34–5, 89, 105, 107–8
Frank, Marcie 131–43
Franks, Augustus Wollaston 175–7, 182–3
Fraterrigo, Elizabeth 152
Frears, Stephen 150
Freedgood, Elaine, and Schmitt, Cannon 123
freedom, religious 128
Freedom to Marry Our Pets (Muñoz and Duggan) 126–7
Freeman, Elizabeth 69, 104, 158–9, 165, 171n8
Freud, Sigmund 7, 9, 16nn4&5, 23, 29n8, 35, 201
Friedan, Betty 57
Friedman, Susan Stanford 33
Frisk (Cooper) 131–4, 136–8, 141–2
fugitive 180
Fuller, Glen, Wilson, Jason and McCrea, Christine 54
Fuss, Diana 10

Gayle, Mike 144
Geldin, Sherri 70

gender bending 199
gender performativity 43, 95–6
Gender Trouble (Butler) 96
Genet, Jean 138
Genette, Gerard 132, 138
genre bending 199, 208
Gentleman's Magazine 181
gentrification 49, 52, 59n3
Gill, Rosalind 144, 148–9
Gilmore, Leigh 200
Gilson, Erinn 193, 196
Glass, Ira 156
GLQ 104
gnomon 169–70
Goldberg, Jonathan 8–9, 15, 21–2, 24, 27–8, 103
Grant, Hugh 148
Graves, Morris 74
Greeson, Jennifer 160
Griffiths, Antony 175
Grossberg, Lawrence 151
Grudin, Anthony E., and Flatley, Jonathan 61–2
Guattari, Félix, and Deleuze, Gilles 112, 124–5, 190
Gumbs, Alexis Pauline 188–9
Gutjahr, Ortrud 145

Hackett, Pat, and Warhol, Andy 79
Halberstam, Judith 178; Muñoz, José Esteban and Eng, David 104
Halliwell, Kenneth 50–8
Halperin, David M. 34
Haraway, Donna 124–5
Hardie, Melissa 48–60
Harrison, Russell 106
Hawkins, Katherine 16n7
Heart is Deceitful Above All Things, The (LeRoy) 139
Heart Sutra 8, 14
Heber, Richard 181–2
Hefner, Hugh 152
hegemonic cluster 99
Hemingway, Ernest 45
Herring, Scott 5–18, 119
Hesford, Victoria 102–15
hetero/homo binary 63, 98, 127
heteronormativity 110–12, 122–3, 127, 129, 152, 154, 159
heterosexist structuralism, stasis of 96
heterosexuality 86, 93, 98–9, 118, 120, 122–4
Heti, Sheila 132, 140–1
High Fidelity (Hornby) 144, 146–50, 153
high-art 160
Highsmith, Patricia 102–3, 106–12, 113nn3,4&6
histeron proteron 24
History of Sexuality (Foucault) 89
Hoarding of Animals, The (Frost *et al.*) 119

Hold Still (Mann) 136
Holmberg, Tora 119–20, 129n3
Homo Academicus (Bourdieu) 104
homo/hetero binary 63, 98, 127
homographesis 27–8
homonationalism 110
homophobic rage 22
homosexuality 27–8, 49, 51, 54, 61–2, 71, 79, 110, 132
homosexualization of American art 61–2, 79
homosociality, lad lit as interface of 145–9
horizontal discourse 199
Hornby, Nick 144–54
hospitality 127–9
How Should a Person Be? (Heti) 141
How to Do Things with Words and Other Materials (Sedgwick) 5, 15, 16n1
How to Draw a Bunny (2002) 72, 74, 77, 80n12
How We Die (Nuland) 15
Howard, Alexander 32–47
Howard Beach situation (1986) 66
humanism, inhuman 28n1
Hungry Woman, The (Moraga) 189
Huysmans, Joris-Karl 42

I Love Dick (Kraus) 195
idealization 204–5
identity 124–8; paradox of 198, 209
If You're Buying, We're Selling campaign 128
impulse, queer 178
In the Penal Colony (Kafka) 72
Indian Penal Code 29n4
individuated Oedipal subject 125
inhuman humanism 28n1
inking up 65–9
inter(in)animation 159, 166
intermedia 157–8, 171n2
intermediality 157–9, 163–6, 170n1, 171n3
interpretive repertoires 149, 154
intimacy, queer 164, 168
intra-action 21, 25
intrahuman connection 20
Irigaray, Luce 191
Is the Rectum a Grave? (Bersani) 22
Isherwood, Christopher 43

Jacob, Naomi 56–7
James, Henry 5
Jameson, Fredric 33–4, 37–8, 45
Janklow, Morton 77–8
Jefferson, Thomas 209
Jewett, Sarah Orne 127
Jim Crow (Basquiat) 79
Johns, Jasper 62
Johnson, Ray 62–72, *63–4*, *67–8*, *70–5*, 74–5, 77–80, *78*, 85–7; cataloguing 63–5; lessons from 69–80
Johnson, Samuel 179

Kahan, Benjamin 61–84, 85–7
Katz, Jonathan D. 61
Kelly, Adam 142n9
Kennedy, Danny 142n3
Kiernan, Brian 91
Kiley, Dean 91–2, 96
kin-making 210–11
Kishi, Madoka 62
Kitchen Table Collective 189
Kittay, Eva 194
Klancher, Jon 181
Klein, Melanie 7, 9, 12–13
Koestenbaum, Wayne 78–9, 142, 142n4, 152
Krafft-Ebing, Richard von 35
Kraus, Chris 195

Lacan, Jacques 39
lad lit 144, 150–4; as interface of masculinity and homosociality 145–9
Ladies Almanack (Barnes) 200
Laing, Olivia 204, 207n2
Lamb, Jonathan 182
Lamp in a Window, A (Capote) 116–18, 123, 127
Laplanche, Jean, and Pontalis, Jean-Bertrand 29n8
Latham, Sean, and Rogers, Gayle 32–3
leathersex 69
Lerner, Ben 132, 139–41
LeRoy, J.T. 138–9
Levy, Ellen 80n3
Lewis, Wyndham 45
Library Association Record, The 53
Light in August (Faulkner) 122–3
Like Andy Warhol (Flatley) 61
Lippold, Richard 71, 86–7
literalism 117–18, 122–6, 128–9
Livingston, Jennie 188
Lloyd, Sarah 176
Lobel, Michael 153
Loftin, Craig 71, 82n40
Long Way Down, A (Hornby) 149
Lord of the Rings, The (Tolkien) 134
Lorde, Audre 189, 200
Lott, Eric 68
Love, Guilt and Reparation and Other Works, 1921–45 (Klein) 9
Love, Heather 105
Love and Theft (Lott) 68
Lover's Discourse, A (Barthes) 198
Love's Last Shift (Cibber) 146
Luciano, Dana 28n1; and Chen, Mel Y. 19–22, 26, 28
Lysons, Daniel 181–2

McCrea, Christine, Fuller, Glen and Wilson, Jason 54
McGirr, Elaine M. 146–7, 149

McInerney, Jay 131
Maciunas, George F. 69, *73*
McLemore, John B. 156–70
McMahon, Elizabeth 92–3
Maerker, Christa 113n6
mail art 62, 68, 70
Making of Americans, The (Stein) 72
Making Things, Practicing Emptiness (Sedgwick) 9
male bonding 148
Man of Mode, The (Etherege) 145–6, 150
Mann, Sally 136–7
Mao, Douglas 40–2; and Bryant, Marsha 32, 37
Mapplethorpe, Robert 136
Maravell, Nicholas 65
marriage plots 121–4
Martin, Biddy 105
Martin, Henry 72
Marxism 107
masculinity: biological-reductionist theory of 148; commercial 152–4; essentialist definition of 145; lad lit as interface of 145–9; normative definition of 145; positivist definition of 145; semiotic definition of 145
masochism 23
Massumi, Brian 90–1
Masten, Jeffrey 78–9
material deviance 6, 119, 124, 183n15
material garbage 7, 15
materialism, vital 125–6
Mayer, So 187–92, 210–11
Medea (Wolf) 187
media 136–8; and objects 134–5
Melanie Klein and the Difference Affect Makes (Sedgwick) 12
memory 136–8, 141, 142n6; involuntary 137; voluntary 137
Mendieta, Ana 196
Mercer, Kobena 61
metalepsis 23–4
metronormativity 171n6
metrosexuality 152
Meyer, Moe 36–8, 43
Meyer, Richard 61
Mickey Mouse 63, 68, 70
middlebrow 160, 171n7
Miller, Nancy K. 10
Minghella, Anthony 102
Minna Unchi (Tarō Gomi) 15
minstrelsy 66, 68
Mitchell, Kaye 193–7, 209
Miyazaki, Hayao 137
modernism 32–4, 36–8, 44–5
modernity 33–4, 105, 107–8
moe 56–7, 59n5
monstrosity 26–7
Moon, Michael, and Sedgwick, Eve 5, 7
Moore, Jackson 88–101

Moraga, Cherríe 189–90
Multiple Personality Disorder (MPD) 57
Muñoz, José Esteban 61, 66–7, 80n1, 111, 178–80, 182; Doyle, Jennifer and Flatley, Jonathan 61; and Duggan, Lisa 127; Eng, David and Halberstam, Judith 104
Music for Chameleons (Capote) 116, 123
My Dog Tulip (Ackerley) 118
My Words to Victor Frankenstein above the Village of Chamounix (Stryker) 26
Myles, Eileen 191

nachträglichkeit 23, 29n8
Nagle, Angela 54
Nam June Paik 63
Name, Billy 65, 75, 79
narrative 137–41; recursions 132–4
Nast, Heidi 122
Nature's Queer Performativity (Barad) 21, 25
Nelson, Maggie 132, 140–1, 186–91, 193–6, 198–201, 203–6, 208–12
Nettleton, Taro 80n1
new lad 148–9, 154
New Literary History 138
New York Correspondence School 62, 64, 74–5, 78–9
New York Magazine 138
New-England Boy's Song about Thanksgiving Day, The (Child) 8
Nicholls, David 144
Nicholls, Peter 42
Nieland, Justus 44
No Future (Edelman) 178
noise 122–4
non-narratives 56–8
normative definition of masculinity 145
normative whiteness 111
Notes on 'Camp' (Sontag) 35
"Nothings" (Johnson) 64
Notley, Alice 193
Nouveaux Romanciers 138
Novel Gazing (Sedgwick) 8
Nuland, Sherwin B. 15

Object Lessons (Wiegman) 89
object panic 119
object relations theory 6–7, 9–16, 37
objectification, fantasy of 106–8
Ochsner, Andrea 144–5, 149
Oedipus (Elvis #1) (Johnson) 63
Ondaatje, Michael 209
Operation Minotaur (Ford) 42
Opie, Catherine 194
Orlando (Woolf) 38, 40
Orton, Joe 50–8
otaku 56–7, 59nn4&5
Otaku (Azuma) 56, 59nn4&5
otherness, significant 124

Overlooking the Ephemeral (Abbate) 178
Oxford Dictionary of National Biography 175
Oxford English Dictionary 25, 138

panic, object 119
Parables for the Virtual (Massumi) 90
paradox of identity 198, 209
paradoxical perverse 112, 113n10
paranoid/schizoid position 11–13, 17n11
Paris is Burning (1990) 188
Parsons, Tony 144
Pasolini, Pier Paolo 187
Pearl, Monica B. 198–202, 209
Perez, Domino Renée 189–90
performativity 89, 91–6, 100, 212; camp 94; gender 43, 95–6; queer 21, 25, 27
Performativity and Performance (Sedgwick) 5
periodization 38
Pero, Allan 35, 37
perversion 103
Peters, Brian M., and Drushel, Bruce E. 35–6
Peters, Fiona 109
Petot, Jean-Michel 16n6
Phillips, Adam 204, 209, 211
Phillpot, Clive 67
photography 133, 136–7, 137, 141, 142n6, 171n9; artistic 48; commercial 48
Pitzulo, Carrie 152–3
Plath, Sylvia 118–20
Playboy 152–3
Playboy and the Making of the Good Life in America (Fraterrigo) 152
plots, marriage 121–4
Poem Is Being Written, A (Sedgwick) 5
politics, and fantasy 112
Pollock, Griselda 64–5
Pontalis, Jean-Bertrand, and Laplanche, Jean 29n8
Poons, Larry 66
Pop 72, 79–80, 80n5
Pop Art 61, 63, 65, 69, 79, 80n4
Pop Out (Doyle et al.) 61
POPism (Warhol and Hackett) 79
positivist definition of masculinity 145
possibility concept 12
Postfeminist Male Singleton 147–8
postmodernity 56
Potvin, John 152–3
Precarious Life (Butler) 195
pregnancy 193–4, 199
Pride and Prejudice (Austen) 149
Professor's House, The (Cather) 12
proto-affective approach 92
Proust, Marcel 132, 137–8, 141, 142n7
psychoanalysis 9–12, 23–4
Puar, Jasbir 104, 110, 124–5
punctum (Barthes) 167

Queer Inhumanisms (Luciano and Chen) 19
queer studies, fantasy of 104–6
Queer Temporalities (Freeman) 104

Rauschenberg, Robert 79–80
Ray Johnson Fan Club (Weinberg) 70
Reading for the Plot (Brooks) 157
readings, sodomitical 22–4
real, effect of 137
realism, limits of 135–8
Reality and Realization (Sedgwick) 8
Recherche du temps perdu, A la (Proust) 132
récit 132, 138
recursions 135–6; narrative 132–4
Red Parts, The (Nelson) 187
Reed, Brian 156–8, 160–70
regimes of representation 149
Relapse, The (Vanbrugh) 151
religious freedom 128
reparative position 11–13, 15, 17n11
reparative reading 38
repertoires, interpretive 149, 154
representation, regimes of 149
restoration comedy 146, 148–9
revision 135–6
Rickards, Maurice 179
Riley, Denise 195
Ripley Underground (Highsmith) 106
Robbins, Harold 55
Robinson, Michael 181
Rogers, Gayle, and Latham, Sean 32–3
Roland Barthes by Roland Barthes (Barthes) 187, 209
Room of One's Own, A (Woolf) 41
Rooney, Monique 156–73; and Davidson, Guy 1–4
Roots (1977) 66
Rose for Emily, A (Faulkner) 123, 171n3
Roth, Martin, and Schäfer, Fabian 57
Rubin, Gayle 82n41
Russell, Gillian 174–85

S-Town (2017) 156–7, 159–61, 163–4, 168, 170
Sade, Marquis de 74–5
sadomasochism 62–3, 68–72, 77–9, 82n42
Sammond, Nicholas 68
Sarah (LeRoy) 139
Sarraute, Nathalie 138
Scarry, Elaine 136–8
Schäfer, Fabian, and Roth, Martin 57
Schenkar, Joan 113n9
Schmitt, Cannon, and Freedgood, Elaine 123
Schneider, Rebecca 159, 166, 168
Schuyff, Peter 72, 74, 78, 86
Secret of Chimneys, The (Christie) 55–6
Sedgwick, Eve 3, 5–7, 9–15, 38, 80n4, 147, 188, 200, 205, 209, 211; and Moon, Michael 5, 7; on shame 88–9, 91, 93, 96–8

See, Sam 45
Self-Portrait with Badges (Blake) 63
Self-Portrait/Cutting (Opie) 194
semiotic definition of masculinity 145
Serial (2014–present) 171n4
Sex and the City (Bushnell) 149
Sex in Public (Berlant and Warner) 99
Sexual Offences Act (1967) 49
sexuality, domain of 117, 128, 129n2
shame 88–101
Shannon Van Wey, William 10
Sharpe, Christina 168
Shepherd, Simon 51–2
Sherman, Stuart 179
Shugart, Helene 147, 152
significant otherness 124
Silver, Kenneth E. 61
Silverberg, Ira 139
Silverman, Kaja 194
Simpsons, The (1989–present) 118, 120
sincerity 140–1, 142n9
sinthome 113n6
skinplay 69
Sloane, Hans 175, 181
Sluts, The (Cooper) 133
snuff 131, 133–8, 141
Social Text 104
sodomitical readings 22–4
sodomy 25–8, 29nn4&5; natural 21–2
Solid Objects (Woolf) 38, 40
Sonnabend, Ileana 80
Sontag, Susan 35–6, 90, 95, 97–8
spacetimemattering 22, 24–6, 28, 29n7
spectacle 149
Spiral Group 67
Stacey, Jackie 203–7, 210–11
Stadler, Matthew 139
state of exception 107, 112
Staves, Susan 146, 148–9
Stein, Gertrude 45, 72, 200
Stepić, Nikola 144–55
stratal configurations 150
Straw, Will 146, 150–1, 153
structuralism, heterosexist 96
Stryker, Susan 26–8
Sturm, Marjorie 139
style 150–1, 154
Suárez, Juan A. 45
Successful Prosecution, A (Connell) 53
Sun Also Rises, The (Hemingway) 45

Talented Mr Ripley, The (Highsmith) 102, 108, 110
temporal lag 158–9, 166
temporality, queer 104, 158, 165, 168
10:04 (Lerner) 139
Tendencies (Sedgwick) 3, 12
Terrorist Assemblages (Puar) 104

Thanksgiving Visitor, The (Capote) 128
Theseus' ship paradox 198
Thigpen, Corbett H., and Cleckley, Hervey M. 57–8
This American Life 156, 162, 171n4
Three Faces of Eve, The (Thigpen and Cleckley) 57
Three Men and Jennie (Jacob) 56
Three Queer Lives (Bailey) 56
Tiger, Lionel 148
timing, queer 166
Tits and Clits Comix 24
Tolkien, J.R.R. 134
Tomkins, Silvan 135
Touching Feeling (Sedgwick) 5–8
Transatlantic Review 52, 55, 56
Trask, Michael 102–3, 113n4, 113n7
Trilling, Lionel 140–1
troll 53–8
Twyborn Affair, The (White) 88–9, 91–101
Tyler, Parker, and Ford, Charles Henri 43–5

Uggams, Leslie 66–7
utopianism, queer 178

Vanbrugh, John 151
Vanita, Ruth 118
verbal objects 136–8
vertigo of critique 89–90
Victorian Dictionary of Slang and Phrase 34
View 42
vinyl 150, 153
visual objects 136–8
vital materialism 125–6
vulnerability 193–6; epistemic 196; ethics of 193, 209; primary 196

Wainwright, Leon 61
Walker, Kara 66
Wallace, David Foster 140
Ware, J. Redding 34
Warhol, Andy 61–3, 65–6, 79, 80n4; and Hackett, Pat 79
Warner, Michael, and Berlant, Lauren 90–1, 99–100, 132

Watson, Jay 122–3
Waugh, Thomas 151, 153
Weather in Proust, The (Sedgwick) 8–9, 11–12
Weinberg, Jonathan 70
Weisbard, Eric 151
What Does Queer Theory Teach Us About X? (Berlant and Warner) 132
What's Queer about Queer Studies Now? (Eng et al.) 104
When Species Meet (Haraway) 124–5
white affect 111
White, Patrick 88–9, 91–4, 99–100
whiteness, normative 111
Whitney, Shiloh Y. 194
Who's Afraid of Virginia Woolf? (Albee) 124
Wiegman, Robyn 17n12, 37, 89–90, 99, 208–12; and Wilson, Elizabeth A. 59n2, 104–6
Wilde, Oscar 35, 86, 127
Wilderson, Frank B. 168
Wilke, Hannah 196
Willa Cather and Others (Goldberg) 12
Willemen, Paul 187
Williams, Mark 92
Wilson, David 175
Wilson, Elizabeth A. 19–31; and Wiegman, Robyn 59n2, 104–6
Wilson, Jason, McCrea, Christine and Fuller, Glen 54
Wilson, William S. 71, 78, 85–7
Winnicott, D.W. 12, 203–4, 210
Wittgenstein, Ludwig 209
Wolf, Christa 187, 189
Wolf Man 23
Women and Performance 8
Woodward, Joanne 57–8
Woolf, Virginia 38–44
World in the Evening, The (Isherwood) 43
world making, queer 90, 99–101

Young and Evil, The (Ford and Tyler) 43–5
Young, Mallory, and Ferriss, Suzanne 149
Young, Timothy 180

Zami (Lorde) 200
Žižek, Slavoj 106–7, 113n6